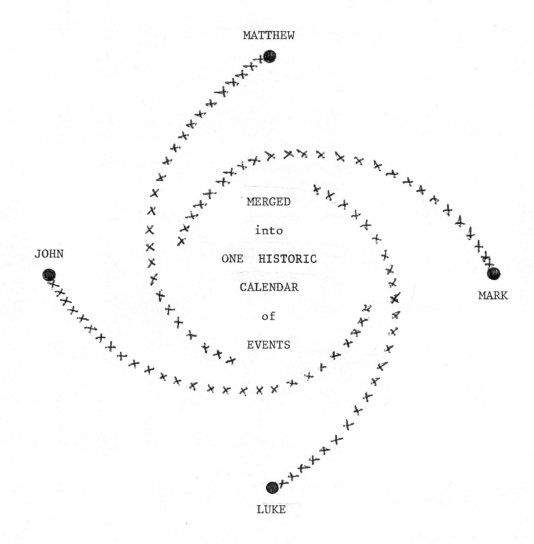

Scan QR Code to learn more about this title

Copyright © 2015 by John Douma

Cover design by Jayme Vincent

The Story of Christmas © Gino Santa Maria. BigStockPhoto.com

All rights reserved. No part of this book may be reproduced or transmitted in any form or by any means whatsoever, including photocopying, recording or by any information storage and retrieval system, without written permission from the publisher and/or author. Contact Inkwater Press at 6750 SW Franklin Street, Suite A, Portland, OR 97223-2542. 503.968.6777

Publisher: Inkwater Press | www.inkwaterpress.com

Hardcover
ISBN-13 978-1-62901-194-3 | ISBN-10 1-62901-194-0

Kindle
ISBN-13 978-1-62901-195-0 | ISBN-10 1-62901-195-9

Printed in the U.S.A.
All paper is acid free and meets all ANSI standards for archival quality paper.

3 5 7 9 10 8 6 4 2

Introduction

We mentally file our knowledge
    according to its value in relation to timing and consequence.

Of course I shall remember!
    How could I forget, being fully aware of its consequential significance.

What Can I say?
    I tried, so hard to remember not to forget, but somehow it slipped my mind.

Some things we remember,
    Other things come to mind, when it is too late;
    Our sub-conscience throws things at us, we had forgot a long time passing.

Some will use a bookmark;
Others fold over the corner of a page,
    to help them to remember where they left off, and intent to continue later.
Hold your finger at a particular page, while researching another page/passage.

It occurred to me, that it should be helpful (so I thought),
If the first 4 gospels of the New Testament (Matthew, Mark, Luke, and John),
    could be merged together, uniting them into one historical calendar of events.

So, I began with the gospel of Matthew (starting at the very beginning),
    and attempted to add to Matthew, the gospels of Mark, Luke, and John.
But there was a serious problem – the events were not in the same order.
This project to merge these 4 gospels, appeared to be a No Go from the Get Go.

It was not until some time later, that I realized,
    that the gospels of Mark, Luke, John, and also the latter half of Matthew,
    had the various events recorded in a similar sequence.

Other observations:
A large portion of the gospel of John consists of speaches
    that were made by Jesus, but are not found in Matthew, Mark, and Luke.
Also, Matthew 16:21 is the beginning of the final journey of Jesus into Jerusalem:
    Who (Lk.9:31) spake of his decease (ie: his departing/exodus),
    which he should accomplish at Jerusalem.
    And the time was come – that he should be received up (Lk.9:51/Lk.13:22).

When events appear to be the same, they could be combined together, provided,
      the conditions (the timing and the number) will so allow it to be.
    Timing: Similar events could have taken place at different times/locations.
    Number: Events that appear to be the same, but took place a number of times;
      The number of times as is recorded in the Bible (Lk.23:22/Lk.20:12).

Alignment of the different events/passages:
Making an effort to retain the order of events as they be recorded in each gospel;
    except for the first halve of Matthew, which (for the most part),
    is adjoined to corresponding Bible passages from Mark, Luke, and John.
There is also Shift between these gospels:
    (ie: when 2 different gospels, each depicting a different event);
    The question is, which event happened first?
    The shift between the various gospels, is diminished or eliminated, contingent,
      on information found in the other gospels, or elsewhere in the Bible.

When we study the Bible (Comparing Scripture with Scripture),   (1 Jn.5:14/Jn.15:7)
We pray for wisdom to better understand;
    and also for correction,
      for we (on our part) make errors, that need to be corrected.

THE LORD IS IN HIS HOLY TEMPLE

Lord, teach us to pray.

After this manner therefore pray ye:

>Our Father,
>>Which art in heaven, hallowed be Thy name.
>>
>>Thy kingdom come.
>>
>>Thy will be done,
>>>in earth, as it is in heaven.
>>
>>Give us this day our daily bread.
>>
>>And forgive us our debts,
>>>as we forgive our debtors.
>>
>>And lead us not into temptation,
>>>but deliver us from evil:
>>
>>For Thine is the kingdom,
>>>and the power, and the glory, for ever.
>>
>>Amen.

Table of Contents (where to find)

Matthew	Page	Matthew	Page	Matthew	Page	Mark	Page	Mark	Page
1:1-25	13	13:52-53	51	26:6-18	126	1:1-6	17	10:39-51	106
2:1-16	15	13:54-55	55	26:18-29	127	1:7-13	18	10:52	107
2:16-23	16	13:56-58	56	26:29	128	1:13	19	11:1-10	109
3:1-10	17	14:1-6	60	26:30-33	129	1:14-22	27	11:11-17	110
3:11-17	18	14:6-14	61	26:34-35	130	1:23-34	28	11:17-18	111
4:1-2	18	14:14-21	62	26:36-39	135	1:35-41	29	11:19-23	112
4:2-11	19	14:22-34	63	26:39-47	136	1:42-45	30	11:23-33	113
4:12-24	27	14:35-36	64	26:48-57	137	2:1-9	30	12:1	113
4:24-25	28	15:1-11	66	26:57-68	138	2:9-18	31	12:1-9	114
5:1-10	34	15:12-28	67	26:69-73	139	2:19-28	32	12:10-12	115
5:10-24	35	15:29-39	68	26:74-75	140	3:1-10	33	12:13-25	116
5:24-44	36	16:1-12	69	27:1-2	140	3:10-19	34	12:25-36	117
5:44-48	37	16:13-26	70	27:2	141	3:19-30	45	12:36-40	118
6:1-8	37	16:27-28	71	27:3-9	140	3:31-35	46	12:41	119
6:9-30	38	17:1-9	71	27:10-15	141	2:35	47	12:42-44	120
6:30-34	39	17:10-17	72	27:16-23	142	4:1-12	47	13:1-11	120
7:1-12	39	17:18-27	73	27:24-32	144	4:13-21	48	13:11-22	121
7:13-27	40	18:1-11	74	27:33-40	145	4:22-32	49	13:23-32	122
7:27-29	41	18:12-33	75	27:40-50	146	4:33-34	50	13:33-37	123
8:1	41	18:33-35	76	27:50-57	147	4:35-41	51	14:1-2	125
8:2-3	29	19:1-2	76	27:58-60	148	5:1	51	14:3-14	126
8:3-4	30	19:3-9	99	F27:61-64	148	5:1-13	52	14:14-25	127
8:5-12	41	19:10-12	100	F27:65-66	149	5:14-25	53	14:25	128
8:12-13	42	19:13-23	103	F28:1	149	5:25-40	54	14:26-29	129
8:14-17	28	19:24-30	104	W27:61-66	149	5:40-43	55	14:30-31	130
8:17	29	20:1-8	104	W28:1	149	6:1-3	55	14:32-35	135
8:18-28	51	20:9-23	105	28:2-8	150	6:3-10	56	14:35-43	136
8:28-32	52	20:23-29	106	28:9-12	151	6:10-11	57	14:44-53	137
8:32-34	53	20:30-34	107	28:13-15	152	6:12-13	58	14:53-65	138
9:1	53	21:1-9	109	28:16-20	156	6:14-21	60	14:66-70	139
9:1-5	30	21:9-11	110			6:21-34	61	14:71-72	140
9:5-14	31	21:12-13	110			6:34-44	62	15:1	140
9:15-17	32	21:13-16	111			6:45-54	63	15:1-6	141
9:18-20	53	21:17-19	110			6:55-56	64	15:7-11	142
9:20-25	54	21:20-21	112			7:1-16	66	15:12-14	143
9:25-38	55	21:21-32	113			7:17-30	67	15:15-21	144
10:1-11	56	21:32-41	114			7:31-37	68	15:22-29	145
10:11-35	57	21:41-46	115			8:1-10	68	15:30-37	146
10:35-42	58	22:1-15	115			8:11-25	69	15:37-43	147
11:1	58	22:15-30	116			8:26-38	70	15:43-46	148
11:2-8	42	22:30-44	117			8:38	71	F15:47	148
11:9-19	43	22:44-46	118			9:1-10	71	F16:1	149
11:20-30	44	23:1-20	118			9:11-24	72	W15:47	149
12:1-9	32	23:20-39	119			9:25-34	73	W16:1	149
12:9-21	33	24:1-9	120			9:34-48	74	16:2-8	150
12:22-34	45	24:9-24	121			9:49-50	76	16:9-10	151
12:34-50	46	24:25-39	122			10:1	76	16:10-12	152
12:50	47	24:40-51	123			10:2-9	99	16:13	153
13:1-14	47	25:1-6	123			10:10-12	100	16:14	154
13:14-23	48	25:7-30	124			10:13-24	103	16:15-20	156
13:24-33	49	25:31-46	125			10:24-31	104		
13:33-52	50	26:1-5	125			10:32-39	105		

Luke	Page	Luke	Page	Luke	Page	John	Page	John	Page
1:1-11	9	8:33-43	53	19:29-36	109	1:1-14	9	15:1-4	131
1:11-32	10	8:43-54	54	19:37-46	110	1:15-21	19	15:4-27	132
1:33-59	11	8:54-56	55	19:46-48	111	1:21-44	20	16:1-22	133
1:59-80	12	9:1-3	56	20:1-8	113	1:45-51	21	16:22-33	134
2:1-5	12	9:4-5	57	20:9-16	114	2:1-14	21	17:1-11	134
2:5-14	13	9:6	58	20:17-20	115	2:14-25	22	17:12-26	135
2:15-37	14	9:7-9	60	20:20-35	116	3:1-11	22	18:1	135
2:37-39	15	9:10-11	61	20:36-42	117	3:12-34	23	18:2-7	136
2:40-52	16	9:11-17	62	20:43-47	118	3:35-36	24	18:8-13	137
3:1	16	9:18-26	70	21:1	119	4:1-23	24	18:13-16	138
3:1-12	17	9:26-36	71	21:2-14	120	4:23-49	25	18:17-23	139
3:13-18	18	9:37-42	72	21:14-23	121	4:50-54	26	18:24	139
3:19-20	27	9:42-47	73	21:24-33	122	5:1-13	58	18:25-26	139
3:21-38	18	9:47-50	74	21:34-38	123	5:13-35	59	18:26-28	140
4:1-2	18	9:51-62	86	22:1-2	125	5:35-47	60	18:28-38	141
4:2-15	19	10:1-9	86	22:3-11	126	6:1-5	61	18:39-40	142
4:16-30	26	10:9-30	87	22:11-20	127	6:5-13	62	19:1-3	142
4:31-32	27	10:30-42	88	22:21-23	128	6:14-21	63	19:3-12	143
4:33-41	28	11:1-8	88	22:24-30	129	6:22-40	64	19:13-17	144
4:42-44	29	11:8-29	89	22:31-38	130	6:40-67	65	19:17-27	145
5:1-13	29	11:30-49	90	22:39-41	135	6:68-71	66	19:28-30	146
5:13-23	30	11:50-54	91	22:41-47	136	7:1-18	76	19:30-38	147
5:23-33	31	12:1-17	91	22:47-54	137	7:19-42	77	19:38-42	148
5:34-39	32	12:17-40	92	22:54-55	138	7:42-53	78		
6:1-6	32	12:41-59	93	22:56-59	139	8:1-18	78	20:1-4	150
6:6-11	33	13:1-24	94	22:59-71	140	8:18-43	79	20:4-17	151
6:12-21	34	13:24-35	95	23:1	140	8:43-59	80	20:18	152
6:22-26	35	14:1-9	95	23:1-4	141	9:1-8	80	20:19-25	153
6:27	36	14:10-31	96	23:5-12	142	9:8-32	81	20:25-31	154
6:28	37	14:32-35	97	23:13-23	143	9:33-41	82	21:1-6	154
6:29-30	36	15:1-19	97	23:24-32	144	10:1-16	82	21:7-23	155
6:31-36	37	15:20-32	98	23:33-35	145	10:17-42	83	21:23-25	156
6:37-42	39	16:1-8	98	23:35-37	146	11:1-2	83		
6:43-49	40	16:8-18	99	23:38	145	11:2-31	84		
6:49	41	16:19-31	100	23:39-46	146	11:32-56	85		
7:1-9	41	17:1-3	100	23:46-50	147	11:56-57	86		
7:10-25	42	17:3-26	101	23:51-54	148	12:1-13	108		
7:26-43	43	17:26-37	102	F23:55-56	148	12:14-19	109		
7:43-50	44	18:1-12	102	W23:55-56	149	12:20-33	111		
8:1-3	44	18:13-24	103	24:1-9	150	12:34-50	112		
8:4-10	47	18:25-30	104	24:10-26	152	13:1	127		
8:11-16	48	18:31-34	105	24:27-43	153	13:2-22	128		
8:17-18	48	18:35-43	106	24:44-48	154	13:23-36	129		
8:19-21	46	19:1	106	24:49-53	156	13:36-38	130		
8:22-25	51	19:2-18	107			14:1-12	130		
8:26-33	52	19:19-28	108			14:12-31	131		

Table of Topics   P.158

Taken from the Gospels of Matthew, Mark, Luke & John

Mt.1	Mk.1	Lk.1	Jn.1		
			1	In the Beginning was the Word,	
			1B	and the Word was with God,	
			1C	and the Word was God.	(He.1:8)
			2	The same was in the beginning with God.	
			3	All things were made by him;	
			3B	and without him - was not any thing made that was made.	
			4	In him was life;	(Jn.5:26)
			4B	and the life was the light of men.	
			5	And the light shineth in the darkness;	
			5B	and the darkness comprehended (ie: get/grasp) it not.	
			6	There was a man sent from God, whose name was John.	
			7	The same came for a witness (to bear witness of the Light),	
			7B	that all through him might believe.	(Acts 4:12)
			8	He was not that Light,	
			8B	but was sent to bear witness of that Light.	
			9	That was the true Light,	
			9B	which lighteth every man that cometh into the world.	
			10	He was in the world, and the world was made by him,	
			10B	and the world knew him not.	
			11	He came unto his own, and his own received him not.	
			12	But as many as received him,	(Phil.2:13)
			12B	to them gave he power to become the sons of God,	
			12C	to them that believe on his name:	
			13	Which were born,	
			13B	not of blood, nor of the will of the flesh,	
			13C	nor of the will of man, but of God.	(1 Jn.3:9)
			14	And the Word was made flesh, and dwelt among us,	
			14B	(and we beheld his glory, the glory as of the	
			14C	only begotten of the Father), full of grace and truth.	
		1		For-as-much as many	
	The	1B		have taken in hand to set forth in order a declaration	
	epistle	1C		of those things which are most surely believed among us,	
	(letter)	2		Even as they delivered them unto us,	
	that	2B		which from the beginning were eyewitnesses,	
	Luke	2C		and ministers of the word;	
	sent	3		It seemed good to me also, having had	
	to	3B		perfect understanding of all things from the very first,	
	Theophilus	3C		to write unto thee - in order, most excellent Theophilus,	
		4		That thou mightest know the certainty of those things,	
		4B		where-in thou hast been instructed.	
		5		There was (in the days of Herod, the king of Judaea),	
	Zacharias	5B		a certain priest named Zacharias, of the course of Abia:	
	and	5C		and his wife was of the daughters of Aaron,	
	Elisabeth	5D		and her name was Elisabeth,	
		6		And they were both righteous before God, walking in all	(Jn.14:15)
		6B		the commandments and ordinances of the Lord blameless.	
		7		And they had no child, because that Elisabeth was barren,	
		7B		and they both were now well stricken in years.	
		8		And it came to pass, that while he executed	
		8B		the priest's office before God (in the order of his course),	
		9		According to the custom of the priest's office, his lot was	
		9B		to burn incense when he went into the temple of the Lord.	
		10		And the whole multitude of the people were praying without	
		10B		at the time of incense.	
		11		And there appeared unto him an angel of the Lord	(Lk.1:19)

Mt.1   Mk.1   Lk.1   Jn.1

	11B	standing on the right side of the altar of incense.
	12	And when Zacharias saw him,
	12B	he was troubled, and fear fell upon him,
	13	But the angel said unto him, Fear not, Zacharias:
	13B	for thy prayer is heard;
	13C	and thy wife Elisabeth shall bear thee a son,
	13D	and thou shalt call his name John.
	14	And thou shalt have joy and gladness;
	14B	and many shall rejoice at his birth.
	15	For he shall be great in the sight of the Lord,
	15B	and shall drink neither wine nor strong drink;
	15C	and he shall be filled with the Holy Ghost,
	15D	even from his mother's womb.
	16	And many of the children of Israel
	16B	shall he turn to the Lord their God.
	17	And he shall go before him in the spirit and power of Elias,
	17B	to turn the hearts of the fathers to the children,
	17C	and the disobedient to the wisdom of the just;
	17D	to make ready a people prepared for the Lord.
	18	And Zacharias said unto the angel, Whereby shall I know this?
	18B	for I am an old man, and my wife well stricken in years.
	19	And the angel answering said unto him, I am Gabriel, that stand
	19B	in the presence of God; and am sent to speak unto thee,
	19C	and to shew thee these glad tidings.
	20	And, behold, thou shalt be dumb, and not able to speak,
	20B	until the day that these things shall be performed,
	20C	because thou believest not my words,
	20D	which shall be fulfilled in their season.
	21	And the people waited for Zacharias, and marvelled
	21B	that he tarried so long in the temple.
	22	And when he came out, he could not speak unto them:
	22B	and they perceived - that he had seen a vision in the temple:
	22C	for he beckoned unto them, and remained speechless.
	23	And it came to pass,
	23B	that, as soon as the days of his ministration
	23C	were accomplished, he departed to his own house.
	24	And after those days his wife Elisabeth conceived,
	24B	and hid herself 5 months, saying,
	25	Thus hath the Lord dealt with me
	25B	in the days wherein he looked on me,
A virgin	25C	to take away my reproach among men.
by the	26	And in the 6th. month the angel Gabriel was sent from God
name	26B	unto a city of Galilee, named Nazareth,
of	27	To a virgin espoused to a man whose name was Joseph,
Mary	27B	of the house of David; and the virgin's name was Mary.
	28	And the angel came in (ie: having come in) unto her (ie: Mary),
	28B	and said, Hail, thou that art highly favoured,
	28C	the Lord is with thee:
	28D	blessed art thou among women.
	29	And when she saw him, she was troubled at his saying,
	29B	and cast in her mind what manner of salutation this should be.
	30	And the angel said unto her, Fear not, Mary:
	30B	for thou hast found favour with God.
	31	And, behold, thou shalt conceive in thy womb,
	31B	and bring forth a son, and shalt call his name JESUS. (Is.9:6)
	32	He shall be great, and shall be called the Son of the Highest:
	32B	and the Lord God shall give unto him
	32C	the throne of his father David:

Mt.1 Mk.1 Lk.1 Jn.1

33	And he shall reign over the house of Jacob for ever;
33B	and of his kingdom there shall be no end.
34	Then said Mary unto the angel,
34B	How shall this be, seeing I know not a man?
35	The angel answered and said unto her,
35B	The Holy Ghost shall come upon thee,
35C	and the power of the highest shall overshadow thee:
35D	therefore also that holy thing which shall be born of thee
35E	shall be called the Son of God.
36	And, behold, thy cousin Elisabeth,
36B	she hath also conceived a son in her old age:
36C	and this is the 6th. month with her, who was called barren.
37	For with God nothing shall be impossible.
38	And Mary said, Behold the handmaid of the Lord;
38B	be it unto me according to thy word.
38C	And the angel departed from her.
39	And Mary arose in those days, and went (with haste)
39B	into the hill country, into a city of Juda;
40	And entered into the house of Zacharias, and saluted Elisabeth.
41	And it came to pass, that, when Elisabeth
41B	heard the salutation of Mary, the babe leaped in her womb;
41C	and Elisabeth was filled with the Holy Ghost;
42	And she spake out with a loud voice,
42B	and said, Blessed art thou among women,
42C	and blessed is the fruit of thy womb.
43	And whence is this to me,
43B	that the mother of my Lord should come to me?
44	For, lo, as soon as the voice of thy salutation
44B	sounded in mine ears, the babe leaped in my womb for joy.
45	And blessed is she that believed:
45B	for there shall be a performance
45C	of those things which were told her from the Lord.
46	And Mary said, My soul doth magnify the Lord,
47	And my spirit hath rejoiced in God my Saviour. (Acts 4:12)
48	For he hath regarded the low estate of his handmaiden:
48B	for, behold,
48C	from henceforth all generations shall call me blessed.
49	For He that is mighty hath done to me great things;
49B	and holy is his name.
50	And his mercy is on them that fear him
50B	from generation to generation.
51	He hath shewed strength with his arm;
51B	he hath scattered the proud in the imagination of their hearts.
52	He hath put down the mighty from their seats,
52B	and exalted them of low degree.
53	He hath filled the hungry with good things;
53B	and the rich he hath sent empty away.
54	He hath holpen his servant Israel, in remembrance of his mercy;
55	As he spake to our fathers, to Abraham, and to his seed for ever.
56	And Mary abode with her about 3 months,
56B	and returned to her own house.
57	Now Elisabeth's full time came that she should be delivered;
57B	and she brought forth a son.
58	And her neighbours and her cousins heard
58B	how the Lord had shewed great mercy upon her;
58C	and they rejoiced with her.
59	And it came to pass, (Gen.17:10)
59B	that on the 8th. day they came to circumcise the child;

⊙ John (at line 57B)

The Gospels of Matthew, Mark, Luke, and John: Merged into One Historic Calendar of Events

Mt.1	Mk.1	Lk.1	Jn.1	
		59C		and they called him Zacharias, after the name of his father.
		60		And the mother answered and said, Not so;
		60B		but he shall be called John.
		61		And they said to her,
		61B		There is none of thy kindred that is called by this name.
		62		They made signs to his father, how he would have him called.
		63		And he asked for a wtiting table, and wrote, saying,
		63B		His name is John. And they marvelled all.
		64		And his mouth was opened immediately, and his tongue loosed,
		64B		and he spake, and praised God.
		65		And fear came on all that dwelt round about them:
		65B		and all these sayings were noised abroad
		65C		throughout all the hill country of Judaea.
		66		And all they that heard – laid them up in their hearts,
		66B		saying, What manner of child shall this be!
		66C		And the hand of the Lord was with him.
Zacharias		67		And his father Zacharias was filled with the Holy Ghost,
(filled		67B		and prophesied, saying,
with the		68		Blessed be the Lord God of Israel;
Holy		68B		for he hath visited and redeemed his people,
Spirit)		69		And hath raised up an horn of salvation (Ps.18:2)
Prophecied		69B		for us – in the house of his servant David;
		70		As he spake by the mouth of his holy prophets,
		70B		which have been since the world began:
		71		That we should be saved from our enemies,
		71B		and from the hand of all that hate us;
		72		To perform the mercy promised to our fathers,
		72B		and to remember his holy covenant;
		73		The oath which he sware to our father Abraham,
		74		That he would grant unto us,
		74B		that we being delivered out of the hand of our enemies
		74C		might serve him without fear,
		75		In holiness and righteousness before him,
		75B		all the days of our life.
		76		And thou, child, shalt be called the prophet of the Highest:
		76B		for thou shalt go before the face of the Lord
		76C		to prepare his ways; (Mal.3:1)
		77		To give knowledge of salvation unto his people
		77B		by the remission of their sins,
		78		Through the tender mercy of our God;
		78B		whereby the dayspring from on high hath visited us,
		79		To give light to them that sit in darkness
		79B		and in the shadow of death,
		79C		to guide our feet into the way of peace.
		80		And the child grew, and waxed strong in spirit,
		80B		and was in the deserts till the day of his shewing unto Israel.
		Lk.2		
		1		And it came to pass in those days,
		1B		that there went out a decree from Caesar Augustus,
		1C		that all the world should be taxed.
		2		This taxing was 1st. made when Cyrenius was governor of Syria.
		3		And all went to be taxed, every one into his own city.
		4		And Joseph also went
		4B		up from Galilee, out of the city of Nazareth,
		4C		into Judaea, unto the city of David, which is called Bethlehem;
		4D		(because he was of the house and lineage of David):
		5		To be taxed

| Mt.1 | Mk.1 | Lk.2 | Jn.1 |

| | | 5B | | with Mary his espoused wife, being great with child.
| | | 6 | | And so it was that, while they were there,
| | | 6B | | the days were accomplished - that she should be delivered.

```
Mt.1   Mk.1          Lk.2    Jn.1
                     5B              with Mary his espoused wife, being great with child.
                     6               And so it was that, while they were there,
                     6B                 the days were accomplished - that she should be delivered.
1                                    The book of the generation
1B           Genealogy                  of Jesus Christ, the son of David, the son of Abraham.
2-6             of                   From Abraham ---------------------- to David (the king),
6-16         Joseph                  From king Solomon (son of David) ---- to Joseph (husband of Mary),
16B                                     Mary - of whom was born Jesus, who is called Christ.

17                                   From Abraham ---- to David                            = 14 generations.
17B                                  David ---- until the carrying away into Babylon = 14 generations.
17C                                  The carrying away into Babylon ---- unto Christ = 14 generations.

18                                   Now the birth of Jesus Christ was on this wise:
18B                                  When as his mother Mary - was espoused to Joseph,
18C                                     (before they came together),
18D                                     she was found with child of the Holy Ghost.
19                                   Then Joseph her husband, being a just man,              (Mt.5:20)
19B                                     and not willing to make her a publick example,
19C                                        was minded to put her away privily.
20                                   But while he thought on these things,
20B          The angel                  behold, the angel of the Lord appeared unto him in a dream,
20C          of the Lord                 saying, Joseph, thou son of David,
20D          appeared                    fear not to take unto thee Mary thy wife:
20E          to Joseph                      for that which is conceived in her is of the Holy Ghost.
21           in a dream.             And she shall bring forth a son,
21B                                     and thou shalt call his name JESUS:
21C                                        for he shall save his people from their sins.
22                                   Now all this was done, that it might be fulfilled
22B                                     which was spoken of the Lord by the prophet,
23                                   saying, behold, a virgin shall be with child,
23B                                     and shall bring forth a son,
23C                                     and they shall call his name Emmanuel,              (Is.7:14)
23D                                        which being interpreted is, God with us.
24                                   Then Joseph being raised from sleep
24B                                     did as the angel of the Lord had bidden him,
24C                                     and took unto him his wife:
25                                   And knew her not till she had brought forth her firstborn son:
25B                                        and he called his name JESUS.

  ⊙JESUS           7                 And she brought forth her firstborn son, and
  the Messiah      7B                   wrapped him in swaddling clothes, and laid him in a manger;
                   7C                        because there was no room for them in the Inn.
  Shepherds        8                  And there were in the same country shepherds abiding in the field,
    abiding        8B                    keeping watch over their flock by night.
    in the         9                  And, lo, the angel of the Lord came upon them,
    field.         9B                    and the glory of the Lord shone round about them:    (Mt.24:30A)
                   9C                    and they were sore afraid,
                   10                 And the angel said unto them, Fear not:
                   10B                   for, behold, I bring you good tidings of great joy,
                   10C                      which shall be to all people.
                   11                 For unto you is born this day in the city of David
                   11B                   a Saviour, which is Christ the Lord.
                   12                 And this shall be a sign unto you; Ye shall find the babe
                   12B                   wrapped in swaddling clothes, lying in a manger.
                   13                 And suddenly there was with the angel a multitude
                   13B                   of the heavenly host praising God, and saying,
                   14                    Glory to God in the highest,
                   14B                      and on earth peace, good will toward men.
```

The Gospels of Matthew, Mark, Luke, and John: Merged into One Historic Calendar of Events

Mt.1   Mk.1   Lk.2   Jn.1

	15	And it came to pass,
	15B	as the angels were gone away from them into heaven,
	15C	The shepherds said one to another,
	15D	Let us now go even unto Bethlehem,
	15E	and see this thing which is come to pass,
	15F	which the Lord hath made known unto us.
	16	And they came with haste,
	16B	and found Mary, and Joseph, and the babe lying in a manger.
	17	And when they had seen it, they made known abroad
	17B	the saying which was told them concerning the child.
	18	And all they that heard it wondered at those things
	18B	which were told them by the shepherds.
	19	But Mary kept all these things, and pondered them in her heart.
	20	And the shepherds returned, glorifying and praising God
	20B	for all the things that they had heard and seen,
	20C	as it was told unto them.
	21	And when 8 days were accomplished (Gen.17:12/Lev.12:3)
25B+	21B	for the circumcising of the child, his name was called JESUS,
	21C	which was so named of the angel
	21D	before he was conceived in the womb.
	22	And when the days of her purification
	22B	were accomlished (according to the law of Moses), (Lev.12:1-5)
	22C	they brought him to Jerusalem, to present him to the Lord
	23	(As it is written in the law of the Lord, Every male
	23B	that openeth the womb shall be called holy to the Lord);
	24	And to offer a sacrifice
	24B	according to that which is said in the law of the Lord,
	24C	A pair of turtledoves, or 2 young pigeons. (Lev.12:6-8)
	25	And, behold, there was a man in Jerusalem,
Simeon	25B	whose name was Simeon; and the same man was just and devout,
	25C	waiting for the consolation of Israel:
	25D	and the Holy Ghost was upon him.
	26	And it was revealed unto him by the Holy Ghost, that he
	26B	should not see death, before he had seen the Lord's Christ.
	27	And he came by the Spirit into the temple:
	27B	and when the parents brought in the child Jesus,
	27C	to do for him after the custom of the law,
	28	Then took he him up in his arms, and blessed God, and said,
	29	Lord, now lettest thou thy servant
	29B	depart in peace, according to thy word:
	30	For mine eyes have seen thy salvation,
	31	which thou hast prepared before the face of all people;
	32	A Light to lighten the Gentiles,
	32B	and the glory of thy people Israel.
	33	And Joseph and his mother marvelled
	33B	at those things which were spoken of him.
	34	And Simeon blessed them,
	34B	and said unto Mary his mother, Behold, this child
	34C	is set for the fall and rising again of many in Israel;
	34D	and for a sign - which shall be spoken against;
	35	Yea, a sword shall pierce through thy own soul also,
	35B	that the thoughts of many hearts may be revealed.
Anna	36	And there was one Anna, a prophetess,
	36B	the daughter of Phanuel, of the tribe of Aser:
	36C	she was of a great age,
	36D	and had lived with an husband 7 years from her virginity;
	37	And she was a widow of about 4 score and 4 (4x20+4=84) years,
	37B	which departed not from the temple,

Mt.1	Mk.1	Lk.2	Jn.1	

```
                  37C            but served God with fastings and prayers night and day.
                  38         And she coming in that instant gave thanks likewise to the Lord,
                  38B            and spake of him - to all them,
                  38C                that looked for redemption in Jerusalem.
                  39         And when they had performed
                  39B            all things according to the law of the Lord,
                  39C            they returned into Galilee, to their own city Nazareth.
Mt.2
 1        Wise men           Now when Jesus was born in Bethlehem of Judaea
 1B         came from            in the days of Herod the king,
 1C           the East.          behold, there came wise men from the east to Jerusalem,
 2                          Saying, Where is he that is born King of the Jews?
 2B                             for we have seen his star in the east,
 2C                             and are come to worship him.
 3                          When Herod the king had heard these things,
 3B                             he was troubled, and all Jerusalem with him.
 4                          And when he had gathered
 4B                             all the chief priests and scribes of the people together,
 4C                             he demanded of them - where Christ should be born.
 5                          And they said unto him, In Bethlehem of Judaea:        (Micah 5:2)
 5B                             for thus it is written by the prophet,
 6                          And thou Bethlehem, in the land of Juda
 6B                             art not the least among the princes of Juda:
 6C                             for out of thee shall come
 6D                                 a Governor, that shall rule my people Israel.
 7                          Then Herod, when he had privily called the wise men,
 7B                             enquired of them diligently what time the star appeared.
 8                          And he sent them to Bethlehem,
 8B                             and said, Go and search diligently for the young child;
 8C                             and when ye have found him,
 8D                             bring me word again, that I may come and worship him also.
 9                          When they had heard the king, they departed; and, lo,
 9B                             the star, which they saw in the east, went before them,
 9C                             till it came and stood over where the young child was.
10                          When they saw the star, they rejoiced with exceeding great joy.
11                          And when they were come into the house,
11B                             they saw the young child with Mary his mother,
11C                             and fell down, and worshipped him:
11D                         And when they had opened their treasures,
11E                             they presented unto him gifts;
11F                                 gold, and frankincense, and myrrh.
12                          And being warned of God in a dream
12B                             that they should not return to Herod,
12C                             they departed into their own country another way.
13                          And when they had departed, behold,
13B       Arise!                the angel of the Lord appeared to Joseph in a dream,
13C       And Flee:             saying, Arise, and take the young child and his mother,
13D          into Egypt.        and flee into Egypt,
13E                             and be thou there until I bring thee word:
13F                             for Herod will seek the young child to destroy him.
14                          When he arose,
14B                             he took the young child and his mother by night,
14C                                 and departed into Egypt:
15                          And was there until the death of Herod:
15B                             that it might be fulfilled which was spoken
15C                             of the Lord by the prophet,
15D                             saying, Out of Egypt have I called my son.

16                          Then Herod, when he saw (ie: perceived)
```

The Gospels of Matthew, Mark, Luke, and John: Merged into One Historic Calendar of Events

Mt.2   Mk.1   Lk.2   Jn.1

16B			that he was mocked by the wise men, was exceeding wroth,
16C	Herod slew		and sent forth, and slew all the children
16D	all the children		that were in Bethlehem, and in all the coast thereof,
16E	from 2 years old		from 2 years old and under, according to the time
16F	and under.		which he had diligently enquired of the wise men.
17			Then was fulfilled
18			that which was spoken by Jeremy the prophet,
18B			saying, In Rama was there a voice heard,
18C			lamentation, and weeping, and great mourning,
18D			Rachel (ie: sheep/ewe) weeping for her children, (Jer.31:15)
18E			and would not be comforted, because they are not.
19			But when Herod was dead, behold,
19B			an angel of the Lord appeared in a dream to Joseph in Egypt,
20			saying, Arise, and take the young child and his mother,
20B			and go into the land of Israel:
20C			for they are dead which sought the young child's life.
21			And he arose, and took the young child and his mother,
21B			and came into the land of Israel.
22			But when he heard that Archelaus did reign in Judaea
22B			in the room of his father Herod,
22C			he was afraid to go thither:
22D			notwithstanding, being warned of God in a dream,
22E	Was Spoken		he turned aside into the parts of Galilee:
23	(not written)		And he came and dwelt in a city called Nazareth:
23B	by the		that it might be fulfilled - which
23C	prophets.		was spoken by the prophets, He shall be called a Nazarene.
		40	And the child grew, and waxed strong in spirit,
		40B	filled with wisdom: and the grace of God was upon him.
		41	Now his parents
	Jesus	41B	went to Jerusalem every year at the feast of the passover.
	12 years	42	And when he was 12 years old,
	old.	42B	they went up to Jerusalem after the custom of the feast.
		43	And when they had fulfilled the days,
		43B	as they returned, the child Jesus tarried behind in Jerusalem;
		43C	and Joseph and his mother knew not of it.
		44	But they, supposing him to have been in the company,
		44B	went a day's journey;
		44C	and they sought him among their kinfolk and acquaintance.
		45	And when they found him not,
		45B	they turned back again to Jerusalem, seeking him.
		46	And it came to pass, that after 3 days they found him
		46B	in the temple, sitting in the midst of the doctors,
		46C	both hearing them, and asking them questions.
		47	And all that heard him
		47B	were astonished at his understanding and answers.
		48	And when they saw him, they were amazed: and his
		48B	mother said unto him, Son, why hast thou thus dealt with us?
		48C	behold, thy father and I have sought thee sorrowing!
		49	And he said unto them, How is it that ye sought me?
		49B	wist ye not that I must be about my Father's business?
		50	And they understood not the saying which he spake unto them.
		51	And he went down with them,
		51B	and came to Nazareth, and was subject unto them:
		51C	But his mother kept all these sayings in her heart. (Lk.2:19)
		52	And Jesus increased in wisdom and stature,
		52B	and in favour with God and man.
		Lk.3	
		1	Now in the 15th. year of the reign of Tiberius Caesar,

Mt.2	Mk.1	Lk.3	Jn.1	
		1B		Pontius Pilate being governor of Judaea, and
		1C		Herod being tetrarch of Galilee, and his brother
		1D		Philip tetrarch of Ituraea and the region of Trachonitis,
		1E		Lysanias the tetrarch of Abilene,
		2		Annas and Caiaphas being the high priests:
		2B		The word of God
		2C		came unto John (the son of Zacharias) in the wilderness.

Mt.3				
1				In those days came John the Baptist,
1B				preaching in the wilderness of Judaea,
2				And saying, Repent ye: for the kingdom of heaven is at hand.

	Mk.1			
	4			John did baptize in the wilderness,
		3		And he came into all the country about Jordan,
	4B	3B		preaching
	4C	3C		the baptism of repentance for the remission of sins:
3				For this is he that was spoken of:
	2	4		As it is written in the prophets,
3B		4B		in the book of the words of Isaias the prophet, saying,
	2B			Behold, I send my messenger before thy face, (Is.40:3-5)
	2C			which shall prepair the way before thee:
3C	3	4C		The voice of one crying in the wilderness,
3D	3B	4D		Prepare ye the way of the Lord, make his paths straight.
		5		Every valley shall be filled,
		5B		and every mountain and hill shall be brought low;
		5C		and the crooked shall be made straight,
		5D		and the rough ways shall be made smooth;
		6		And all flesh shall see the salvation of God.
	1			The beginning of the gospel of Jesus Christ, the Son of God:
4	6			And John was clothed with (his raiment of) camel's hair,
4B	6B			and a leather girdle (girdle of a skin) about his loins;
4C	6C			and he did eat (his meat was) locust and wild honey.
5	5	Baptizing		And there went out to him
5B	5B	in the		all (the land of) Judaea, and (they of) Jerusalem,
5C		river of		and all the region round about Jordan:
6	5C	Jordan		And were (all) baptized of him in the river of Jordan,
6B	5D			confessing their sins.
7				But when he saw
7B				many of the Pharisees and Sadducees come to his baptism;
7C				he said unto them
		7		(to the multitude that came forth to be baptized of him),
7D		7B		O generation of vipers,
7E		7C		who has warned you to flee from the wrath to come?
8		8		But bring forth therefore fruits meet (worthy) of repentance;
9		8B		And begin (think) not
9B		8C		to say within yourselves, We have Abraham to our father:
9C		8D		For I say unto you, That God is able
9D		8E		of these stones to raise up children unto Abraham.
10		9		And now also the axe is laid unto the root of the trees:
10B		9B		every tree therefore which bringeth not forth good fruit
10C		9C		is hewn down, and cast into the fire.
		10		And the people asked him, saying, What shall we do then?
		11		He answered and said unto them, (Mt.3:2)
		11B		He that hath 2 coats, let him impart to him that has none;
		11C		and he that hath meat, let him do likewise. (1 Thes.2:8)
		12		Then came also publicans (ie: tax collectors) to be baptized,
		12B		and said unto him, Master, what shall we do?

Mt.3	Mk.1	Lk.3	Jn.1	
		13		And he said unto them,
		13B		Exact no more than that which is appointed you.
		14		And the soldiers likewise demanded of him,
		14B		saying, And what shall we do?
		14C		And he said unto them,
		14D		Do violence to no man, neither accuse any falsely;
		14E		and be content with your wages.
		15		And as the people were in expectation,
		15B		and all men mused in their hearts of John,
		15C		whether he were the Christ, or not:
	7	16		John answered (he preached), saying unto them all,
11B	7B	16C		There cometh one mightier than I, after me,
11C				whose shoes I am not worthy to bear;
	7C	16D		the latchet of whose shoes
	7D	16E		I am not worthy (to stoop down, and) to unloose:
11A	8	16B		I indeed baptize(d) you with water - unto repentance,
11D	8B	16F		but, he shall baptize you with the Holy Ghost, and fire:
12		17		Whose fan is in his hand, and he will throughly purge his floor,
12B		17B		and will gather the (his) wheat into his (the) garner;
12C		17C		but the chaff he will burn (burn up) with fire unquenchable.
		18		And many other things
		18B		in his exhortation preached he unto the people.
				John also told Herod (the tetrarch) his fault. (See Lk.3:19,20)
		21		Now when all the people were baptized:
	9	21B		And it came to pass in those days,
13	9B			that Jesus came from Nazareth of Galilee
13B				to Jordan unto John - to be baptized of him. (? Mk.1:5)
14				But John forbad him, saying,
14B				I have need to be baptized of thee, and comest thou to me?
15				Jesus answering said unto him, Suffer it to be so now:
15B				for thus it becometh us to fulfil all righteousness.
15C				Then he suffered;
16	9C	21C		and Jesus also was baptized of John in the Jordan.
16B	10			And straightway coming up out of the water:
		21D		And praying,
16C	10B	21E		and, lo, he saw the heavens opened unto him:
16D	10C	22		And he saw the Spirit of God (the Holy Ghost)
16E	10D	22B		descending (in a bodily shape) like a dove,
16F	10E	22C		descending, and lighting upon him: (Jn.1:32,33)
17	11	22D		And lo there came a voice from heaven,
17B	11B	22E		saying, This is (Thou art) my beloved Son,
17C	11C	22F		in whom (in thee) I am well pleased.
		23		And Jesus himself began to be about 30 years,
Genealogy		23B		(being - as was supposed, the son of Joseph.)
of		23C		which was of Heli.
Jesus		38-31		Shown in reverse: From Adam (which was of God) ----- to David.
		31-23		Shown in reverse: From Nathan (son of David) ------- to Heli.
Mt.4		Lk.4		
		1		And Jesus being full of the Holy Ghost returned from the Jordan:
1	12	1B		And then (immediately) he (Jesus) was led up of (by) the Spirit;
1B	12B	1C		and driveth him into the wilderness, (Mt.3:1,3/Lk.8:29)
1C				to be tempted of the devil.
	13			And he was there in the wilderness (He.3:8,17/Rev.12:6)
	13B	2		40 days, being tempted of Satan (the devil); (Acts 7:30,36-45)
	13C			and was with the wild beasts: (Acts 28:4)
		2B		And in those days he did eat nothing:
2				And when he had fasted 40 days and 40 nights:

Mt.4	Mk.1	Lk.4	Jn.1	
2B		2C		And when they were ended, he was afterward an hungered:
3		3		And when the devil (the tempster) came to him,
3B		3B		he said unto him, If thou be the Son of God, (Mt.3:17)
3C		3C		command that this stone (these stones) be made bread.
4		4		But he (Jesus) answered him, saying,
4B		4B		It is written, That man shall not live by bread alone,
4C		4C		but by every word that proceedeth out of the mouth of God
5		9		Then the devil taketh him up into the holy city (to Jerusalem),
5B		9B		and setteth him on a pinnacle of the temple,
6		9C		and saith unto him, If thou be the Son of God,
6B	Thou	9D		cast thyself down from thence:
6C	shalt	10		For it is written,
6D	not	10B		He shall give his angels charge over (concerning) thee,
	tempt	10C		to keep thee: (Ps.91:11,12)
6E	the	11		And in their hands they shall bear thee up,
6F	LORD	11B		lest at any time thou dash thy foot against a stone.
7	your	12		And Jesus answering said unto him,
7B	God.	12B		It is written again (it is said),
7C		12C		Thou shalt not tempt the Lord thy God. (De.6:16)
8		5		Again, the devil taketh him up into an (exceeding) high mountain,
8B		5B		and shewed him all the kingdoms of the world,
		5C		in a moment of time,
8C				and the glory of them.
9		6		And the devil said unto him, All these things (all the power)
9B		6B		will I give thee, and the glory of them:
		6C		for that is delivered unto me;
		6D		and to whomsoever I will give it:
9C		7		If thou wilt fall down and therefore worship me,
		7B		all shall be thine.
10		8		And Jesus answered and said unto him,
10B		8B		Get thee hence (behind me), Satan: (Mk.8:33)
10C		8C		for it is written, Thou shalt worship the Lord thy God,
10D		8D		and him only shalt thou serve.
		13		And when the devil had ended all the temptation,
11				then the devil leaveth him,
		13B		he departed from him for a season (ie: a time).
11B	13D			And, behold, the angels came and ministered unto him.
		14		And Jesus returned in the power of the Spirit into Galilee:
		14B		and there went out a fame of him
		14C		through all the region round about.
		15		And he taught in their synagogues, being glorified of all.
			15	John bare witness of him, and cried, saying,
			15B	This was he of whom I spake, He that cometh after me
			15C	is preferred before me: for he was before me.
			16	And of his fulness have all we received, and grace for grace.
			17	For the law was given by Moses,
			17B	but grace and truth came by Jesus Christ.
			18	No man hath seen God at any time;
			18B	the only begotten Son,
			18C	which is in the bossem of the Father - he hath declared Him.
			19	And this is the record (ie: testimony/witness) of John,
			19B	when the Jews sent priests and Levites
			19C	from Jerusalem - to ask him, Who art thou?
			20	And he (ie: John) confessed and denied not;
			20B	but confessed, I am not the Christ.
			21	And they asked him, What then?
			21B	Art thou Elias? And he saith, I am not.

The Gospels of Matthew, Mark, Luke, and John: Merged into One Historic Calendar of Events

Mt.4   Mk.1   Lk.4   Jn.1

21C	Art thou that prophet? And he answered, No.
22	Then said they unto him, Who art thou?
22B	that we may give an answer to them that sent us.
22C	What sayest thou of thyself?
23	He said, I am the voice of one crying in the wilderness,
23B	Make straight the way of the Lord,
23C	as said the prophet Esaias. (Is.40:3)
24	And they which were sent were of the Pharisees.
25	And they asked him, and said unto him, Why baptizest thou then,
25B	if thou be not that Christ, nor Elias, neither that prophet?
26	John answered them, saying, I baptize with water:
26B	but there standeth one among you, whom ye know not;
27	He it is, who coming after me - is preferred before me,
27B	whose shoe's latchet I am not worthy to unloose.
28	These things were done in Bethabara
28B	beyond Jordan, where John was baptizing.
29	The next day John seeth Jesus coming unto him,
29B	and saith, Behold the Lamb of God,
29C	which taketh away the sin of the world.
30	This is he of whom I said,
30B	After me cometh a man
30C	which is preferred before me: for he was before me. (Jn.1:27)
31	And I knew him not:
31B	but that he should be made minifest to Israel,
31C	therefore, am I come baptizing (ie: washing) with water.
32	And John bare record, saying, I saw the Spirit descending
32B	from heaven like a dove, and it abode upon him.
33	And I knew him not: but he that sent me to baptize with water,
33B	the same said unto me, Upon whom thou shalt see
33C	the Spirit descending, and remaining on him,
33D	the same is he which baptizeth with the Holy Ghost.
34	And I saw, and bare record - that this is the Son of God.

John
and 2 of
  his disciples,
  Andrew and ???

35	The next day again, stood John and 2 of his disciples; (Jn.1:40)
36	and looking upon Jesus as he walked,
36B	he saith, Behold the Lamb of God!
37	And the 2 disciples heard him speak, and they followed Jesus.
38	Then Jesus turned, and saw them following,
38B	and saith unto them, What seek ye?
38C	They said unto him, Rabbi,
38D	(which is to say, being interpreted, Master),
38E	where dwellest thou?
39	He (ie: Jesus) saith unto them, Come and see.
39B	They came and saw where he dwelt,
39C	and abode with him that day: for it was about the 10th. hour.
40	One of the 2 which heard John, and followed him (ie: Jesus),
40B	was Andrew (the brother of Simon Peter).

Simon Peter

41	He first findeth his brother Simon, and saith unto him, We have
41B	found the messias (which is, being interpreted, the Christ).
42	And he brought him to Jesus.
42B	And when Jesus beheld him,
42C	he said, Thou art Simon the son of Jona: thou
42D	shalt be called Cephas (which is by interpretation, Peter).
43	The day following
43B	Jesus would (ie: desired to) go forth into Galilee,

Philip,
  follow me.

43C	and findeth Philip, and saith unto him, Follow me.
44	Now Philip was of Bethsaida, the city of Andrew and Peter.

Mt.4	Mk.1	Lk.4	Jn.1

	45 Philip findeth Nathanael,
	45B and saith unto him, We have found him,
	45C of whom Moses - in the law, and the prophets, did write,
	45D Jesus of Nazareth, the son of Joseph. (Lk.3:23)
Na-than'a-el	46 And Nathanael said said unto him,
	46B Can there any good thing come out of Nazareth? (Jn.7:52)
	46C Philip saith unto him, Come and see.
	47 Jesus saw Nathanael coming to him, and saith of him,
	47B Behold an Israelite indeed, in whom is no guile!
	48 Nathanael saith unto him, Whence knowest thou me?
	48B Jesus answered and said unto him,
	48C Before that Philip called thee,
	48D when thou wast under the fig tree, I saw thee.
	49 Nathanael answered and saith unto him,
	49B Rabbi, thou art the Son of God; (Mt.16:16)
	49C thou art the King of Israel. (Jn.6:14,15)
	50 Jesus answered and said unto him, Because I said unto thee,
	50B I saw thee under the fig tree - believest thou?
	50C thou shalt see greater things than these.
	51 And he (ie: Jesus) saith unto him, Verily, verily, I say unto you,
	51B Hereafter ye shall see heaven open, and the angels of God
	51C ascending and descending upon the Son of man.
	Jn.2
	1 And on the 3rd. day there was a marriage in Cana of Galilee;
	1B and the mother of Jesus was there:
	2 And Jesus was also called, and his disciples, to the marriage.
	3 And when they wanted (ie: to be in want of = insufficient) wine,
	3B the mother of Jesus saith unto him, They have no wine.
	4 Jesus saith unto her, Woman,
	4B what have I to do with thee? mine hour is not yet come.
	5 His mother saith unto the servants,
	5B Whatsoever he saith unto you, do.
	6 And there were set there 6 waterpots of stone,
	6B (after the manner of the purifying of the Jews),
	6C containing 2 or 3 firkins apiece.
	7 Jesus saith unto them, Fill the waterpots with water.
	7B And they filled them up to the brim.
	8 And he saith unto them,
	8B Draw out now, and bear unto the governor of the feast.
The water	8C And they bare (ie: to bring forth/carry) it.
turned	9 When the ruler (ie: governor) of the feast had tasted
into wine.	9B the water that was made wine, and knew not whence it was:
	9C (but the servants which drew the water knew);
	9D the governor of the feast called the bridegroom,
This	10 And saith unto him,
the	10B Every man at the beginning - doth set forth good wine;
beginning	10C and when men have well drunk, then that which is worse:
of	10D but thou hast kept the good wine until now.
miracles.	11 This, beginning of miracles - did Jesus in Cana of Galilee,
	11B and manifested forth his glory;
	11C and his disciples believed on him. (Jn.1:41)
	12 After this he went down to Capernaum, (Lk.4:31)
	12B he, and his mother, and his brethren, and his disciples:
	12C And they continued there not many days. (Jn.7:3,5)
	13 And the Jews' passover was at hand:
	13B And Jesus went up to Jerusalem, and
	14 found in the temple those that sold oxen and sheep and doves,

The Gospels of Matthew, Mark, Luke, and John: Merged into One Historic Calendar of Events

Mt.4　　Mk.1　　Lk.4　　Jn.2

14B	and the changers of money sitting:
15	And when he made a scourge (ie: a whip) of small cords
15B	he drove them all out of the temple,
15C	and the sheep, and the oxen;
15D	and poured out the changers' money, and overthrew the tables;
16	And said unto them that sold doves, Take these things hence;
16B	make not my Father's house an house of merchandise.
17	And his disciples remembered - that it was written,
17B	The zeal of thine house hath eaten me up.　　　　(Ps.69:9)
18	Then answered the Jews and said unto him,
18B	What sign shewest thou unto us,
18C	seeing that thou doest these things?
19	Jesus answered and said unto them,
19B	Destroy this temple, and in 3 days I will raise it up.
20	Then said the Jews, 46 years was this
20B	temple in building, and wilt thou rear it up in 3 days?
21	But he (ie: Jesus) spake of the temple of his body.　(Mt.17:23)
22	When therefore he was risen from the dead,
22B	his disciples remembered that he had said this unto them;
22C	and they believed the scripture,
22D	and the word which Jesus had said.
23	Now when he (ie: Jesus) was in Jerusalem at the passover,
23B	in the feast many believed in his name
23C	when they saw the miracles which he did.
24	But Jesus did not commit himself unto them,
24B	because he knew all men,　　　　　　　　　　(Jn.6:15,26)
25	And needed not that any should testify of man:
25B	for he knew (ie: perceived/understood) what was in man.

Jn.3

Must be born again to have the ability to SEE!

1	There was a man of the Pharisees,
1B	named Nicodemus, a ruler of the Jews:　　　　　(Jn.19:39)
2	The same came to Jesus by night, and said unto him
2B	Rabbi, we know that thou art a teacher come from God;
2C	for no man can do these miracles
2D	that thou doest, except God be with him.
3	Jesus answered and said unto him,
3B	Verily, verily, I say unto thee,
3C	Except a man be born again, he cannot see the kingdom of God.
4	Nicodemus saith unto him, How can a man be born when he is old?
4B	Can he enter the 2nd. time into his mother's womb, and be born?
5	Jesus answered, Verily, verily, I say unto thee,
5B	Except a man be born of Water and the Spirit,　(Jn.4:10,14)
5C	he cannot enter into the kingdom of God.　(1 Jn.5:8)
6	That which is born of the flesh is flesh;
6B	and that which is born of the Spirit is spirit.　(Gal.4:29)
7	Marvel not that I said unto thee, Ye must be born again.
8	The wind bloweth where it listeth,
8B	and thou hearest the sound thereof,
8C	but canst not tell whence it cometh, and whither it goeth:
8D	So is every one that is born of the Spirit.
9	Nicodemus answered and said unto him, How can these things be?
10	Jesus answered and said unto him,
10B	Art thou a master of Israel, and knowest not these things?
11	Verily, verily, I say unto thee,
11B	We speak that we do know, and testify that we have seen;
11C	and ye receive not our witness (ie: testimony).

Mt.4   Mk.1   Lk.4   Jn.3

	12	If I have told you earthly things, and ye believe not,
	12B	how shall ye believe, if I tell you heavenly things?
	13	And no man hath ascended up to heaven, but he that came down
Even so must	13B	from heaven, even the Son of man which is in heaven. (Jn.1:18)
the Son of man	14	And as Moses lifted up the serpent in the wilderness, (Num.21:8,9)
be lifted up.	14B	even so must the Son of man be lifted up:
	15	That whosoever believeth in him
	15B	should not perish (ie: be destroyed), but have eternal life.
	16	For God so (ie: in this manner) loved the world,
	16B	that he gave his only begotten (ie: born) Son, that whosoever
	16C	believeth on him should not perish, but have everlasting life.
	17	For God sent not his Son into the world to condemn the world;
	17B	but that the world through him might be saved. (Acts 4:12)
	18	He that believeth on him is not condemned;
	18B	but he that believeth not - is condemned already, because he
	18C	hath not believed in the name of the only begotten Son of God.
	19	And this is the condemnation (ie: accusation/judgment),
	19B	that light is come into the world, (Jn.1:4,9)
	19C	and men loved darkness rather than light,
	19D	because their deeds were evil. (Rom.3:11,12)
	20	For every one that doeth evil hateth the light,
	20B	neither cometh to the light,
	20C	lest his deeds should be reproved (ie: he be told his faults).
	21	But he that doeth (ie: worketh) truth cometh to the light,
The disciples	21B	that his deeds may be manifest,
of Jesus	21C	that they are wrought in God. (Phil.2:13)
baptized	22	After these things came Jesus and his disciples into the land of
in Judaea	22B	Judaea; and there he tarried with them, and baptized. (Jn.4:2)
John baptized	23	And John also was baptizing in Aenon (near to Salim), because
at the	23B	there was much water there: And they came, and were baptized.
Aenon Springs	24	For John was not yet cast into prison.
	25	Then there arose a question
	25B	between some of John's disciples and the Jews about purifying.
	26	And they came unto John, and said unto him, Rabbi (ie: Master),
	26B	he that was with thee beyond Jordan,
	26C	to whom thou bearest witness,
	26D	behold, the same baptizeth, and all come to him.
	27	John answered and said,
	27B	A man can receive nothing, except it be given him from heaven.
	28	Ye yourselves bear me witness, that I said,
	28B	I am not the Christ, but that I am sent before him.
	29	He that hath the bride is the bridegroom:
	29B	but the friend of the bridegroom,
	29C	which standeth and heareth him,
	29D	rejoiceth greatly because of the bridegroom's voice:
	29E	This my joy therefore is fulfilled.
	30	He must increase, but I must decrease.
	31	He that cometh from above - is above all:
	31B	He that is of the earth is earthly, and speaketh of the earth:
	31C	He that cometh from heaven - is above all.
	32	And what he hath seen and heard, that he testifieth;
	32B	and no man receiveth his testimony.
	33	He that received his testimony
	33B	hath set to his seal that God is true.
	34	For he whom God hath sent speaketh the words of God: (Jn.14:24)
	34B	for God giveth him the Spirit - not by measure.

Mt.4   Mk.1   Lk.4   Jn.3

	35	The Father loveth the Son,
	35B	and hath given all things into his hand.
	36	He that believeth on the Son hath everlasting life:
	36B	and he that believeth not the Son shall not see life;
	36C	but the wrath of God abideth on him. (Lk.17:26,27)

Jn.4

Sychar is a city of Samaria.	1	When therefore the Lord knew how the Pharisees had heard
	1B	that Jesus made and baptized more disciples than John
	2	(though Jesus himself baptized not, but his disciples),
	3	he left Judaea, and departed again into (ie: toward) Galilee.
	4	And he must needs go through Samaria:
	5	Then cometh he to a city of Samaria, which is called Sychar,
	5B	near to the parcel of ground that Jacob gave to his son Joseph.
	6	Now Jacob's well was there:
	6B	Jesus therefore, being wearied (ie: laboured) with his journey,
	6C	sat thus on the well:
	6D	And it was about the 6th. hour.
	7	There cometh a woman of Samaria to draw water:
	7B	Jesus saith unto her, Give me to drink.
	8	(For his disciples were gone away unto the city to buy meat.)
	9	Then saith the woman (of Samaria) unto him,
	9B	How is it that thou, being a Jew,
	9C	askest drink of me, which am a woman of Samaria?
	9D	For the Jews have no dealings with the Samaritans.
	10	Jesus answered and said unto her,
	10B	If thou knewest the gift of God, (Jn.3:16)
	10C	and who it is that saith to thee, Give me to drink; (Mt.16:16)
	10D	thou wouldest have asked of him, (1 Jn.5:14)(1 Thes.5:17,18)
	10E	and he would have given thee living water. (Rev.7:17)

Cities
of
Galilee
 -Cana
 -Capernaum
 -Nazareth

Cities
of
Samaria
 -Sychar

Cities
of
Judaea
 -Jerusalem

11	The woman saith unto him, Sir,
11B	thou hast nothing to draw with, and the well is deep:
11C	from whence then hast thou that living water?
12	Art thou greater than our father Jacob, who gave us the well,
12B	and drank thereof himself, and his children, and his cattle?
13	Jesus answered and said unto her,
13B	Whosoever drinketh of this water shall thirst again:
14	But whosoever drinketh of the water
14B	that I shall give him - shall never thirst;
14C	but the water that I shall give him, shall be in him
14D	a well of water springing up into everlasting life.
15	The woman saith unto him, Sir, give me this water,
15B	that I thirst not, neither come hither to draw.
16	Jesus saith unto her, Go, call thy husband, and come hither.
17	The woman answered and said, I have no husband. (1 Cor.14:35)
17B	Jesus said unto her, Thou hast well said, I have no husband:
18	For thou hast had 5 husbands;
18B	and he whom thou now hast is not thy husband:
18C	in that saidst thou truly.
19	The woman saith unto him, Sir, I perceive that thou art a prophet.
20	Our fathers worshipped in this mountain; and ye say,
20B	that in Jerusalem is the place where men ought to worship.
21	Jesus said unto her, Woman, believe me,
21B	the hour cometh, when ye shall neither in this mountain,
21C	nor yet at Jerusalem, worship the Father.
22	Ye worship, ye know not what:
22B	we know what we worship: for salvation is of the Jews.
23	But the hour cometh, and now is, when the true worshippers

Mt.4　Mk.1　Lk.4　Jn.4

	23B	shall worship the Father in Spirit and in truth:
	23C	for the Father seeketh such to worship him.
	24	God is a Spirit: and they
	24B	that worship him must worship him in spirit and in truth.
	25	The woman saith unto him,
	25B	I know that Messaias cometh, which is called Christ:
	25C	when he is come, he will tell us all things.
	26	Jesus saith unto her, I that speak unto thee am he.
	27	And upon this came his disciples,
	27B	and marvelled that he talked with the woman: yet no man said,
	27C	What seekest thou? or, Why talkest thou with her?
	28	The woman then left her waterpot, and went into the city,
	29	and saith to the men, Come, see a man,
	29B	which told me all things that I ever did:
	29C	Is not this the Christ?
	30	Then they went out of the city, and came unto him.
	31	In the mean while his disciples prayed him, saying, Master, eat.
	32	He said unto them, I have meat to eat - that ye know not of.
	33	Therefore said the disciples one to another,
Yet 4 month	33B	Hath any man brought him ought (ie: something) to eat?
and then	34	Jesus saith unto them, My meat is to do　　(Mt.5:17/Jn.17:4)
cometh	34B	the will of him that sent me, and to finish his work.
Harvest?	35	Say not ye, There are yet 4 month, and then cometh harvest.
	35B	Behold, I say unto you, Lift up your eyes, and look
	35C	on the fields; for they are white already to harvest.
	36	And he that reapeth receiveth wages,
	36B	and gathereth fruit unto life eternal: that both
	36C	he that soweth and he that reapeth - may rejoice together.
	37	And herein is that saying true, One soweth, and another reapeth.
	38	I set you to reap that whereon ye bestowed no labour:
	38B	Other men laboured, and ye are entered into their labours.
	39	And many of the Samaritans (of that city)
	39B	believed on him for the saying of the woman,
	39C	which testified, He told me all that ever I did.
	40	So when the Samaritans were come unto him.
	40B	they besought him that he would tarry with them:
	40C	And he abode there 2 days.
	41	And many more believed because of his own word;
	42	And said unto the woman,
	42B	Now we believe, not because of thy saying:
	42C	for we have heard him ourselves, and know
	42D	that this is indeed the Christ, the Saviour of the world.
	43	After 2 days he departed hence, and went into Galilee:
	44	For Jesus himself testified,
Jesus came	44B	that a prophet hath no honour in his own country.　(Lk.4:23)
into Galilee.	45	Then when he was come into Galilee, the Galileans received him,
	45B	having seen all the things that he did at Jerusalem
	45C	at the feast: for they also went unto the feast.　(Jn.2:13,23)
Cana of Galilee.	46	So Jesus came again into Cana of Galilee,
	46B	where he had made the water into wine.　(Jn.2:1-11)
	46C	And there was a certain nobleman, whose son was sick at Capernaum:
	47	When he heard that Jesus was come out of Judaea into Galilee,
	47B	he went unto him, and besought him - that he would come down,
	47C	and heal his son: for he was at the point of death.
	48	Then Jesus said unto him,
	48B	Except ye see signs and wonders, ye will not believe.
	49	The nobleman saith unto him, Sir, come down ere my child die.

Mt.4   Mk.1   Lk.4   Jn.4

	50	Jesus saith unto him, Go thy way; thy son liveth.

```
                      50    Jesus saith unto him, Go thy way; thy son liveth.
                      50B   And the man believed
                      50C     the word that Jesus had spoken unto him, and he went away.
                      51    And as he was now going down,
                      51B     his servants met him, and told him, saying, Thy son liveth.
                      52    Then enquired he of them the hour when he began to amend.
                      52B   And they said unto him,
                      52C     Yesterday at the 7th. hour the fever left him.
                      53    So, the father knew
                      53B     that it was at that same hour, in which Jesus said unto him,
                      53C       Thy son liveth: And himself believed, and his whole house.
                      54    This again, a 2nd. miracle
                      54B     that Jesus did, when he came out of Judaea into Galilee.

  Jesus         16          And he (ie: Jesus) came to Nazareth, where he was brought up:
    stood up    16B         And, as his custom was, he went into the synagogue
    to read.    16C           on the sabbath day:  And he stood up for to read.
                17          And there was delivered unto him the book of the prophet Esaias.
                17B         And when he had opened the book,
                17C           he found the place where it was written,            (Is.61:1,2)
                18          The Spirit of the Lord is upon me, because
                18B           he hath anointed me to preach the gospel to the poor;
                18C           he hath sent me to heal the broken-hearted,
                18D             to preach deliverance to the captives,
                18E               and recovering of sight to the blind,
                18F             to set at liberty them that are bruised,
                19             to preach the acceptable year of the Lord.
                20          And he closed the book, and he gave it again
                20B           to the minister (ie: servant/officer), and sat down.
                20C           And the eyes of all of them
                20D             that were in the synagogue were fastened on him.
                21          And he (ie: Jesus) began to say unto them,
                21B           This day is this scripture fulfilled in your ears.
                22          And all bare him witness, and wondered
                22B           at the gracious words which proceeded out of his mouth.
                22C           And they said, Is not this Joseph's son?
                23          And he said unto them, Ye will surely say unto me this proverb,
                23B           Physician, heal thyself:
                23C           whatsoever we have heard done in Capernaum,          (Jn.4:46-52)
                23D             do also here in thy country (ie: thy home-land/turf)
                24          And he said, Verily I say unto you,
                24B           No prophet is accepted in his own country.    (Jn.1:11/Jn.4:44)
                25          But I tell you of a truth,
                25B           many widows were in Israel - in the days of Elias,
                25C           when the heaven was shut up 3 years and 6 months,
                25D           when great famine was throughout all the land;
                26            But unto none of them was Elias sent, save unto      (1 Ki.17)
                26B             Sarepta (a city in Sidon), unto a woman that was a widow.
                27          And many lepers were in Israel
                27B           in the time of Eliseus the prophet;                  (2 Ki.5)
                27C           And none of them was cleansed, saving Naaman the Syrian.
                28          And all they in the synagogue,
                28B           when they heard these things - were filled with wrath,
                29          And they rose up, and thrust him out of the city, and led him
                29B           unto the brow of the hill whereon their city was built,
                29C             that they might cast him down headlong.
                30          But he passing through the midst of them - went his way.
```

Mt.4	Mk.1	Lk.4	Jn.4	
		Lk.3		
		19		
John		19B		But Herod the tetrarch, being reproved by him (ie: John)
shut up		19C		for Herodias (his brother Philip's wife),
in prison.		20		and for all the evils which Herod had done;
				Added yet this above all, that he shut up John in prison.
	14			Now after that John was cast into prison:
12				When Jesus had heard that John was cast into prison,
12B	14B			He (ie: Jesus) departed into Galilee: (Jn.4:45)
13				And leaving Nazareth, he came and dwelt in Capernaum, which is
13B				upon the sea coast, in the borders of Zabulon and Nephthalim:
14				That it might be fulfilled
14B				which was spoken by Esaias the prophet, saying,
15				The land of Zabulon, and the land of Nephthalim,
15B				the way of the sea, beyond Jordan, Galilee of the Gentiles;
16				The people which sat in darkness - saw a great light;
16B				and to them which sat in the region and shadow of death
16C				light is sprung up.
17				From that time Jesus began to preach,
	14C	Jesus		preaching the gospel of the kingdom of God:
17B	15	began to		And to say (saying),
	15B	preach.		The time is fulfilled,
17C	15D			Repent ye, and believe the gospel:
17D	15C			For the kingdom of heaven (the kingdom of God) is at hand.
18	16	Simon		And Jesus, walking (as he walked) by the sea of Galilee,
18B	16B	&		he saw 2 brethren, Simon (called Peter) and Andrew,
18C	16C	Andrew		casting a net into the sea: for they were fishers (fisher men).
19	17			And Jesus said unto them, Come ye after (follow) me, (Jn.1:43)
19B	17B	Jesus said,		and I will make you to become fishers of men.
20	18	Follow me.		And straightway
20B	18B			they left (forsook) their nets, and followed him.
21	19			And going on from thence (when he had gone a little farther),
21B		James		he saw 2 other brethren,
21C	19B	&		James (the son of Zebedee) and John his brother;
21D	19C	John		who also were in a ship;
21E	19D			in the ship with Zebedee their father, mending nets.
21F	20	And they		And straightway he (ie: Jesus) called them.
22		immediately		And they immediately left the ship and their father,
	20B	followed him.		(they left their father in the ship with the hired servants.)
22B	20C			and went after (followed) him.
	21	31		And they came down to (went into) Capernaum (a city of Galilee):
	21B			And straightway on the sabbath day he entered into the synagogue,
		31B		and taught them on the sabbath days.
	22	32		And they were astonished at his doctrine:
		32B		for his word was with power;
	22B			For he taught them as one that had authority,
	22C			and not as the scribes.
23				And Jesus went about all Galilee, teaching in their synagogues,
23B				and preaching the gospel of the kingdom,
23C				and healing all manner of sickness
23D				and all manner of disease among the people.
24				And his fame went throughout all Syria:
24B				And they brought unto him all sick people
24C				that were taken with divers diseases and torments,

Mt.4	Mk.1	Lk.4	Jn.4	
24D				and those which were possessed with devils,
24E				and those which were lunatick,
24F				and those that had the palsy;
24G				and he healed them.
25				And there followed him great multitudes of people – from
25B				Galilee, and Decapolis, and Jerusalem,
25C				and Judaea, and beyond Jordan.
	23	33		And in the (their) synagogue there was a man,
	23B	33B		with an unclean spirit – of an devil,
	23C	33C		and he cried out with a loud voice,
	24	34		Saying, Let us alone;
	24B	34B		what have we to do with thee,
	24C	34C		thou Jesus of Nazareth? art thou come to destroy us?
	24D	34D		I know thee who thou art, the Holy One of God.
	25	35		And Jesus rebuked him,
	25B	35B		saying, Hold thy peace, and come out of him.
	26	35C		And when the unclean spirit (the devil)
	26B	35D		had thrown him in the midst (torn him)
	26C	35E		and cried with a loud voice, he came out of him,
		35D		and hurt him not.
	27	36		And they were all amazed,
	27B	36B		insomuch that they spake (questioned) among themselves, saying,
	27C	36C		What thing is this? What new doctrine is this?
	27D	36D		What a word is this?
	27E	36E		For with authority and power
	27F	36F		commandeth he even the unclean spirits,
	27G	36G		and they do obey him, and they come out.
	28	37		And immediately the fame of him went out (spread abroad)
		37B		into every place of the country round about,
	28B			throughout all the region round about Galilee.
	29	38		And forthwith he arose and they came out of the synagogue,
	29B	38B	Simon's	and entered into Simon's house (the house of Simon and Andrew)
	29C		wife's	with James and John.
	30	38C	mother.	But Simon's wife's mother was taken (lay sick) with a great fever;
	30B	38D		and anon they tell him of her (they besought him for her):
Mt.8				
14				And when Jesus was come into Peter's house,
14B				he saw his wife's mother laid, and sick of a fever.
15	31	39		And he came (stood over her) and touched (took) her by the hand,
	31B	39B		and rebuked the fever, and lifted her up;
15B	31C	39C		and immediately the fever left her and she arose,
15C	31D	39D		and she ministered unto them.
16	32	40		Now, when the sun was setting (when the even was come):
16B	32B	40B		They (all they that had any sick) brought them unto him,
	32C	40C		all that were diseased (divers diseases),
		40D		and he laid his hands on every one of them, and healed them:
16C	32D			And many of them – that were possessed with devils.
	33			And all the city were gathered at the door:
	34			And he healed many that were sick of divers diseases.
16D				And he cast out the spirits with his word;
	34B	41		And devils he cast out (they came out) of many,
		41B		and saying (crying out), Thou art the Christ, the Son of God:
	34C	41C		And he rebuking them suffered them (the devils) not to speak,
	34D	41D		because (for) they knew him, that he was Christ.
16D				And healed all that were sick: That it might be fulfilled
17				which was spoken by Esaias the prophet, (Is.53:4)

Mt.8	Mk.1	Lk.4	Jn.4	
17B				saying, Himself took our infirmities and bare our sicknesses.
	35			And in the morning,
	35B			rising up a great while before day, he went out, (Mt.6:5,6)
	35C	42		and departing into a desert/solitary place, and there prayed.
		42B		And the people sought him.
	36			And Simon and they that were with him followed after him.
	37			And when they had found him,
	37B			they said unto him, All men seek for thee.
		42C		And the people came unto him, and stayed him,
		42D		that he should not depart from them.
	38	43		And he (ie: Jesus) said unto them,
	38B			Let us go into the next towns, that I may preach there also:
	38C			for therefore came I forth.
		43B		I must preach the kingdom of God to other cities also:
		43C		for therefore am I sent.
	39	44		And he preached in their synagogues of (throughout all) Galilee,
	39B			and cast out devils.
		Lk.5		
		1		And it came to pass, that, as the people pressed upon him
		1B		to hear the word of God, and he stood by the lake of Gennesaret.
		2		And saw 2 ships standing by the lake:
		2B		but the fishermen were gone out of them,
Jesus		2C		and were washing their nets.
taught		3		And he entered into one of the ships, which was Simon's,
out of		3B		and prayed him that he would thrust out a little from the land.
a ship.		3C		And he sat down, and taught the people out of the ship.
		4		Now when he had left speaking, he said unto Simon,
		4B		Launch out into the deep, and let down your nets for a draught.
		5		And Simon answering said unto him, Master,
		5B		we have toiled all the night, and have taken nothing:
A great		5C		nevertheless at thy word I will let down the net.
multitude		6		And when they had this done, they
of fishes,		6B		inclosed a great multitude of fishes: and their net brake.
Broken nets.		7		And they beckoned unto their partners
		7B		which were in the other ship,
Help us!		7C		that they should come and help them.
Ships		7D		And they came, and filled both the ships,
over-full.		7E		so that they began to sink.
		8		When Simon Peter saw it, he fell down at Jesus' knees,
		8B		saying, Depart from me; for I am a sinful man, O Lord.
		9		For he was astonished, and all that were with him,
		9B		at the draught of the fishes which they had taken:
		10		And so was also James, and John (the sons of Zebedee),
		10B		which were partners with Simon.
I will		10C		And Jesus said unto Simon,
make U		10D		Fear not; from henceforth thou shalt catch men.
fishers		11		And when they had brought their ships to land,
of men!		11B		they forsook all, and followed him.
		12		And it came to pass, when he was in a certain city:
2	40	12B		And, behold, there came a leper (a man full of leprosy) to him;
		12C		who seeing Jesus, falling on his face
2B	40B	12D		beseeching him, and kneeling down to (worshipped) him,
2C	40C	12E		and saying unto him, Lord,
2D	40D	12F		if thou wilt, thou canst make me clean.
3	41	13		And Jesus, moved with compassion,
3B	41B	13B		put forth his hand, and touched him,
3C	41C	13C		and saith unto him, I will; be thou clean.

Mt.8	Mk.1	Lk.5	Jn.4	
	42			And as soon as he had spoken,
3D	42B	13D		and, immediately the leprosy departed from him,
3E	42C			and he was cleansed.
	43	14		And he (Jesus) straitly (ie: strictly/stringently), charged him,
	43B			and forthwith (ie: immediately/straightway) sent him away;
4	44			And Jesus saith unto him
4B	44B	14B		See thou tell no (say nothing to any) man:
4C	44C	14C		but go thy way and shew thyself to the priest,
4D	44D	14D		and offer the gift for thy cleansing
4E	44E	14E		those things which (according as) Moses commanded,
4F	44F	14F		for a testimony unto them.
	45			But he went out, and began to publish it much,
	45B			and to blaze abroad (ie: spread abroad) the matter.
		15		But so much the more - went there a fame abroad of him:
		15B		and great multitudes came together
		15C		to hear, and to be healed by him of their infirmities.
	45C			Insomuch that Jesus could no more openly enter into the city:
		16		And he withdrew himself into the wilderness, and prayed.
	45D			But he was without (ie: outside) in desert places:
	45E			And they came to him from every quarter.

Mt.9	Mk.2			
	1			And again (after some days) he entered into Capernaum:
1C				And he came into his own city:
	1B			and it was noised that he was in the house.
	2			And straightway many were gathered together,
	2B			insomuch that there was no room to receive them,
	2C			no, not so much as about the door:
	2D			and he preached the word unto them.
There has		17		And it came to pass on a certain day, as he was teaching,
to be		17B		that there were Pharisees and doctors of the law sitting by,
another		17C		which were come out of every town
way in.		17D		of Galilee, and Judaea; and Jerusalem:
		17E		And the power of the Lord was present to heal them.
2	3	18		And, behold, they come unto him,
2B	3B	18B		bringing one sick of the (taken with a) palsy
2C		18C		which was (lying on a bed) borne of four:
		18D		And they sought means to
		18E		to bring him in, and to lay him before him.
	4	19		And when they could not
	4B	19B		come nigh unto him for the press (multitude):
		19C		They went upon the housetop
	4C			and they uncovered the roof - where he (ie: Jesus) was:
	4D			And when they had broken it up,
	4E	19D		they let him (the sick of the palsy) down with the bed (couch)
	4F	19E		whereon he lay - through the tiling, in the midst before Jesus.
2D	5	20		And Jesus seeing their faith, said unto the sick of the palsy,
2E	5B	20B		Son (man), be of good cheer; thy sins be forgiven thee.
3	6	21		And, behold, there were certain of the scribes (and Pharisees)
3B	6B	21B		sitting there - began to reason in their hearts (said within
3C	7	21C		themseves), Who is this. Why does this man speak blasphemies?
3D	7B	21D		This man blasphemeth, who can forgive sins but God only!
	8			And immediately
4	8B	22		when Jesus perceived in his spirit (knowing their thoughts),
	8C			that they so (ie: in this manner) reasoned within themselves;
4B	8D	22B		He answering said unto them, What (why) reason ye
4C	8E	22C		these things (wherefore think ye evil) in your hearts?
5	9	23		For whether is it easier - to say to the sick of the palsy,

Mt.9	Mk.2	Lk.5	Jn.4	
5B	9B	23B		Thy sins be forgiven thee;
5C	9C	23C		or to say, Rise up (arise), and take up thy bed, and walk?
6	10	24		But that ye may know
6B	10B	24B		that the Son of man has power on earth to forgive sins:
6C	10C	24C		Then saith he (he saith) to the sick of the palsy,
6D	11	24D		I say unto thee, Arise, and take up
6E	11B	24E		thy bed (couch), and go thy way unto thine house.
7	12	25		And immediately he arose (rose up before them),
7B	12B	25B		and took up that whereon he lay (his bed),
	12C			and went forth before them all;
7C		25C		and departed to his own house, glorifying God.
8				But when the multitude saw it,
8B				they marvelled,
8C	12D	26		insomuch that they were all amazed, and they glorified God.
8D				which had given such power unto men.
		26B		And they were filled with fear,
	12E			saying, We never saw it on this fashion;
		26C		saying, We have seen strange things to day.
	13			And he went forth again by the sea side;
	13B			and all the multitude resorted unto him, and he taught them.
9		27		And after these things, Jesus went forth (passed) from thence:
9B	14	27B		And as he passed by, he saw a man,
9C	14B	27C	Matthew	a publican (ie: a tax collector), named Levi (Matthew)
	14C			the son of Alpheus
9D	14D	27D		sitting at the receipt of custom (ie: tax office);
9E	14E	27E		And he (ie: Jesus) saith unto him, Follow me.
		28		And he left all,
9F	14F	28B		and he arose (rose up), and followed him.
		29		And Levi made him a great feast in his own house:
10	15			And it came to pass, that, as Jesus sat at meat in his house,
		29B		And there was a great company
	15D			(for there were many, and they followed him);
10B	15B	29C		Behold, many publicans and others (sinners) came, and
10C	15C	29D		sat down also, together with Jesus and his disciples.
11	16	30		And when the scribes and Pharisees, saw
	16B			him eat with publicans and sinners,
11B	16C	30B		they said to (murmered against) his disciples, saying,
11C	16D	30C		Why is it that he (why do you)
11D	16E	30D		eat and drink with publicans and sinners?
12	17	31		But when Jesus heard it, he answering said unto them,
12B	17B	31B		They that be whole have no need of the physician;
12C	17C	31C		but they that are sick.
13				But go ye and learn what it is (meaneth),
13B				I will have mercy, and not sacrifice:
13C	17D	32		For, I came not to call the righteous,
13D	17E	32B		but sinners to repentance.
	18			And the disciples of John and of the Pharisees used to fast:
	18B	33		Then they come and say (they said) unto him,
	18C			Why do the disciples of John and the Pharisees fast.
	18D			but thy disciples fast not?
		33B		Why do the disciples of John fast often, and making prayers,
		33C		and likewise they of the Pharisees,
		33D		but thine eat and drink?
14				Then came to him the disciples of John, saying,
14B				Why do we and the Pharisees fast oft,
14C				but thy disciples fast not?

Mt.9	Mk.2	Lk.5	Jn.4	
15	19	34		And he (Jesus) said unto them,
15B	19B	34B		Can (ye make) the children of the bridechamber fast (mourn),
15C	19C	34C		as long as (while) the bridegroom is with them?
	19D			As long as they have the bridegroom with them,
	19E			they cannot fast.
	20	35		But the days will come,
	20B	35B		when the bridegroom shall be taken away from them,
	20C	35C		and then shall they fast in those days. (Is.58:6,7)
		36		And he spake also a parable unto them:
16	21	36B		No man also seweth a piece of new cloth on an old garment;
		36C		If otherwise, then the new maketh a rent;
		36D		The piece that was out of the new agreeth not with the old:
16B	21B			Else the new piece (that which is put in) that filled it up
16C	21C			taketh from the garment (the old), and the rent is made worse.
17	22	37		Neither do men put (no man putteth) new wine into old bottles;
17B	22B	37B		else the new wine will break (doth burst) the bottles,
17C	22C	37C		and the wine runneth out (be spilled),
17D	22D	37D		and the bottles shall perish (will be marred):
17E	22E	38		But they put new wine (new wine must be put) into new bottles;
17F		38B		and both are preserved.
		39		No man also having drunk old wine
		39B		straightway desireth new: for he saith, The old is better.

Mt.12		Lk.6		
		1		And it came to pass on the 2nd. sabbath (after the first),
1	23	1B		that he (Jesus) went through the corn fields on/in the sabbath;
1B	23B			and his disciples (were hungered) and began, as they went,
1C	23C	1C		to pluck the ears of corn, and to eat,
		1D		and did eat, rubbing them in their hands.
2	24	2		When the Pharisees saw - they (certain of them) said unto him,
		2B		Why do ye that which is not lawful:
2B	24B			Behold, why do thy disciples do that which is not lawful
2C	24C	2C		to do upon the sabbath day(s).
3	25	3		And Jesus answering them said,
3B	25B	3B		Have ye never (not) read - so much as this, what David did,
3C	25C	3C		when he (himself) had need and was an hungred,
3D	25D	3D		he, and they that were with him?
4	26	4		How he went into (entered into) the house of God,
	26B			(in the days of Abiathar the priest);
4B	26C	4B		And did take and eat the shewbread, (1 Sam.21:4-6)
	26F	4C		and gave also to them that were with him:
4C	26D	4D		Which is not lawful for him to eat,
4D				neither for them which were with him,
4E	26E	4E		but only for the priests?
5				Or have ye not read in the law,
5B				how that on the sabbath days the priests in the temple
5C				profane the sabbath, and are blameless? (Num.28:9,10)
6				But I say unto you,
6B				That in this place - is one greater than the temple.
7				But if ye had known what it meaneth,
7B				I will have mercy, and not sacrifice, (Mt.9:13)
7C				ye would not have condemned the guiltless.
	27	5		And he said unto them,
	27B			The sabbath was made for man, and not man for the sabbath:
8	28	5B		Therefore the Son of man is Lord also of the sabbath day.
	Mk.3			
9				And when he was departed thence:
		6		And, it came to pass also on another sabbath,

Mt.12	Mk.3	Lk.6	Jn.4	
9B	1	6B		that he entered again into the (their) synagogue and taught:
10	1B	6C		And, behold, there was a man whose right hand was withered:
10B				And they (ie: the Pharisees) asked him (ie: Jesus) saying,
10C				Is it lawful to heal on the sabbath days?
	2	7		And they (the scribes and Pharisees) watched him,
	2B	7B		whether he would heal him on the sabbath day;
10D	2C	7C		that they might find an accusation against him.
		8		But he knew their thoughts:
11				And he said unto them,
11B				What man shall there be among you, that shall have one sheep,
11C				and if it fall into a pit on the sabbath day,
11D				will he not lay hold on it, and lift it out?
12				How much then - is a man better than a sheep?
12B				Wherefore it is lawful to do well on the sabbath days.
	3	8B		Then saith he to the man (which had the withered hand),
	3B	8C		Rise up, and stand forth in the midst.
		8D		And he arose and stood forth.
	4	9		Then Jesus saith unto them,
		9B		I will ask you one thing;
	4B	9C		Is it lawful on the sabbath days to do good, or to do evil?
	4C	9D		to save a life or to destroy (to kill)?
	4D			But they held their peace (ie: they remained silent).
	5	10		And looking round about - upon them all,
	5B			with anger, being grieved for the hardness of their hearts,
13	5C	10B		Then saith he unto the man, Stretch forth thy hand.
13B	5D	10C		And he so did, he stretched it out (forth):
13C	5E	10D		And his hand was restored whole as (like) the other.
14	6	They		And (then) the Pharisees went forth (out),
14B	6B	took		and straightway took counsel with the Herodians against him,
14C	6C	counsel		how they might destroy him.
		11		And they were filled with madness; (Acts 9:1)
		11B		and communed one with another - what they might do to Jesus.
15				But when Jesus knew it, he withdrew himself from thence:
15B				and great multitudes followed him, and he healed them all;
16				And charged them - that they should not make him known:
17				That it might be fulfilled
17B				which was spoken by Esaias the prophet, saying,
18				Behold my servant, whom I have chosen;
18B				my beloved, in whom my soul is well pleased:
18C				I will put my spirit upon him,
18D				and he shall shew judgment to the Gentiles.
19				He shall not strive, nor cry;
19B				neither shall any man hear his voice in the streets.
20				A bruised reed shall he not break,
20B				and smoking flax shall he not quench,
20C				till he send forth judgment unto victory. (Is.42:1-4)
21				And in his name shall the Gentiles trust.
	7			But Jesus withdrew himself (with his disciples) to the sea:
	7B			and a great multitude from Galilee followed him,
	8			And from Judaea, and from Jerusalem, and from Idumaea,
	8B			and beyond the Jordan,
	8C			and they about Tyre and Sidon, a great multitude:
	8D			when they had heard what great things he did, came unto him.
	9			And he spake to his disciples,
	9B			that a small ship should wait on him
	9C			because of the multitude, lest they should throng him.
	10			For he had healed many;
	10B			insomuch that they pressed upon him

The Gospels of Matthew, Mark, Luke, and John: Merged into One Historic Calendar of Events

Mt.12　Mk.3　Lk.6　Jn.4

	10C		for to touch him, as many as had plagues.
	11		And unclean spirits,
	11B		when they saw him, fell down before him,
	11C		and cried, saying, Thou art the Son of God.
	12		And he straitly charged them
	12B		that they should not make him known.

Mt.5

		12	And it came to pass in those days:　　　　　(Lk.6:12,17/Mt.8:1)
1			And seeing the multitudes,
1B	13	12B	he (ie: Jesus) goeth (went) up into a mountain - to pray,
		12C	and continued all night in prayer to God.
1C		13	And, when it was day (when he was set),
		13B	he called unto him his disciples;
	13B	13C	And of them (calleth unto him whom he would), he chose 12,
1D	13C		and they (his disciples) came unto him:
	14	13D	He ordained 12, whom also he named apostles;
	14B		that they should be with him,
	14C	12 disciples	and that he might send them forth to preach;
	15	ordained,	And to have power to heal sicknesses,
	15B	as Apostles.	and to cast out devils.
	16	14	┌ Simon　(who he also named/surnamed Peter)
	18	14	└ Andrew (the brother of Simon)
	17	14	┌ James　(the son of Zebedee)　　　┐ he surnamed them Boanerges
	17	14	└ John　　(the brother of James)　┘　(ie: The sons of thunder).
	18	14	Philip
	18	14	Bartholomew
	18	15	Matthew
	18	15	Thomas
	18	15	James　(the son of Alphaeus)
	18	15	Simon　(called Zelotes) the Canaanite.
	18	16	Judas　(brother of James)/Lebbaeus surnamed Thaddaeus. (Mt.10:3)
	19A	16	Judas Iscariot (which also was the traitor).
And		17	And he came down with them, and stood in the plain:　　(Mt.8:1)
they		17B	And the company of his disciples,
stood		17C	and a great multitude of people
in the		17D	out of all Judaea and Jerusalem,
Plain.		17E	and from the sea coast of Tyre and Sidon,
(perhaps a		17F	which came to hear him, and to be healed of their diseases;
plateau?)		18	And they were vexed (ie: beset/harassed)
		18B	with unclean spirits - and they were healed.
		19	And the whole multitude sought to touch him:
		19B	for there went virtue out of him: and he healed them all.
		20	And he lifted up his eyes on his disciples:
2		20B	And he opened his mouth, and taught them, and said,
3		20C	Blessed be the (ye) poor - in spirit:
3B		20D	for your's (their's) is the kingdom of God (of heaven).
4			Blessed are they that mourn: for they shall be comforted.
5			Blessed are the meek: for they shall inherit the earth.
6		21	Blessed are ye that hunger (now) and thirst after righteousness:
6B		21B	for ye (they) shall be filled.
		21C	Blessed are ye that weep now: for ye shall laugh.
7			Blessed are the merciful: for they shall obtain mercy.
8			Blessed are the pure in heart: for they shall see God.
9			Blessed are the peacemakers:
9B			for they shall be called the children of God.
10			Blessed are they which are persecuted for righteousness' sake:

| Mt.5 | Mk.3 | Lk.6 | Jn.4 |

```
10B                            for their's is the kingdom of heaven.
11            22      Blessed are ye - when men shall hate you,
              22B        and when they shall separate you, and shall reproach you,
              22C        and cast out your name as evil;
11B                      when men shall revile you and persecute,           (1 Pe.3:17)
11C                      and shall say all manner of evil against you falsely,
11D           22D            for my sake (for the Son of man's sake).
12            23      Rejoice, ye in that day,
12B           23B        and leap for joy (be exceeding glad);
12C           23C            for, behold, your reward is great in heaven:
12D           23D        for so (in like manner) persecuted they (ie: their fathers)
12E           23E            the prophets - which were before you.
              24      But woe unto you that are rich!                      (Mt.6:19,20)
              24B         for ye have received your consolation (ie: comfort/fill).
              25      Woe unto you that are full!  for ye shall hunger.
              25B     Woe unto you that laugh now!  for ye shall mourn and weep.
              26      Woe unto you, when all men shall speak well of you!
              26B         for so did their fathers to the false prophets.
13                    Ye are the salt of the earth:
13B                       but if the salt have lost his savour,
13C                           wherewith shall it be salted?
13D                       it is thenceforth good for nothing, but to be cast out,
13E                       and to be trodden under foot of men.             (Mal.4:3)
14                    Ye are the light of the world.
14B                       A city that is set on an hill cannot be hid.
15                    Neither do men light a candle, and put it under a bushel,
15B                       but on a candlestick;
15C   Jesus Christ        and it giveth light unto all that are in the house.
16      came to      Let your light so shine before men,
16B     fulfil           that they may see your good works,
16C      -the Law        and glorify your Father, which is in heaven.
17       -the Prophets. Think not that I am come to destroy the law, or the prophets:
17B                       I am not come to destroy, but to fulfil.          (Jn.4:34)
18                    For verily I say unto you, Till heaven and earth pass,
18B                       one jot or one title shall in no wise pass from the law,
18C                           till all be fulfilled.
19                    Whosoever therefore shall break one of these least commandments,
19B                       and shall teach men so,
19C                           he shall be called the least in the kingdom of heaven:
19D                       But whosoever shall do and teach them.
19E                           the same shall be called great in the kingdom of heaven.
20                    For I say unto you, That except your righteousness
20B                       shall exceed the righteousness of the scribes and Pharisees,
20C                       ye shall in no case enter into the kingdom of heaven.
21                    Ye have heard that it was said by them of old time,
21B                       Thou shalt not kill;
21C                       and whosoever shall kill shall be in danger of the judgment:
22                    But I say unto you,
22B                       That whosoever is angry with his brother without a cause
22C                           shall be in danger of the judgment:
22D                       And whosoever shall say to his brother, Raca,
22E                           shall be in danger of the council:
22F                       But whosoever shall say, Thou fool,
22G                           shall be in danger of hell fire (ie: gehenna).(Mt.10:28)
23                    Therefore if thou bring thy gift to the altar,
23B                       and there rememberest
23C                           that thy brother hath ought against thee;
24                    Leave there thy gift before the altar,
```

Mt.5   Mk.3   Lk.6   Jn.4

24B		Agree	and go thy way; first be reconciled to thy brother,
24C		with thine	and then come and offer thy gift.
25		adversary.	Agree with thine adversary quickly,
25B			whiles thou art in the way with him;
25C			Lest at any time the adversary deliver thee to the judge,
25D			and the judge deliver thee to the officer,
25E			and thou be cast into prison.
26			Verily I say unto thee,
26B			Thou shalt by no means come out thence,
26C			till thou hast paid the uttermost farthing.
27			Ye have heard that it was said by them of old time,
27B			Thou shalt not commit adultery:
28			But I say unto you, (James 2:10)
28B			That whosoever looketh on a woman to lust after her
28C			hath committed adultery with her already in his heart.
29			And if thy right eye offend thee,
29B			pluck it out, and cast it from thee:
29C			for it is profitable for thee that one of thy members
29D			should perish, and not thy whole body should be cast into hell.
30			And if thy right hand offend thee,
30B			cut it off, and cast it from thee:
30C			for it is profitable for thee that one of thy members
30D			should perish, and not thy whole body should be cast into hell.
31			It hath been said, Whosoever shall put away his wife,
31B			let him give her a writing of divorcement:
32			But I say unto you, That whosoever shall put away (ie: divorce)
32B			his wife (saving for the cause of fornication)
32C			causeth her to commit adultery:
32D			And whosoever shall mary her
32E			that is divorced committeth adultery.
33			Again, ye have heard that it hath been said by them of old time,
33B			Thou shalt not forswear thyself,
33C			but shall perform unto the Lord thine oaths:
34		Swear Not!	But I say unto you, Swear not at all;
34B			neither by heaven; for it is God's throne:
35			nor by the earth; for it is His footstool:
35B			neither by Jerusalem; for it is the city of the great King.
36			Neither shalt thou swear by thy head,
36B			because thou canst not make one hair white or black.
37			But let your communication be, Yea, yea; Nay, nay:
37B			for whatsoever is more than these cometh of evil.
38			Ye have heard that it hath been said,
38B			An eye for an eye, and a tooth for a tooth:
39			But I say unto you, That ye resist not evil: (Prov.20:22)
39B	29		And unto him (whosoever) that smiteth thee on thy (right) cheek,
39C	29B		turn to him (offer) also the other.
40			If any man will sue thee at the law, and take away thy coat,
40B			let him have thy cloke also.
	29C		And him that taketh away thy cloke,
	29D		forbid him not to take thy coat also.
41			And whosoever shall compel thee to go a mile, go with him twain.
42	30		Give to him (every man) that asketh of thee,
42B			and from him that would borrow of thee turn not thou away;
	30B		and of him that taketh away thy goods - ask them not again.
43			Ye have heard that it hath been said,
43B			Thou shalt love thy neighbour, and hate thine enemy.
44	27		But I say unto you which hear, (Mt.13:9)
44C	27B		Love your enemies, do good to them that hate you;

Mt.5	Mk.3	Lk.6	Jn.4	
44B		28		Bless them that curse you,
44D		28B		and pray for them (Rom.12:20/Prov.25:21)
44E		28C		which despitefully use you and persecute you;
45				That ye may be the children of your Father which is in heaven:
45B		Sunshine & Rain		for he maketh his sun to rise on the evil and on the good,
45C				and sendeth rain on the just and on the unjust.
		31		And as ye would that men should do to you,
		31B		do ye also to them likewise.
46		32		For if ye love them which love you, what thank (reward) have ye?
46B				do not even the publicans the same? (Lk.19:8)
		32B		for sinners also love those that love them. (Mt.9:10)
47				And if ye salute your brethren only,
47B				what do ye more than others? do not even the publicans so?
		33		And if ye do good to them
		33B		which do good to you, what thank have ye?
		33C		for sinners also do even the same.
		34		And if ye lend to them
		34B		of whom ye hope to receive, what thank have ye?
		34C		for sinners also lend to sinners, to receive as much again.
		35		But love your enemies, (Rom.5:10)
		35B		and do good, and lend, hoping for nothing again;
		35C		and your reward shall be great, (1 Pe.3:18/Mt.5:45)
		35D		and ye shall be the children of the Highest:
		35E		for He is kind - unto the unthankful and to the evil.
		36		Be ye therefore merciful, as your Father also is merciful.
48				Be ye therefore perfect,
48B				even as your Father which is in heaven is perfect.
Mt.6				
1				Take heed
1B				that ye do not your alms before men, to be seen of them:
1C				otherwise ye have no reward of your Father which is in heaven.
2				Therefore when thou doest thine alms,
2B				do not sound a trumpet before thee,
2C				as the hypocrites do in the synagogues and in the streets,
2D				that they may have glory of men.
2E				Verily I say unto you, They have their reward.
3				But when thou doest alms,
3B				let not thy left hand know what thy right hand doeth:
4				That thine alms may be in secret:
4B				and thy Father
4C				which seeth in secret himself shall reward thee openly.
5				And when thou prayest, thou shalt not be as the hypocrites:
5B				for they love to pray standing in the synagogues
5C				and in the corners of the streets,
5D		Enter into		that they may be seen of men.
5E		thy closet		Verily I say unto you, They have their reward. (Mt.16:27)
6		and shut		But thou, when thou prayest,
6B		thy door.		enter into thy closet, and when thou hast shut thy door,
6C				pray to thy Father which is in secret;
6D				And thy Father which seeth in secret shall reward thee openly.
7				But when ye pray, use not vain repetitions, as the heathen:
7B				for they think that they shall be heard for their much speaking.
8				Be not ye therefore like unto them:
8B				for your Father knoweth
8C				what things ye have need of, before ye ask him.

Mt.6   Mk.3   Lk.6   Jn.4

9		After this manner therefore pray ye:
9B	The	Our Father which art in heaven, Hallowed be thy name. (Lk.11:2-4)
10	Lord's	Thy kingdom come.
10B	prayer.	Thy will be done in earth, as it is in heaven.
11		Give us this day our daily bread.
12		And forgive us our debts, as we forgive our debtors.
13		And lead us not into temptation, but deliver us from evil:
13B		For thine is the kingdom,
13C		and the power, and the glory, for ever. Amen.
14	Do you have	For if ye forgive men their trespasses,
14B	it in you	your heavenly Father will also forgive you: (Mk.11:26)
15	to forgive?	But if ye forgive not men their trespasses,
15B		neither will your Father forgive your trespasses.
16	Fasting.	Moreover when ye fast, be not, as the hypocrites, (Is.58:6,7)
16B		of a sad countenance; for they disfigure their faces,
16C		that they may appear unto men to fast.
16D		Verily I say unto you, They have their reward.
17		But thou, when thou fastest, anoint thine head, and wash thy face;
18		that thou appear not unto men to fast,
18B		but unto the Father which is in secret:
18C		And thy Father, which seeth in secret, shall reward thee openly.
19	Earthly treasures	Lay not up for yourselves treasures upon earth,
19B	versus	where moth and rust doth corrupt,
19C	Heavenly treasure.	and where thieves break through and steal:
20		But lay up for yourselves treasures in heaven,
20B		where neither moth nor rust doth corrupt,
20C		and where thieves do not break through nor steal:
21		For where your treasure is, there will your heart be also.
22		The light of the body is the eye:
22B	Stay focussed!	if therefore thine eye be single, (Lk.11:34) (Acts 4:12)
22C	on the	thy whole body shall be full of light.
23	cross	But if thine eye be evil,
23B	of Christ.	thy whole body shall be full of darkness.
23C		If therefore the light that is in thee be darkness,
23D		how great is that darkness!
24	Obvious,	No man can serve 2 masters:
24B	Logic.	for either he will hate the one, and love the other;
24C		or else he will hold to the one, and despise the other.
24D		Ye cannot serve God and mammon.
25	Be not	Therefore I say unto you, Take no thought for your life,
25B	anxious	what ye shall eat, or what ye shall drink;
25C	(worried)	nor yet for your body, what ye shall put on.
25D		Is not the life more than meat, and the body than raiment?
26	Be of	Behold the fowls of the air:
26B	good	for they sow not, neither do they reap, nor gather into barns;
26C	courage	yet your heavenly Father feedeth them.
26D	Hope in the LORD	Are ye not much better than they? (Gen.1:27)
27	Wait on the LORD	Which of you (by taking thought)
27B	Ps.31:24	can add one cubit unto his stature?
28	Ps.27:14	And why take ye thought for raiment? (Ps.27:14 & 31:24)
28B		Consider the lilies of the field, how they grow;
28C		they toil not, neither do they spin:
29		And yet I say unto you, that even Solomon in all his glory
29B		was not arrayed like one of these.
30		Wherefore, if God so clothe the grass of the field,
30B		which to day is, and to morrow is cast into the oven,

Mt.6	Mk.3	Lk.6	Jn.4	
30C				shall he not much more clothe you, O ye of little faith?
31				Therefore take no thought, saying,
31B				What shall we eat? or, What shall we drink?
31C				or, Wherewithal shall we be clothed?
32				For after all these things do the Gentiles seek:
32B				for your heavenly Father knoweth
32C				that ye have need of all these things.
33				But seek ye first the kingdom of God, and his righteousness;
33B				and all these things shall be added unto you.
34				Take therefore no thought for the morrow: (Lk.12:15-19)
34B				for the morrow shall take thought for the things of itself.
34C				Sufficient unto the day is the evil thereof. (Col.3:6-8)
Mt.7				
1		37		Judge not, that ye be not (and ye shall not be) judged;
2				for with what judgment ye judge, ye shall be judged:
		37B		Condemn not, and ye shall not be condemned: (James 5:1,5)
		37C		Forgive, and ye shall be forgiven:
		38		Give, and it shall be given unto you;
		38B		good measure, pressed down, and shaken together,
		38C		and running over, shall men give into your bosom.
2B		38D		And with what measure that ye mete
2C		38E		withal (the same) it shall be measured to you again.
		39		And he spake a parable unto them:
		39B		Can the blind lead the blind?
		39C		shall they both not fall into the ditch?
		40		The disciple is not above his master:
		40B		but every one that is perfect shall be as his master.
3		41		And why beholdest thou the mote that is in thy brother's eye,
3B		41B		but considerest (perceivest) not
3C		41C		the beam that is in thine own eye?
4		42		Or how wilt (canst) thou say to thy brother,
4B		42B		Brother, let me pull out the mote that is in thine eye,
4C		42C		and, behold (thou thyself beholdest not),
4D		42D		the beam that is in thine own eye.
5		42E		Thou hypocrite, cast out first the beam out of thine own eye:
5B		42F		and then shalt thou see clearly
5C		42G		to cast (pull) out the mote out of thy brother's eye.
6				Give not that which is holy unto the dogs, (Phil.3:2)
6B				neither cast ye your pearls before swine, lest they
6C				trample them under their feet, and turn again and rend you.
7				Ask, and it shall be given you; (James 1:5) (1 Jn.5:14)
7B				Seek, and ye shall find;
7C				Knock, and it shall be opened unto you:
8				For every one that asketh receiveth; and
8B				He that seeketh fineth; and
8C				To him that knocketh it shall be opened.
9				Or what man is there of you,
9B				whom if his son ask bread, will he give him a stone?
10				Or if he ask a fish, will he give him a serpent?
11				If ye then,
11B				being evil, know how to give good gifts unto your children,
11C				how much more shall your Father which is in heaven
11D				give good things to them that ask him?
12				Therefore all things whatsoever
12B	The Golden Rule			ye would that men should do to you, do ye even so to them:
12C				For this is the law and the prophets. (Mt.5:17,18)

Mt.7	Mk.3	Lk.6	Jn.4	
13				Enter ye in at the strait (ie: narrow) gate:
13B				for wide is the gate, and broad is the way, that leadeth to
13C				destruction, and many there be which go in thereat:
14				Because strait is the gate, and narrow is the way,
14B				which leadeth unto life, and few there be that find it.
15			Believe	Beware of false prophets, which come to you in sheep's clothing,
15B			not	but inwardly they are ravening wolves. (Mt.24:24)
16			every	Ye shall know them by their fruits. (Rev.22:18,19)
16B			spirit.	Do men gather grapes of thorns, or figs of thistles?
17				Even so - every good tree bringeth forth good fruit;
17B				but a corrupt tree bringeth forth evil fruit. (Lk.3:7,8)
18		43		A good tree bringeth not (cannot bring) forth evil (corrupt) fruit,
18B		43B		neither doth a corrupt tree bring forth good fruit.
		44		For every tree is known by his own fruit:
		44B		for of thorns men do not gather figs,
		44C		nor of a bramble bush gather they grapes.
19				Every tree that bringeth not forth good fruit
19B				is hewn down, and cast into the fire.
20				Wherefore by their fruits ye shall know them.
		45		A good man out of the good treasure of his heart
		45B		bringeth forth that which is good;
		45C		and an evil man out of the evil treasure of his heart
		45D		bringeth forth that which is evil:
		45E		For of the abundance of the heart his mouth speaketh.
		46		And why call ye me, Lord, Lord!
		46B		and do not the things which I say?
21				Not every one that saith unto me, Lord, Lord,
21B				shall enter into the kingdom of heaven;
21C				but he that doeth the will of my Father which is in heaven.
22				Many will say to me in that day,
22B				Lord, Lord, have we not prophesied in thy name?
22C				and in thy name cast out devils?
22D				and in thy name done many wonderful works?
23				And then will I profess unto them, I never knew you:
23B				depart from me, ye that work iniquity.
24		47	Hear	Therefore whosoever cometh to me
24B		47B	&	and heareth my sayings (these sayings of mine), and doeth them;
		47C	Obey	I will show you to whom he is like.
24C		48		I will liken him unto (he is like) a wise man,
24D		48B		which built an house (his house) upon the rock;
		48C		and digged deep, and laid the foundation on the rock:
25				And the rain descended:
25B		48D		And when the flood(s) came (arose),
		48E		the stream beat vehemently upon (ie: against) that house;
25C				and the winds blew, and beat upon that house,
		48F		and could not shake it,
25D		48G		and it fell not: for it was founded upon the rock.
26		49		But he (every one)
26B		49B		that heareth these sayings of mine, and doeth them not,
26C		49C		shall be likened unto a foolish man,
		49D		that without a foundation
26D		49E		built an (his) house upon the sand (earth).
27				And the rain descended, and the floods came,
27B		49F		and the stream did beat vehemently against his house,
				and the winds blew, and beat upon that house;
27C		49G		and it (immediately) fell:

Mt.7	Mk.3	Lk.6	Jn.4	
27D		49H		And the fall of it (the ruin of that house) was great.
		Lk.7		
28				And it came to pass,
28B		1		When Jesus had ended these (all his) sayings
		1B		in the audience of the people,
28C				the people were astonished at his doctrine:
29				For he taught them
29B				as one having authority, and not as the scribes.
Mt.8				
1				When he was come down
1B				from the mountain, great multitudes followed him. (Lk.6:12,17)
5		1C		And when Jesus was entered into Capernaum:
5B		2		A (certain) centurion,
		2B		whose servant was dear to him, was sick and ready to die:
		3		When he heard of Jesus, he
5C				-came unto him, beseeching him:
		3B		-sent unto him the elders of the Jews, beseeching him
		3C		that he would come and heal his servant.
		4		And when they came to Jesus, they besought him instantly,

```
┌─────────────────────────────────────────────────────────────────────────────┐
│ Note:                    There came unto him a centurion, saying, ------.  (Mt.8:5) │
│                          The elders of the Jews (sent on his behalf) said, --. (Lk.7:2,3) │
│        How can we make                                                      │
│        sense of this  ── The elders of the Jews which he sent - to represent him. │
│        situation?            speaking on his behalf, as if he were there in person. │
│                          And in addition they (on their part) spake well of him. │
└─────────────────────────────────────────────────────────────────────────────┘
```

Mt	Mk	Lk	Jn	
6				And saying, Lord, my servant
6B				lieth at home sick of the palsy, grievously tormented.
		4B		Saying, that he was worthy for whom he should do this;
		5		for he loveth our nation, and he hath built us a synagogue.
7				And Jesus said unto him, I will come and heal him.
		6		Then Jesus went with them.
		6B		And when he was now not far from the house,
8		6C		The centurion
8B				-answered and said, Lord,
		6D		-sent friends to him, saying unto him, Lord,
		6E		Trouble not thyself: for,
8C		6F		I am not worthy
8D		6G		that thou shouldest come/enter under my roof.
		7		Wherefore neither thought I myself worthy to come unto thee:
8E		7B		but say in a word (speak the word only),
8F		7C		and my servant shall be healed.
9		8		For I also am a man set under authority, having soldiers under me;
9B		8B		and I say to this one, Go, and he goeth;
9C		8C		and to another, Come, and he cometh;
9D		8D		and to my servant, Do this, and he doeth it.
10		9		When Jesus heard these things, he marvelled at him; and he
10B		9B		turned him about, and said unto the people that followed him,
10C		9C		Verily I say unto you,
10D		9D		I have not found so great faith, no not in Israel.
11				And I say unto you,
11B				That many shall come from the east and west,
11C				and shall sit down
11D				with Abraham, and Isaac, and Jacob, in the kingdom of heaven.
12				But the children of the kingdom
12B				shall be cast out into outer darkness:

Mt.8	Mk.3	Lk.7	Jn.4	
12C				there shall be weeping and gnashing of teeth.
13				And Jesus said unto the centurion, Go thy way;
13B				and as thou hast believed, so be it done unto thee.
13C				And his servant was healed in the self same hour.
		10		And they that were sent, returning to the house,
		10B		found the servant whole – that had been sick.
		11		And it came to pass the day after,
		11B		that he went into a city called Nain;
		11C		and many of his disciples went with him, and much people.
		12		Now when he came nigh to the gate of the city.
		12B		behold, there was a dead man carried out,
		12C		the only son of his mother, and she was a widow:
		12D		and much people of the city was with her.
		13		And when the Lord saw her,
		13B		he had compassion on her, and said unto her, Weep not.
		14		And he came and touched the bier:
		14B		and they that bare him stood still.
		14C		And he said, Young man, I say unto thee, Arise:
		15		And he that was dead sat up, and began to speak:
		15B		And he delivered him to his mother.
		16		And there came a fear on all; and they glorified God,
		16B		saying, That a great prophet is risen up among us;
		16C		and, That God hath visited his people.
		17		And this rumour of him went forth throughout all Judaea,
		17C		and throughout all the region round about.
		18		And the disciples of John shewed him (ie: John) all these things.
Mt.11				
2				Now when John had heard in prison – the works of Christ:
2B		19		John calling 2 of his disciples, sent them to Jesus,
		19B		saying, Art thou he that should come? or look we for another?
		20		When the men were come unto him,
		20B		they said, John the Baptist hath sent us unto thee,
3		20C		saying (and they said unto him),
3B		20D		Art thou he that should come? or look we for another?
		21		And in that same hour
		21B		he cured many of their infirmities and plagues,
		21C		and of evil spirits; and unto many blind he gave sight.
4		22		Jesus answered and said unto them.
4B		22B		Go your way, and tell (shew) John again those things
4C		22C		which ye do hear and see (have seen and heard):
		22D		How that
5		22E		the blind receive their sight,
5B		22F		the lame walk,
5C		22G		the lepers are cleansed,
5D		22H		the deaf hear,
5E		22I		the dead are raised up,
5F		22J		the poor have the gospel preached unto them.
6		23		And blessed is he, whosoever shall not be offended in me.
7		24		And as they (the messengers of John) departed (were departed):
7B		24B		Jesus began to say unto the people (multitude) concerning John,
7C		24C		But what went ye out into the wilderness for to see?
7D		24D		A reed shaken with the wind?
8		25		But what went ye out for to see?
8B		25B		A man clothed in soft raiment?
8C				Behold, they that wear soft clothing are in kings' houses:
		25C		Behold, they which are gorgeously apparelled,
		25D		and live delicately, are in kings' courts.

Mt.11	Mk.3	Lk.7	Jn.4	
9		26		But what went ye out for to see?
9B		26B		A prophet?
9C		26C		Yea, I say unto you, and much more than a prophet.
10		27		For this is he, of whom it is written,
10B		27B		Behold, I send my messenger before thy face,
10C		27C		which shall prepare thy way before thee. (Mal.3:1)
11		28		For (verily) I say unto you,
11B		28B		Among them (those) that are born of women
11C		28C		there is not (has not risen)
11D		28D		a greater prophet than John the Baptist:
11E		28E		But (notwithstanding) he that is least
11F		28F		in the kingdom of God (kingdom of heaven) is greater than he.
12				And from the days of John the Baptist until now
12B				the kingdom of heaven suffereth violence,
12C				and violent take it by force.
13				For all the prophets and the law - prophesied until John.
14				And (if ye will receive it), this is Elias, which was for to come.
15				He that hath ears to hear, let him hear. (Lk.8:18)
		29		And all the people that heard him, and the publicans (Mt.21:32)
		29B		justified God, being baptized with the baptism of John.
		30		But the Pharisees and lawyers rejected the
		30B		counsel of God against themselves, being not baptized of him.
		31		And the Lord said,
16		31B		Where unto then shall I liken the men of this generation?
		31C		and to what are they like?
16B		32		They are like unto children sitting in the market place,
16C		32B		and calling one to another (unto their fellows),
17		32C		saying, We have piped unto you, and ye have not danced;
17B		32D		we have mourned unto you, and ye have not wept (lamented).
18		33		For John the Baptist came neither eating bread nor drinking wine;
18B		33B		and they (ye) say, He hath a devil.
19		34		The Son of man come (came) eating and drinking;
19B		34B		and they (ye) say, Behold a gluttonous man,
19C		34C		and a winebibber, a friend of publicans and sinners!
19D		35		But wisdom is justified of all her children. (Rom.7:24)
		36		And one of the Pharisees desired him - that he would eat with him.
		36B		And he went into the Pharisee's house, and sat down to meat.
		37		And, behold, a woman in the city, which was a sinner, (1 Tim.1:15)
		37B		when she knew that Jesus sat at meat
		37C		in the Pharisee's house, brought an alabaster box of ointment;
		38		And standing behind at his feet, weeping;
		38B		and began to wash his feet with tears,
		38C		and did wipe them with the hairs of her head,
		38D		and kissed his feet, and anointed them with the ointment.
		39		Now when the Pharisee - which had bidden him saw it,
		39B		he spake (within himself), saying, This man, if
		39C		he were a prophet, would have known who and what manner
		39D		of woman this is that toucheth him: for she is a sinner.
		40		And Jesus answering said unto him,
		40B		Simon, I have somewhat to say unto thee.
		40C		And he (ie: Simon) saith, Master, say on.
		41		There was a certain creditor which had 2 debtors:
		41B		the one owed 500 pence, and the other 50.
		42		And when they had nothing to pay, he frankly forgave them both.
		42B		Tell me therefore, which of them will love him most?
		43		Simon answered and said,
		43B		I suppose that he, to whom he forgave most (ie: more).

Mt.11   Mk.3   Lk.7   Jn.4

		43C	And he (ie: Jesus) said unto him, Thou hast rightly judged.
		44	And he turned to the woman,
		44B	and said unto Simon, Seest thou this woman?
		44C	I entered into thine house, thou gavest me no water for my feet:
		44D	But she hath washed my feet with tears,
		44E	and wiped them with the hairs of her head.
		45	Thou gavest me no kiss: but this woman
		45B	since the time I came in hath not ceased to kiss my feet.
		46	My head with oil thou didst not anoint:
		46B	but this woman hath anointed my feet with ointment.
		47	Wherefore I say unto thee, Her sins,
		47B	which are many, are forgiven; for she loved much:
		47C	but to whom little is forgiven, the same loveth little.
		48	And he said unto her, Thy sins are forgiven.
		49	And they that sat at meat with him – began to say
		49B	within themselves, Who is this that forgiveth sins also?
		50	And he said to the woman. Thy faith hath saved thee; go in peace.

Lk.8
```
      1      And it came to pass afterward,
      1B        that he went throughout every city and village, preaching
      1C        and shewing the glad tidings of the kingdom of God:    (Lk.4:43)
      1D     And the 12 were with him.
      2      And certain women,
      2B        which had been healed of evil spirits and infirmities,
      2C        Mary (called Magdalene), out of whom went 7 devils, and
      3         Joanna, the wife of Chuza Herod's steward, and
      3B        Susanna, and many others,
      3C           which ministered unto him of their substance.
```

20   Then began he to upbraid (ie: reproach/revile) the cities wherein
20B   most of his mighty works were done, because they repented not:
21   Woe unto thee, Chorazin! Woe unto thee, Bethsaida!
21B   for if the mighty works,
21C   which were done in you, had been done in Tyre and Sidon,
21D   they would have repented long ago in sackcloth and ashes.
22   But I say unto you, It shall be more tolerable
22B   for Tyre and Sidon at the day of judgment, than for you.
23   And thou, Capernaum,
23B   which art exalted unto heaven, shalt be brought down to hell:
23C   for if the mighty works, which have been done in thee,
23D   had been done in Sodom, it would have remained until this day.
24   But I say unto you, That it shall be more tolerable   (Mt.6:11)
24B   for the land of Sodom in the day of judgment, than for thee.

25   That which is   At that time Jesus answered and said,
25B   revealed   I thank thee, O Father, Lord of heaven and earth,
25C   unto some   because thou hast hid these things   (Lk.10:21) (2 Cor.3:14)
25D   Remains   from the wise and prudent, and hast revealed them unto babes.
26   a mystery   Even so, Father: for so it seemed good in thy sight.
27   to others.   All things are delivered unto me of my Father: (Lk.10:22)
27B   and no man knoweth the Son, but the Father;
27C   Neither knoweth any man the Father, save the Son,
27D   and he to whomsoever the Son will reveal him.
28   Come unto me, all ye that labour and are heavy laden,
28B   and I will give you rest.
29   Take my yoke upon you,
29B   and learn of me; for I am meek and lowly in heart:
29C   And ye shall find rest unto your souls;
30   for my yoke is easy, and my burden is light.

Mt.11	Mk.3	Lk.8	Jn.4	
	19B			And they went into an house.
	20			And the multitude cometh together again,
	20B			so that they could not so much as eat bread.
	21			And when his friends heard of it,
	21B			they went out to lay hold on him:
	21C			for they said, He is beside himself.

Mt.12

22				Then was brought unto him
22B				one possessed with a devil, blind and dumb: and he healed him,
22C				insomuch that the blind and dumb both spake and saw.
23				And all the people
23B				were amazed, and they said, Is not this the son of David?
	22			The scribes which came down from Jerusalem
	22B			said, He hath Be-elzebub,
	22C			and by the prince of the devils casteth he out devils.
24				But when the Pharisees heard it,
24B				they said, This fellow doth not cast out devils,
24C				but by Beelzebub the prince of the devils. (Mk.3:22)
25				And Jesus knew their thoughts:
25B	23			And he called them unto him, and said unto them in parables,
	23B			How can Satan cast out Satan?
25C	24			And if a kingdom (every kingdom) be divided against itself,
25D	24B			that kingdom cannot stand - it is brought to desolation:
25E	25			And if a house (every city or house)
25F	25B			divided against itself cannot (shall not) stand.
26				And if Satan cast out Satan, he is
26B				divided against himself; how shall then his kingdom stand?
	26			And if Satan rise up against himself,
	26B			and be divided, he cannot stand, but has an end.
27				And if I by Beelzebub cast out devils,
27B				by whom do your children cast them out?
27C				therefore they shall be your judges.
28				But, if I cast out devils by the Spirit of God,
28B				then the kingdom of God is come unto you.
29				Or, how else can one enter
29B	27B			into a strong man's house and spoil his goods?
29C	27			No man can enter - and spoil his goods, except he will first
29D	27C			bind the strong man, and then he will spoil his house.
30				He that is not with me is against me;
30B				and he that gathereth not with me scattereth abroad.
31	28			Wherefore (verily) I say unto you, All manner of sin
31B	28C			and blasphemy (wherewith soever they shall blaspheme),
31C	28B			shall be forgiven unto men (unto the sons of men):
31D				But the blasphemies against the Holy Ghost (ie: Holy Spirit)
31E				shall not be forgiven unto men.
32				And whosoever speaketh a word against the Son of man,
32B				it shall be forgiven him:
32C	29			But he/whosoever blasphemes (speaketh against) the Holy Ghost,
	29C			(But, is in danger of eternal damnation; (Mt.7:1/Jude :9)
	30			because they said, he hath an unclean spirit.) (Mk.3:22)
32D	29B			it shall not (it shall never) be forgiven him, (Lk.12:10)
32E				neither in this world (ie: age), neither in the world to come.
33				Either make the tree good, and his fruit good;
33B				or else make the tree corrupt, and his fruit corrupt:
33C				for the tree is known by his fruit. (Mt.7:16-20)
34				O generation of vipers, (Mt.23:33-36)
34B				how can ye, being evil, speak good things?

```
Mt.12   Mk.3   Lk.8   Jn.4

34C                           for out of the abundance of the heart the mouth speaketh.
35                         A good man out of the good treasure of the heart
35B                              bringeth forth good things:
35C                           and an evil man out of the evil treasure
35D                              bringeth forth evil things.
36                         But I say unto you,                              (1 Jn.4:1/He.4:12)
36B                           That every idle word that men shall speak,
36C                              they shall give account thereof in the day of judgment.
37                            For by thy words thou shalt be justified,
37B                              and by thy words thou shalt be condemned.

38                         Then certain of the scribes and of the Pharisees answered,
38B                           saying, Master, we would see a sign from thee.
39                         But he (ie: Jesus) answered and said unto them,
39B                           An evil and adulerous generation seeketh after a sign;
39C                           and there shall no sign be given to it,
39D                           but the sign of the prophet Jonas:
40                         For as Jonas was 3 days and 3 nights in the whale's belly;
40B                           so shall the Son of man
40C                           be 3 days and 3 nights in the heart of the earth.
41                         The men of Nineveh shall rise in judgment
41B                           with this generation, and shall condemn it:
41C                           because they repented at the preaching of Jonas;
41D                           and, behold, a greater than Jonas is here.
42                         The queen of the south shall rise up in the judgment
42B                           with this generation, and shall condemn it:
42C                           for she came from the uttermost parts of the earth
42D                           to hear the wisdom of Solomon;                 (1 Ki.10:1-5)
42E                           and, behold, a greater than Solomon is here.
43                         When the unclean spirit is gone out of a man,
43B                           he walketh through dry places, seeking rest, and findeth none.
44                         Then he saith, I will return into my house from whence I came out;
44B                           and when he is come, he findeth it empty, swept, and garnished.
45                         Then goeth he, and taketh with himself 7 other spirits
45B                           more wicked than himself, and they enter in and dwell there:
45C                           and the last state of that man - is worse than the first.
45D                           Even so shall it be also unto this wicked generation.

46                         While he (ie: Jesus) yet talked to the people:
46B     31     19          Behold, there came then his mother and his brethren,
46C     31B                   and stood (standing) without
               19B                  (and could not come at him for the press.)
46D     31C                   desiring to speak with him, sent unto him, calling him.
               20          And it was told him:
47                         Then, one said unto him,
47B                           Behold, thy mother and thy brethren
47C                              stand without desiring to speak with thee;
        32     20B         And the multitude sat about him, said unto him,
        32B    20C            Behold, thy mother and thy brethren
        32C    20D               without seek for (desire to see) thee.
48      33     21          And he answered and said unto him/them that told him, saying,
48B     33B                   Who is my mother? and who are my brethren?
        34                 And he looked round about on them which sat about him:
49                         And he stretched forth his hand toward his disciples,
49B     34B                   and said, Behold my mother and my brethren!
               21B            My mother and brethren
               21C               are these which hear the word of God, and do it.
50      35                 For whosoever shall do the will of
50B     35B                   my God (my Father which is in heaven),
```

Mt.12	Mk.3	Lk.8	Jn.4	
50C	35C			the same is my brother, and sister, and mother.
Mt.13	Mk.4			
1				The same day
1B				went Jesus out of the house, and sat by the sea side.
	1			And he began again to teach by the sea side:
2	1B			And great multitude(s) were gathered together unto him,
2B	1C			so that he went into (entered) a ship, and sat - in the sea;
2C	1D			and the whole multitude stood on the land (shore) by the sea.
		4		And when much people
		4B		were gathered together, and were come to him out of every city:
3	2			And he taught (spake) many things unto them in parables:
	2B	4C		And in his doctrine he said unto them by a parable,
3B	3	5		Hearken (ie: hear), behold, a sower went out to sow his seed:
4	4	5B		And it came to pass, as (when) he sowed:
4B	4B	5C		Some seed fell by the wayside;
		5D		and it was trodden down,
4C	4C	5E		and the fowls of the air came and devoured it/them up.
5	5			And some fell on (upon) stony places (ground),
5B	5B			where it had not much earth;
5C	5C			and forthwith (immediately) it sprung up,
5D	5D			because it had no depth (no deepness) of earth:
6	6			But when the sun was come up, it was scorched;
6B	6B			And because it had no root, it withered away.
		6		And some fell uon a rock;
		6B		and as soon as it was sprung up,
		6C		it withered away, because of lack of moisture.
7	7	7		And some fell among thorns;
7B	7B	7B		and the thorns grew up (sprang up) with it, and choked it/them:
	7C			And it yielded no fruit.
8	8	8		And other fell on good ground,
	8B	8B		and did yield fruit, that sprang up and increased;
		8C		And bare fruit an hundred fold:
8B	8C			And brought forth fruit, some 30, and some 60, and some 100.
		8D		And when he had said these things:
	9	8E		He said unto them, he cried,
9	9B	8F		He who hath ears to hear, let him hear!
10	10	9		And when he was alone, the/his disciples came,
	10B			(they that were about him with the 12),
10B	10C	9B		and asked of him the parable, and said unto him, saying,
		9C		What might this parable be?
10C				Why speakest thou unto them in parables?
11	11	10		And he answered and said unto them,
11B	11B	10B		Because it is given unto you to know
11C	11C	10C		the mysteries of the kingdom of God (the kingdom of heaven):
11D	11D	10D		But to others (them that are without), (Mt.11:25)
11E	11E	10E		it is not given - all these things are done in parables:
12				For whosoever hath,
12B				to him shall be given, and he shall have more abundance:
12C				But whosoever hath not,
12D				from him shall be taken away even that he hath.
13				Therefore speak I to them in parables:
13B	12	10F		That seeing (they may see) but not perceive (ie: they see not);
13C	12B	10G		And hearing (they may hear) but not understand (ie: they hear not);
	12C			Lest at any time they should be converted,
	12D			and their sins should be forgiven them.
14				And in them is fulfilled the prophecy of Isaias, which saith,
14B				By hearing ye shall hear, and shall not understand;

Mt.13	Mk.4	Lk.8	Jn.4	
14C				and seeing ye shall see, and shall not perceive:
15				For this people's heart is waxed gross (ie: fat/thick),
15B				and their ears are dull of hearing,
15C				and their eyes they have closed: (Is.6:10/Acts 28:25-27)
15D				Lest at any time
15E				they should see with their eyes and hear with their ears,
15F				and should understand with their heart,
15G				and should be converted, and I should heal them.
	13			And he said unto them, Know ye not this parable?
	13B			and how then will ye know all parables?
16				But blessed are your eyes, for they see;
16B				and your ears, for they hear. (Mk.4:34)
17				For verily I say unto you,
17B				That many prophets and righteous men have desired
17C				to see the things which ye see, and have not seen; and
17D				to hear the things which ye hear, and have not heard:
18				Hear ye therefore the parable of the sower.
		11		Now the parable is this:
		11B		The seed is the word of God.
	14			The sower soweth the word. (Mt.4:23)
19F	15	12		And these are they (he which received seed) by the way side
	15B	12B		where the word is sown, are those that hear:
19A	15C			But when they have heard (when one heareth)
19B				the word of the kingdom, and understandeth it not; (Mt.13:13)
19C	15D	12C		Then Satan (the devil, the wicked one) cometh immediately,
19D	15E			and taketh (catches) away the word
19E	15F	12D		(that was sown in their hearts) out of their hearts:
		12E		Lest they should believe and be saved.
20	16			And these are they, that received the seed upon stony places:
20B	16B			Who, when they have heard the word,
20C	16C			anon (immediately) receive it with gladness (joy);
21	17			And having no root in themselves, and so endure but for a time;
21B	17B			Afterward, when tribulation (affliction) or persecution ariseth
21C	17C			for the word's sake (because of the word):
21D	17D			By and by (immediately) they are offended.
		13		And they on the rock:
		13B		These are they, which, when they hear, receive the word with joy;
		13C		And these have no root, which for a while believe,
		13D		And in time of temptation fall away.
22	18	14		And these are they, that received seed which fell among the thorns:
22B	18B	14B		Are such, as hear the word, go forth,
		14C		and are choked with cares and riches, and pleasures of life:
22C	19			The cares of this world, and the deceitfulness of riches,
22D	19B			and the lusts of other things entering in, choke the word,
22E	19C	14D		and it becometh unfruitful (bring no fruit to perfection).
23	20	15		And these are they, that received seed on/in good ground:
23B	20B			Are they, that hear the word, and receive and understand it;
		15B		and in an honest and good heart, having heard the word, keep it,
23C	20C	15C		which also beareth, and bringeth forth fruit with patience:
23D	20D			Some an 100 fold, some 60, and some 30.
	21			And he (ie: Jesus) said unto them,
	21B			Is a candle brought to be put under a bushel,
	21C			or under a bed? and not to be set on a candlestick?
		16		No man, when he hath lighted a candle,
		16B		covereth it with a vessel, or putteth it under a bed;
		16C		but setteth it on a candlestick,
		16D		that they which enter in - may see the light.

Mt.13	Mk.4	Lk.8	Jn.4	
	22	17B		For there is nothing hid, which shall not be manifested;
	22B	17		Neither any thing kept secret,
	22C	17C		that shall not be known, but that it should come abroad.
	23			If any man have ears to hear, let him hear.
	24			And he said unto them, Take heed what ye hear;
	24B			with what measure ye mete, it shall be measured to you:
	24C			And unto you that hear shall more be given.
		18		Take heed therefore how ye hear:
	25	18B		For he that (whosoever) hath, to him shall be given: and
	25B	18C		To him that (whosoever) hath not, from him shall
	25C	18D		be taken even that which he hath (seemeth to have).
	26			And he said, So is the kingdom of God,
	26B			as if a man should cast seed into the ground;
	27			And should sleep, and rise night and day,
	27B			and the seed should spring and grow up, he knoweth not how.
	28			For the earth bringeth forth fruit of herself;
	28B			first the blade,
	28C			then the ear, after that the full corn in the ear.
	29			But when the fruit is brought forth, immediately
	29B			he putteth in the sickle, because the harvest is come.
24				Another parable put he forth unto them,
24B				saying, The kingdom of heaven
24C				is likened unto a man which sowed good seed in his field:
25				But while men slept, his enemy came
25B				and sowed tares among the wheat, and went his way.
26				But when the blade was sprung up,
26B				and brought forth fruit, then appeared the tares also.
27				So the servants of the householder came and said unto him,
27B				Sir, didst not thou sow
27C				good seed in thy field? from whence then hath it tares?
28				He said unto them, An enemy hath done this.
28B				The servants said unto him,
28C				Wilt thou then that we go and gather them up?
29				But he said, Nay; lest while ye gather up the tares,
29B				ye root up also the wheat with them.
30				Let both grow together until the harvest:
30B				And in the time of harvest
30C				I will say to the reapers, Gather ye together first the tares,
30D				and bind them in bundles - to burn them:
30E				But gather the wheat into my barn.
31	30			Another parable put he forth unto them, saying,
	30B			Where unto shall we liken the kingdom of God?
	30C			or with what comparison shall we compare it?
31B	31			The kingdom of heaven (the kingdom of God)
31C	31B			is like to a grain of mustard seed,
31D				which a man took and sowed in the field;
32	31C			which, when it is sown in the earth, which indeed
32B	31D			is the least of all (less than) the seeds that be in the earth.
	32			But when it is sown,
	32B			it groweth up and becomes greater than all herbs:
32C				When it is grown it is the greatest among herbs,
32D	32C			and shooteth out branches, and becometh a tree:
32E	32D			so that the birds (fowls) of the air
	32E			may lodge under the shadow of it,
32F				come and lodge in the branches thereof.
33				Another parable spake he unto them;

```
Mt.13   Mk.4   Lk.8   Jn.4
```

33B				The kingdom of heaven is like unto leaven,
33C				which a woman took,
33D				and hid in 3 measures of meal, till the whole was leavened.
34				All these things spake Jesus unto the multitude in parables:
	33			With many such parables
	33B			spake he the word unto them, as they were able to hear it.
34B	34			And without a parable spake he not unto them:
35				That it might be fulfilled which was spoken by the prophet, saying,
35B				I will open my mouth in parables;
35C				I will utter things which have been
35D				kept secret from the foundation of the world.
36				Then Jesus sent the multitude away, and went into the house:
36B				And his disciples came unto him,
36C				saying, Declare unto us the parable of the tares of the field.
	34B			And when they were alone he expounded all things to his disciples.
37				Jesus answered and said unto them,
37B				He that soweth the good seed is the Son of man; (Mt.13:24C)
38				The field is the world (ie: the kosmos);
38B				The good seed are the children of the kingdom;
38C				but the tares are the children of the wicked one;
39				the enemy that sowed them is the devil:
39B				The harvest is the end of the world (ie: the end of the age);
39C				and the reapers are the angels.
40				As therefore the tares are gathered and burned in the fire;
40B				so shall it be in the end of the world.
41				The Son of man shall send forth his angels,
41B				and they shall gather out of his kingdom
41C				all things that offend, and them which do iniquity; (1 Cor.6:9)
42				And shall cast them into a furnace of fire; (Mt.3:12)
42B				there shall be wailing and gnashing of teeth.
43				Then shall the righteous shine forth as the sun (Eph.1:4)
43B				in the kingdom of their Father.
43C				Who has ears to hear, let him hear.
44				Again, the kingdom of heaven is like unto treasure hid in a field;
44B				the which when a man hath found, he hideth, and for joy thereof
44C				goeth and selleth all that he hath, and buyeth that field.
45				Again, the kingdom of heaven
45B				is like unto a merchant man, seeking goodly pearls:
46				Who, when he had found one pearl of great price, went and
46B				sold all that he had, and bought it. (Phil.2:7)
47				Again, the kingdom of heaven is like a net,
47B				that was cast into the sea, and gathered of every kind;
48				Which, when it was full, they drew to shore, and sat down, and
48B				gathered the good into vessels, but cast the bad away.
49				So shall it be at the end of the world:
49B				The angels shall come forth,
49C				and sever the wicked from the just,
50				And shall cast them into the furnace of fire:
50B				there shall be wailing and gnashing of teeth.
51				Jesus saith unto them, Have ye understood all these things?
51B				They said unto him, Yea, Lord.
52				Then said he unto them, Therefore every scribe

> Note: (a) scribe (ie: a writer, or somebody well versed in the Scriptures).
>   (to) scribe (ie: to/to be - number(ed), count(ed), declare(d), speak (told).

52B				which is
52C				instructed (ie: to teach/make disciples) (Mt.28:19/Acts 14:21)

Mt.13	Mk.4	Lk.8	Jn.4		
52D				unto the kingdom of heaven	(Mt.13:44/Mt.19:12)
52E				is like unto a man that is an householder,	(Mt.12:35)
52F				which bringeth forth out of his treasure things new and old.	
53				And it came to pass,	
53B				when Jesus had finished these parables, he departed thence.	

Mt.8				
		22		Now it came to pass on a certain day,
	35			And the same day, when the even was come,
18				Now when Jesus saw great multitudes about him,
18B	35B			he gave commandment to depart (pass over) unto the other side.
19				And a certain scribe came, and said unto him,
19B				Master, I will follow thee whither-so-ever thou goest.
20				And Jesus saith unto him,
20B				The foxes have holes, and the birds of the air have nests;
20C				but the Son of man hath not where to lay his head.
21				And another of his disciples said unto him,
21B				Lord, suffer me first to go and bury my father.
22				But Jesus said unto him,
22B				Follow me; and let the dead bury their dead.
	36			And when they had sent away the multitude;
23		22B		And when he was entered into a ship, his disciples followed him.
		22C		And he said unto them,
		22D		Let us go over unto the other side of the lake.
	36B			(they took him even as he was in the ship.)
		22E		And they launched forth:
	36C			and there were also with him - other little ships.
		23		But as they sailed, he fell asleep.
24				And, behold,
24B	Tsunami			there arose a great tempest (ie: earthquake) in the sea
				Note: An earthquake in the sea = a tsunami.
	37	23B		and there arose (came down) a great storm of wind on the lake:
24C				insomuch that the ship was covered with the waves:
	37B			And the waves beat into the ship,
	37C	23C		so that they now became full, filled with water;
		23D		and were in jeopardy.
24D	38			And Jesus was in the hinder part of the ship, asleep on a pillow:
25	38B	24		And his disciples came to him, and they awake (awoke) him,
25B	38C	24B		and say unto him,
		24C		Master, master, we perish!
25C				Lord, save us: we perish!
	38D			Master, carest thou not that we perish?
26				And he saith unto them,
26B				Why are ye fearful, O ye of little faith?
26C	39	24D		And he arose, and rebuked the wind(s) and the raging of the water,
	39B			and said unto the sea, Peace, be still.
26D	39C	24E		And (they ceased) the wind ceased, and there was a great calm.
	40	25		And he said unto them,
		25B		Where is your faith?
	40B			Why are ye so fearful? How is it that ye have no faith?
	41	25C		And they being afraid, feared exceedingly;
27	41B	25D		and they (the men) marvelled (wondering) saying one to another,
27B	41C	25E		What manner of man is this!
27C	41D			that even the wind(s) and the sea obey him!
		25F		for he commandeth even the winds and water,
		25G		and they obey him.
	Mk.5			
	1			And he/they came over unto the other side of the sea:

Mt.8	Mk.5	Lk.8	Jn.4	
28				When he/they arrived (were come/came over)
28B		26B		unto the other side of the sea (over against Galilee);
28C	1B	26A		They arrived in the country of the Gadarenes/Gergesenes:
28D				There met him 2 possessed with devils;
28E		Two men		coming out of the tombs:
28F				Exceeding fierce, so that no man might pass by that way.
				Note: Did Jesus confront these 2 together, or one at a time?
	2			And when he was come out of the ship, immediately,
	2B			there met him a man (out of the tombs) with an unclean spirit;
	3			who had his dwelling among the tombs:
	3B			And no man could bind him, no, not with chains;
	4			because that he had been often bound with fetters and chains,
	4B			And the chains had been plucked asunder by him,
	4C			and the fetters broken in pieces:
	4D			neither could any man tame him.
	5	This		And always, night and day, he was in the mountains,
	5B	man		and in the tombs, crying, and cutting himself with stones.
	6	ran		When he saw Jesus afar off, he ran and worshipped him:
		27		And when he went forth to land:
		27B		There met him out of the city a certain man,
		27C		which had devils a long time, and ware no clothes,
		27D		neither abode in any house, but in the tombs:
		28		When he saw Jesus, he cried out, and fell down before him:
	7			And he cried out with a loud voice, and said,
		28		And with a loud voice, said,
29				And, behold, they cried out saying,
29B	7B	28B		What have I (we)
29C	7C	28C		to do with thee, Jesus, thou Son of the Most High God?
29D				Art thou come hither to torment us before the time?
	7D			I adjure thee by God, that thou torment me not:
		28D		I beseech thee, torment me not.
	8	29		For he had said (he had commanded) the unclean spirit,
	8B	29B		Come out of the man, thou unclean spirit.
		29C		For often-times it had caught him:
		29D		(and he was kept bound with chains and in fetters);
		29E		and he brake the bands,
		29F		and was driven of the devil into the wilderness.
	9	30		And Jesus asked him, saying, What is thy name?
	9B	30B		And he answered him, saying, My name is Legion:
	9C	30C		for we are many (because many devils were entered into him).
	10	31		And he/they besought him,
	10B			much, that he would not send them away out of the country:
		31B		that he would not command them to go out into the deep.
30	11	32		Now, there was there (a good way off from them),
	11B			nigh unto the mountains,
30B	11C	32B		many (a great herd of) swine feeding on the mountain.
31	12	32C		But, all the devils besought him, saying,
31B	12B	32D		If thou cast us out, send us (suffer us)
31C	12C	32E		to go away (that we may enter) into the herd of swine.
	13	32F		And forthwith Jesus (suffered them)
32	13B			gave them leave; and he said unto them, Go!
	13C	33		And the unclean spirits (devils) went out of the man:
32B				And when they were come out
32C	13D	33B		they entered (went into) the herd of swine;
32D	13E	33C		And, behold, the whole herd of swine
32E	13F	33D		ran violently down a steep place into the sea/lake:
	13G			(They were about 2000) and were choked in the sea.

Mt.8	Mk.5	Lk.8	Jn.4	
32F		33E		and were choked, and perished in the waters.
33	14	34		When they that kept (fed) the swine,
33B	14B	34B		when they saw what was done, they fled:
33C	14D	34D		And went their ways unto the city, and into the country,
33D	14C	34C		and told everything,
33E				and what was befallen to the possessed of the devils.
	14E	35		And they went out to see what it was that was done:
	15	35B		And they come to Jesus, and him (they found the man),
	15B			that was possessed with the devil,
		35C		out of whom the devils were departed;
	15C	35D		And him that had the legion, sitting at the feet of Jesus,
	15D	35E		and clothed, and in his right mind:
	15E	35F		And they were afraid.
	16	36		And they also which saw it, told them how (by what means)
	16B	36B		it befell to him that was possessed with the devil was healed;
	16C			and also concerning the swine.
34				And, behold, the whole city came out to meet Jesus:
		37		Then the whole multitude
		37B		of the country of the Gadarenes round about,
34B	17	37C		when they saw him besought him (they began to pray him),
34C	17B	37D		that he would depart from them, out of their coasts:
		37E		For they were taken with great fear.

Mt.9				
1		37F		And he entered (went up into) the ship returning (to pass over):
	18			And when he was come into the ship,
	18B	38		the man that had been possessed with the devil
		38B		(out of whom the devils were departed),
	18C	38C		besought (prayed) him that he might be with him.
	19	38D		Howbeit Jesus suffered (ie: allowed) him not, but sent him away,
	19B	39		saying, Return to thine house (go home to thy friends),
	19C	39B		and tell them, shew how great things the Lord (God)
	19D	39C		hath done for (unto) thee, and hath had compassion on thee.
	20	39D		And he departed (he went his way),
	20B	39E		and began to publish in Decapolis (throughout the whole city),
	20C	39F		how great things Jesus had done for (unto) him:
	20D			And all men did marvel.
1B	21			And Jesus passed over
	21B			again by ship unto the other side:
		40		And it came to pass, that, when Jesus was returned,
		40B		the people received him; for they were all waiting for him.
	21C			Much people gathered unto him: and he was nigh unto the sea.
18				While he spake these things unto them,
18B	22	41		behold, there came (cometh) a certain ruler:
	22B	41B		One of the rulers of the synagogue, a man named Ja-i'rus;
	22C	41C		and when he saw him, he fell down at Jesus' feet,
	23	41D		and besought him greatly, that he would come into his house:
18C	23B			And he worshipped him, saying,
18D	23C			My little daughter lieth at the point of death - even now dead;
18E	23D			I pray thee, come and lay thy hand(s) upon her,
18F	23E			that she may be healed; and she shall live.
		42		(For he had one only daughter,
		42B		about 12 years of age, and she lay a dying.)
19	24			And Jesus arose, and followed him (Jesus went with him);
19B	24B			and so did his disciples, and much people followed him:
	24C	42C		But as he went the people thronged him.
20	25	43		And, behold, a certain woman,

Mt.9	Mk.5	Lk.8	Jn.4
20B	25B	43B	
	26		
	26B	43C	
	26C		
		43D	
	27		
20C	27B	44	
20D	27C	44B	
21	28		
21B	28B		
	29	44C	
	29B	44D	
	29C		
	30		
	30B		
22	30C		
	30D	45	
		45B	
	31	45C	
	31B	45D	
	31C	45E	
		46	
		46B	
	32		
	33	47	
	33B	47B	
22B	33C	47C	
	33D	47D	
		47E	
22C	34	48	
22D	34B	48B	
	34C	48C	
22E			
	35	49	
	35B	49B	
	35C	49C	
	35D	49D	
	36	50	
	36B	50B	
	36C	50C	
		50D	
	37		
	37B		
	38		
	38B		
23	39	51	
23B			
		51B	
		51C	
		52	
24	39B	52B	
24B	39C	52C	
24C	39D	52D	
24D	40	53	
		54	
25	40B		
	40C		
	40D		

which was diseased with (having) an issue of blood 12 years:
And had suffered many things of many physicians,
    and had spent all her living (all she had) upon physicians;
    and was nothing bettered, but rather grew worse,
        neither could be healed of any.
When she heard of Jesus,
    came in the press (ie: people/multitude) behind,
    and touched the border (the hem) of his garment:
    for she said (within herself),
    if I may but touch his garment (clothes), I shall be whole.
And immediately (straightway)
    the issue (fountain) of her blood was stanched (dried up),
    and she felt in her body that she was healed of that plague.
And Jesus, immediately knowing (in himself)
    that virtue (ie: power) had gone out of him,
    turned him about in the press;
    and Jesus said, Who touched me? Who touched my clothes?
When all denied,
    Peter and they that were with him (his disciples) said unto him,
    Master, thou seest the multitude thronging thee, and press,
        and sayest thou, Who touched me?
And Jesus said, somebody hath touched me:
    for I perceive that virtue is gone out of me.
And Jesus looked round about to see her that had done this thing.
But when the woman saw that she was not hid,
    she came fearing and trembling, knowing what was done in her:
And when Jesus saw her, she fell down before him, and declared
    all the truth unto him, before all the people, for what cause
    she had touched him, and how she was healed immediately.
And he (ie: Jesus) said unto her, Daughter,
    be of good comfort: thy faith hath made thee whole;
    go in peace, and be whole of thy plague.
And the woman was made whole from that hour.
And while he yet spake,
    there cometh one from the ruler of the synagogue's house,
    saying to him, Thy daughter is dead;
        trouble not (why troublest) thou the Master any further?
But when (as soon as) Jesus heard the word that was spoken,
    he saith unto (answered him) the ruler of the synagogue,
    Fear not (be not afraid) only believe,
        and she shall be made whole.
And he suffered no man to follow him,
    save Peter, and James, and John (the brother of James).
And he cometh to the house of the ruler of the synagogue,
    and seeth the tumult, and them that wept and wailed greatly.
And when Jesus came into (was come in) the ruler's house,
    he saw the minstrels and the people making a noise:
    He (ie: Jesus) suffered no man to go in, save Peter and James,
        and John, and the father and the mother of the maiden.
And all wept, and bewailed her:
He saith unto them, Give place (ie: Go aside/depart);
    Weep not! Why make ye ado and weep?
        for she (the maid/damsel) is not dead, but sleepeth.
And they laughed him to scorn, knowing that she was dead.
And he (ie: Jesus) put them all out.
But when he had put them all out (when the people were put forth),
    he taketh the father and the mother of the damsel,
    and them that were with him;

Mt.9	Mk.5	Lk.8	Jn.4	
25B	40E			and entereth in (he went in) where the damsel was lying.
25C	41	54B		And he (ie: Jesus) took her (the damsel) by the hand,
	41B	54C		and he said unto her (and called, saying),
	41C			Talitha cumi (which is, being interpreted),
	41D	54D		Damsel (Maid), I say unto thee, arise.
		55		And her spirit came again, (Jam.2:26)
25D	42	55B		and straightway she (the damsel/maid) arose and walked;
	42B			for she was of the age of 12 years.
	42C			And they were astonished with a great astonishment.
		56		And her parents were astonished.
	43C	55C		And he commanded to give her (that something be given her) to eat.
	43A	56B		And he charged them
	43B			straitly (ie: greatly) that no man should know it; (Mk.5:23)
		56C		that they should tell no man what was done.
26				And the fame thereof went abroad into all the land.
27				And when Jesus departed thence, 2 blind men followed him,
27B				crying, and saying, Thou Son of David, have mercy on us.
28				And when he was come into the house, the blind men came to him:
28B				Jesus saith unto them, Believe ye that I am able to do this?
28C				They said unto him, Yea, Lord.
29				Then touched he their eyes,
29B				saying, According to your faith be it unto you.
30				And their eyes were opened; and Jesus straitly charched them,
30B				saying, See that no man know it.
31				But they, when they were departed,
31B				spread abroad his fame in all that country.
32				As they went out, behold,
32B				they brought to him a dumb man possessed with a devil.
33				And when the devil was cast out, the dumb spake:
33B				And the multitudes marvelled,
33C				saying, It was never so seen in Israel.
34				But the Pharisees said, (Mk.3:22)
34B				He casteth out devils through the prince of the devils.
35				And Jesus went about all the cities and villages,
35B				teaching in their synagogues,
35C				and preaching the gospel of the kingdom,
35D				and healing every sickness and every disease among the people.
	The			
36	harvest			When he saw the multitudes,
36B	is plenteous,			he was moved with compassion on them, because they fainted,
36C	The			and were scattered abroad, as sheep having no shepherd.
37	labourers			Then saith he unto his disciples,
37B	are not many.			The harvest truly is plenteous, but the labourers are few;
38				Pray ye therefore the Lord of the harvest,
38B				that he will send forth labourers into the harvest.
Mt.13	Mk.6			
	1			And he went out from thence,
54	1B			and came into his own country: and his disciples follow him.
	2			And when the sabbath day was come,
54B	2B			he began to teach them in their synagogue.
54C	2C			And many hearing him were astonished, saying,
54D	2D			From whence hath this man these things?
54E	2E			that even such mighty works are wrought by his hands?
55				Is not this the carpenter's son? Is not his mother called Mary?
	3			Is not this the carpenter, the son of Mary?
55B	3B			And his brethren (the brother of)
55C	3C			James, and Joses, and Juda(s), and Simon?

The Gospels of Matthew, Mark, Luke, and John: Merged into One Historic Calendar of Events

Mt.13	Mk.6	Lk.8	Jn.4		
56	3D			and his sisters, are they not all with us?	
56B				Whence then hath this man all these things?	
57	3E			And they were offended in him.	
57B	4			But Jesus said unto them,	
57C	4B			A prophet is not without honour, save/but in his own country,	
57D	4C			and among his own kin, and in his own house.	(Jn.7:5)
	5			And he could there do no mighty work	
58				(He did not many mighty works there),	
58B				because of their unbelief;	
	5B			Save that he	
	5C			laid his hands upon a few sick folk and healed them.	
	6			And he marvelled because of their unbelief.	
	6B			And he went round about the villages, teaching.	

Mt.10		Lk.9			
1	7	1		And he called together unto him his 12 disciples,	
	7B			and began to send them forth by 2 and 2;	
1B	7C	1B		And he gave them power and authority	
1C	7D	1C		over all devils (unclean spirits) to cast them out;	
1D				And to heal all manner of sickness,	
1E		1D		and to cure all manner of disease.	
2				Now the names of the 12 apostles are these;	(Mk.3:14)
2B				The 1st. Simon, who is called Peter,	Peter
2C				and Andrew his brother;	Andrew
2D				James the son of Zebedee,	James
2E				and John his brother;	John
3				Philip,	Philip
3B				and Bartholomew;	Bartholomew
3C				Thomas,	Thomas
3D				and Matthew the publican;	Matthew
3E				James the son of Alphaeus,	James
3F				and Lebbaeus, surnamed Thaddaeus	Lebbaeus
4				Simon the Canaanite,	Simon
4B				and Judas, who also betrayed him.	Judas
5		2		And he sent them (these 12) forth,	
		2B		to preach the kingdom of God, and to heal the sick.	
5B	8	3		And he said unto them (he commanded them), saying,	
5C				Go not into the way of the Gentiles,	
5D				and into any city of the Samaritans enter ye not:	
6				But go rather to the lost sheep of the house of Israel.	
7				And as ye go, preach,	
7B				saying, The kingdom of heaven is at hand,	
8				Heal the sick, cleanse the lepers,	
8B				Raise the dead, cast out devils:	
8C				Freely ye have received, freely give.	
	8B			Take nothing for your journey, save your staff only!	
10	8C	3B		Take nothing for your journey, no staff, nor scrip, nor bread:	
	8D	3C		No money in your purse,	
9				provide neither gold, nor silver, nor bronze in your purses:	
	9			Be shot with sandals,	
10B	9B	3D		and not put on (have) 2 coats apiece, nor shoes, nor staves:	
10C				for the workman is worthy of his meat.	

Note: Were they allowed to take their staff?
Perhaps, if it be a stick used to walk, and not a rod for defence.

	10			And he (ie: Jesus) said unto them,	
11				And into whatsoever city or town ye shall enter,	
11B				enquire who in it is worthy:	

Mt.10	Mk.6	Lk.9	Jn.4

	10B	4	
11C	10C	4B	
12			
13			
13B			
14	11	5	
14B	11B	5B	
14C	11C	5C	
15	11D		
15B	11E		
15C	11F		
16			
16B			
17			
17B			
17C			
18			
18B			
19			
19B	Do Not Rehearse!		
19C			
20			
20B			
21			
21B			
21C			
21D			
22			
22B			
23			
23B			
23C			
24			
24B			
25			
25B			
25C			
25D			
26			
26B			
27			
27B			
28			
28B			
28C			
28D			
29			
29B			
30			
31			
32			
32B			
33			
33B			
34			
34B			
35			
35B			

In what place soever, and whatever house ye shall enter into;
   there abide till ye go thence-forth (depart) from that place.
And when ye come into an house, salute it:
   And if the house be worthy, let your peace come upon it;
   but if it be not worthy, let your peace return to you.
And whosoever shall (will) not receive you, nor hear your words;
   when ye go (depart thence) out of that house or city, shake off
   the very dust from under your feet for a testimony against them.
Verily I say unto you,
   It shall be more tolerable for the land of Sodom and Gomorrha
   in the day of judgment, than for that city.   (Lk.10:12)
Behold, I send you forth as sheep in the midst of wolves:
   be ye therefore wise as serpents, and harmless as doves.
But beware of men:
   for they will deliver you up to the councils,
   and they will scourge you in their synagogues;
And ye shall be brought before governors and kings for my sake,
   for a testimony against them and the gentiles.
But when they deliver you up,
   take no thought how or what ye shall speak:
   for it shall be given you in that same hour what ye shall speak.
   For it is not ye that speak,   (Lk.21:14,15)
      but the Spirit of your Father which speaketh in you.
And the brother shall
   deliver up the brother to death, and the father the child;
   and the children shall rise up against their parents,
      and cause them to be put to death.
And ye shall be hated of all men for my name's sake:
   but he that endures to the end shall be saved.
But when they persecute you in this city, flee ye into another:
   for verily I say unto you, Ye shall not have gone over
   the cities of Israel, till the Son of man be come.
The disciple is not above his master,
   nor the servant above his lord.
   It is enough for the disciple that he be as his master,
      and the servant as the lord.
If they have called the master of the house Be-el'ze-bub,
   how much more shall they call them of his household?
Fear them not therefore: for there is nothing covered,
   that shall not be revealed; and hid, that shall not be known.
What I tell you in darkness, that speak ye in light:
   and what ye hear in the ear, that preach ye upon the housetops.
And fear not them which kill the body,
   but are not able to kill the soul:
   but rather fear him which is able to destroy
      both soul and body in hell (ie: Gehenna).   (Mt.5:22)
Are not 2 sparrows sold for a farthing? and not one of them
   shall fall on the ground without your Father. (Lk.12:6/Mt.6:26)
But the very hairs of your head are all numbered.
   Fear ye not therefore, ye are of more value than many sparrows.
Whosoever therefore shall confess me before mem,
   him will I confess also before my Father which is in heaven.
But whosoever shall deny me before men,
   him will I also deny before my Father which is in heaven.
Think not that I am come
   to send peace on earth: I came not to send peace, but a sword.
For I am come to set a man at variance against his father,
   and the daughter against her mother,

Mt.10	Mk.6	Lk.9	Jn.4	
35C				and the daughter in law against her mother in law.
36				And a man's foes shall be they of his own household.
37				He that loveth father or mother more than me is not worthy of me:
37B				and he that loveth
37C				son or daughter more than me is not worthy of me.
38				And he that taketh not his cross,
38B				and followeth after me, is not worthy of me.
39				He that findeth his life shall lose it: (Mt.10:33)
39B				and he that loseth his life for my sake shall find it.
40				He that receiveth you receiveth me,
40B				and he that receiveth me receiveth him that sent me.
41				He that receiveth a prophet in the name of a prophet
41B				shall receive a prophet's reward;
41C				And he that receiveth a righteous man in the name of
41D				a righteous man shall receive a righteous man's reward.
42				And whosoever shall give to drink unto one of these little ones
42B				a cup of cold water only in the name of a disciple,
42C				verily I say unto you, he shall in no wise lose his reward.
Mt.11				
1				And it came to pass,
1B				when Jesus had made an end of commanding his 12 disciples,
1C				he departed thence to teach and to preach in their cities.
	6			And they (ie: the 12) departed, and went through the towns:
	12			and they went out, and preached that men should repent;
	6B			preaching the gospel, and healing every where.
	13			And they cast out many devils,
	13B			and anointed with oil many that were sick, and healed them.
			Jn.5	
			1	After this there was a feast of the Jews;
			1B	and Jesus went up to Jerusalem.
			2	Now there is at Jerusalem by the sheep market, a pool, which
			2B	is called in the Hebrew tongue Be-thes'da, having 5 porches.
			3	In these lay a great multitude of impotent (ie: weak/sick) folk,
			3B	of blind, halt, withered, waiting for the moving of the water.
			4	For an angel (at a certain season/time)
			4B	went down into the pool, and troubled (ie: agitated) the water:
			4C	Whosoever then (after the troubling of the water) stepped in
			4D	first was made whole of whatsoever disease he had.
			5	And a certain man was there, which had an infirmity 38 years.
			6	When Jesus saw him lie, and knew that he had been so now
			6B	for a long time; he saith unto him, Wilt thou be made whole?
			7	The impotent man answered him, Sir, I have no man,
			7B	when the water is troubled, to put me into the pool:
			7C	but while I am coming, another steppeth down before me.
			8	Jesus saith unto him, Rise, take up thy bed, and walk.
			9	And immediately the man was made whole,
			9B	and took up his bed, and walked:
			9C	On the same day was the sabbath.
			10	The Jews therefore said unto him that was cured,
			10B	It is the sabbath day:
			10C	it is not lawful for thee to carry thy bed.
			11	He answered them, He that made me whole,
			11B	the same said unto me, Take up thy bed, and walk.
			12	Then asked they him, What man is that
			12B	which said unto thee, Take up thy bed, and walk?
			13	And he that was healed wist not who it was, for Jesus

Mt.11　Mk.6　Lk.9　Jn.5

13B	had conveyed himself away, a multitude being in that place.
14	Afterward Jesus findeth him in the temple,
14B	and said unto him, Behold, thou art made whole:
14C	sin no more, lest a worse thing come unto thee.
15	The man departed, and told the Jews that it was Jesus,
15B	which had made him whole.
16	And therefore did the Jews persecute Jesus,
16B	and sought to slay him,
16C	because he had done these things on the sabbath day.
17	But Jesus answered them, My Father worketh hitherto, and I work!
18	Therefore the Jews sought the more to kill him,
18B	because he not only had broken the sabbath, but said also
18C	that God was his Father, making himself equal with God.
19	Then answered Jesus and said unto them,
19B	Verily, verily, I say unto you, The Son
19C	can do nothing of himself, but what he seeth the Father do:
19D	For what things soever he doeth,
19E	these also doeth the Son likewise.
20	For the Father loveth the Son,
20B	and sheweth him all things that himself doeth:
20C	And he will
20D	shew him greater works than these, that ye may marvel.
21	For as the Father raiseth up the dead,
21B	and quickeneth - even so the Son quickeneth whom he will.
22	For the Father judgeth no man,
22B	but he committed (ie: granted/gave) all judgment unto the Son:
23	That all men should honour the Son,
23B	even as they honour the Father.
23C	He that honoureth not the Son
23D	honoureth not the Father which hath sent him.
24	Verily, verily, I say unto you,
24B	He that heareth my word, and believeth on him that sent me,
24C	hath everlasting life, and shall not come into condemnation;
24D	but is passed from death unto life.
25	Verily, verily, I say unto you,
25B	The hour is coming, and now is,
25C	when the dead shall hear the voice of the Son of God:
25D	And they that hear shall live.
26	For as the Father hath life in himself;
26B	so hath he given to the Son to have life in himself;
27	And hath given him authority to execute judgment also,
27B	because he is the Son of man.
28	Marvel not at this: for the hour is coming,
28B	in the which all that are in the graves shall hear his voice,
29	And shall come forth;
29B	they that have done good, unto the resurrection of life;
29C	and they that have done evil,
29D	unto the resurrection of damnation.
30	I can of mine own self do nothing: as I hear, I judge:
30B	and my judgment is just; because I seek not mine own will,
30C	but the will of the Father which hath sent me.
31	If I bear witness of myself, my witness is not true.
32	There is another that beareth witness of me;
32B	and I know that the witness which he witnesseth of me is true.
33	Ye sent unto John, and he bare witness unto the truth.
34	But I receive not testimony from man:
34B	but these things I say, that ye might be saved.
35	He was a burning and a shining light:

Mt.11　Mk.6　Lk.9　Jn.5

			35B	and ye were willing for a season to rejoice in his light.
			36	But I have greater witness than that of John:
			36B	for the works which the Father hath given me to finish,
			36C	the same works that I do,
			36D	bear witness of me, that the Father hath sent me.
			37	And the Father himself,　　　　(Jn.12:45/Jn.8:51/Jn.6:40/He.9:28)
			37B	which hath sent me, hath borne witness of me.
			37C	Ye have neither heard his voice at any time, nor seen his shape.
			38	And ye have not his word abiding in you:
			38B	for whom he hath sent, him ye believe not.
			39	Search the Scriptures;

　　The
　　　love
　　　　of God
　　　　　was not
　　　　　　in them.

```
                    39B        for in them ye think ye have eternal life:
                    39C           and they are they which testify of me.
                    40     And ye will not come to me, that ye might have life.
                    41     I receive not honour from men.
                    42     But I know you, that ye have not the love of God in you.
                    43     I am come in my Father's name, and ye receive me not:
                    43B       If another shall come in his own name, him ye will receive.
                    44     How can ye believe, which receive honour one of another,
                    44B       and seek not the honour that cometh from God only?
                    45     Do not think that I will accuse you to the Father:
                    45B       there is one that accuseth you, even Moses, in whom ye trust.
                    46     For had ye believed Moses,
                    46B       ye would have believed me: for he wrote of me.     (De.18:17-19)
                    47     But if ye believe not his writings, how shall ye believe my words?

Mt.14
 1       14      7         And at that time king Herod (the tetrarch) heard
 1B              7B           of the fame of Jesus - of all that was done by him,
         14B                     (for his name was spread abroad):
                 7C        And he was perplexed, because
                 7D           that it was said of some, that John was risen from the dead:
                 8            And of some, that Elias had appeared; and of others,
                 8B              that one of the old prophets was risen again.
                 9         And Herod said, John have I beheaded: but who is this,
                 9B           of whom I hear such things?  And he desired to see him.
 2       14C               And he said unto his servants,
 2B      14D                  That (this is) John the Baptist, he is/was risen from the dead,
 2C      14E                  and therefore mighty works do shew forth themselves in him.
         15                Others said, That it is Elias;
         15B               And others said, That it is a prophet, or as one of the prophets.
         16                But when Herod heard, he said, IT IS John, whom I beheaded:
         16B                  he is risen from the dead!
 3       17                For Herod himself had sent forth, and laid hold upon John,
 3B      17B                  and bound him, and put him in prison              (Lk.3:19,20)
 3C      17C                    for Herodias' sake, his brother Philip's wife:
         17D                       for he had married her.
 4       18                For John had said unto Herod,
 4B      18B                  It is not lawful for thee to have thy brother's wife.
         19                Therefore Herodias had a quarrel (ie: a vendetta) against him,
         19B                  and would have killed him; but she could not:
         20                For Herod feared John,
         20B                  knowing that he was a just man and an holy, and observed him:
         20C                  And when he heard him, he did many things, and heard him gladly.
 5                         And when he would have put him to death,
 5B                           he feared the multitude, because they counted him as a prophet.
 6       21                And when a convenient day was come (when Herod's birthday was kept)
```

Mt.14	Mk.6	Lk.9	Jn.5	
	21B			that Herod (on his birthday) made a supper
	21C			to the lords, high captains, and chief estates of Galilee:
6B	22			And when the daughter of the said Herodias came in, and danced
6C	22B			before them, and pleased Herod and them that sat with him.
7				Whereupon he (the king) promised with an oath
7B				to give her whatsoever she would ask.
	22C			The king said unto the damsel (ie: maiden),
	22D			Ask of me whatsoever thou wilt, and I will give it thee.
	23			And he sware unto her, Whatsoever thou shalt ask of me,
	23B			I will give it thee, unto the half of my kingdom.
	24			And she went forth, and said unto her mother, What shall I ask?
	24B			And she (ie: her mother) said, The head of John the Baptist.
	25			And she came in straightway with haste unto the king,
8	25B			and (being before instructed of her mother), asked saying,
	25C			I will that thou give me by and by (ie: immediately/straightway)
8B	25D			in a charger the head of John the Baptist.
9	26			And the king was exceeding sorry;
9B	26B			nevertheless, for his oath's sake,
9C	26C			and for their sakes which sat with him at meat,
9D	26D			he would not reject her, he commanded it to be given.
10	27	John		And immediately the king sent an executioner,
	27B	was		and commanded his head to be brought:
10B	27C	beheaded.		And he went and beheaded him (John) in the prison.
11	28			And his head was brought in a charger, and given to the damsel:
11B	28B			and she (the damsel) brought it (gave it) to her mother.
	29			And when his disciples heard of it,
12	29B			they (his disciples) came and took up his corpse (the body),
12B	29C			and buried it (laid it in a tomb); and went and told Jesus.
	30	10		And the apostles (when they were returned)
	30B	10B		gathered themselves together unto Jesus, and told him
	30C	10C		all things, both what they had done and what they had taught.
13				When Jesus heard of it,
	31			He said unto them,
	31B			Come ye yourselves apart into a desert place, and rest a while:
	31C			for there were many coming and going,
	31D			and they had no leisure so much as to eat.
			Jn.6	
			1	After these things,
13B	32	10D		He (ie: Jesus) took them, and he/they departed thence by ship,
			1B	Jesus went over the sea of Galilee (ie: the sea of Tiberias):
13C	32B	10E		and went aside privately (by ship) into a desert place apart,
		10F		(a desert place belonging to the city called Bethaida).
	33			And the people saw them departing, and many knew him,
	33B			and ran afoot thither out of all cities,
	33C			and outwent them, and came together unto him.
13D	11			And when the people had heard thereof (when they knew it),
13E	11B			they followed him on foot out of the cities.
			2	And a great multitude followed him, because
The			2B	they saw his miracles which he did on them that were diseased.
Passover			3	And Jesus went up into a mountain,
was nigh.			3B	and there he sat with his disciples.
			4	And the passover, a feast of the Jews, was nigh.
14	34			And Jesus went forth (when he came out):
			5	When Jesus then lifted up his eyes,
14B	34B			and saw much people (a great multitude),
			5B	a great company come unto him:
			5C	He (ie: Jesus) saith unto Philip,

Mt.14	Mk.6	Lk.9	Jn.6	
			5D	Whence shall we buy bread, that these may eat?
			6	And this he said to prove (ie: try/examine) him:
			6B	for he himself knew what he would do.
			7	Philip answered him, Two hundred pennyworth of bread is not
			7B	sufficient for them, that every one of them may take a little.
14C	34C			And Jesus was moved with compassion toward them,
	34D			because they were as sheep not having a shepherd:
		11C		And he received them,
	34E			and he began to teach them many things,
		11D		and spake unto them of the kingdom of God,
14D		11E		and he healed their sick (them that had need of healing).
15	35	12		As the day began to wear away (was now far spent), it was evening:
15B	35B	12B		His disciples (the 12) came unto him, and said unto him,
15D	35D			the time (ie: the hour) is now past (far passed):
15E	36	12C		Send them (the multitude) away,
15F	36B	12E		that they may go into the country round about,
15G	36C	12D		and into the towns (villages)
15H	36D	12F		and lodge, and get (buy) themselves victuals (bread);
15C	35C,E	12G		we are here in a desert place, and they have nothing to eat.
16	37	13		But Jesus answered and said unto them,
16B	37B	13B		They need not depart; give ye them to eat.
	37C			And they say unto him, Shall we go
	37D			and buy 200 pennyworth of bread, and give them to eat?
	38			He saith unto them, How many loaves have ye? go and see.
17	38B	13C		And (when they knew) they say unto him,
17B	38C	13D		We have here no more but 5 loaves and 2 fishes;
		13E		except we should go and buy meat for all this people.
			8	One of his disciples,
5000+ did eat.			8B	Andrew (Simon Peter's brother) saith unto him,
A surplus			9	There is a lad here,
of 12 baskets.			9B	which hath 5 barley loaves, and 2 small fishes:
			9C	but what are they among so many?
18				He (ie: Jesus) said, Bring them hither to me.
			10C	Now there was much grass in the place.
		14		They were (a multitude) of about 5000 men:
	39	14B	10A	And he (ie: Jesus) commanded (said to them) his disciples,
	39B	14C	10B	to make them/the men (to make all) sit down
	39C	14D		by companies (50 in a company) upon the green grass.
			10D	So they (the men) sat down, in number about 5000:
	40			And they sat down in ranks, by hundreds, and by fifties:
19				And he commanded the multitude to sit down in the grass;
		15		and they did so, they made them all to sit down.
19B	41	16		And when he had taken the 5 loaves and the 2 fishes:
			11	And Jesus took the loaves,
19C	41B	16B	11B	and looking up to heaven, gave thanks, blessed and brake them;
19D	41C	16C	11C	And he distibuted (gave the loaves) to his disciples,
19E	41D	16D	11D	and the disciples to the multitude (them that were set down);
	41E		11E	And likewise the 2 fishes,
	41F		11F	divided he among them all: as much as they would.
20	42	17		And they did eat, and were all filled.
			12	When they were filled, he said unto his disciples,
			12B	Gather up the fragments that remain, that nothing be lost.
20B	43	17B	13	Therefore they gathered them together; and they took up, and
20C'E	43B	17C,E	13B	filled 12 baskets with the fragments of the barley loaves,
	43C			and of the fishes;
20D		17D	13C	which remained (over and above) unto them that had eaten:
21	44			And they that did eat (of the loaves) were about 5000 men,
21B				besides women and children.

Mt.14	Mk.6	Lk.9	Jn.6	
			14	Then those men, when they had seen the miracles that Jesus did,
			14B	said, This is
			14C	of a truth that prophet that should come into the world.
			15	Jesus therefore perceived (ie: knew) that they
			15B	would come and take him by force, to make him a king:
22	45			And straightway Jesus constrained (ie: compelled)
22B	45B			his disciples to get into the ship,
22C	45C			and to go (before him) unto the other side, unto Bethsaida,
22D	45D			while he sent away the people (the multitude).
23	46			And when he had sent them (the multitudes) away,
			15C	he departed again into a mountain, himself alone
23B	46B			he went up into a mountain apart to pray.
23C	47		16	When the evening was come,
			16B	His disciples went down to the sea,
			17	and entered into a ship,
			17B	and went over the sea toward Capernaum.
24	47B			The ship was now in the midst of the sea.
			17C	And it was now dark, and Jesus was not come to them.
			18	And the sea arose by reason of a great wind that blew:
24B				the ship tossed with the waves: for the wind was contrary.
23D	47C			And he (ie: Jesus) was there all alone on the land:
	48			and he saw them toiling in rowing;
	48B			for the wind was contrary unto them.
			19	So when they had rowed about 25 or 30 furlongs;
25	48C			And (in or about) the 4th. watch of the night
25B	48D			he (Jesus) cometh unto them walking upon the sea,
	48E			and he would have passed by them.
26	49		19B	And the disciples saw him (Jesus) walking upon the sea.
			19C	And drawing nigh unto the ship, and they were afraid:
	49B			They supposing it was a spirit,
26C	49C			cried out for fear, saying, It is a spirit!
26B	50			For they all saw him, and were troubled.
27	50B		20	And straightway (immediately) Jesus spake unto them,
27B	50C		20B	saying, Be of good cheer: it is I; be not afraid.
28				And Peter answered him and said,
28B	On the sea			Lord, if it be thou, bid me come unto thee on the water.
29	toward Capernaum			And he (ie: Jesus) said, Come.
29B				And when Peter was come down out of the ship,
29C				he walked on the water, to go to Jesus.
30				But when he saw the wind boisterous, he was afraid;
30B	Lord Save Me!			and beginning to sink, he cried, saying, Lord, save me!
31				And immediately Jesus stretched forth his hand,
31B				and caught him, and said unto him,
31C				O thou of little faith, wherefore didst thou doubt?
			21	Then they willingly received him into the ship:
	51			He (ie: Jesus) went up unto them into the ship.
32	51B			And when they were come into the ship, the wind ceased.
33				Then they (that were in the ship) came and worshipped him,
33B				saying, Of a truth thou art the Son of God.
	51C			And they
	51D			were sore amazed in themselves beyond measure, and wondered.
	52			For they considered not the miracle of the loaves:
	52B			for their heart was hardened (ie: blinded). (Rom.11:7)
			21B	And immediately the ship was at the land whither they went.
34	53			And when they were gone over (had passed over),
34B	53B			they came into the land of Gennesaret, and drew to the shore.
	54			And when they were come out of the ship, straightway

The Gospels of Matthew, Mark, Luke, and John: Merged into One Historic Calendar of Events

Mt.14 Mk.6 Lk.9 Jn.6

	55			they knew him, and ran through that whole region round about:
35				And when the men of that place had knowledge of him,
35B				they sent out - into all that country round about;
	55B			And began to carry
	55C			about in beds those that were sick, to where they heard he was;
35C				and brought unto him all that were diseased:
	56			Whithersoever he entered, into villages,
	56B			or cities, or country, they laid the sick in the streets,
36	56C			And besought him, that they might only touch
36B	56D			if it were but the border (the hem) of his garment:
36C	56E			And as many as touched him were made perfectly whole.

	22	The day following,
	22B	when the people which stood on the other side of the sea,
	22C	saw that there was none other boat there,
	22D	save that one whereinto his disciples were entered;
	22E	And that Jesus went not with his disciples into the boat,
	22F	but his disciples were gone away alone;
	23	(Howbeit there came other boats from Tiberias nigh unto the place,
	23B	where they did eat bread, after that the Lord had given thanks:)
Others also	24	When the people therefore saw that Jesus was not there,
took shipping	24B	neither his disciples, they
to Capernaum.	24C	also took shipping, and came to Capernaum, seeking for Jesus.
	25	And when they had found him on the other side of the sea,
	25B	they said unto him. Rabbi, when camest thou hither?
	26	Jesus answered them and said, Verily, verily,
	26B	I say unto you, Ye seek me, not because ye saw the miracles,
	26C	but because ye did eat of the loaves, and were filled.
	27	Labour not for the meat (ie: food) which perishes, but for
	27B	that meat which endureth unto everlasting life, (Mt.6:19,20)
	27C	which the Son of man shall give unto you: (Jn.3:27)
	27D	for him hath God the Father sealed. (Jn.4:10/Jn.6:51)
	28	Then said they unto him,
	28B	What shall we do, that we might work the works of God?
	29	Jesus answered and said unto them, This is the work of God,
	29B	that ye believe on him whom he hath sent. (Mt.21:37/Jn.3:16,17)
	30	They said therefore unto him, What sign shewest thou then, that
	30B	we may see, and believe thee? what dost thou work? (De.13:1,2)
	31	Our fathers did eat manna in the desert; as it is written,
	31B	He gave them bread from heaven to eat. (Ps.78:24,25)
	32	Then Jesus said unto them, Verily, verily, I say unto you,
	32B	Moses gave you not that bread from heaven;
	32C	but my Father giveth you the true bread from heaven.
	33	For the bread of God is he which cometh down from heaven,
	33B	and giveth life unto the world.
	34	Then said they unto him, Lord, evermore give us this bread.
	35	And Jesus said unto them, I am the bread of life:
Come	35B	He that cometh to me shall never hunger; and
& Believe.	35C	He that believeth on me shall never thirst.
	36	But I said unto you, That ye also have seen me, and believe not.
	37	All that the Father giveth me shall come to me;
	37B	and him that cometh to me, I will in no wise cast out.
	38	For I came down from heaven, not to do mine own will,
	38B	but the will of him that sent me. (Jn.4:34/Jn.5:36/Jn.17:4)
	39	And this is the Father's will which hath sent me,
	39B	that of all which he hath given me I should lose nothing,
	39C	but should raise it up again at the last day.
	40	And this is the will of him that sent me,
	40B	that every one which seeth the Son,

Mt.14 Mk.6 Lk.9 Jn.6

	40C and believeth on him, may have everlasting life:
	40D And I will raise him up at the last day.
	41 The Jews then murmured at him,
	41B because he said, I am the bread which came down from heaven.
	42 And they said, Is not this Jesus, (Mt.13:55,56)

```
                             40C       and believeth on him, may have everlasting life:
                             40D         And I will raise him up at the last day.
                             41      The Jews then murmured at him,
                             41B       because he said, I am the bread which came down from heaven.
                             42      And they said, Is not this Jesus,                      (Mt.13:55,56)
                             42B       the son of Joseph, whose father and mother we know?
                             42C       How is it then that he saith, I came down from heaven?
                             43      Jesus therefore answered
                             43B       and said unto them, Murmur not among yourselves.
   No man can                44        No man can come to me,
      come - unless,         44B       except the Father which hath sent me draw him:
                             44C           and I will raise him up at the last day.  (1 Th.4:14,16)
                             45      It is written in the prophets, And they shall be all taught of God.
                             45B       Every man therefore
                             45C       that hath heard, and learned of the Father, cometh unto me.
                             46      Not that any man hath seen the Father,                 (Jn.14:8,9)
                             46B       save he which is of God, he hath seen the Father.
                             47      Verily, verily, I say unto you,
                             47B       He that believeth on me hath everlasting life.
                             48      I am that bread of life.
                             49      Your fathers did eat manna in the wilderness, and are dead.
                             50      This is the bread which cometh down from heaven,       (Jn.3:13)
                             50B        that a man may eat thereof, and not die.
                             51      I am the living bread which came down from heaven:
                             51B       if any man eat of this bread, he shall live for ever:
                             51C         And the bread that I will give is my flesh,
                             51D            which I will give for the life of the world.
                             52      The Jews therefore strove among themselves,
                             52B       saying, How can this man give us his flesh to eat?
                             53      Then Jesus said unto them, Verily, verily,
                             53B       I say unto you, Except ye eat the flesh of the Son of man,
                             53C       and drink his blood ye have no life in you.          (Mt.13:10-16)
                             54      Whoso eateth my flesh, and drinketh my blood, hath eternal life;
                             54B       and I will raise him up at the last day.
                             55         For my flesh is meat indeed, and my blood is drink indeed.
                             56         He that eateth my flesh, and drinketh my blood,    (Lk.22:19,20)
                             56B           dwelleth in me, and I in him.
                             57      As the living Father hath sent me, and I live by the Father:
                             57B        so he that eateth me, even he shall live by me.
                             58      This is that bread which came down from heaven:
                             58B        not as your fathers did eat manna, and are dead:
                             58C        He that eateth of this bread shall live for ever.
   Many of                   59      These things said he in the synagogue, as he taught in Capernaum.
      his disciples          60      Many therefore of his disciples, when they had heard this,
                             60B        said, This is an hard saying; who can hear it?
                             61      When Jesus knew in himself that his disciples murmured at it,
                             61B        said unto them, Doth this offend you?  And what if
                             62      ye shall see the Son of man ascend up to where he was before?
   His words are             63      It is the spirit that quickeneth; the flesh profiteth nothing:
      Spirit & Life.         63B        the words that I speak unto you, are spirit, and they are life.
                             64      But there are some of you that believe not.
                             64B        (For Jesus knew from the beginning who they were
                             64C            that believed not, and who should betray him.)
                             65      And he said, Therefore said I unto you, that no man
                             65B        can come unto me, except it were given unto him of the Father.
                             66      From that time
       went back.            66B        many of his disciples went back, and walked no more with him.
                             67      Then said Jesus unto the twelve, Will ye also go away? (Mt.26:56)
```

The Gospels of Matthew, Mark, Luke, and John: Merged into One Historic Calendar of Events

Mt.14	Mk.6	Lk.9	Jn.6	
			68	Then Simon Peter answered him, Lord,
			68B	to whom shall we go? thou hast the words of eternal life.
			69	And we believe and are sure,
			69B	that thou art that Christ, the Son of the living God.
			70	Jesus answered them,
			70B	Have not I chosen you twelve, and one of you is a devil?
			71	He spake of Judas Iscariot (the son of Simon):
			71B	for he it was (being one of the 12) that should betray him.

Mt.15	Mk.7		
1	1		Then came together unto him (to Jesus) the Pharisees,
1B	1B		and certain of the scribes which were of (came from) Jerusalem.
	2		And when they saw some of his disciples eat bread - defiled,
	2B		that is to say, with unwashen hands, they found fault.
	3		For the Pharisees, and all the Jews, except they wash
	3B		their hands oft, eat not: holding the tradition of the elders.
	4		And when they come from the market, except they wash, they eat not.
	4B		And many other things there be,
	4C		which they have received to hold,
	4D		as the washing of cups, and pots, brasen vessels, and of tables.
	5		Then the Pharisees and the scribes asked him,
2	5B		Why do thy disciples transgress (walk not according to)
2B	5C		the tradition of the elders?
2C			For they wash not their hands when they eat bread
	5D		but eat bread with unwashed hands?
3	6		But he answered and said unto them,
3B			Why do ye also transgress the commandment of God by your tradition?
7	6B		Ye hypocrites, well did Esaias prophesy of you,
7B	6C		saying (as it is written),
8	6D		This people
8B			draweth nigh unto me with their mouth, and
8C	6E		honoureth me with lips, but their heart is far from me.
9	7		But (howbeit) in vain do they worship me,
9B	7B		teaching for doctrines, the commandments of men.
	8		For laying aside the commandment of God,
	8B		ye hold the tradition of men, as the washing of pots and cups,
	8C		and many other such like things ye do.
	9		And he said unto them, Full well ye reject
	9B		the command of God, that ye may keep your own tradition.
4	10	When	For God commanded (Moses said),
4B	10B	man-made	saying, Honour thy father and thy mother; and, he that (whoso)
4C	10C	traditions	curseth father or mother, Let him die the death.
5	11	supersede	But ye say, If a man (whosoever) shall say unto his
5B	11B	the	father or mother, It is Corban (that is to say, it is a gift);
5C	11C	Scriptures.	It is a gift, by whatsoever thou mightest be profited by me:
	12		And ye suffer him no more to do ought for his father or mother,
6			and honour not his father or his mother, and he shall be free.
6B	13		Making (thus have ye made) the word (the commandment) of God
6C	13B		of none effect through/by your tradition,
	13C		which ye have delivered: and many such like things do ye.
10	14		And when he had called all the people (the multitude), he said
10B	14B		unto them, Hearken unto me (hear me) every one, and understand:
	15		There is nothing from without a man, that entereth into him
11			(not that which goeth into the mouth),
11B	15B		that can defile him (the man);
11C	15C		But that which cometh out of him (out of his mouth),
11D	15D		this (these are they) that defileth a man.
	16		If any man have ears to hear, let him hear.

Mt.15	Mk.7	Lk.9	Jn.6

```
         17                    And when he was entered into the house, from the people;
12                             Then came his disciples, and said unto him, Knowest thou
12B                               that the Pharisees were offended, after they heard this saying?
13                             But he (ie: Jesus) said, Every plant
13B                               which my heavenly Father hath not planted shall be rooted up.
14                               Let them alone: they be blind leaders of the blind.
14B                                And if the blind
14C                                   lead the blind, they both shall fall into the ditch.
         17B                   His disciples asked him concerning the parable:
15                             And Peter answering, said unto him, Declare unto us this parable.
16       18                    And Jesus said unto them, Are ye also yet without understanding?
17       18B                     Do ye not perceive (not yet understand),
17B      18C                       that whatsoever thing entereth
17C      18D                       from without into a man (into the mouth), cannot defile him,
17D      19                        because it entereth not into the heart, but into the belly, and
17E      19B                       goeth out (is cast out) into the draught - purching all meats
18       20                    But those things which proceed/cometh out of the mouth of the man,
18B      20B                     come forth from the heart, and they defile the man.
19       21                    For from within, out of the heart of men,
19B      21B                     proceed evil thoughts, adulteries, fornications, murders,
19C      22                        thefts, false witness, blasphemies, covetousness, wickedness,
         22B                       deceit, lasciviousness (ie: wantonness/filthy conversation),
         22C                       an evil eye, blasphemy, pride, foolishness:
20       23                    All these evil things come from within, and devile the man;
20B                               but to eat with unwashed hands defileth not a man.

21       24                    And Jesus arose from thence,
21B      24B                     and departed/went into the borders (coasts) of Tyre Sidon,
         24C                     And entered into an house,
         24D                        and would have no man know: but he could not be hid.
22       25                    And, behold, a woman of Canaan came out of the same coasts,
         25B                     whose young daughter had an unclean spirit, heard of him:
22B                            And cried unto him,
22C                               saying, Have mercy on me, O Lord, thou Son of David;
22D                                 my daughter is grievously vexed with a devil.
23                             But he answered her not a word.
23B                              And his disciples came and besought him, saying,
23C                                 Send her away; for she crieth after us.
24                             But he answered and said,
24B                              I am not sent but unto the lost sheep of the house of Israel.
25                             Then came she and worshipped him,
25B      25C                     and she fell at his feet, saying, Lord, help me!
         26                      The woman was a Greek, a Syrophenician by nation;
         26B                     and she besought him
         26C                        that he would cast forth the devil out of her daughter.
26       27                    But Jesus answered and said unto her,
         27B                     Let the children first be filled;
26B      27C                     for it is not meet to
26C      27D                        take the children's bread, and to cast it unto the dogs.
27       28                    And she answered and said unto him,
27B      28B                     Truth/Yes, Lord: yet the dogs under the table eat of
27C      28C                     the children's crumbs - which fall from their master's table.
28       29                    And Jesus answered and said unto her,
28B                              O woman, great is thy faith: be it unto thee even as thou wilt.
         29B                     For this saying go thy way;
         29C                        the devil is gone out of thy daughter.
28C                            And her daughter was made whole from that very hour.
         30                    And when she was come to her house, she found the devil gone out,
         30B                       and her daughter laid upon the bed.
```

The Gospels of Matthew, Mark, Luke, and John: Merged into One Historic Calendar of Events

| Mt.15 | Mk.7 | Lk.9 | Jn.6 |

29	31		And Jesus departed from thence, the coasts of Tyre and Sidon,
	31B		he came unto the
	31C		sea of Galilee, through the midst of the coasts of Decapolis.
	32		And they bring unto him one that was deaf,
	32B		and had an impediment in his speech;
	32C		And they beseech him to put his hand upon him.
	33		And he took him aside from the multitude,
	33B		and put his fingers into his ears,
	33C		and spit, and touched his tongue;
	34		And looking up to heaven,
	34B		he sighed, and saith unto him, Eph'pha-tha, that is, Be opened.
	35		And straightway his ears were opened,
	35B		and the string of his tongue was loosed, and he spake plain.
	36		And he charged them
	36B		that they should tell no man: but the more he charged them,
	36C		so much the more a great deal they published it;
	37		And were beyond measure astonished, saying,
	37B		He hath done all things well:
	37C		He maketh both deaf to hear, and the dumb to speak.
29B			And he came nigh unto the sea of Galilee
29C			and went up into a mountain, and sat down there.
30			And great multitudes came unto him, having with them those
30B			that were lame, blind, dumb, maimed, and many others,
30C			and cast them down at Jesus' feet; and he healed them:
31			Insomuch that the multitude wondered,
31B			when they saw the dumb to speak, the maimed to be whole,
31C			the lame to walk, and the blind to see: (Mt.11:4-6)
31D			And they glorified the God of Israel.
	Mk.8		
	1		In those days
	1B		the multitude (being very great), and having nothing to eat,
32	1C		Then Jesus called his disciples unto him, and saith unto them,
32B	2		I have compassion on the multitude, because they continue
32C	2B		with me now (have now been) 3 days, and have nothing to eat:
	3		And if I send them away fasting to their own houses,
	3B		they will faint by the way, for divers of them came from far:
32D			I will not send them away fasting, lest they faint in the way.
33	4		And his disciples say unto (answered) him,
33B			Whence should we have so much bread?
33D	4B		From whence can a man satisfy (as to fill) these,
33C,E	4C		so great a multitude with bread here in the wilderness?
34	5	4000 did eat.	And he (Jesus) asked (saith unto) them, How many loaves have ye?
34B	5B	A surplus	And they said, 7 and a few little fishes.
35	6	of 7 baskets.	And he (ie: Jesus) commanded
35B	6B		the people (the multitude) to sit down on the ground:
36A,C	6C		And he took the 7 loaves, and gave thanks, and brake them,
36D	6D		and gave to his disciples to set before them/the multitude;
36E	6E		and they did set them before the people/the multitude.
36B	7		And they had a few small fishes; and he blessed,
	7B		and commanded to set them also before them.
37	8		So they did all eat, and were filled: and they took up
37B	8B		the broken (ie: fragments) that was left 7 baskets full.
38	9		And they that did eat (had eaten)
38B	9B		were 4000 men (about 4000), beside women and children:
39	9C		And he (ie: Jesus) sent them (the multitude) away.
39B	10		And straightway he took (entered into a) ship with his disciples,
39C	10B		and came into the parts of Dalmanutha, the coasts of Magdala.
Mt.16			

Mt.16	Mk.8	Lk.9	Jn.6	
1	11			And the Pharisees (also with the Sadducees) came forth,
	11B			and began to question with him,
1B	11C,E			and tempting desired him (seeking of him),
1C	11D			that he would shew them a sign from heaven.
2				He answered and said unto them, When it is evening,
2B				ye say, It will be fair weather: for the sky is red.
3				And in the morning, It will be foul weather to day,
3B				for the sky is red and lowring.
3C				O ye hypocrites, ye can discern the face of the sky;
3D				but can ye not discern the signs of the times?
	12			And he sighed deeply in his spirit,
	12B			and saith, Why doth this generation seek after a sign?
	12C			Verily, verily, I say unto you,
4				A wicked and adulterous generation seeketh after a sign;
4B	12D			and there shall no sign be given unto it (this generation),
4C				but the sign of the prophet Jonas. (Mt.12:40)
4D	13			And he left them, and departed:
	13B			and entering into the ship again departed to the other side,
5				And when the disciples were come to the other side,
5B	14			and they (the disciples) had forgotten to take bread,
	14B			neither had they in the ship with them more than one loaf.
6	15			Then Jesus said unto them (and he charged them), saying,
6B	15B			Take heed, and beware of the leaven of the Pharisees,
6C	15C			and of the Sadducees; and of the leaven of Herod.
7	16			And they reasoned among themselves,
7B	16B			saying, It is because we have taken no bread.
8	17			And when Jesus perceived (knew it), he saith unto them,
8B	17B			O ye of little faith, why
8C	17C			reason ye among yourselves - because ye have brought no bread?
	17D			Perceive ye not yet,
	17E			neither understand? have ye your heart yet hardened?
	18			Having eyes, see ye not? and having ears, hear ye not?
9	18B			Do ye not yet understand, neither (and do ye not) remember,
9B	19			when I brake the 5 loaves among 5000, (Mt.14:17-21)
9C	19B			and how many baskets full of fragments took ye up?
	19C			They say unto him, Twelve.
10	20			And when the 7 loaves among the 4000, (Mt.15:34-38)
	20B			and how many baskets full of fragments took ye up?
	20C			And they said, Seven.
11	21			And he said unto them, How is it that ye do not understand?
11B				that I spake it not to you concerning bread.
11C		Jesus		But, that ye should
11D		spake		beware of the leaven of the Pharisees and of the Sadducees.
12		to them		Then understood they
12B		in Parables.		how that he bade them not beware of the leaven of bread,
12C				but of the doctrine of the Parisees and of the Sadducees.
	22			And he cometh to Bethsaida:
	22B			And they bring
	22C			a blind man unto him, and besought him to touch him.
	23			And he took
	23B			the blind man by the hand, and led him out of the town;
	23C			And when he spit on his eyes, and put his hands upon him,
	23D			he asked him if he saw ought (ie: any thing).
	24			And he looked up, and said, I see men as trees, walking.
	25			After that again,
	25B			he put his hands upon his eyes, and made him look up:
	25C			And he was restored, and saw every man clearly.

```
Mt.16   Mk.8   Lk.9   Jn.6
```

	26		And he sent him away to his house, saying,
	26B		Neither go into the town, nor tell it to any in the town.
	27		And Jesus went out,
	27B		and his disciples, into the towns of Caesarea Philippi:
	27C		And by the way,
13			When Jesus came into the coasts of Caesarea Philippi;
		18	And it came to pass,
		18B	as he was alone praying, his disciples were with him:
13B	27D	18C	He asked his disciples, saying unto them,
13C	27E	18D	Whom say men (the people) that I the Son of man am?
14	28	19	And they answering said,
14B	28B	19B	some say John the Baptist; some Elias, and others, Jeremias;
14C	28C	19C	or that one of the old prophets is risen again.
15	29	20	And he (ie: Jesus) saith unto them, But whom say ye that I am?
16	29B	20B	And Simon Peter answereth and saith unto him,
16B	29C	20C	Thou art the Christ, the Son of the living God.
17			And Jesus answered and said unto him,
17B			Blessed art thou, Simon Bar-jona: for flesh and blood hath not
17C			revealed it unto thee, but my Father which is in heaven.
18			And I say also unto thee, That thou art Peter,
18B			And upon this rock I will build my church;
18C			and the gates of hell shall not prevail against it.
19			And I will give unto thee the keys of the kingdom of heaven:
19B			and whatsoever thou shalt bind on earth (1 Jn.5:14)
19C			shall be (ie: shall having been) bound in heaven;
19D			and whatsoever thou shalt loose on earth
19E			shall be (ie: shall having been) loosed in heaven.
20	30	21	Then he straitly charged his disciples, and commanded them,
20B	30B	21B	that they should tell no man that he was Jesus the Christ.
21	Toward Jerusalem.		From that time forth began Jesus to shew unto his disciples
21B	31		(he began to teach them), how that he must go unto Jerusalem;
21C	31B	22	and that, the Son of man must suffer many things, and
21D	31C	22B	be rejected of the elders, and the chief priests, and scribes,
21E	31D	22C	and be slain/killed, and be raised after 3 days (the 3rd. day).
	32		And he spake that saying openly.
22	32B		Then Peter took him, and began to rebuke him,
22B			saying, Be it far from thee, Lord: this shall not be unto thee.
23	33		But when he had turned about, and looked on his disciples,
23B	33B		he rebuked Peter, saying,
23C	33C		Get thee behind me, Satan: for thou art an offense unto me:
23D	33D		for thou savourest not the things that be of God,
23E	33E		but those things that be of men.
	34		And when he had called the people unto him with his disciples:
24	34B	23	He said unto them (to his disciples and to them all),
24B	34C	23B	If any (whosoever) will come after me, let
24C	34D	23C	him deny himself, and take up his cross daily, and follow me.
25	35	24	For whosoever will save his life shall lose it:
25B	35B	24B	but, whosoever will lose his life for my sake and the gospel's,
25C	35C	24C	the same shall save (shall find) it.
26	36	25	For what shall it profit a man (for what is man advantaged),
26B	36B	25B	if he gain the whole world and lose his own soul (lose himself),
26C	37		Or what shall a man give in exchange for his soul?
		25C	Or be cast away (ie: receive damage/suffer loss, the loss of)?
	38	26	Whosoever therefore shall be ashamed of me and my words,
	38B		in this adulterous and sinful generation;
	38C	26B	Of him also shall the Son of man be ashamed, when he cometh:
27			For the Son of man shall come,

Assembly by John Douma

Mt.16	Mk.8	Lk.9	Jn.6	
		26C		in his own glory, and in his Father's, and of the holy angels;
27B	38D			in the glory of his Father with his angels (the holy angels);
27C				And then he shall reward every man according to his works.
	Mk.9			
	1	27		And he said unto them, But I tell you of a truth,
28	1B	27B		Verily I say unto you, That there be
28B	1C	27C		some of them that stand here, which shall not taste of death,
28C				till they have seen the Son of man coming in his kingdom:
	1D	27D		till they have seen the kingdom of God come with power.
Mt.17				
		28		And it came to pass
1	2	28B		after 6 days (about an 8 days after these sayings):
1B	2B	28C		Jesus taketh Peter, and James, and John his brother,
		28D		and went up into a mountain to pray;
1C	2C			and bringeth them up into an high mountain apart by themselves.
		29		And as he prayed,
		29B		the fashion of his countenance was altered,
2	2D			and he was transfigured before them:
2B				And his face did shine as the sun,
2C	3	29C		And his raiment became shinning, exceeding white
	3B			as snow; so as not fuller on earth can white them;
2D		29D		white as the light, white and glistering.
3	4	30		And, behold, there appeared unto them,
3B	4B	30B		two men (Elias with Moses), and they were talking to Jesus:
		31		Who appeared in glory, and spake of his decease (ie: departing)
		31B		which he should accomplish at Jerusalem.
		32		But Peter, and they that were with him, were heavy with sleep:
		32B		and when they were awake,
		32C		they saw his glory, and the 2 men that stood with him.
		33		And it came to pass, as they departed from him,
4	5	33B		Then answered Peter, and said unto Jesus, Lord, Rabbi, Master,
4B	5B	33C		it is good for us to be here:
4C	5C	33D		And, let us (if thou wilt), make here 3 tabernacles;
4D	5D	33E		one for thee, and one for Moses, and one for Elias:
		33F		Not knowing what he said,
	6			for he wist not what to say, for they were sore afraid.
5		34		While he thus (yet) spake,
5B	7	34B		behold, there came a bright cloud, and over shadowed them:
		34C		And they feared as they entered into the cloud.
5C	7B	35		And behold, there came a voice out of the cloud, which said,
5D	7C	35B		This is my beloved Son, in whom I am well pleased; hear ye him.
6				And when the disciples heard it,
6B				they fell on their face, and were sore afraid.
	8	36		And suddenly (when the voice was passed),
7				Jesus came and touched them, and said, Arise, and be not afraid.
8	8B			And when they had lifted up their eyes (looked round about),
8B	8C			they saw no man anymore, save Jesus only,
	8D	36B		Jesus was found alone - with themselves.
9	9			And as they came down from the mountain, Jesus charged them,
9B	9B			saying, Tell the vision (what things they had seen) to no man,
9C	9C			until the Son of man be risen from the dead.
	10			And they kept that saying with themselves, questioning
	10B			one with another, what the rising from the dead should mean.
		36C		And they kept it close (ie: they kept silence),
		36D		And told no man
		36E		in those days - any of those things which they had seen.

The Gospels of Matthew, Mark, Luke, and John: Merged into One Historic Calendar of Events

Mt.17	Mk.9	Lk.9	Jn.6

Mt.17	Mk.9	Lk.9	
10	11		And his disciples asked him,
10B	11B		saying, Why then say the scribes that Elias must first come?
11	12		And Jesus answered and told them (said unto them),
11B	12B		Elias indeed cometh first and restoreth all things;
	12C		and how it is written of the Son of man, that he must
	12D		suffer many things, and be set at nought (ie: be despised).
12	13		But I say unto you, That Elias is indeed already come,
12B			and they knew him not, (Mt.11:12-15/Mal.4:5,6)
12C	13B		and they have done unto him whatsoever they listed (ie: wilt);
	13C		as it is written of him.
12D			Likewise shall also the Son of man suffer of them:
13			Then the disciples
13B			understood that he spake unto them of John the Baptist.
		37	And it came to pass, that on the next day, when
		37B	they were come down from the hill (ie: mountain): (Mk.9:2)
14			And when they were come to the multitude:
	14		And when he (ie: Jesus) came to his disciples,
	14B		he saw a great multitude about them,
	14C		and the scribes questioning with them.
	15	37C	And straightway all the people (much people),
	15B		when they beheld him, were greatly amazed,
	15C	37D	and running to him (met him) saluted him.
	16		And he asked the scribes, What question ye with them?
14B		38	And, behold, there came to him a man,
	17	38B	one of the multitude (company) answered
14C	17B	38C	kneeling down to him, and said (cried out, saying), Master,
		38D	I beseech thee, look upon my son: for he is mine only child.
	17C		I have brought unto thee my son, which hath a dumb spirit.
15			Lord, have mercy on my son: for he is lunatick, and sore vexed:
15B			for oft-times he falleth into the fire, and oft into the water.
	18	39	And, lo, a spirit taketh him (and wheresoever he taketh him),
		39B	and he suddenly crieth out;
	18B	39C	and it (he) teareth him that he foameth again,
	18C		and gnasheth with his teeth, and pineth (ie: withereth) away:
		39D	And bruising him hardly departeth from him.
16			I brought him to thy disciples,
	18D	40	And spake to (besought) thy disciples
	18E	40B	that they should cast him out;
16B	18F	40C	And they could not cure him.
17	19	41	Then he (Jesus) answereth him,
17B	19B	41B	and saith, O faithless and perverse generation,
17C	19C	41C	how long shall I be with you? and how long shall I suffer you?
17D	19D	41D	Bring him (thy son) hither unto me.
	20		And they brought (ie: bring/bringing) him unto him:
	20B	42	And as he was yet a coming, when he saw him,
	20C	42B	straightway the spirit (the devil) threw him down and tare him,
	20D		and he fell on the ground, and wallowed (ie: to roll) foaming.
	21	Rolling	And he (ie: Jesus) asked his father,
	21B	and	How long is it ago since this came unto him?
	21C	Foaming.	And he said, Of a child.
	22		And ofttimes it hath cast him into the fire,
	22B		and into the waters, to destroy him: but
	22C		if thou canst do any thing, have compassion on us, and help us.
	23		Jesus said unto him,
	23B		If thou canst believe,
	23C		all things are possible to him that believeth.
	24		And straightway the father of the child cried out,
	24B		and said with tears, Lord, I believe; help thou mine unbelief.

Mt.17	Mk.9	Lk.9	Jn.6	
	25			When Jesus saw that the people came running together,
18	25B	42C		he (Jesus) rebuked the foul (unclean) spirit (the devil),
	25C			saying unto him, Thou dumb and deaf spirit, I charge thee,
	25D			come out of him, and enter no more into him.
	26			And the spirit cried,
18B	26B			and rent him sore, and he came (departed) out of him:
	26C			And he was as one dead; insomuch that many said, He is dead.
	27			But Jesus took him by the hand, and lifted him up; and he arose.
18C		42D		And the child was healed (cured) from that very hour,
		42E		and delivered him again to his father.
	28			And when he was come into the house,
19	28B			then came the disciples to Jesus apart (privately),
19B	28C			and said (they asked him), Why could we not cast him out?
20	29			And he (Jesus) said unto them,
20B				Because of your unbelief: for verily I say unto you,
20C				If ye have faith as a grain of mustard seed, ye shall
20D				say unto this mountain, Remove hence to yonder place;
20E				and it shall remove: and nothing shall be impossible unto you.
21	29B			Howbeit, this kind can come forth
21B	29C			by nothing (goeth not out) but by prayer and fasting.
	30			And they departed thence, and passed through Galilee:
22				And while they abode in Galilee;
		43		and they were all amazed at the mighty power of God.
		43B		But while they wondered every one at all things which Jesus did;
	30B			And he (ie: Jesus) would not that any man should know it,
22B	31	43C		for Jesus taught his disciples, and said unto them,
		44		Let these sayings sink down into your ears;
22C	31B	44B		for the Son of man is (shall be) betrayed (delivered)
22D	31C	44C		into the hands of men:
23	31D			And they shall kill him (and after that he is killed),
23B	31E			and (he shall rise) the 3rd. day he shall be raised.
23C				And they (ie: his disciples) were exceeding sorry.
	32	45		But they understood not the saying,
		45B		and it was hid from them, that they perceived it not:
	32B	45C		And they feared (were afraid) to ask him of that saying.
		46		Then there arose
		46B		a reasoning among them, which of them should be greatest.
24	33			And he/they came (were come) to Capernaum:
24B				They that received tribute money came to Peter,
24C				and said, Doth not your master pay tribute?
25				He (ie: Peter) saith, Yes.
25B				And when he was come into the house,
25C				Jesus prevented (ie: fore-spake) him, saying,
25D				What thinkest thou, Simon? of whom do the kings of the earth
25E				take custom or tribute? of their own children, or of strangers?
26				Peter saith unto him, Of strangers.
26B				Jesus saith unto him,
26C				Then are the children free.
27				Notwithstanding, lest we should offend them, go thou to the sea,
27B				and cast an hook, and take up the fish that first cometh up;
27C				And when thou hast opened his mouth, thou shalt find
27D				a piece of money: that take, and give unto them for me and thee.
		47		And Jesus, perceiving the thought of their heart:
	33B			And being in the house, he asked them,
	33C			What was it that ye disputed among yourselves by the way?
	34			But they held their peace: for by the way they

Mt.17	Mk.9	Lk.9	Jn.6	
		34C		had disputed among themselves who be the greatest. (Lk.9:46)
Mt.18				
	35			And he sat down, and called the 12:
1				At the same time came the disciples unto Jesus,
1B				saying, Who is the greatest in the kingdom of heaven?
	35B			And Jesus saith unto them, If any man desire
	35C			to be first, the same shall be last of all, and servant of all.
2				And Jesus called a little child unto him,
2B	36	47B		And he took the child, and set him (by him) in the midst of them:
3	36B	48		And when he had taken him in his arms, he said unto them,
3B				Verily I say unto you,
3C				Except ye be converted, and become as little children,
3D				ye shall not enter into the kingdom of heaven.
4				Whosoever therefore shall humble himself as this little child,
4B				the same is greatest in the kingdom of heaven.
5	37	48B		And whosoever shall receive one such (this) little child,
5B	37B	48E		one of such little children, in my name receiveth me.
	37C	48F		And whosoever
	37D	48G		shall receive me, receiveth (not me, but) him that sent me:
		48H		For he that is least among you all, the same shall be great.
	38	49		And John answered him, and said,
	38B	49B		Master, we saw one casting out devils in thy name,
	38C			and he followeth not us;
	38D	49C		And we forbade him, because he followeth not with us.
	39	50		And Jesus said unto him, Forbid him not:
	39B			for there is no man which shall do a miracle in my name.
	39C			that can lightly (ie: quickly) speak evil of me.
	40	50B		For he that is not against us is on our part (is for us).
	41			For whosoever shall give you
	41B			a cup of water to drink in my name, because ye belong to Christ,
	41C			verily I say unto you, he shall not lose his reward. (Mt.10:42)
6	42			But whosoever shall offend
6B	42B			one of these little ones that/which believe in me,
6C	42C			It is/were better for him
6D	42D			that a millstone were hanged about his neck, and he were cast
6E	42E			into the sea, and that he were drowned in the depth of the sea.
7				Woe unto the world
7B				because of offences! for it must needs be that offences come;
7C				but woe to that man by whom the offence cometh!
8	43,45			Wherefore if thy hand or thy foot offend thee,
8B	43,45			cut it/them off, and cast them from thee;
8C	43,45			It is better for thee to enter into life halt or maimed,
8D	43,45			rather than having 2 hands or 2 feet
8E	43,45			to go (be cast) into hell (everlasting fire);
	43,45			Into the fire that never shall be quenched:
	44,46			Where their worm dieth not, and the fire is not quenched.
9	47			And if thine eye offend thee,
9B	47B			pluck it out, and cast it from thee;
9C	47C			It is better for thee
9D	47D			to enter into life (into the kingdom of God) with one eye,
9E	47E			rather than having 2 eyes to be cast into hell fire;
	48			Where their worm dieth not, and the fire is not quenched.
10				Take heed that ye despise not one of these little ones;
10B				for I say unto you, That in heaven their angels
10C				do always behold the face of my Father which is in heaven:
11				For the Son of man is come to save that which was lost.

Mt.18 Mk.9 Lk.9 Jn.6

12	How think ye?
12B	If a man have an 100 sheep, and one of them be gone astray,
12C	doth he not leave the 90 and 9 (90+9=99), and goeth into
12D	the mountains, and seeketh that which is gone astray?
13	And if so be that he find it,
13B	verily I say unto you, he rejoiceth more of that sheep,
13C	than of the 90 and 9 which went not astray.
14	Even so it is not the will of your Father which is in heaven,
14B	that one of these little ones should perish.
15	Moreover if thy brother shall trespass against thee,
15B	go and tell him his fault between thee and him alone;
15C	if he shall hear thee, thou hast gained thy brother.
16	But if he will not hear thee, take with thee 1 or 2 more, that
16B	in the mouth of 2 or 3 witnesses every word may be established.
17	And if he shall neglect to hear them, tell it unto the church:
17B	but if he neglect to hear the church, let him be unto thee
17C	as an heathen and a publican. (Mt.5:46/Mt.9:11/Lk.3:12,13)
18	Verily I say unto you,
18B	Whatsoever ye shall bind on earth (Mt.16:19B)
18C	shall be (ie: shall having been) bound in heaven:
18D	and whatsoever ye shall loose on earth
18E	shall be (ie: shall having been) loosed in heaven.
19	Again I say unto you, That if 2 of you
19B	shall agree on earth as touching anything that they shall ask,
19C	it shall be done for them of my Father which is in heaven.
20	For where 2 or 3 are together
20B	in my name, there am I in the midst of them.
21	Then came Peter to them, and said, Lord, how oft shall
21B	my brother sin against me, and I forgive him? till 7 times?
22	Jesus saith unto him,
22B	I say not unto thee, Until 7 times: but, Until 70 times 7.
23	Therefore is the kingdom of heaven likened
23B	unto a certain king, which would take account of his servants.
24	And when he had begun to reckon,
24B	one was brought unto him, which owed him 10,000 talents.
25	But forasmuch as he had not to pay,
25B	His lord commanded him to be sold, and his wife, and children,
25C	and all that he had, and payment be made.
26	The servant therefore fell down, and worshipped him,
26B	saying, Lord, have patience with me, and I will pay thee all.
27	Then the lord of that servant was moved with compassion,
27B	and loosed him, and forgave him the debt.
28	But the same servant went out, and
28B	found one of his fellowservants, which owed him an 100 pence:
28C	And he laid his hands on him,
28D	and took him by the throat, saying, Pay me that thou owest.
29	And his fellowservant fell down at his feet, and besought him,
29B	saying, Have patience with me, and I will pay thee all.
30	And he would not: but went
30B	and cast him into prison, till he should pay the debt.
31	So when his fellowservants
31B	saw what was done, they were very sorry,
31C	and came and told unto their lord all that was done.
32	Then his lord, after that he had called him, said unto him,
32B	O thou wicked servant, I forgave thee all that debt,
32C	because thou desiredst (ie: besought) me:
33	Shouldest not thou also have had

Mt.18	Mk.9	Lk.9	Jn.6	
33B				compassion on thy fellowservant, even as I had pity on thee?
34				And his lord was wroth, and delivered him to the tormentors,
34B				till he should pay all that was due unto him.
35				So likewise shall my heavenly Father do also unto you, if ye from
35B				your hearts forgive not every one his brother their trespasses.
	49			For every one shall be salted with fire,
	49B			and every sacrifice shall be salted with salt.
	50			Salt is good: but if
	50B			the salt have lost his saltness, wherewith will ye season it?
	50C			Have salt in yourselves, and have peace one with another.

Mt.19	Mk.10			
1				And it came to pass, that when Jesus had finished these sayings,
1B	1			and he arose from thence: he departed from Galilee;
1C	1B			and cometh (came) into the coasts of Judaea,
1D	1C			by the farther side of the Jordan (beyond the Jordan).
	1D			And the people resort unto him again;
2				And great multitudes followed him; and he healed them there:
	1E			and as he wont (ie: customary), he taught them again.

			Jn.7	
The Feast of			1	After these things Jesus walked in Galilee:
-Unleavened bread			1B	for he would not walk in Jewry (ie: Judaea),
-Weeks			1C	because the Jews sought to kill him. (Mk.3:6/Jn.5:18)
-Tabernacles			2	Now the Jews' feast of tabernacles was at hand. (De.16:16)
			3	His brethren therefore said unto him,
			3B	Depart hence, and go into Judaea,
			3C	that thy disciples also may see the works that thou doest.
			4	For there is no man that doeth any thing in secret,
			4B	and he himself seeketh to be known openly.
His brethren			4C	If thou do these things, shew thyself to the world.
believed not!			5	For neither did his brethren believe in him. (Mk.3:21)
			6	Then Jesus said unto them,
			6B	My time is not yet come: but your time is alway ready.
			7	The world cannot hate you; but me it hateth,
			7B	because I testify of it, that the works thereof are evil.
			8	Go ye up unto this feast:
			8B	I go not up yet unto the feast;
			8C	for my time is not yet fully come.
			9	When he had said these words unto them, he abode still in Galilee.
			10	But when his brethren were gone up - then went he
No-one			10B	also up unto the feast, not openly, but as it were in secret.
spake openly			11	Then the Jews sought him at the feast, and said, Where is he?
about Jesus,			12	And there was much murmuring among the people concerning him:
for they all			12B	some said, He is a good man:
feared			12C	others said, Nay; but he deceiveth the people.
the Jews.			13	Howbeit no man spake openly of him for fear of the Jews. (Jn.9:22)
			14	Now about the midst of the feast Jesus went
			14B	up into the temple, and taught. And the Jews marvelled,
			15	saying, How knoweth this man letters, having never learned?
				(Note: Jesus having never learned was well versed in grammar.)
			16	Jesus answered them, and said,
			16B	My doctrine is not mine, but his that sent me.
			17	If any man will do his will, he shall know of the doctrine,
			17B	whether it be of God, or whether I speak of myself.
			18	He that speaketh of himself seeketh his own glory:
			18B	but he that seeketh the glory of him that sent him,
			18C	the same is true, and no unrighteousness is in him.

Mt.19 Mk.10 Lk.9   Jn.7

	19	Did not Moses give you the law, (Jn.5:45/Acts 7:53)
	19B	yet none of you keepeth the law? Why go ye about to kill me?
	20	The people answered and said,
	20B	Thou hast a devil: who goeth about to kill thee?
	21	Jesus answered and said unto them,
	21B	I have done one work, and ye all marvel.
	22	Moses therefore gave unto you circumcision
	22B	(not because it is of Moses, but of the fathers):
	22C	And ye on the sabbath day circumcise a man.
	23	If a man on the sabbath day receive circumcision,
	23B	that the law of Moses should not be broken;
	23C	are ye angry at me,
	23D	because I have made a man every whit whole on the sabbath day?
	24	Judge not according to the appearance, (Mt.7:1)
	24B	but judge righteous judgment. (Mt.7:2/Acts 4:19)
	25	Then said some of them of Jerusalem,
	25B	Is not this he, whom they seek to kill?
	26	But, lo, he speaketh boldly, and they say nothing unto him.
	26B	Do the rulers know indeed that this is the very Christ?
	27	Howbeit we know this man whence he is: (Mk.6:3)
	27B	but when Christ cometh, no man knoweth whence he is.
	28	Then cried Jesus in the temple as he taught,
	28B	saying, Ye both know me, and ye know whence I am:
	28C	and I am not come of myself,
	28D	but he that sent me is true, whom ye know not.
	29	But I know him: for I am from him, and he hath sent me.
	30	Then they sought to take him:
	30B	but no man laid hands on him, because his hour was not yet come.
	31	And many of the people believed on him,
	31B	and said, When Christ cometh,
	31C	will he do more miracles than these which this man hath done?
	32	The Pharisees heard
	32B	that the people murmured such things concerning him; and
	32C	the Pharisees and the chief priests sent officers to take him.
	33	Then said Jesus unto them, Yet a little while am I with you.
	33B	and then I go unto him that sent me. Ye shall seek me,
	34	and shall not find me: and where I am, thither ye cannot come.
	35	Then said the Jews among themselves,
	35B	Whither will he go, that we shall not find him? will he go
	35C	unto the dispersed among the Gentiles, and teach the Gentiles?
	36	What manner of saying is this that he said, Ye shall seek me,
	36C	and shall not find: and where I am, thither ye cannot come?
	37	In the last day, the great day of the feast, (Jn.7:2/Lev.23:34-36)
	37B	Jesus stood and cried, saying,
	37C	If any man thirst, let him come unto me, and drink.
Rivers	38	He that believeth on me, as the scripture hath said,
of Living Water	38B	Out of his belly shall flow rivers of Living Water.
	39	(But this spake he of the Spirit, (Joel 2:29-32)
	39B	which they that believe on him should receive:
	39C	for the Holy Ghost was not yet given;
	39D	because that Jesus was not yet glorified.)
	40	Many of the people therefore, when
	40B	they heard this saying, said, Of a truth this is the Prophet.
	41	Others said, This is the Christ.
	41B	But some said,
	41C	Shall Christ come out of Galilee? Hath not
	42	the scripture said, That Christ cometh of the seed of David,

The Gospels of Matthew, Mark, Luke, and John: Merged into One Historic Calendar of Events

Mt.19 Mk.10 Lk.9   Jn.7

	42B	and out of the town of Bethlehem, where David was? (Mt.2:5,6)
	43	So there was a division among the people because of him.
	44	And some of them
	44B	would have taken him; but no man laid hands on him. (Jn.7:30)
	45	Then came the officers to the chief priests and Pharisees;
	45B	and they said unto them, Why have ye not brought him?
	46	The officers answered, Never man spake like this man. (Mt.7:28,29)
	47	Then answered them the Pharisees, Are ye also deceived?
	48	Have any of the rulers, or of the Pharisees believed on him?
	49	But this people who knoweth not the law are cursed. (Jn.5:39)
	50	Nicodemus (he that came to Jesus by night, being one of them),
	51	saith unto them, Doth our law judge any man, (Jn.3:1,2)
	51B	before it hear him, and know what he doeth? (Jn.19:39)
	52	They answered and said unto him, Art thou also of Galilee?
	52B	Search, and look: for out of Galilee ariseth no prophet.
	53	And every man went unto his own house.

Jn.8

	1	Jesus went unto the mount of Olives.
	2	And early in the morning he came again into the temple, and
	2B	all the people came unto him; and he sat down, and taught them.
	3	And the scribes and Pharisees
	3B	brought unto him a woman taken in adultery;
	3C	And when they had set her in the midst, they say unto him,
	4	Master, this woman was taken in adultery, in the very act.
	5	Now Moses in the law commanded us, that such should be stoned:
	5B	But what sayest thou? (Lev.20:10/He.9:10/Jn.8:11/Mt.1:19)
	6	This they said, tempting him, that they might have to accuse him.
	6B	But Jesus stooped down, and with
	6C	his finger wrote on the ground, as though he heard them not.
	7	So when they continued asking him, he lifted up himself,
	7B	and said unto them, He that is without sin among you,
	7C	let him first cast a stone at her.
	8	And again he stooped down, and wrote on the ground.
	9	And they which heard it, being convicted by their own conscience,
	9B	went out one by one, beginning at the eldest even unto the last:
	9C	And Jesus was left alone, and the woman standing in the midst.
	10	When Jesus had lifted up himself, and saw none but the woman,
	10B	he said unto her, Woman,
	10C	where are those thine accusers? hath no man condemned thee?
	11	She said, No man, Lord.
	11B	And Jesus said unto her,
Sin No More!	11C	Neither do I condemn thee: go, and sin no more.
	12	Then spake Jesus again unto them,
	12B	saying, I am the light of the world, he that followeth me
	12C	shall not walk in darkness, but shall have the light of life.
	13	The Pharisees therefore said unto him,
	13B	Thou bearest record of thyself; thy record is not true.
	14	Jesus answered and said unto them,
	14B	Though I bear record of myself, yet my record is true:
	14C	for I know whence I came, and whither I go;
	14D	but ye cannot tell whence I come, and whither I go. (Jn.3:13)
	15	Ye judge after the flesh; I judge no man.
	16	And yet if I judge, my judgment is true:
	16B	for I am not alone, but I and the Father that sent me.
	17	It is also written in your law,
	17B	that the testimony of 2 men is true:
	18	I am one that bear witness of myself,

Mt.19　Mk.10　Lk.9　Jn.8

18B	and the Father that sent me beareth witness of me.
19	Then said they unto him, Where is thy Father?
19B	Jesus answered, Ye neither know me, nor my Father:　(Mt.11:27)
19C	if ye had known me, ye should have known my Father also.
20	These words
20B	spake Jesus in the treasury, as he taught in the temple:
20C	And no man laid hands on him; for his hour was not yet come.
21	Then said Jesus again unto them,
21B	I go my way, and ye shall seek me, and shall die in your sins:
21C	Whither I go, ye cannot come.
22	Then said the Jews, Will he kill himself?
22B	because he saith, Whither I go, ye cannot come.
23	And he (ie: Jesus) said unto them,
23B	Ye are from beneath; I am from above:
23C	Ye are of this world; I am not of this world.
24	I said therefore unto you, that ye shall die in your sins:
24B	for if ye believe not that I am He, ye shall die in your sins.
25	Then said they unto him, Who art thou?
25B	And Jesus saith unto them,
25C	Even the same that I said unto you from the beginning.
26	I have many things to say and to judge of you:
26B	But he that sent me is true; and
26C	I speak to the world those things which I have heard of him.
27	They understood not that he spake to them of the Father.
28	Then said Jesus unto them,
28B	When ye have lifted up the Son of man, then　(Mt.28:2-4,11-13)
28C	shall ye know that I am he, and that I do nothing of myself;
28D	but as my Father hath taught me, I speak these things.
29	And he that sent me is with me: the Father hath
29B	not left me alone; for I do always those things that please him.
30	As he spake these words, many believed on him.
31	Then said Jesus to those Jews which believed on him,
31B	If ye continue in my word, then are ye my disciples indeed.
32	And ye shall know the truth, and the truth shall make you free.
33	They answered him,
33B	We be Abraham's seed, and were never in bondage to any man:
33C	how sayest thou, Ye shall be made free?
34	Jesus answered them, Verily, verily,
34B	I say unto you, Whosoever committeth sin is the servant of sin.
35	And the servant abideth not in the house for ever:
35B	but the son abideth ever.
36	If the Son therefore shall make you free, ye shall be free indeed.
37	I know that ye are Abraham's seed;
37B	but ye seek to kill me, because my word hath no place in you.
38	I speak that which I have seen with my Father:
38B	and ye do that which ye have seen with your father.
39	They answered and said unto him, Abraham is our father. (Gen.17:5)
39B	Jesus said unto them,
39C	If ye were Abraham's children, ye would do the works of Abraham.
40	But now ye seek to kill me,
40B	a man that hath told you the truth, which I have heard of God:
41	this did not Abraham. Ye do the deeds of your Father.
41B	Then said they to him,
41C	We be not born of fornication; we have one Father, even God.
42	Jesus said unto them, If God were your Father, ye would love me:
42B	For I proceeded forth and came from God;
42C	neither came I of myself, but he sent me.
43	Why do ye not understand my speech?

Abraham's Seed,

  but

  not

Abraham's Children.

Mt.19 Mk.10 Lk.9 Jn.8

43B	even because ye cannot hear my word.
44	Ye are of your father the devil,
44B	and the lusts of your father ye will do.
44C	He was a murderer from the beginning,
44D	and abode not in the truth, because there is no truth in him.
44E	When he speaketh a lie, he speaketh
44F	of his own - for he is a liar, and the father of it.
45	And because I tell the truth, ye believe me not.
46	Which of you convinceth me of sin?
46B	and if I tell the truth, why do ye not believe me?
47	He that is of God heareth God's words:
47B	ye therefore hear them not, because ye are not of God.
48	Then answered the Jews, and said unto him,
48B	Say we not well that thou art a Samaritan, and hast a devil?
49	Jesus answered, I have not a devil;
49B	But I honour my Father, and ye do dishonour me.
50	And I seek not mine own glory:
50B	there is one that seeketh and judgeth.
51	Verily, verily, I say unto you,
51B	If a man keep my saying, he shall never see death. (Jn.11:26)
52	Then said the Jews unto him, Now we know that thou hast a devil.
52B	Abraham is dead, and the prophets; and thou
52C	sayest, If a man keep my saying, he shall never taste of death.
53	Art thou greater than our father Abraham, which is dead?
53B	and the prophets are dead: Whom makest thou thyself?
54	Jesus answered, If I honour myself, my honour is nothing:
54B	It is my Father that honoureth me;
54C	of whom ye say, that he is your God: Yet ye have not known him;
55	But I know him: and if I should say,
55B	I know him not, I shall be a liar like unto you:
55C	But I know him, and keep his saying.
56	Your father Abraham
56B	rejoiced to see my day: and he saw it, and was glad.
57	Then said the Jews unto him,
57B	Thou art not yet 50 years old, and hast thou seen Abraham?
58	Jesus said unto them, Verily, verily,
58B	I say unto you, Before Abraham was, I am. (Eph.3:9/Jn.17:5)
59	Then took they up stones to cast at him:
59B	But Jesus hid himself, and went out of the temple,
59C	going through the midst of them, and so passed by.

Jn.9

	1	And as Jesus passed by, he saw a man which was blind from birth.
The Reason	2	And his disciples asked him, saying, Master, who did sin,
is so designed	2B	this man, or his parents, that he was born blind? (Lk.13:1-5)
as to fulfil	3	Jesus answered, Neither hath this man sinned, nor his parents:
the purpose!	3B	but that the works of God should be made manifest in him.
	4	I must work the works of him that sent me, while it is day:
	4B	The night cometh, when no man can work. (Rev.11:7/Rev.8:1)
	5	As long as I am in the world, I am the light of the world.
	6	When he had thus spoken,
	6B	he spat on the ground, and made clay of the spittle,
	6C	and he anointed the eyes of the blind man with the clay,
	7	And said unto him,
	7B	Go, wash in the pool of Siloam, (ie: by interpretation, Sent).
	7C	He went his way therefore, and washed, and came seeing.
	8	The neighbours therefore,
	8B	and they which before had seen him that he was blind, said,

Mt.19　Mk.10　Lk.9　Jn.9

8C	Is not this he that sat and begged?
9	Some said, This is he: others said, He is like him:
9B	But he said, I am he.
10	Therefore said they unto him, How were thine eyes opened?
11	He answered and said,
11B	A man that is called Jesus made clay, and anointed mine eyes,
11C	and said unto me, Go to the pool of Siloam, and wash:
11D	And I went and washed, and I received sight.
12	Then said they unto him, Where is he?
12B	He said, I know not.
13	They brought to the Pharisees him that aforetime was blind.
14	And it was the sabbath day
14B	when Jesus made the clay, and opened his eyes.
15	Then again the Pharisees
15B	also asked him how he had received his sight.
15C	He said unto them,
15D	He put clay upon mine eyes, and I washed, and I see.
16	Therefore said the Pharisees,
16B	This man is not of God, because he keepeth not the sabbath day.
16C	Others said, How can a man that is a sinner do such miracles?
16D	And there was a division among them.
17	They say unto the blind man again,
17B	What sayest thou of him, that he hath opened thine eyes?
17C	He said, He is a prophet.
18	But the Jews did not believe concerning him,
18B	that he had been blind, and received his sight, until
18C	they called the parents of him that had received his sight.
19	And they asked them, saying, Is this your son,
19B	who ye say was born blind? How then doth he now see?
20	His parents answered them and said,
20B	We know that this is our son, and that he was born blind:
21	But by what means he now seeth, we know not;
21B	or who has opened his eyes, we know not:
21C	He is of age; ask him: he shall speak for himself.
22	These words spake his parents, because they feared the Jews:
22B	for the Jews had agreed already, that if any man did confess
22C	that he was Christ, he should be put out of the synagogue.
23	Therefore said his parents, He is of age; ask him.
24	Then again called they the man that was blind, and said unto him,
24B	Give God the praise: we know that this man is a sinner.
25	He answered and said, Whether he be a sinner or no, I know not:
25B	one thing I know, that, where as I was blind, now I see.
26	Then said they to him again,
26B	What did he to thee? how opened he thine eyes?
27	He answered them, I have told you already, and ye did not hear?
27B	wherefore would ye hear it again?
27C	will ye also be his disciples?
28	Then they reviled him, and said,
28B	Thou art his disciple; but we are Moses' disciples.
29	We know that God spake unto Moses:
29B	as for this fellow, we know not from whence he is.
30	The man answered and said unto them,
30B	Why herein is a marvellous thing, that ye know not
30C	from whence he is, and yet he hath opened mine eyes.
31	Now, we know that God heareth not sinners: but if any man
31B	be a worshipper of God, and doeth his will, him he heareth.
32	Since the world began was it not heard
32B	that any man opened the eyes of one that was born blind.

Mt.19	Mk.10	Lk.9	Jn.9	

			33	If this man were not of God, he could do nothing.
Who do you			34	They answered and said unto him,
think you are?			34B	Thou wast altogether born in sins, and doest thou teach us?
			34C	And they cast him out.

35   Jesus heard that they had cast him out; and when he had found him,
35B   he said unto him, Dost thou believe on the Son of God?
36   He answered and said, Who is he, Lord, that I might believe on him?
37   And Jesus said unto him,
37B   Thou hast both seen him, and it is he that talketh with thee.
38   And he said, Lord, I believe. And he worshipped him.
39   And Jesus said,
39B   For judgment I am come into the world, (Mt.10:34-39)
39C   that they which see not, might see; (Mt.11:25/Mt.21:16)
39D   and that they which see, might be made blind.
40   And some of the Pharisees which were with him heard these words,
40B   and said unto him, Are we blind also?
41   Jesus said unto them, (Rom.5:12-14/Rom.2:11-15/Ez.3:18-21)
41B   If ye were blind, ye should have no sin: (Jn.15:22-24)
41C   but now ye say, We see; therefore your sin remaineth.

Jn.10

His sheep hear His voice, and he leadeth them out.

1   Verily, verily, I say unto you,
1B   He that entereth not by the door into the sheepfold, but
1C   climbeth up some other way, the same is a thief and a robber.
2   But he that entereth in by the door is the shepherd of the sheep.
3   To him the porter openeth; and the sheep hear his voice:
3B   and he calleth his own sheep by name, and leadeth them out.
4   And when he putteth forth his own sheep, he goeth before them,
4B   and the sheep follow him: for they know his voice. (Rev.18:4)
5   And a stranger will they not follow, but will flee from him:
5B   for they know not the voice of strangers. (Mt.24:24)
6   This parable spake Jesus unto them: but they
6B   understood not what things they were which he spake unto them.
7   Then said Jesus unto them again, Verily, verily, I say unto you,
7B   I am the door of the sheep.
8   All that ever came before me are thieves and robbers: (Acts 4:12)
8B   but the sheep did not hear them. (Jn.10:27)
9   I am the door:
9B   by me if any man enter in, he shall be saved,
9C   and shall go in and out, and find pature. (Ps.23:1-6)
10   The thief cometh
10B   not, but for to steal, and to kill, and to destroy:
10C   I am come that they
10D   might have life, and that they might have it more abundantly.
11   I am the good shepherd:
11B   the good shepherd giveth his life for the sheep.
12   But he that is an hireling,
12B   and not the shepherd (whose own the sheep are not),
12C   seeth the wolf coming, and leaveth the sheep, and fleeth:
12D   And the wolf catcheth them, and scattereth the sheep.
13   The hireling fleeth,
13B   because he is an hireling, and careth not for the sheep.

I have other sheep which are not of this Fold.

14   I am the good shepherd, and know my sheep, and am known of mine.
15   As the Father knoweth me, even so know I the Father: (Mt.11:27)
15B   And I lay down my life for my sheep. (Is.53:5,10,11)(Mt.20:28)
16   And other sheep I have, which are not of this fold: (Rom.11:25)
16B   them also I must bring, and they shall hear my voice;
16C   and there shall be one fold, and one shepherd. (Mt.8:11)

Mt.19　Mk.10　Lk.9　　Jn.10

	17	Therefore doth my Father love me,　　　　　　(Mt.22:37,39)(Acts 13:33)
	17B	because I lay down my life, that I might take it again.
	18	No man taketh it from me, but I lay it down of myself.
	18B	I have power to lay it down, and I have the power to take it again.
	18C	This commandment have I received of my Father.　　　　　(Jn.14:31)
	19	There was therefore
	19B	again a division among the Jews for these sayings.
	20	And many of them said,
	20B	He hath a devil, and is mad; why hear ye him?
	21	Others said, These are not the words of him that hath a devil;
	21B	can a devil open the eyes of the blind?

	22	And it was at Jerusalem:
	22B	the feast of the dedication (ie: the renewal of the temple),
It was winter.	22C	And it was winter.
	23	And Jesus walked in the temple - in Solomon's porch.
	24	Then came the Jews round about him,
	24B	and said unto him, How long dost thou make us to doubt?
	24C	If thou be the Christ, tell us plainly.
	25	Jesus answered them, I told you, and ye believed not: the
	25B	works that I do in my Father's name, they bear witness of me.
	26	But ye believe not,
	26B	because ye are not of my sheep, as I said unto you.
Safe,	27	My sheep hear my voice, and I know them, and they follow me:
-in the hand	28	And I give unto them eternal life; and they shall
of the Son,	28B	never perish, neither shall any man pluck them out of my hand.
-in the hand	29	My Father, which gave them me, is greater than all;
of the Father.	29B	and no man is able to pluck them out of my Father's hand.
They Are One.	30	I and my Father are one.
	31	Then the Jews took up stones again to stone him.
	32	Jesus answered them,
	32B	Many good works have I shewed you from my Father;
	32C	for which of these works do ye stone me?
	33	The Jews answered him, saying,
	33B	For a good work we stone thee not; but for blasphemy;
	33C	and because that thou, being a man, makest thyself God.
	34	Jesus answered them,
	34B	Is it not written in your law, I said, Ye are gods?　　　　(Ps.82:6)
	35	If he called them gods, unto whom the word of God came,
	35B	(and the scripture cannot be broken); (Is.45:5,18,21,22)
	36	Say ye of him, whom the Father hath sanctified, and sent into
	36B	the world, Thou blasphemest; because I said, I am the Son of God?
	37	If I do not the works of my Father, believe me not.
	38	But if I do (though ye believe me not),
	38B	believe the works: that ye may know,
	38C	and believe that the Father is in me, and I in him.
	39	Therefore they
	39B	sought again to take him: but he escaped out of their hand,
	40	and went away again beyond the Jordan,
	40B	into the place where John at first baptized: And there he abode.
	41	And many resorted (ie: came) unto him, and said,
	41B	John did no miracle: but all things that John spake
	42	of this man were true. And many believed on him there.

	Jn.11	
	1	Now a certain man was sick, named Lazarus,
	1B	of Bethany, the town of Mary and her sister Martha,　　(Jn.12:3)
	2	(It was that Mary which anointed the Lord with ointment, and

Mt.19 Mk.10 Lk.9 Jn.11

2B	wiped his feet with her hair.) whose brother Lazarus was sick:
3	Therefore his sisters sent unto him, saying,
3B	Lord, behold, he whom thou lovest is sick.
4	When Jesus heard, he said,
4B	This sickness is not unto death, but for the glory of God,
4C	that the Son of God might be glorified thereby. (Jn.9:3)
5	Now Jesus loved Martha, and her sister, and Lazarus.
6	When he had heard therefore that he was sick,
6B	he abode 2 days still in the same place where he was.
7	Then after that
7B	saith he to his disciples, Let us go into Judaea again.
8	His disciples say unto him, Master, the Jews of late (ie: now)
8B	sought to stone thee; and goest thou thither again? (Jn.10:39)
9	Jesus answered, Are there not 12 hours in the day?
9B	If any man walk in the day,
9C	he stumbleth not, because he seeth the light of this world.
10	But if a man walk in the night,
10B	he stumbleth, because there is no light in him.
11	These things said he: and after that
11B	he saith unto them, Our friend Lazarus sleepeth;
11C	but I go, that I may awake him out of sleep.
12	Then said his disciples, Lord, if he sleep, he shall do well.
13	(Howbeit Jesus spake of his death: but they
13B	thought that he had spoken of taking of rest in sleep.)
14	Then said Jesus unto them plainly, Lazarus is dead.
15	And I am glad for your sakes that I was not there,
15B	to the intent ye may believe; nevertheless let us go unto him.
16	Then said Thomas (which is called Didymus), unto his
16B	fellow disciples, Let us also go, that we may die with him.
17	Then when Jesus came,
17B	he found that he had lain in the grave 4 days already.
18	Now Bethany was nigh unto Jerusalem, about 15 furlongs off:
19	And many of the Jews came
19B	to Martha and Mary, to comfort them concerning their brother.
20	Then Martha, as soon as she heard that Jesus was coming,
20B	went and met him: but Mary sat still in the house.
21	Then said Martha unto Jesus, Lord,
21B	if thou hadst been here, my brother had not died.
22	But I know, that even now,
22B	whatsoever thou wilt ask of God, God will give it thee.
23	Jesus saith unto her, Thy brother shall rise again.
24	Martha saith unto him, I know
24B	that he shall rise again in the resurrection at the last day.
25	Jesus said unto her, I am the resurrection, and the life:
25B	he that believeth in me, though he were dead, yet shall he live:
26	And whosoever
26B	liveth and believeth in me shall never die. Believest thou this?
27	She said unto him, Yea, Lord: I believe that thou art the Christ,
27B	the Son of God, which should come into the world. (Mt.16:16)
28	And when she had so said,
28B	she went her way, and called Mary her sister secretly,
28C	saying, The Master is come, and calleth for thee.
29	As soon as she heard, she arose quickly, and came to him.
30	Now Jesus was not yet come into the town,
30B	but was in that place where Martha met him.
31	The Jews then which were with her in the house, and comforted her,
31B	when they saw Mary, that she rose up hastily and went out,
31C	followed her, saying, She goeth unto the grave to weep there.

Mt.19 Mk.10 Lk.9   Jn.11

	32	Then when Mary was come where Jesus was,
	32B	and saw him, she fell down at his feet, saying unto him,
	32C	Lord, if thou hadst been here, my brother had not died.
	33	When Jesus therefore saw her weeping,
	33B	and the Jews (which came with her) also weeping,
	33C	he groaned in the spirit, and was troubled.
	34	And said, where have ye laid him?
	34B	They said unto him, Lord, come and see.
Jesus wept.	35	Jesus wept. (Lk.19:41/Jn.11:35)
	36	Then said the Jews, Behold how he loved him!
	37	And some of them said,
	37B	Could not this man, which opened the eyes of the blind,
	37C	have caused that even this man should not have died?(Jn.10:1-7)
	38	Jesus therefore again groaning in himself cometh to the grave.
	38B	It was a cave, and a stone lay upon it.
	39	Jesus said, Take ye away the stone.
	39B	Martha (the sister of him that was dead) saith unto him, Lord,
	39C	by this time he stinketh: for he hath been dead 4 days.
	40	Jesus saith unto her, Said I not unto thee, that, if thou wouldest
	40B	believe, thou shouldest see the glory of God? (Jn.11:4,39-45)
	41	Then they took away the stone from where the dead was laid.
	41B	And Jesus lifted up his eyes,
	41C	and said, Father, I thank thee - that thou hast heard me.
	42	And I knew that thou hearest me always:
	42B	but, because of the people which stand by I say it,
	42C	that they may believe that thou hast sent me.
	43	And when he thus had spoken,
	43B	he cried with a loud voice, Lazarus, come forth.
	44	And he that was dead came forth, bound hand and foot
	44B	with grave-clothes: and his face was bound about with a napkin.
	44C	Jesus saith unto them, Loose him, and let him go.
	45	Then many of the Jews which came to Mary,
	45B	and had seen the things which Jesus did, believed on him.
	46	But some of them went to the Pharisees,
	46B	and told them what things Jesus had done.
Act now, or	47	Then gathered the chief priests and the Pharisees a council:
All men will	47B	And said, What do we? for this man doeth many miracles. (Mt.16:1)
believe on him!	48	If we let him thus alone, all men will believe on him: and
	48B	the Romans shall come and take away both our place and nation.
	49	And one of them, named Caiaphas, being the high priest
	49B	that same year, said unto them, Ye know nothing at all,
	50	Nor consider that it is expedient for us, that one man
	50B	should die for the people, and that the whole nation perish not.
	51	And this spake he not of himself: but being high priest that year,
	51B	he prophesied that Jesus should die for that nation;
	52	And not for that nation only,
	52B	but that also he should gather together in one (Jn.10:16)
	52C	the children of God that were scattered abroad.
	53	Then from that day forth
	53B	they took counsel together for to put him to death,
	54	Jesus therefore walked no more openly among the Jews;
	54B	but went thence unto a country near to the wilderness, into
	54C	a city called Ephraim, and there continued with his disciples.
	55	And the Jews' passover was nigh at hand:
	55B	and many went out of the country
	55C	up to Jerusalem before the passover, to purify themselves.
	56	Then sought they for Jesus,

The Gospels of Matthew, Mark, Luke, and John: Merged into One Historic Calendar of Events

Mt.19 Mk.10 Lk.9 Jn.11

	56B	and spake among themselves, as they stood in the temple,
	56C	What think ye, that he will not come to the feast? (Jn.7:1)
	57	Now both the chief priests and the Pharisees
	57B	had given a commandment, that, if any man knew where he were,
	57C	he should shew it, that they might take him.

Jesus facing Jerusalem.		
	51	And it came to pass,
	51B	when the time was come that he should be received up,
	51C	he stedfastly set his face to go to Jerusalem,
	52	and sent messengers before his face:
	52B	And they went, and entered
	52C	into a village of the Samaritans, to make ready for him.
	53	And they did not receive him, (Jn.10:16/Jn.8:48)
	53B	because his face was as though he would go to Jerusalem.
	54	And when his disciples James and John saw this,
	54B	they said, Lord, wilt thou that we command fire
	54C	to come down from heaven, and consume them, even as Elias did?
	55	But he turned, and rebuked them, and said,
	55B	Ye know not what manner of spirit ye are of. (Num.14:24)
	56	For the Son of man
	56B	is not come to destroy men's lives, but to save them.
	56C	And they went to another village.
	57	And it came to pass, that as they went in the way:
	57B	A certain man said unto him, (Mt.8:19,20)
	57C	Lord, I will follow thee whithersoever thou goest.
	58	And Jesus said unto him,
	58B	Foxes have holes, and the birds of the air have nests;
	58C	but the Son of man hath not where to lay his head.
	59	And he said unto another, Follow me. (Mt.8:21,22)
	59B	But he said, Lord, suffer me first to go and bury my father.
	60	Jesus said unto him, Let the dead bury the dead:
	60B	but go thou and preach the kingdom of God.
	61	And another also said, Lord, I will follow thee; but let me
	61B	first go bid them farewell, which are at home at my house.
	62	And Jesus said unto him, No man, having put his hand to
	62B	the plough, and looking back, is fit for the kingdom of God.

Lk.10

1	After these things, the Lord appointed other 70 also;
1B	And sent them 2 and 2 before his face
1C	into every city and place, whither he himself would come.
2	Therefore said he unto them, (Mt.9:37,38)
2B	The harvest truly is great, but the labourers are few:
2C	Pray ye therefore the Lord of the harvest,
2D	that he would send forth labourers into his harvest.
3	Go your ways: behold, I send you forth as lambs among wolves.
4	Carry neither purse, nor scrip, nor shoes: (Mt.10:5-15/Mk.6:7-11)
4B	and salute no man by the way.
5	And into whatsoever house ye enter,
5B	first say, Peace be to this house.
6	And if the son of peace be there, your peace shall rest upon it:
6B	(if not, it shall turn to you again.)
7	And in the same house remain, eating and drinking such things
7B	as they give: for the labourer is worthy of his hire (ie: wage).
7C	Go not from house to house.
8	And into whatsoever city ye enter,
8B	and they receive you, eat such things as are set before you:
9	And heal the sick that are therein,

Mt.19 Mk.10 Lk.10 Jn.11

	9B	and say unto them, The kingdom of God is come nigh unto you.
	10	But into whatsoever city ye enter, and they receive you not,
	10B	Go your ways out into the streets of the same,
	11	and say, Even the very dust of your city, which cleaveth on us,
	11B	we do wipe off against you:
	11C	Notwithstanding be ye sure of this,
	11D	that the kingdom of God is come nigh unto you.
	12	But I say unto you, that it shall
	12B	be more tolerable in that day for Sodom, than for that city.
	13	Woe unto thee, Chorazin! Woe unto thee, Bethsaida! (Mt.11:21-23)
	13B	for if the mighty works had been done in Tyre and Sidon,
	13C	which have been done in you, they had a great while ago
	13D	repented, sitting in sackcloth and ashes.
	14	But it shall be more tolerable (Lk.12:42-48)
	14B	for Tyre and Sidon, at the judgment, than for you.
	15	And thou, Capernaum, which art exalted to heaven,
	15B	shall be thrust down to hell.
	16	He that heareth you heareth me; (Mt.10:40/Jn.3:20)
	16B	and he that despiseth you despiseth me;
	16C	and he that despiseth me despiseth him that sent me.

The 70 returned with joy.

	17	And the 70 returned (ie: come again) with joy, saying,
	17B	Lord, even the devils are subject unto us through thy name.
	18	And he said unto them,
	18B	I beheld Satan as lightning fall from heaven.
	19	Behold, I give unto you power to tread on
	19B	serpents and scorpions, and over all the power of the enemy:
	19C	and nothing shall by any means hurt you. (Mk.16:15-18)
	20	Notwithstanding in this rejoice not,
	20B	that the spirits are subject unto you;
	20C	But, rather rejoice, because your names are written in heaven.
	21	In that hour Jesus rejoiced in spirit, (Mt.11:25-27)
	21B	and said, I thank thee, O Father, Lord of heaven and earth,
	21C	that thou hast hid these things from the wise and prudent,
	21D	and hast revealed them unto babes:
	21E	Even so, Father; for so it seemed good in thy sight.
	22	All things are delivered to me of my Father:
	22B	and no man knoweth who the Son is, but the Father;
	22C	and who the Father is, but the Son,
	22D	and he to whom the Son will reveal him.
	23	And he turned him unto his disciples, and said privately,
	23B	Blessed are the eyes which see the things that ye see:
	24	For I tell you, that many prophets and kings have desired
	24B	to see those things which ye see, and have not seen;
	24C	and to hear those things which ye hear, and have not heard.
	25	And, behold, a certain lawyer stood up, and tempted him, saying,
	25B	Master, what shall I do to inherit eternal life? (Mt.22:35-40)
	26	He said unto him, What is written in the law? how readest thou?
	27	And he answering said, (De.6:5/Lev.18:5/Lev.19:18)
	27B	Thou shalt love the LORD thy God with all thy heart,
	27C	and with all thy soul, and with all thy strength,
	27D	and with all thy mind; and thy neighbour as thyself.
	28	And he (ie: Jesus) said unto him,
	28B	Thou hast answered right: this do, and thou shalt live.

Who is my neighbour?

	29	But he, willing to justify himself,
	29B	said unto Jesus, And who is my neighbour?
	30	And Jesus answering said,

Mt.19 Mk.10 Lk.10 Jn.11

	30B	A certain man went down from Jerusalem to Jericho,
	30C	and fell among thieves, which stripped him of his raiment,
	30D	and wounded him, and departed, leaving him half dead.
	31	And by chance there came down a certain priest that way:
	31B	and when he saw him, he passed by on the other side.
	32	And likewise a Levite, when he was at the place,
	32B	came and looked on him, and passed by on the other side.
	33	But a certain Samaritan, as he journeyed, came where he was:
	33B	And when he saw him, he had compassion on him,
	34	And went to him,
	34B	and bound up his wounds, pouring in oil and wine,
	34C	And set him on his beast,
	34D	and brought him to an inn, and took care of him.
	35	And on the morrow when he departed,
	35B	he took out 2 pence, and gave them to the host, and said
	35C	unto him, Take care of him; and whatsoever thou spendest more,
	35D	when I come again, I will repay (ie: pay) thee.
	36	Which now of these 3, thinkest thou,
	36B	was neighbour unto him that fell among the thieves?
	37	And he said, He that shewed mercy on him.
	37B	Then said Jesus unto him, Go, and do thou likewise.
	38	Now it came to pass, as they went,
	38B	that he entered into a certain village: (Jn.11:1)
	38C	And a certain women named Martha received him into her house.
	39	And she had a sister called Mary, (Jn.12:3)
	39B	which also sat at Jesus' feet, and heard his word.
	40	But Martha was cumbered about much serving, and came to him,
	40B	and said, Lord, dost thou not care that my sister (Mk.4:38)
	40C	hath left me to serve alone? bid her therefore that she help me.
	41	And Jesus answered and said unto her, Martha, Martha,
	41B	thou art careful and troubled about many things:
	42	But one thing is needful: and Mary hath chosen that good part,
	42B	which shall not be taken away from her. (Jn.6:63)
	Lk.11	
Lord,	1	And it came to pass, that, as he was praying in a certain place,
teach us	1B	when he ceased, one of his disciples said unto him,
to pray!	1C	Lord, teach us to pray, as John also taught his disciples.
	2	And he (ie: Jesus) said unto them, When ye pray, say, (Mt.6:9-13)
	2B	Our Father which art in heaven, Hallowed be thy name.
	2C	Thy kingdom come.
	2D	Thy will be done, as in heaven, also upon the earth.
	3	Give us day by day our daily bread.
	4	And forgive us our sins;
	4B	for we also forgive every one that is indebted to us.
	4C	And lead us not into temptation; but deliver us from evil.
	5	And he said unto them,
	5B	Which of you shall have a friend, and shall go unto him
	5C	at midnight, and say unto him, Friend, lend me 3 loaves;
	6	For a friend of mine in his journey is come to me,
	6B	and I have nothing to set before him.
	7	And he from within shall answer and say, Trouble me not:
	7B	the door is now shut,
	7C	and my children are with me in the bedroom;
	7D	I cannot rise and give thee.
	8	I say unto you,
	8B	Though he will not rise and give him, because he is his friend,
	8C	yet because of his importunity (ie: continual urging) (Lk.18:5)

Mt.19 Mk.10 Lk.11 Jn.11

8D	he will rise and give him as many as he needeth.
9	And I say unto you,
9B	Ask, and it shall be given you; (Mt.7:7-12)
9C	Seek, and ye shall find;
9D	Knock, and it shall be opened unto you.
10	For every one that asketh receiveth;
10B	And he that seeketh findeth;
10C	And to him that knocketh it shall be opened.
11	And which of you that is a father,
11B	If a son shall ask bread, will give him a stone? or,
11C	If he ask a fish, will he for a fish give him a serpent? or,
12	If if he shall ask an egg, will he offer him a scorpion?
13	If ye then, being evil,
13B	know how to give good gifts unto your children:
13C	How much more shall your heavenly Father
13D	give the Holy Spirit to them that ask him?
14	And he was casting out a devil, and it was dumb. (Mt.12:22-30)
14B	And it came to pass, when the devil was gone out, (Mt.9:32-34)
14C	the dumb spake: And the people wondered. (Mk.3:22-30)
15	But some of them said, He casteth
15B	out devils through Beelzebub, the chief of the devils.
16	And others, tempting him, sought of him a sign from heaven.
17	But he (ie: Jesus), knowing their thoughts, said unto them,
17B	Every kingdom divided against itself is brought to desolation;
17C	and a house divided against a house falleth.
18	If Satan also be divided against himself,
18B	how shall his kingdom stand? because ye say,
18C	that I cast out devils through Beelzebub.
19	And if I by Beelzebub cast out devils, by whom do your sons
19B	cast them out? therefore shall they be your judges.
20	But if I with the finger of God cast out devils, no doubt
20B	the kingdom of God is come upon you. (Lk.10:9,11)
21	When a strong man
21B	armed keepeth his palace, his goods are in place:
22	But when a stronger than he - shall come upon him,
22B	and overcome him, he taketh from him all his armour
22C	wherein he trusted, and divideth his spoils.
23	He that is not with me is against me:
23B	and he that gathereth not with me scattereth.
24	When the unclean spirit is gone out of the man,
24B	he walketh through dry places, seeking rest; and finding none,
24C	he saith, I will return unto my house whence I came out.
25	And when he cometh, he findeth it swept and garnished. (Lk.21:5)
26	Then goeth he, and taketh to him 7 other spirits (Mt.12:43-45)
26B	more wicked than himself; and they enter in, and dwell there:
26C	And the last state of that man is worse than the first.
27	And it came to pass, as he spake these things,
27B	a certain woman of the company lifted up her voice,
27C	and said unto him, Blessed is the womb that bare thee,
27D	and the paps (ie: breasts) which thou hast sucked.
28	But he said, Yea rather,
28B	blessed are they that hear the word of God, and keep it.
29	And when the people were gathered thick together, (Mt.12:38-42)
29B	He (ie: Jesus) began to say, This is an evil generation:
29C	they seek a sign; and there shall
29D	no sign be given it, but the sign of Jonas the prophet.

| Mt.19 | Mk.10 | Lk.11 | Jn.11 |

So shall		30	For as Jonas was a sign unto the Ninevites,
also the		30B	so shall also the Son of man be to this generation.
Son of man		31	The queen of the south shall rise up in the judgment
be a Sign		31B	with the men of this generation, and condemn them:
to this		31C	For she came from the utmost parts of the earth (1 Ki.10:1)
generation.		31D	to hear the wisdom of Solomon;
		31E	And, behold, a greater than Solomon is here.
		32	The men of Nineve shall rise up (Jonah 3:5)
		32B	in the judgment with this generation, and shall condemn it:
		32C	for they repented at the preaching of Jonas;
		32D	and, behold, a greater than Jonas is here.
		33	No man, when he hath lighted a candle, putteth it in (Mt.5:14-16)
		33B	a secret place, neither under a bushel, but on a candle stick,
		33C	that they which come in may see the light.
Good		34	The light (ie: candle/lamp) of the body is the eye: therefore
or		34B	when thine eye is single, thy whole body is full of light;
Evil.		34C	but when thine eye is evil, thy body also is full of darkness.
		35	Take heed therefore (2 Cor.11:14,15)(Num.14:24/Num.32:12)
		35B	that the light which is in thee be not darkness.
		36	If thy whole body therefore be full of light,
		36B	having no part dark, the whole shall be full of light,
		36C	as when the bright shinning of a candle doth give thee light.
		37	And as he spake,
		37B	a certain Pharisee besought him to dine with him:
		37C	And he went in, and sat down to meat.
		38	And when the Pharisee saw (he marvelled) (Mt.15:2/Mk.7:1-3)
		38B	that he (ie: Jesus) had not first washed before dinner.
		39	And the Lord said unto him, Now do ye Pharisees (Mt.23:25)
		39B	make clean the outside of the cup and the platter;
		39C	but your inward part is full of ravening and wickedness.
		40	Ye fools, did not he that made - that which is without,
		40B	make that which is within also?
		41	But rather give alms of such things as ye have;
		41B	and, behold, all things are clean unto you.
Woe		42	But woe unto you, Pharisees!
		42B	for ye tithe mint and rue and all manner of herbs, (Mt.23:23)
		42C	and pass over judgment and the love of God:
		42D	these ought ye to have done, and not to leave the other undone.
Woe		43	Woe unto you, Pharisees! (Mt.23:6,7/Lk.20:46)
		43B	for ye love the uppermost seats in the synagogues,
		43C	and greetings in the markets.
Woe		44	Woe unto you, scribes and Pharisees, hypocrites! (Mt.23:27)
		44B	for ye are as graves which appear not (ie: are not seen),
		44C	and the men that walk over them are not aware of them.
		45	Then answered one of the lawyers, and said unto him,
		45B	Master, thus saying - thou reproachest us also?
Woe		46	And he said, Woe unto you also, ye lawyers!
		46B	for ye lade men with burdens grievous to be borne, (Mt.23:4)
		46C	and ye yourselves
		46D	touch not the burdens with one of your fingers.
Woe		47	Woe unto you! for ye build (Mt.23:29-31)
		47B	the sepulchres of the prophets, and your fathers killed them.
		48	Truly ye bear witness that ye allow the deeds of your fathers:
		48B	for they indeed killed them, and ye build their sepulchres.
		49	Therefore also said the wisdom of God,
		49B	I will send them prophets and apostles, (Mt.23:34-36)
		49C	and some of them they shall slay and persecute:

Mt.19 Mk.10 Lk.11 Jn.11

	50	That the blood of all the prophets, which was shed from
	50B	the foundation of the world, may be required of this generation:
	51	From the blood of Abel unto the blood of Zacharias,
	51B	which perished between the altar and the temple: (Mt.24:34)
	51C	Verily I say unto you, It shall be required of this generation.
Woe	52	Woe unto you, lawyers! (Lk.7:30/Lk.14:3)(Mt.23:13)
	52B	for ye have taken away the key of knowledge: ye entered not in
	52C	yourselves, and them that were entering in ye hindered.
	53	And as he (ie: Jesus) said these things unto them,
	53B	The scribes and the Pharisees began to urge him vehemently,
	53C	and to provoke him to speak of many things:
	54	Laying wait for him, and seeking
	54B	to catch something out of his mouth, that they might accuse him.

	Lk.12	
	1	In the mean time,
Their	1B	When there were gathered together an innumerable
doctrine	1C	multitude of people, insomuch that they trode one upon another,
which is	1D	He (ie: Jesus) began to say unto his disciples first of all,
hypocrisy.	1E	Beware ye of the leaven of the Pharisees, which is hypocrisy.
	2	For there is nothing covered, that shall not be revealed;
	2B	neither hid, that shall not be known. (1 Cor.4:5/Mt.7:1)
	3	Therefore whatsoever ye have spoken in darkness (Mt.10:25-28)
	3B	shall be heard in the light; and that which ye have spoken
	3C	in the ear in closets - shall be proclaimed upon the housetops.
	4	And I say unto you my friends, Be not afraid of them that
	4B	kill the body, and after that have no more that they can do.
	5	But I will forewarn you whom ye shall fear: Fear him, which
	5B	after he hath killed hath power to cast into hell (ie: gehenna).
	5D	Yea, I say unto you, Fear him.
	6	Are not 5 sparrows sold for 2 farthings, (Mt.10:29)
	6B	and not one of them is forgotten before God?
	7	But even the very hairs of your head are all numbered.
	7B	Fear not therefore: ye are of more value than many sparrows.
	8	Also I say unto you,
	8B	Whosoever shall confess me before men, (1 Jn.4:15)
	8C	him shall the Son of man also confess before the angels of God:
	9	But he that denieth me before men (2 Jn:7)
	9B	shall be denied before the angels of God.
	10	And whosoever shall speak a word against the Son of man,
	10B	it shall be forgiven him: but unto him that blasphemeth
	10C	against the Holy Ghost - it shall not be forgiven. (Mk.3:22-30)
	11	And when they bring you (Mt.10:16-20/Mk.13:9-11/Lk.21:12-15)
	11B	unto the synagogues, and unto magistrates, and powers,
	11C	Take ye no thought (Mt.10:19,20/Mk.13:11/Lk.21:14,15)
	11D	how or what thing ye shall answer, or what ye shall say:
	12	For the Holy Ghost (ie: Holy Spirit)
	12B	shall teach you in the same hour what ye ought to say.
	13	And one of the company said unto him, Master,
	13B	speak to my brother, that he divide the inheritance with me.
	14	And he he said unto him,
	14B	Man, who made me a judge or a divider over you?
	15	And he saith unto them, Take heed, and beware of covetousness:
	15B	for a man's life consisteth (Jn.1:4/Jn.3:16)
	15C	not in the abundance of the things which he possesseth.
	16	And he (ie: Jesus) spake a parable unto them, saying,
	16B	The ground of a certain rich man brought forth plentifully:
	17	And he thought within himself, saying, What shall I do,

Mt.19 Mk.10 Lk.12 Jn.11

	17B	because I have no room where to bestow my fruits?
	18	And he said,
So	18B	This will I do: I will pull down my barns, and build greater;
is he	18C	and there will I bestow all my fruits and my goods.
that	19	And I will say to my soul, Soul, thou hast much goods laid up
layeth	19B	for many years; take thine ease, eat, drink and be merry.
up	20	But God said unto him, Thou fool,
treasure	20B	this night thy soul shall be required of thee:
for	20C	then, whose shall those things be, which thou hast provided?
himself.	21	So is he - that, layeth up treasure for himself, (Gen.11:4)
	21B	and is not rich toward God. (Mt.6:19,20)
	22	And he (ie: Jesus) said unto his disciples, (Mt.6:24-34)
	22B	Therefore I say unto you, Take no thought for yout life,
	22C	what ye shall eat; neither for the body, what ye shall put on.
	23	The life is more than meat, and the body is more than raiment.
	24	Consider the ravens:
	24B	For they neither sow nor reap;
	24C	which neither have storehouse nor barn; and God feedeth them:
	24D	How much more are ye better than the fowls?
	25	And which of you
	25B	with taking thought can add to his stature one cubit?
	26	If ye then be not able to do
	26B	that thing which is least, why take ye thought for the rest?
	27	Consider the lilies how they grow:
	27B	they toil not, they spin not; and yet I say unto you, that
	27C	Solomon in all his glory was not arrayed like one of these,
	28	If then God so clothe the grass, which
	28B	is to day in the field, and to morrow is cast into the oven;
	28C	How much more will he clothe you, O ye of little faith?
	29	And seek not ye what ye shall eat,
	29B	or what ye shall drink, neither be ye of doubtful mind.
	30	For all these things do the nations of the world seek after:
	30B	and your Father knoweth that ye have need of these things.
Seek ye	31	But rather seek ye the kingdom of God; (Mt.6:33) (Mk.10:15/Mt.7:21)
first	31B	and all these things shall be added unto you.
the	32	Fear not, little flock; (Mt.10:28)
Kingdom	32B	for it is your Father's good pleasure to give you the kingdom.
of God.	33	Sell that ye have, and give alms; (Mt.6:1-4,19-21)
	33B	provide yourselves bags which wax not old,
	33C	a treasure in the heavens that faileth not,
	33D	where no thief approacheth, neither moth corrupteth.
	34	For where your treasure is, there will your heart be also.
	35	Let your loins be girded about, and your lights burning;
	36	And ye yourselves like unto men that wait for the lord,
	36B	when he will return from the wedding; that when
	36C	he cometh and knocketh, they may open unto him immediately.
Blessed	37	Blessed are those servants, (Ex.12:11/Mt.25:4/Rev.16:15/Rev.3:3)
are	37B	whom the Lord when he cometh shall find watching:
those	37C	Verily, I say unto you, that, he shall gird himself, and make
servants.	37E	them to sit down to meat, and will come forth and serve them.
	38	And if he shall come in the 2nd. watch, or come
	38B	in the 3rd. watch, and find them so, blessed are those servants.
	39	And this know, that if the goodman of the house had known
	39B	what hour the thief would come, he would have watched,
	39C	and not have suffered his house to be broken through.
	40	Be ye therefore ready also: (1 Thes.5:4-6)
	40B	for the Son of man cometh at an hour when ye think not.

Mt.19 Mk.10 Lk.12 Jn.11

41	Then Peter said unto him,
41B	Lord, speakest thou this parable unto us, or even to all?
42	And the Lord said,
42B	Who then is that faithful and wise steward,
42C	whom his lord shall make ruler over his household,
42D	to give them their portion of food (wheat/corn) in due season?
43	Blessed is that servant,
43B	whom his lord (when he cometh) shall find so doing.
44	Of a truth I say unto you, (1 Thes.5:4,5/Rev.3:3/Lk.12:37)
44B	that he will make him ruler over all that he hath.
45	But, if that servant say in his heart, My lord delayeth his coming;
45B	And shall begin to beat the menservants and maidens,
45C	and to eat and drink, and to be drunken;
46	The lord of that servant
46B	will come in a day when he looketh not for him,
46C	and at an hour when he is not aware, and will cut him in sunder,
46D	and will appoint him his portion with the unbelievers.
47	And that servant, (James 4:17)
47B	which knew his lord's will, and prepared not himself, neither
47C	did according to his will, shall be beaten with many stripes.
48	But he that knew not, and did commit
48B	things worthy of stripes, shall be beaten with few stripes.
48C	For unto whomsoever
48D	much is given, of him shall be much required: And to whom men
48E	have committed much, of him they ask the more.
49	I am come to send fire on earth; (2 Pe.3:10)
49B	and what will I, if it be already kindled?
50	But I have a baptism to be baptized with; (Mt.20:22)
50B	and how am I straitened (ie: pressed) till it be accomplished!
51	Suppose ye that I am come to give peace on earth?
51B	I tell you, Nay; but rather division:
52	From henceforth there shall be
52B	5 in one house divided, 3 against 2, and 2 against 3.
53	The father shall be divided against the son,
53B	and the son against the father;
53C	The mother against the daughter
53D	and the daughter against the mother;
53E	The mother in law against her daughter in law,
53F	and the daughter in law against her mother in law.
54	And he (ie: Jesus) said also to the people,
54B	When ye see a cloud rise out of the west, (Mt.16:2,3)
54C	straightway ye say, There cometh a shower; and so it is.
55	And when ye see the south wind blow,
55B	ye say, There will be heat; and it cometh to pass.
56	Ye hypocrites,
56B	ye can discern the face of the sky and of the earth;
56C	but how is it that ye do not discern this time?
57	Yea, and why even of yourselves judge ye not what is right?
58	When thou goest with thine adversary to the magistrate,
58B	As thou art in the way,
58C	give diligence - that thou mayest be delivered from him;
58D	lest he hale (ie: to drag) thee to the judge,
58E	and the judge deliver thee to the officer,
58F	and the officer cast thee into prison.
59	I tell thee, thou
59B	shalt not depart thence, till thou hast paid the very last mite.
Lk.13	

The Gospels of Matthew, Mark, Luke, and John: Merged into One Historic Calendar of Events

Mt.19 Mk.10 Lk.13 Jn.11

	1	There were present
	1B	at that season (ie: time) some that told him of the Galileans,
	1C	whose blood Pilate had mingled with their sacrifices.
	2	And Jesus answering said unto them,
	2B	Suppose ye that these Galileans were sinners (Rom.3:9-12)
	2C	above all the Galileans, because they suffered such things?
	3	I tell you, Nay:
	3B	but, except ye repent, ye shall all likewise perish.
18 people.	4	Or those 18, upon whom the tower in Siloam fell, and slew them,
	4B	think ye that they were sinners
	5	above all men that dwelt in Jerusalem? I tell you, Nay:
	5B	but, except ye repent, ye shall all likewise perish.
	6	He (ie: Jesus) spake also this parable; (Mt.3:10/Mt.16:27)
	6B	A certain man had a fig tree planted in his vineyard;
	6C	and he came and sought fruit thereon; and found none.
	7	Then said he unto the dresser of his vineyard,
	7B	Behold, these 3 years I come seeking fruit on this fig tree,
	7C	and find none: Cut it down; why cumbereth it the ground?
	8	And he (ie: the dresser of the vineyard) answering said unto him,
	8B	Lord, let it alone this year also, till I shall
	9	dig about it, and dung it: and it bear well:
	9B	And if not, then after that - thou shalt cut it down.
	10	And he was teaching in one of the synagogues on the sabbath.
	11	And, behold,
18 years.	11B	there was a woman which had a spirit of infirmity 18 years,
	11C	and was bowed together, and could in no wise lift up herself.
	12	And when Jesus saw her, he called her to him,
	12B	and said unto her, Woman, thou art loosed from thine infirmity.
	13	And he laid his hands on her:
	13B	and immediately she was made straight, and glorified God.
	14	And the ruler of the synagogue answered with indignation,
	14B	because that Jesus had healed on the sabbath day, and said
	14C	unto the people, There are 6 days in which men ought to work:
	14D	in them therefore come and be healed, and not the sabbath day.
	15	The Lord then answered him, and said, (Mt.12:11,12/Lk.14:5)
	15B	Thou hypocrite, doth not each one of you on the sabbath loose
	15C	his ox or his ass from the stall, and lead him away to watering?
	16	And ought not this woman (being a daughter of Abraham),
	16B	whom Satan hath bound, lo, these 18 years,
	16C	be loosed from this bond on the sabbath day?
	17	And when he (ie: Jesus)
	17B	had said these things, all his adversaries were ashamed:
	17C	And all the people rejoiced
	17D	for all the glorious things that were done by him.
	18	Then said he (ie: Jesus), Unto what is the kingdom of God like?
	18B	and whereunto shall I resemble it? (Mt.13:31,32/Mk.4:30-32)
	19	It (ie: the kingdom of God) is like a grain of mustard seed,
	19B	which a man took, and cast into his garden;
	19C	and it grew, and waxed (ie: became) a great tree; (Dan.2:34,35)
	19D	and the fowls of the air lodged in the branches of it.
	20	And again he said, Whereunto shall I liken the kingdom of God?
	21	It is like leaven, which a woman took (Mt.13:33,34)
Journeying	21B	and hid in 3 measures of meal, till the whole was leavened.
toward	22	And he went through the cities and villages, teaching,
Jerusalem.	22B	and journeying toward Jerusalem.
	23	Then said one unto him, Lord, are there few that are saved?
	24	And he said unto them, Strive to enter in at the strait gate:

Mt.19 Mk.10 Lk.13 Jn.11

	24B	for many (I say unto you), (Rom.9:13-16)
	24C	will seek to enter in, and shall not be able. (Mt.7:13,14)
	25	When once the master of the house is risen up,
	25B	and ye begin to stand without,
	25C	and to knock at the door, saying, Lord, Lord, open unto us;
	25D	And he shall answer and say unto you, I know not whence ye are:
I went	26	Then shall ye begin to say,
to church?	26B	We have eaten and drunk in thy presence,
	26C	and thou hast taught in our streets.
	27	But he shall say, I tell you, I know not whence ye are;
	27B	depart from me, all ye workers of iniquity.
	28	There shall be weeping and gnashing of teeth,
	28B	when ye shall see Abraham, and Isaac, and Jacob, and all the
	28C	prophets, in the kingdom of God, but ye yourselves thrust out.
	29	And they shall come from the East, and from the West,
	29B	and from the North, and from the South,
	29C	and shall sit down in the kingdom of God.
	30	And, behold, there are last which shall be first, (Mt.19:30)
	30B	and there are first which shall be last. (Mt.20:16)
	31	The same day there came certain of the Pharisees, saying unto him,
	31B	Get thee out, and depart hence: for Herod will kill thee.
	32	And he said unto them, Go ye, and tell that fox, Behold,
	32B	I cast out devils, and I do cures to day and to morrow,
	32C	and the 3rd. day I shall be perfected (ie: fulfilled).
	33	Nevertheless,
	33B	I must walk to day, and to morrow, and the day following: for
	33C	it cannot be that a prophet perish (ie: die) without Jerusalem.
	34	O Jerusalem, Jerusalem, which killest the prophets,
	34B	and stonest them that are sent unto thee; (Mt.23:37-39)
	34C	How often would I have gathered thy children together, as
	34D	a hen doth gather her brood under her wings, and ye would not!
	35	Behold, your house is left unto you desolate (ie: a wilderness):
	35B	And verily I say unto you,
	35C	Ye shall not see me, until the time come when ye shall say,
	35D	Blessed is he that cometh in the name of the Lord.
	Lk.14	
	1	And it came to pass, as he (ie: Jesus) went into the house
	1B	of one of the chief Pharisees to eat bread on the sabbath day:
	1C	And they watched him.
	2	And, behold, there was a certain man before him - which
	2B	had the dropsy (ie: Generalized Edema, excessive fluid/water).
	3	And Jesus answering spake unto the lawyers and Pharisees,
	3B	saying, Is it lawful to heal on the sabbath day?
	4	And they held their peace (ie: they remained silent).
	4B	And he (Jesus) took him, and healed him, and let him go;
	5	And answered them, saying, (Mt.12:11,12/Lk.13:15)
	5B	Which of you shall have an ass or an ox fallen into a pit,
	5C	and will not straightway pull him out on the sabbath day?
	6	And they could not answer him again to these things.
	7	And he (ie: Jesus) put forth a parable to those who were bidden,
	7B	(when he marked how they chose out the chief rooms);
	8	saying unto them, When thou art bidden (ie: invited)
	8B	of any man to a wedding, sit not down in the highest room;
	8C	lest a more honourable man than thou be bidden of him;
	9	And he that bade thee and him
	9B	come and say to thee, Give this man place;
	9C	and thou begin with shame to take the lowest room.

Mt.19 Mk.10 Lk.14 Jn.11

	10	But when thou art bidden, go and sit down in the lowest room;
	10B	that when he that bade thee cometh, he may say unto thee,
	10C	Friend, go up higher: Then shalt thou have worship (ie: glory)
	10D	in the presence of them that sit at the table with thee.
	11	For whosoever exalteth himself shall be abased; and he that
	11B	humbleth himself shall be exalted. (Mt.23:11,12/Lk.18:13,14)
	12	Then said he (ie: Jesus) also to him that bade him,
	12B	When thou makest a dinner or a supper, call not thy friends, nor
	12C	thy brethren, neither thy kinsmen, nor thy rich neighbours;
	12D	lest they also bid thee again, and a recompence be made thee.
	13	But when thou makest a feast,
	13B	call the poor, the maimed, the lame, the blind:
	14	And thou shalt be blessed; for they cannot recompence thee:
	14B	for thou shalt be recompenced at the resurrection of the just.
	15	And when one of them that sat at meat with him heard these things,
	15B	he said unto him (ie: he said unto Jesus),
	15C	Blessed is he that shall eat bread in the kingdom of God.
	16	Then said he (ie: Jesus) unto them, (Mt.22:2-5,8-10)
	16B	A certain man made a great supper, and bade many:
	17	And sent his servant at supper time to say
	17B	to them that were bidden, Come; for all things are now ready.
Thank U,	18	And they all with one consent began to make excuse.
but	18B	The first said unto him, I have bought a piece of ground,
No Thank U.	18C	and I must needs go and see it: I pray thee have me excused.
	19	And another said, I have bought 5 yoke of oxen,
	19B	and I go to prove them: I pray thee have me exused.
	20	And another said,
	20B	I have married a wife, and therefore I cannot come.
	21	So, that servant came, and shewed his lord these things.
	21B	Then the master of the house being angry said to his servant,
	21C	Go out quickly into the streets and lanes of the city,
	21D	and bring in hither the poor, and the maimed,
	21E	and the halt (ie: cripple), and the blind.
	22	And the servant said, Lord,
	22B	it is done as thou hast commanded, and yet there is room.
	23	And the lord said unto the servant,
Compel them	23B	Go out into the highways and hedges,
to come in.	23C	and compel them to come in - that my house may be filled.
	24	For I say unto you, That none of those men
	24B	which were bidden shall taste of my supper.
	25	And there went great multitudes with him:
	25B	And he turned, and said unto them,
	26	If any man come to me, and hate not his father, and mother,
	26B	and wife, and children, and brethren, and sisters,
	26C	yea, and his own life also, he cannot be my disciple.
	27	And whosoever doth not bear his cross,
	27B	and come after me, cannot be my disciple. (Mk.8:34)
	28	For which of you,
	28B	intending to build a tower, sitteth not down first,
	28C	and counteth the cost, whether he have sufficient to finish it?
	29	Lest haply (ie: lest at any time),
	29B	after he hath laid the foundation, and is not able to finish it,
	29C	all that behold it began to mock him, saying,
	30	This man began to build, and was not able to finish.
	31	Or what king, going to make war against another king, sitteth
	31B	not down first, and consulteth whether he be able with 10,000
	31C	to meet him that cometh against him with 20,000?

Mt.19 Mk.10 Lk.14 Jn.11

32	Or else, while the other is yet a great way off,
32B	he sendeth an ambassage, and desireth conditions of peace.
33	So likewise, whosoever he be of you that forsaketh not all
33B	that he hath, he cannot be my disciple.
34	Salt is good: but if salt (Mt.5:13/Mk.9:50/Col.4:6)
34B	have lost his savour, wherewith shall it be seasoned?
35	It is neither fit for the land, nor yet for the dunghill;
35B	but men cast it out.
35C	He that hath ears to hear, let him hear.

Lk.15

1	Then drew near unto him
1B	all the publicans and sinners - for to hear him.
2	And the Pharisees and scribes murmured, (Lk.5:30-32/Lk.7:37,39)
2B	saying, This man receiveth sinners, and eateth with them.
3	And he (ie: Jesus) spake this parable unto them, saying,
4	What man of you, having an 100 sheep, and if he (Mt.18:11-14)
4B	lose one of them, doth not leave the 90 and 9 in the wilderness,
4C	and go after that which is lost, until he find it?
5	And when he hath found it,
5B	he layeth it on his shoulders, rejoicing.
6	And when he cometh home, he
6B	calleth together his friens and neighbours, saying unto them,
6C	Rejoice with me; for I have found my sheep which was lost.
7	I say unto you, that likewise
7B	joy shall be in heaven over one sinner that repenteth, more
7C	than over 90 and 9 just persons, which need no repentance.
8	Or what woman having 10 pieces of silver,
8B	if she lose one piece, doth not light a candle,
8C	and sweep the house, and seek diligently till she find it?
9	And when she hath found it,
9B	she calleth her friends and neighbours together, saying,
9C	Rejoice with me; for I have found the piece which I had lost.
10	Likewise, I say unto you, there is joy in the (Rev.8:1)
10B	presence of the angels of God over one sinner that repenteth.
11	And he said, A certain man had 2 sons:
12	And the younger of them said to his father, Father,
12B	give me the portion of goods that falleth to me.
12C	And he divided unto them his living.
13	And not many days after the younger son
13B	gathered all together, and took his journey into a far country;
13C	and there wasted his substance with riotous living.
14	And when he had spent all,
14B	there arose a mighty famine in that land;
14C	and he began to be in want.
15	And he went and joined himself to a citizen of that country;
15B	and he sent him into his fields to feed swine.
16	And he would fain (ie: desiring)
16B	have filled his belly with the husks that the swine did eat:
16C	And no man gave unto him.
17	And when he came to himself,
17B	he said, How many hired servants of my father's
17C	have bread enough and to spare; and I perish with hunger!
18	I will arise and go to my father,
18B	and I will say unto him, Father, I have sinned against heaven,
19	and before thee, and am no more worthy to be called thy son:
19B	Make me as one of thy hired servants.

Mt.19 Mk.10 Lk.15 Jn.11

20	And he arose, and went to his father.
20B	But when he was yet a great way off, his father saw him, and
20C	had compassion, and ran, and fell on his neck and kissed him.
21	And the son said unto him, Father, I have sinned against heaven,
21B	and in thy sight, and am no more worthy to be called thy son.
22	But the father said to his servants,
22B	Bring forth the best robe, and put it on him;
22C	and put a ring on his hand, and shoes on his feet:
23	And bring hither the fatted calf, and kill it;
23B	and let us eat, and be merry:
24	For this my son was dead, and is alive again;
24B	he was lost, and is found. And they began to be merry.
25	Now his elder son was in the field: and as he came
25B	and drew nigh to the house, he heard musick and dancing.
26	And he called
26B	one of the servants, and asked what these things meant.
27	And he said unto him, Thy brother is come;
27B	and thy father hath killed the fatted calf,
27C	because he hath received him safe and sound.
28	And he was angry, and would not go in:
28B	Therefore came his father out, and intreated him.
29	And he answering said to his father,
29B	Lo, these many years do I serve thee,
29C	neither transgressed I at any time thy commandment:
29D	and yet thou never gavest me a kid,
29E	that I might make merry with my friends:
30	But as soon as this thy son was come,
30B	which hath devoured thy living with harlots,
30C	thou hast killed for him the fatted calf.
31	And he said unto him,
31B	Son, thou art ever with me, and all that I have is thine.
32	It was meet (ie: ought) that we should make merry, and be glad:
32B	For this thy brother was dead, and is alive again;
32C	and was lost, and was found.

Lk.16

1	And he (ie: Jesus) said also unto his disciples,
1B	There was a certain rich man, which had a steward;
1C	and the same was accused unto him that he had wasted his goods.
2	And he called him,
2B	and said unto him, How is it that I hear this of thee?
2C	Give an account of thy stewardship;
2D	for thou mayest be no longer steward.
3	Then the steward (within himself) said, What shall I do?
3B	for my lord taketh away
3C	from me the stewardship: I cannot dig; to beg I am ashamed.
4	I am resolved (ie: I perceive/understand/know) what to do,
4B	that, when I am put out of the stewardship,
4C	they (ie: the debtors) may receive me into their houses.
5	So he called every one of his lord's debtors unto him,
5B	And he said unto the first, How much owest thou unto my lord?
6	And he said, An 100 measures of oil.
6B	And he said unto him,
6C	Take thy bill, and sit down quickly, and write 50.
7	Then said he to another, And how much owest thou?
7B	And he said, An 100 measures of oil.
7C	And he said unto him,
7D	Take thy bill, and write fourscore (ie: 4x20=80).
8	And the lord commended (ie: praised)

Mt.19   Mk.10   Lk.16   Jn.11

		8B	the unjust steward, because he had done wisely:
		8C	For the children of this world (ie: of this age)
		8D	are in their generation wiser than the children of Light.
		9	And I say unto you,
		9B	Make to yourselves friends of the mammon of unrighteousness;
		9C	that, when ye fail
		9D	they may receive you into everlasting habitations.
		10	He that is faithful
		10B	in that which is least - is faithful also in much:
		10C	And he that is unjust in the least is unjust also in much.
		11	If therefore
		11B	ye have not been faithful in the unrighteous mammon,
		11C	who will commit to your trust the true riches?
		12	And if ye have not been faithful in that which is another man's,
		12B	who shall give you that which is your own?
		13	No servant can serve 2 masters:
		13B	for either he will hate the one, and love the other;
		13C	or else he will hold to the one, and despise the other.
		13D	Ye cannot serve God and mammon. (Mt.6:24)
			(Note: Mammon = a Chaldee word that was used by Jesus Christ.)
		14	And the Pharisees also,
		14B	who were covetous, heard all these things: And they derided him.
		15	And he (ie: Jesus) said unto them, Ye are they which
		15B	justify yourselves before men; but God knoweth your hearts:
		15C	For that which
		15D	is highly esteemed among men is abomination in the sight of God.
		16	The law and the prophets were until John: (Mt.11:13/Acts 3:24)
		16B	since that time the kingdom of God is preached, (Mt.11:12)
		16C	and every man presseth (ie: suffereth violence) into/in it.
		17	And it is easier (Mt.5:17,18)
		17B	for heaven and earth to pass, than one title of the law to fail.
3	2		And the Pharisees (also) came unto him,
3B	2B,D		and asked him (tempting him) saying unto him, Is it lawful
3C	2C		for a man to put away (ie: divorce) his wife - for every cause?
	3		And he answered and said unto them, What did Moses command you?
	4		And they said, Moses suffered (ie: to permit/give licence)
	4B		to write a bill of divorce, and to put her away.
4	5		And he (Jesus) answered and said unto them,
	5B		For the hardness of your heart he wrote you this precept.
4B	6B		Have ye not read, that he (God) which made them
4C	6A,C		at/from the beginning of creation made them male and female.
5	7		And said, For this cause shall a man
5B	7B		leave his father and mother, and shall cleave to his wife;
5C	8		and the twain shall be one flesh:
6	8B		so then (wherefore) they are no more twain, but one flesh.
6B	9		What therefore God hath joined together,
6C	9B		let not man put asunder (ie: not separate). (Mal.2:16)
7			They say unto him, Why did Moses then (De.24:1/Mt.5:31)
7B			command to give a writing of divorcement, and to put her away?
8			He saith unto them, Moses because of the hardness of your hearts
8B			suffered you to put away (ie: divorce) your wives:
8C			but from the beginning it was not so.
9	18		And I say unto you, Whosoever putteth (shall put) away his wife,
9B			except it be for fornication,
9C	18B		and shall marry another, committeth adultery:
9D	18C		And whoso married her
9E	18D		which is put away from her husband, committeth adultery.

The Gospels of Matthew, Mark, Luke, and John: Merged into One Historic Calendar of Events | 99

Mt.19　Mk.10　Lk.16　Jn.11

	10		And in the house his disciples asked him again of the same matter.
	11		And he saith unto them,　　　　　　　　　　　　　　　　(Mk.4:34)
	11B		Whosoever shall put away (ie: divorce) his wife,
	11C		and marry another, committeth adultery against her.
	12		And if a woman shall put away (ie: divorce) her husband,
	12B		and be married to another, she committeth adultery.
10			His disciples say unto him,
10B			If the case of the man be so (ie: in this manner)
10C			with his wife, it is not good to marry.
11			But he said unto them, All men cannot
11B			receive this saying, save they to whom it is given.
12			For there are some eunuchs,
12B			which were so born from their mother's womb:
12C			And there are some eunuchs, which were made eunuchs of men:
12D			And there be eunuchs which have made themselves eunuchs
12E			for the kingdom of heaven's sake.
12F			He that is able to receive it, let him receive it. (1 Cor.7:32)

		19	There was a certain rich man,
		19B	which was clothed in purple and fine linen, and
		19C	fared sumptuously (ie: to make merry and in splendor) every day:
		20	And there was a certain beggar named Lazarus,
		21	which laid at his gate full of sores, and desiring to be fed
		21B	with the crumbs which fell from the rich man's table:
		21C	moreover the dogs came and licked his sores.　(Rev.16:2)
		22	And it came to pass, that the begger died,
		22B	and was carried by the angels into Abraham's bosom:
		22C	The rich man also died, and was buried;
		23	and in hell he lift up his eyes, being in torments,
		23B	and seeth Abraham afar off, and Lazarus in his bosom.
		24	And he cried and said, Father Abraham, have mercy on me,
		24B	and send Lazarus, that he may dip the tip of his finger
		24C	in water, and cool my tongue; for I am tormented in this flame.
		25	But Abraham said, Son, remember that thou in thy lifetime
		25B	receivedst thy good things, and likewise Lazarus evil things:
		25C	but now he is comforted, and thou art tormented.
		26	And beside all this,
		26B	between us and you there is a great gulf fixed:
		26C	so that they which would pass from hence to you cannot;
		26D	neither can they pass to us, that would come from thence.
		27	Then he said, I pray thee therefore, father,
		27B	that thou wouldest send him to my father's house:
		28	For I have 5 brethren; that he may testify unto them,
		28B	lest they also come into this place of torment.
		29	Abraham saith unto him,
		29B	They have Moses and the prophets; let them hear them.
		30	And he said, Nay, father Abraham:
		30B	but if one went unto them from the dead, they will repent.
		31	And he said unto him, If they hear not Moses and the prophets,
		31B	neither will they be persuaded, though one rose from the dead.
		Lk.17	
		1	Then said he (ie: Jesus) unto his disciples,
		1B	It is impossible but (ie: it must be) that offences will come:
		1C	but woe unto him, through whom they come!
		2	It were better for him that a millstone
		2B	were hanged about his neck, and he be cast into the sea,
		2C	than that he should offend one of these little ones. (Mk.9:42)
		3	Take heed to yourselves:

Mt.19　Mk.10　Lk.17　Jn.11

	3B	If thy brother trespass against thee, rebuke him;
	3C	and if he repent, forgive him.
	4	And if he trespass against thee 7 times in a day,
	4B	and 7 times in a day turn again to thee, saying, I repent;
	4C	thou shalt forgive him.
	5	And the apostles said unto the Lord, Increase our faith.
	6	And the Lord said,
	6B	If ye had faith as a grain of mustard seed, ye might say
	6C	unto this sycamine tree, Be thou plucked up by the root,
	6D	and be thou planted in the sea; and it should obey you.
	7	But which of you, having a servant plowing or feeding cattle,
	7B	will say unto him by and by (ie: anon/straightway/immediately),
	7C	when he is come from the field, Go and sit down to meat?
	8	But, will he not say unto him, Make ready wherewith I may sup,
	8B	and gird thyself, and serve me, till I have eaten and drunken;
	8C	and afterward shalt thou not eat and drink?
	9	Doth he thank that servant because he (ie: that servant) did
	9B	the things that were commanded him? I trow (ie: I think) not.
	10	So likewise ye, when
	10B	ye shall have done all those things which are commanded you,
	10C	say, Unprofitable servants we be,
	10D	for we have done that which was our duty to do.
	11	And it came to pass, as he went to Jerusalem, that
	11B	He passed through the midst of Samaria and Galilee.
	12	And as he entered into a certain village,
	12B	there met him 10 men that were lepers, which stood afar off:
	13	And they lifted up their voices,
	13B	and said, Jesus, Master, have mercy on us.
	14	And when he (ie: Jesus) saw them,
	14B	he said unto them, Go shew yourselves unto the priests.
	14C	And it came to pass, that, as they went, they were cleansed.
	15	And one of them, when he saw that he was healed,
	15B	turned back, and with a loud voice glorified God,
	16	And fell down on his face at his feet, giving him thanks:
	16B	And he was a Samaritan.　　　　　　　　(Lk.10:33/Jn.4:9)
	17	And Jesus answering said, Were there not 10 cleansed?
	18	but where are the nine? There are not found
	18B	that returned to give glory to God, save this stranger.
	19	And he (ie: Jesus) said unto him.
	19B	Arise, go thy way: thy faith hath made thee whole.
	20	And when he was demanded of the Pharisees,
The	20B	when the kingdom of God should come.
Kingdom	20C	He answered them and said,
of God	20D	The kingdom of God cometh not with observation:
is within	21	Neither shall they say, Lo here! or, lo there!
you.	21B	for, behold, the kingdom of God is within you.
	22	And he said unto the disciples.
	22B	The days will come, when ye shall desire to see
	22C	one of the days of the Son of man, and ye shall not see it.
	23	And they shall say to you,
	23B	See here; or, see there: go not after them, nor follow them.
	24	For as the lightning, that lighteneth out of
	24B	one part under heaven, shineth unto the other part under heaven;
	24C	so shall also the Son of man be in his day.
	25	But first must he
	25B	suffer many things, and be rejected of this generation.
	26	And as it was in the days of Noe (ie: Noah),

Mt.19 Mk.10 Lk.17 Jn.11		
In the	26B	so shall it be also in the days of the Son of man.
days of	27	They did eat, they drank, they married wives, (James 5:7)
the Son	27B	they were given in marriage, until the day that Noe entered
of man:	27C	into the ark, and the flood came, and destroyed them all.
(before),	28	Likewise also as it was in the days of Lot; they did eat, they
That Day	28B	drank, they bought, they sold, they planted, they builded;
the	29	But the same day that Lot went out of Sodom it rained fire and
Son of man	29B	brimstone from heaven, and destroyed them all. (Jude :7)
be	30	Even thus shall it be
revealed.	30B	in the day when the Son of man is revealed.
	31	In that day, he (Mt.24:33-42/Mk.13:14-20)
	31B	which shall be upon the housetop, and his stuff in the house
	31C	let him not come down to take it away:
	31D	and he that is in the field,
	31E	let him likewise not return back. (Rev.18:4)
	32	Remember Lot's wife.
	33	Whosoever shall seek to save his life shall lose it; and
	33B	Whosoever shall lose his life shall preserve it. (Mt.10:39)
	34	I tell you, in that night there shall be
	34B	Two in one bed;
	34C	one shall be taken, and the other shall be left.
	35	Two shall be grinding together;
	35B	the one shall be taken, and the other left.
Shall	36	Two shall be in the field;
be left	36B	the one shall be taken, and the other left.
where?	37	And they answered and said unto him, Where, Lord?
	37B	And he said unto them,
	37C	Wheresoever the body is,
	37D	thither will the eagles be gathered together. (Mt.24:28)
	Lk.18	
Pray	1	And he (ie: Jesus) spake a parable unto them to this end,
without	1B	that men ought always to pray, and not to faint: saying,
ceasing.	2	There was in a city a judge,
	2B	which feared not God, neither regarded man:
	3	And there was a widow in that city;
	3B	and she came unto him, saying, Avenge me of mine adversary.
	4	And he would not for a while.
	4B	But afterward,
	4C	he said within himself, Though I fear not God, nor regard man;
	5	Yet because this widow troubleth me, I will avenge her,
	5B	lest by her continual coming she weary me.
	6	And the Lord (ie: the Lord Jesus) said,
	6B	Hear what the unjust judge saith.
	7	And shall not God avenge his own elect, which cry
	7B	day and night unto him, though he bear long with them?
	8	I tell you that He will avenge them speedily.
	8B	Nevertheless when
	8C	the Son of man cometh, shall he find faith on the earth?
	9	And he spake this parable unto certain which trusted
	9B	in themselves that they were righteous, and despised others:
	10	Two men went up into the temple to pray;
	10B	(the one a Pharisee, and the other a publican). (Lk.3:12,13)
	11	The Pharisee stood and prayed thus with himself,
	11B	God, I thank thee, that I am not as other men are,
	11C	extortioners, unjust, adulterers, or even as this publican.
	12	I fast twice in a week (ie: 2x in the sabbath), (Mk.2:28)
	12B	I give tithes of all that I possess.

Mt.19	Mk.10	Lk.18	Jn.11	
		13		And the publican (ie: tax collector), standing afar off,
		13B		would not lift up so much as his eyes unto heaven, but
		13C		smote upon his breast, saying, God be merciful to me a sinner.
		14		I tell you, this man
		14B		went down to his house justified rather than the other:
		14C		For every one that exalteth himself shall be abased;
		14D		and he that humbleth himself shall be exalted.
13	13	15		And then they brought little/young children (also infants) to him,
	13B	15B		that he should/would touch them:
13B				that he should put his hands on them, and pray:
		15C		But when the disciples saw it,
13C	13C	15D		they (the disciples) rebuked those that brought them.
	14			But when Jesus saw it, he was much displeased,
14	14B	16		And he (Jesus) called them, and said unto them, Suffer (ie: let)
14B	14C	16B		the little children to come unto me, and forbid them not:
14C	14D	16C		for of such is the kingdom of heaven (the kingdom of God).
	15	17		Verily I say unto you,
	15B	17B		Whosoever shall not receive the kingdom of God
	15C	17C		as a little child, he shall not (in no wise) enter therein.
	16			And he took them up in his arms,
15	16B			and he laid his hands on them, and blessed them,
15B				and departed thence.
	17			And when he was gone forth into the way,
16	17B	18		And, behold, there came one running (a certain ruler),
16B	17C	18B		And kneeled to him, and said unto him (asked him),
16C	17D	18C		saying, Good Master, what good thing shall I do,
16D	17E	18D		to inherit (that I may have) eternal life?
17	18	19		And Jesus said unto him,
17B	18B	19B		Why callest thou me good? none is good, save one, that is God:
17C				but if thou wilt enter into life, keep the commandments.
18				He saith unto him, Which?
18B	19	20		Jesus said, Thou knowest the commandments,
18D	19B	20B		Do not (thou shalt not) commit adultery,
18C	19C	20C		Do not (thou shalt do no) murder,
18E	19D	20D		Do not (thou shalt not) steal,
18F	19E	20E		Do not (thou shalt not) bear false witness:
	19F			Defraud not,
19	19G	20F		Honour thy father and thy mother,
19B				And thou shalt love thy neighbour as thyself.
20	20	21		And he (the young man) answered and saith unto him, Master,
20B	20B	21B		all these things have I observed/kept from my youth up:
20C				what lack I yet?
	21	22		Now when Jesus heard these things, beholding him loved him;
21	21B	22B		And Jesus said unto him,
21B	21C	22C		Yet lackest thou one thing: if thou wilt be perfect,
21C	21D	22D		go thy way, sell whatsoever (all) thou hast,
21D	21E	22E		and distribute (give it) unto the poor, and thou shalt have
21E	21F	22F		treasure in heaven: and come, take up the cross, and follow me.
22	22	23		But when the young man heard that saying he was sad;
22B	22B	23B		and he became very sorrowful, and went away grieved:
22C	22C	23C		for he had great possessions (he was very rich).
	23	24		But when Jesus saw that he was very sorrowful, looked round about,
23	23B	24B		Then said Jesus unto his disciples, Verily, I say unto you,
23B	23C	24C		That a rich man (they that have riches)
23C	23D	24D		shall hardly enter into the kingdom of heaven (kingdom of God).
	24			And the disciples were astonished at his words.
	24B			But Jesus answereth again, and saith unto them,

Mt.19	Mk.10	Lk.18	Jn.11
	24C		
	24D		
24			
24B	25	25	
24C	25B	25B	
25		26	
25B	26		
25C	26B	26B	
26	27	27	
26B	27B	27B	
26C	27C	27C	
27	28	28	
27B	28B	28B	
27C			
28	29	29	
28B			
28C			
28D			
28E			
29	29B	29B	
29B	29C	29C	
29C			
	29D		
		29D	
29D	30	30	
	30B	30B	
	30C		
	30D		
	30E	30C	
29E	30F	30D	
30	31		

```
                    Children, how hard is it for them that
                trust in riches to enter into the kingdom of God!  (1 Tim.6:17)
            And again I say unto you,
                It is easier for a camel to go through the eye of a needle,
                than for a rich man to enter into the kingdom of God.
            And when they (his disciples) heard it,
                and they were astonished out of measure (exceedingly amazed),
                saying among themselves, Who then can be saved?
            But Jesus beheld (looking upon) them; he saith unto them,
                The things which are impossible with men are possible with God:
                    for with God all things are possible.
            Then answered Peter and said (began to say) unto him, Lo/Behold,
                we have left (forsaken) all, and have followed thee;
                what shall we have therefore?
            And Jesus answered and said unto them, Verily I say unto you, That,
                ye which have followed me, in the regeneration (ie: rebirth)
                when the Son of man shall sit in the throne of his glory,
                ye also shall sit upon 12 thrones, judging the 12 tribes
                of Israel.  (Note: the 12 who followed him. Mt.24:13/Acts 1:26)
            And every one that hath left (forsaken) houses, or brethren, or
                sisters, or father, or mother, or wife, or children, or lands,
                    for my name's sake,
                    for my sake, and the gospel's,
                    for the kingdom of God's sake,
                        who shall receive manifold more (receive an 100 fold).
            Now in this present time,
                houses, and brethren, and sisters, and mothers, and children,
                and lands, with persecutions;          (2 Tim.3:12/Mt.5:45)
            And in the world to come
                    and, shall inherit eternal (everlasting) life.
            But many that are first shall be last; and the last first.
```

> Note: Occasionally, as in Mk.10:29,30 and Lk.18:29,30.
> A double negative is used, which is equal to a positive.
> (e.g. There is no man --- who shall not: Indicating all will.)
> It may be more simple to use positive instead of a double neg.

Mt.20

Mt.20	
1	
1B	
1C	
2	
2B	One Penny
3	(coinage)
3B	-a pence
4	-a dinarius
4B	The wages
5	paid for
5B	one day
6	of work.
6B	
6C	
7	
7B	
7C	
8	
8B	
8C	
8D	

```
            For the kingdom of heaven
                is like unto a man that is an householder, which went out
                early in the morning to hire labourers into his vineyard.
            And when he had agreed with the labourers
                for a penny a day, he sent them into the vineyard.
            And he went out about the 3rd. hour,
                and saw others standing idle in the marketplace;
            And said unto them, Go ye also into the vineyard, and
                whatsoever is right I will give you.  And they went their way.
            Again he went out
                about the 6th. and the 9th. hour, and he did likewise.
            And about the 11th. hour
                he went out, and found others standing idle,
                and saith unto them, Why stand ye here all the day idle?
            They say unto him, Because no man hath hired us.
            He saith unto them, Go ye also into the vineyard;
                and whatsoever is right, that shall ye receive.
            So when even was come;
            The lord of the vineyard saith unto his steward,
                Call the labourers, and
                give them their hire, beginning from the last unto the first.
```

Mt.20	Mk.10	Lk.18	Jn.11	
9				And when they came that were hired about the 11th. hour,
9B				they received every man a penny.
10				But when the 1st. came,
10B				(they supposed that they should have received more.)
10C				and they likewise received every man a penny.
11				And when they had received it,
11B				they murmured against the goodman of the house.
12				saying, These last have wrought but one hour,
12B				and thou hast made them equal unto us,
12C				which have borne the burden and heat of the day.
13				But he answered one of them, and said, Friend,
13B				I do thee no wrong: didst not thou agree with me for a penny?
14				Take that thine is, and go thy way:
14B				I will give unto this last, even as unto thee.
15				Is it not lawful for me to do what I will with mine own?
15B				Is thine eye evil, because I am good?
16				So the last shall be first, and the first last:
16B				For many be called, but few chosen.
17				And Jesus going up to Jerusalem:
	32			And they were in the way going up to Jerusalem;
	32B			And Jesus went before them: and they were amazed;
	32C			and as they followed, they were afraid.
17B	32D	31		And he (ie: Jesus) took again the 12 disciples apart in the way,
	32E			and began to tell them what things should happen unto him.
17C		31B		And said unto them,
18	33	31C		Behold, we go up to Jerusalem;
		31D		and all things that are written by
		31E		the prophets concerning the Son of man shall be accomplished.
18B	33B			And the Son of man shall be betrayed (delivered)
18C	33C			unto the chief priests and unto the scribes;
18D	33D			and they shall condemn him to death,
19	33E	32		and he shall be delivered unto the Gentiles,
19B	34A	32B		and they shall mock him, and he be spitefully entreated,
	34C	32C		and shall spit upon him,
19C	34B	33		and they shall scourge him,
19D	34D	33B		and shall put him to death (kill), and to crucify him:
19E	34E	33C		And the 3rd. day he shall rise again.
		34		And they understood none of these things: and this saying was
		34B		hid from them, neither knew they the things which were spoken.
20				Then came to him the mother of Zebedee's children with her sons,
20B				worshipping him, and desiring a certain thing of him.
	35			And James and John (the sons of Zebedee) come unto him,
	35B			saying, Master, we would that thou
	35C			shouldest do for us whatsoever we shall desire.
	36			And he said unto them, What would ye that I should do for you?
	37			They said unto him,
	37B			Grant unto us that we may sit, one on thy right hand,
	37C			and the other on thy left hand, in thy glory.
21				And he said unto her, What wilt thou?
21B				She saith unto him,
21C				Grant that these my 2 sons may sit, the one on thy right hand,
21D				and the other on the left, in thy kingdom.
22	38			But Jesus answered and said unto them, Ye know not what ye ask:
22B	38B			can ye (are ye able to) drink of the cup that I shall drink of?
22C	38C			and to be baptized with the baptism that I am baptized with?
22D	39			And they said unto him, We are able.
23	39B			And Jesus said unto them,

| Mt.20 | Mk.10 | Lk.18 | Jn.11 |

23B	39C		Ye shall indeed drink of my cup (the cup that I drink of); and
23C	39D		ye shall be baptized with the baptism that I am baptized with:
23D	40		But to sit on my right hand, and on my left hand,
23E	40B		is not mine to give: but it shall be
23F	40C		given to them for whom it is prepared of my Father.
24	41		And when the 10 heard it,
24B	41B		They began to be/were moved with indignation (much displeased)
24C	41C		against the 2 brethren, James and John.
25	42		But Jesus called them to him, and saith unto them,
25B	42B		Ye know that they (the princes of the Gentiles), (Lk.22:25)
	42C		which are accounted to rule over the Gentiles,
25C	42D		exercise dominion/lordship over (upon) them;
25D	42E		And they that are great (their great ones)
25E	42F		exercise authority upon them.
26	43		But so shall it NOT be among you:
26B	43B		But whosoever will be great among you,
26C	43C		shall be (let him be) your minister (ie: your servant):
27	44		And whosoever of you (among you) will be the chiefest (ie: first),
27B	44B		shall be (let him be) your servant (ie: bondman) of all.
28	45		For even (even as) the Son of man came not to be ministered unto,
			but to minister, and to give his life a ransom for many.
		35	And it came to pass, that as he was come nigh unto Jericho,
		35B	a certain blind man sat by the way side begging:
		36	And hearing the multitude pass by, he asked what it meant.
		37	And they told him, that Jesus of Nazareth passed by.
		38	And he cried, saying, Jesus, thou son of David, have mercy on me.
		39	And they
		39B	which went before rebuked him, that he should hold his peace:
		39C	But he cried so much the more,
		39D	Thou son of David, have mercy on me.
		40	And Jesus stood, and commanded him to be brought unto him:
		40B	And when he was come near, he (ie; Jesus) asked him,
		41	saying, What wilt thou that I shall do unto thee?
		41B	And he said, Lord, that I may receive my sight.
		42	And Jesus said unto him,
		42B	Receive thy sight: thy faith hath saved thee. And immediately
		43	he received his sight, and followed him, glorifying God:
		43B	And all the people (when they saw it) gave praise unto God.
		Lk.19	
	46	1	And they came to Jericho; entered, and passed through Jericho.
29	46B		And as he/they departed from (went out of) Jericho,
	46C		with his disciples and a great number of people:
29B			A great multitude followed him.
	46D		Blind Bartimaeus (the son of Timaeus) sat by the way side begging.
	47		And when he heard that it was Jesus of Nazareth, he began to
	47B		cry out, and say, Jesus, thou son of David, have mercy on me.
	48		And many charged (ie: rebuked) him that he should hold his peace:
	48B		But he cried a great deal the more,
	48C		Thou son of David, have mercy on me.
	49		And Jesus stood still, and commanded him to be called.
	49B		And they call the blind man,
	49C		saying unto him, Be of good comfort, rise; he calleth thee.
	50		And he, casting away his garment, rose, and came to Jesus.
	51		And Jesus answered and said unto him,
	51B		What wilt thou that I should do unto thee?
	51C		The blind man said unto him, Lord, that I might receive my sight.

Mt.20 Mk.10 Lk.19 Jn.11

	52		And Jesus said unto him,
	52B		Go thy way; thy faith hath made thee whole.
	52C		And immediately he received his sight,
	52D		and followed Jesus in the way.
30	Two blind men		And behold, 2 blind men sitting by the way side,
30B			When they heard that Jesus passed by,
30C			cried out, saying, Have mercy on us, O Lord, thou son of David.
31			And the multitude
31B			rebuked them, because they should hold their peace:
31C			But they cried the more,
31D			saying, Have mercy on us, O Lord, thou son of David.
32			And Jesus stood still, and called them,
32B			and said, What will ye that I shall do unto you?
33			They say unto him, Lord, that our eyes may be opened.
34			So Jesus had compassion on them, and touched their eyes:
34B			And immediately
34C			their eyes received sight, and they followed him.
	Zacchaeus	2	And, behold, there was a man named Zacchaeus,
		2B	which was the chief among the publicans, and he was rich.
		3	And he sought to see Jesus who he was; and he could not for
		3B	the press (ie: multitude), because he was little of stature.
		4	And he ran before, and climbed up
		4B	into a sycomore tree to see him: for he was to pass that way.
		5	And when Jesus came to the place, he looked up,
		5B	and saw him, and said unto him, Zacchaeus, make haste,
		5C	and come down; for to day I must abide at thy house.
		6	And he made haste, and came down, and received him joyfully.
		7	And when they saw it, they murmured, saying, (Mt.9:10,11/Mt.11:19)
		7B	That he was gone to be guest with a man that is a sinner.
		8	And Zacchaeus stood, and said unto the Lord;
		8B	Behold, Lord, the half of my goods I give to the poor;
		8C	and if I have taken any thing from any man (Lk.3:12,13)
		8D	by false accusation, I restore him fourfold.
		9	And Jesus said unto him, This day is salvation
		9B	come to this house, forsomuch as he also is a son of Abraham.
		10	For the Son of man is come
		10B	to seek and to save that which was lost.
What		11	And as they heard these things, he added and spake a parable,
they		11B	because he was nigh to Jerusalem, and because they thought
thought.		11C	that the kingdom of God should immediately appear.
		12	He said therefore (ie: because they expect the kingdom of God now),
		12B	A certain nobleman went into
		12C	a far country to receive for himself a kingdom, and to return.
		13	And he called his 10 servants, and delivered them 10 pounds,
		13B	and said unto them, Occupy (ie: do business) till I come.
		14	But his citizens hated him, and sent a message after him,
		14B	saying, We will not have this man to reign over us.
		15	And it came to pass,
		15B	that when he was returned, having received the kingdom,
		15C	then he commanded these servants
		15D	to be called unto him, to whom he had given the money,
		15E	that he might know how much every man had gained by trading.
		16	Then came the 1st. saying, Lord, thy pound hath gained 10 pounds.
		17	And he said unto him, Well done, thou good servant: (Mt.25:21)
		17B	because thou hast been faithful in very little,
		17C	have thou authority over 10 cities.
		18	And the 2nd. came, saying, Lord, thy pound hath gained 5 pounds.

Mt.20 Mk.10 Lk.19 Jn.11

	19	And he said likewise to him, Be thou also over 5 cities.
	20	And another came, saying, Lord, behold, here is thy pound,
	20B	which I have kept laid up in a napkin:
	21	For I feared (ie: be afraid of) thee, because (Mt.25:24,25)
	21B	thou art an austere (ie: stern) man: thou takest up that
	21C	thou layedst not down, and reapest that thou didst not sow.
	22	And he saith unto him, (Jn.9:41/Jn.15:22-24)
	22B	Out of thine own mouth will I judge thee, thou wicked servant.
	22C	Thou knewest that I was an austere man,
	22D	taking up that I laid not down, and reaping that I did not sow:
	23	Wherefore then gavest not thou my money into the bank,
	23B	that at my coming I might have required mine own with usury?
	24	And he said unto them that stood by,
	24B	Take from him the pound, and give it to him that hath 10 pounds.
	25	(And they said unto him, Lord, he hath 10 pounds!)
	26	For I say unto you,
	26B	That unto every one which hath shall be given; and from him
	26C	that hath not, even that he hath shall be taken away from him.
	27	But those mine enemies, which would not that I should reign
	27B	over them, bring hither, and slay them before me. (Lk.19:14)
	28	And when he had thus spoken,
	28B	he went before, ascending up to Jerusalem.

Jn.12
1   Then Jesus (6 days before the passover) came to Bethany,
1B   where Lazarus was,
1C   which had been dead - whom he (ie: Jesus) raised from the dead.
2   There they made him a supper; and Martha served:
2B   but Lazarus was one of them that sat at the table with him.
3   Then took Mary a pound of ointment of spikenard,
3B   very costly, and anointed the feet of Jesus,
3C   and wiped his feet with her hair: (Jn.11:2)
3D   And the house was filled with the odour of the ointment.

The Tongue
  dancing
  and twisting
  to the beat
  of the desires
  of the heart.

4   Then saith one of his disciples,
5   Judas Iscariot (Simon's son), which should betray him, Why was
5B   not this ointment sold for 300 pence, and given to the poor?
6   This he said, not that he cared for the poor; but because
6B   he was a thief, and had the bag, and bare what was put therein.
7   Then said Jesus, Let her alone:
8   Against the day of my burying hath she kept this. For the poor
8B   always ye have with you; but me ye have not always.
9   Much people of the Jews therefore knew that he was there:
9B And they came - not for Jesus' sake only, but that they might
9C   see Lazarus also, whom he had raised from the dead.

10 But the chief priests
10B   consulted that they might put Lazarus also to death:
11   Because that by reason of him   (Jn.11:47,48)
11B   many of the Jews went away, and believed on Jesus.

12 On the next day:
12B Much people that were come to the feast,
12C   when they heard that Jesus was coming to Jerusalem,
13   took branches of the palm trees, and went forth to meet him,
13B   And cried, Hosanna: Blessed be
13C   the king of Israel that cometh in the name of the Lord.

Mt.21 Mk.11

Mt.21	Mk.11	Lk.19	Jn.12	
		29		And it came to pass,
1	1			When he/they drew (came) nigh unto Jerusalem,
1B	1B	29B		nigh to Bethphage and Bethany,
1C	1C	29C		at the mount called the mount of Olives,
1D	1D	29D		Then he (Jesus) sendeth forth 2 of his disciples;
2	2	30		And saith unto them, Go your way into the village over against you:
2B	2B	30B		And as soon as ye be entered into it, and
2C				straightway ye shall find an ass tied, and a colt with her:
	2C	30C		ye shall find a colt tied, whereon yet never man sat:
2D	2D	30D		loose him, and bring unto me.
3				And if any man say ought (ie: say any-thing) unto you,
	3	31		If any man ask (say unto) you, Why do ye do this/loose him?
3B	3B	31B		Thus shall ye say (say ye) unto him,
3C	3C	31C		That/Because, the Lord hath need of him/them.
3D	3D			And straightway he will send him/them hither.
4				All this was done, that
4B				it might be fulfilled which was spoken by the prophet, saying,
5				Tell ye the daughter of Sion, (Zeck.9:9/Zeph.3:14,15)
5B				Behold, thy King cometh unto thee, meek, and sitting upon
5C				an ass, and a colt the foal of a beast of burden.
6	4	32		And they (the disciples) that were sent went their way,
6B				and did as Jesus had commanded them,
		32B		and found even as he had said unto them
	4B			And found the colt tied by the door, without (ie: outside),
	4C			in a place where 2 ways meet; and they loose him.
		33		And as they were loosening the colt,
	5	33B		Certain of them (the owners thereof) that stood there
	5B	33C		said unto them, What do ye loosing (why loose ye) the colt?
	6	34		And they said unto them
	6B	34B		(even as Jesus had commanded), The Lord has need of him.
	6C			And they let them go.
7	7	35		And they brought him/the colt (the ass and the colt) to Jesus:
7B				and put on them their clothes,
	7B	35B		and they cast their garments on him (upon the colt);
7C		35C		And they set him/Jesus thereon (ie: on the clothes/garments):
	7C			And he sat upon him (ie: a colt whereon yet never a man sat).
			14	And Jesus, when he had found a young ass, sat thereon.
			14B	As it is written,
			15	Fear not, daughter of Sion:
			15B	behold, thy King cometh, sitting on an ass's colt.
			16	These things understood not his disciples at the first:
			16B	but when Jesus was glorified, (Jn.14:26/Jn.16:13)
			16C	then remembered they that these things were written of him,
			16D	and that they had done these things unto him.
			17	The people therefore that was with him, when he called Lazarus
Therefore			17B	out of his grave, and raised him from the dead, bare record.
the Pharisees			18	For this cause the people also met him,
became very			18B	for that they heard that he had done this miracle.
frustrated.			19	The Pharisees therefore said among themselves, Perceive ye
			19B	how ye prevail nothing? behold, the world is gone after him.
8	8			And many, a very great multitude:
8B	8B	36		And as he went, they spread their garments/clothes in the way;
8C	8C			and others cut down branches
8D	8D			off/from the trees, and strawed them in the way.
9	9			And they (the multitude) that went before, and they that followed,
9B	9B			cried, saying, Hosanna to the son of David:
9C	9C			Blessed is he that cometh in the name of the Lord:
	10			Blessed be the kingdom of our father David,

Mt.21	Mk.11	Lk.19	Jn.12	
	10B			that cometh in the name of our Lord:
9D	10C			Hosanna in the highest.
		37		And when he was come nigh,
They		37B		even now at the descent of the mount of Olives,
began to		37C		The whole multitude of the disciples
rejoice		37D		began to rejoice and praise God with a loud voice
and		37E		for all the mighty works that they had seen;
praise		38		Saying, Blessed be the King that cometh in the name
God.		38B		of the Lord: peace in heaven, and glory in the highest.
		39		And some of the Pharisees from among the multitude
		39B		said unto him, Master, rebuke thy disciples.
		40		And he (ie: Jesus) answered and said unto them,
		40B		I tell you that, If these should hold their peace,
		40C		the stones would immediately cry out.
Jesus wept		41		And when he was come near, he beheld the city, and wept over it,
over		42		Saying, If thou hadst known, even thou - at least in this thy day,
Jerusalem.		42B		the things which belong unto thy peace!
		42C		But now they are hid from thine eyes.
		43		For the days shall come upon thee, (Lk.21:16-20/Mt.24:2)
		43B		that thine enemies shall cast a trench about thee,
		43C		and compass thee round, and keep thee in on every side.
		44		And shall lay thee even with the ground,
		44B		and thy children within thee;
		44C		And they shall not leave in thee one stone upon another;
		44D		because, thou knewest not the time of thy visitation.
	11			Jesus entered into Jerusalem:
10				And when he was come into Jerusalem,
10B				all the city was moved, saying, Who is this?
11				And the multitude said,
11B				This is Jesus the prophet of Nazareth of Galilee.
	11B			And Jesus went into the temple:
	11C			And when he had looked round about upon all things,
	11D			(and now the eventide was come):
17	11E			He left them, and went out of the city into Bethany with the 12;
17B				and he lodged there.
18	12			And on the morrow (in the morning) as he returned to the city,
18B	12B			when they were come from Bethany, he was hungry:
19	13			And seeing in the way, afar off - a fig tree having leaves,
	13B			he came, if haply he might find any thing thereon:
19B	13C			And when he came to it, he found nothing but leaves;
	13D			for the time of figs was not.
19C	14			And Jesus answered and said unto it,
19D				Let no fruit grow on thee henceforward for ever;
	14B			No man eat fruit of thee hereafter for ever.
	14C			And his disciples heard it.
19E				And presently (ie: immediately) the fig tree withered.
	15			And they come to Jerusalem:
12	15B	45		And Jesus went into the temple of God,
12B	15C	45B		and began to cast out
12C	15D	45C		all of them that sold and bought in the temple,
12D	15E			and overthrew the tables of the money-changers,
12E	15F			and the seats of them that sold doves;
	16			And would not suffer (ie: let) that any man
	16B			should carry any vessel through the temple.
13	17	46		And he taught, saying unto them,
13B	17B	46B		It is written, (Is.56:7/Jer.7:11)

Mt.21	Mk.11	Lk.19	Jn.12	
13C	17C	46C		My house is/shall be called of all nations the house of prayer:
13D	17D	46D		but ye have made it a den of thieves.
14				And the blind and the lame
14B				came to him in the temple; and he healed them.
15				And when the chief priests and scribes
15B				saw the wonderful things that he did,
15C	Out			and the children crying (ie: calling out, speak loudly)
15D	of			in the temple, and saying, Hosanna to the son of David:
15E	the			They (ie: the priests and the scribes) were sore displeased,
16	mouth			and said unto him, Hearest thou what they say?
16B	of			And Jesus said unto them
16C	babes.			Yea; have ye never read, Out of the mouth
16D				of babes and sucklings thou hast perfected praise? (Ps.8:2)
		47		And he taught daily in the temple,
	18			and the scribes and the chief priests heard it:
		47B		But the chief priests and scribes and the chief of the people
	18B	47C		sought how they might destroy him,
		48		and could not find what they might do:
	18C	48B		For they feared him, because all the people
	18D			was astonished at his doctrine,
		48C		were very attentive to hear him.

Certain Greeks			20	And there were certain Greeks
came to worship			20B	among them that came up to worship at the feast:
at the Feast.			21	The same came therefore
			21B	to Philip (which was of Bethsaida of Galilee), (Jn.1:44)
			21C	and desired (ie: besought/asked) him,
			21D	saying, Sir, we would see Jesus.
			22	Philip cometh and telleth Andrew:
			22B	and again Andrew and Philip tell Jesus.
			23	And Jesus answered them, saying, (Jn.13:31,32)
			23B	The hour is come, that the Son of man should be glorified.
			24	Verily, verily, I say unto you,
			24B	Except a corn (ie: a grain) of wheat
			24C	fall into the ground and die, it abideth alone:
			24D	but if it die, it bringeth forth much fruit.
			25	He that loveth his life shall lose it; (Mk.8:35)
			25B	and he that hateth his life in this world
			25C	shall keep it unto life eternal.
			26	If any man serve me, let him follow me;
			26B	and where I am, there shall also my servant be:
			26C	If any man serve me, him will my Father honour.
			27	Now is my soul troubled;
			27B	and what shall I say, Father, save me from this hour?
			27C	but for this cause came I unto this hour. (Mt.26:37-39)
A voice			28	Father, glorify thy name. (Jn.17:1,5)
from heaven			28B	Then came there a voice from heaven,
for your sakes			28C	saying, I have both glorified it, and will glorify it again.
			29	The people therefore, that stood by,
			29B	and heard it, said it thundered: (Ex.20:18/Ps.29:3)
			29C	others said, An angel spake to him.
			30	Jesus answered and said, This voice came not because of me,
			31	but for your sakes. Now is the judgment of this world.
			31B	Now shall the prince of this world be cast out. (Jn.16:11)
			32	And I, if I be lifted up from the earth, will draw all men unto me.
			33	This he said, signifying what death he should die. (Jn.3:14)

Mt.21   Mk.11   Lk.19   Jn.12

			34	The people answered him,
			34B	We have heard out of the law that Christ abideth for ever:
			34C	and how sayest thou, The Son must be lifted up?
			34D	Who is this Son of man?
			35	Then Jesus said unto them,
			35B	Yet a little while is the light with you. (Jn.1:9/Jn.8:12)
			35C	Walk while ye have the light, lest darkness come upon you:
			35D	for he that walketh in darkness knoweth not whither he goeth.
			36	While ye have light,
			36B	believe in the light, that ye may be children of light.
			36C	These things spake Jesus,
			36D	and departed, and did hide himself from them.
			37	But though he had
			37B	done so many miracles before them, yet they believed not on him.
			38	That the saying of Isaias the prophet might be fulfilled,

He hath
  blinded
    their eyes,
      and hardened
        their hearts.

			38B	which he spake, Lord, who hath believed our report? (Rom.10:16)
			38C	and to whom hath the arm of the Lord been revealed? (Is.53:1)
			39	Therefore they could not believe, because that Isaias said again,
			40	He hath blinded their eyes, and hardened their heart;
			40B	that they should not see with their eyes, nor understand with
			40C	their heart, and be converted, and I should heal them.
			41	These things said (2 Pe.1:7,9)(2 Thes.2:10,11)(2 Cor.4:4)
			41B	Esaias, when he saw his glory, and spake of him.(Is.6:1)

They loved the
  praise of men
  more than the
  praise of God.

			42	Nevertheless among the chief rulers also many believed on him:
			42B	but because of the Pharisees they did not confess him, lest
			42C	they should be put out of the synagogue: (Jn.7:13/Jn.9:22)
			43	For they loved the praise of men more than the praise of God.
			44	Jesus cried and said, He that
			44B	believeth on me, believeth not on me, but on him that sent me.
			45	And he that seeth me seeth him that sent me. (Jn.8:19/Jn.14:9)
			46	I am come a light into the world,
			46B	that whosoever believeth on me should not abide in darkness.
			47	And if any man hear my words, and believe not, I judge him not:
			47B	for I came not to judge the world, but to save the world.
			48	He that rejecteth me,
			48B	and receiveth not my words, hath one that judges him: the word
			48C	that I have spoken, the same shall judge him in the last day.
			49	For I have not spoken of myself;
			49B	but the Father which sent me, he - gave me commandment,
			49C	what I shall say, and what I shall speak. (Jn.7:16/Jn.14:10)

Jesus spake
  as the Father
    commanded him.

			50	And I know that his commandment is life everlasting:
			50B	whatsoever I speak therefore, (2 Cor.3:6/Jn.6:63)
			50C	even as the Father said unto me, so I speak. (Jn.14:24B)
		19		And when even was come, he went out of the city.
		20		And in the morning, as they passed by,
	20	20B		when they (the disciples) saw
		20C		the fig tree dried up from the roots;
20B				They marvelled, saying,
20C				How soon is the fig tree withered away!
		21		And Peter calling to remembrance said unto him, Master,
		21B		behold, the fig tree which thou cursedst is withered away.
21	22			And Jesus answering saith unto them, Have faith in God.
21B	23			For, verily I say unto you,
21C				If ye have faith, and doubt not,
21D				ye shall not only do this which is done to the fig tree;

Mt.21	Mk.11	Lk.19	Jn.12	
21E	23B			but also if ye (whosoever) shall say unto
21F	23C			this mountain, Be thou removed, and be thou cast into the sea,
	23D			and shall not doubt in his heart, but shall
	23E			believe that those things which he saith shall come to pass,
21G	23F			he shall have whatsoever he saith, it shall be done:
22				And all things whatsoever ye shall ask in prayer,
22B				believing, ye shall receive. (1 Jn.5:14/James 1:5;4:2,3)
	24			Therefore I say unto you, What things soever ye desire,
	24B			when ye pray, believe that ye receive, and ye shall have.
	25			And when ye stand praying,
	25B			forgive, if ye have ought against any: that your Father also
	25C			which is in heaven may forgive you your trespasses.
	26			But if ye do not forgive, neither will
	26B			your Father which is in heaven forgive your trespasses.

		Lk.20		
	27			And they came again to Jerusalem:
		1		And it came to pass, on one of those days,
23	27B			when he (ie: Jesus) was walking in (come into) the temple,
23		1B		and as he taught (was teaching) the people in the temple,
23D		1C		and preached the gospel;
23B	27C	1D		The chief priests and the scribes
23C	27D	1E		came upon (unto) him, with the elders,
23E	28	2		And spake unto him, saying, Tell us,
23F	28B	2B		by what authority doest thou these things? and/or who
23G	28C	2C		is he that gave thee this authority to do these things?
24	29	3		And Jesus answered and said unto them,
24B	29B	3B		I will also ask of you one thing (one question),
24C	29C			which, if ye tell/answer me, and I in like wise
24D	29D			will tell you by what authority I do these things.
	30B	3C		Answer me:
25	30A	4		The baptism of John, whence was it from heaven, or of men?
25B	31	5		And they reasoned with themselves,
25C	31B	5B		saying, If we shall say, From heaven;
25D	31C	5C		he will say unto us, Why then did ye not believe him?
26	32	6		But if we shall say, Of men (they feared the people);
26B	32B	6B		all the people will stone us:
		6C		For they (ie: the people) be persuaded,
26C	32C	6D		(for all counted/hold) that he (John) was a prophet indeed.
27	33	7		And they answered and said unto Jesus,
27B	33B	7B		We cannot tell (they could not tell whence it was).
27C	33C	8		And Jesus answering saith unto them,
27D	33D	8B		Neither tell I you by what authority I do these things.

	Mk.12			
	1			And he (ie: Jesus) began to speak unto them by parables.
28				But what think ye? A certain man had 2 sons;
28B				And he came to the first,
28C				and said, Son, go work to day in my vineyard.
29				He answered and said, I will not:
29B				but afterward he repented, and went.
30				And he came to the second, and said likewise.
30B				And he answered and said, I go, sir; and went not.
31				Whether of them twain did the will of his father?
31B				They say unto him, The first.
31C				Jesus saith unto them, Verily I say unto you, that the publicans
31D				and the harlots go into the kingdom of God before you.(Mt.5:20)
32				For John came unto you
32B				in the way of righteousness, and ye believed him not:

Mt.21 Mk.12 Lk.20 Jn.12

32C			But the publicans and the harlots believed him:
32D			And ye, when ye had seen,
32E			repented not afterward, that ye might believe him.
33			Hear another parable.
		9	Then began he to speak to the people this parable:
33B	1B	9B	There was a certain man (a householder) which planted a vineyard,
33C	1C		and hedged it (set a hedge) round about,
33D	1D		and digged a place for a winefat (digged a wine press in it),
33E	1E		And built a tower,
33F	1F		and let it forth/out to husbandmen:
33G	1G		And went into a far country, for a long time.
34	2	10	And at the season (when the time of the fruit drew near),
34B	2B	10B	He sent his servants to the husbandmen, that they might receive
34C	2C	10C	from the husbandmen of the fruit of the vineyard.
35			The husbandmen took his servant(s):
35B	3	10D	And beat one (they caught/took him),
	3B	10E	and the husbandmen beat him, and sent him away empty.
		11	And again he sent another servant.
		11B	and they beat him also,
		11C	and entreated him shamefully, and sent him away empty.
		12	And again he sent a third,
		12B	and they wounded him also, and cast him out.
	4		And again he sent another servant,
35D	4B		and (they stoned another) at him they cast stones,
	4C		and wounded him in the head,
	4D		and send him away shamefully handled.
	5		And again he sent another,
35C	5B		and (they killed another) him they killed.
36	5C		And again he sent other servants (many others/more than the first);
36B			And they did unto them likewise,
	5D		beating some, and killing some.
		13	Then said the lord of the vineyard, What shall I do?
	6		Having yet therefore one son, his Wellbeloved.
		13B	I will send my beloved son;
37	6B		And he sent him to them last (last of all) saying,
37B	6C	13C	It may be that they will reverence him - when they see him.
38		14	But, when the husbandmen saw him (the son),
38B	7	14B	those husbandmen said (reasoned) among themselves,
38C		14C	saying, This is the heir; Come, let us kill him, and let us
38D		14D	seize on his inheritance (the inheritance shall be ours).
39	8		And they took/caught him,
39B	8B	15	and they slew (killed) him, and cast him out of the vineyard.
40	9	15B	When therefore the lord of the vineyard cometh, what shall
40B	9B	15C	therefore the lord of the vineyard do unto those husbandmen?
	9C	16	He shall come and destroy these husbandmen,
	9D	16B	and shall give the vineyard unto others.
		16C	And when they heard, they said, God forbid (ie: It must not be).

> Note: they (the people) understood (they felt the pain)
> of the lord of the vineyard, and responded, It must not
> be (ie: this should not have happened). And they gave
> their approval for what he did to correct the situation.

41			And they say unto him,
41B			He will miserably destroy those wicked men,
41C			and will let out his vineyard unto other husbandmen,

Mt.21	Mk.12	Lk.20	Jn.12	
41D				which shall render him the fruits in their seasons.
42		17		And he (ie: Jesus) beheld them, and saith unto them,
42B	10			Did you not/never read the scripture(s)?
		17B		What is this then that is written,
42C	10B	17C		The stone which the builders rejected
42D	10C	17D		the same is become the head of the corner:
42E	11			This was the Lord's doing, and it is marvellous in our eyes?
43				Therefore say I unto you,
43B				The kingdom of God shall be taken from you,
43C				and given to a nation bringing forth the fruits thereof.
44		18		And whosoever shall fall on this/that stone shall be broken,
44B		18B		but on whomsoever it shall fall, it will grind him to powder.
45				And when the chief priests and Pharisees had heard his parables,
45B	12C	19D		for they perceived (they knew)
45C	12D	19E		that he spake (had spoken) this parable of/against them:
		19A		And the chief priests and the scribes
		19B		that same hour sought to lay hands on him;
46	12A			But when they sought to lay hands (hold) on him,
46B	12B	19C		they feared the people (the multitude),
46C				because they took him for a prophet.

Mt.22				
		20		And they watched him.
1				And Jesus answered and spake unto them again by parables,
2				and said, The kingdom of heaven is like unto a certain king,
2B				which made a marriage for his son,
3				And sent forth his servants to call them that
3B				were bidden to the wedding: and they would not come.
4				Again, he sent forth other servants, saying,
4B				Tell them which are bidden, Behold, I have prepared my dinner:
4C				my oxen and my fatlings are killed,
4D				and all things are ready: Come unto the marriage.
5				But they made light of it, and went their ways,
5B				one to his farm, another to his merchandise:
6				And the remnant took his servants, and
6B				entreated them spitefully, and slew (ie: killed) them.
7				But when the king heard there of, he was wroth:
7B				and he sent forth his armies,
7C				and destroyed those murderers, and burned up their city.
8				Then saith he to his servants, The wedding is ready,
8B				but they which were bidden were not worthy.
9				Go ye therefore into the highways,
9B				and as many as ye shall find, bid to the marriage.
10				So those servants went out into the highways, and
10B				gathered together all as many as they found, both bad and good:
10C				and the wedding was furnished with guests.
11				And when the king came in to see the guests,
11B				he saw there a man which had not on a wedding garment:
12				And he saith unto him, Friend,
12B				how camest thou in hither not having a wedding garment?
12C				And he was speechless.
13				Then said the king to his servants, Bind him hand and foot,
13B				and take away, and cast him into outer darkness;
13C				there shall be weeping and gnashing of teeth.
14				For many are called, but few are chosen.
	12E			And they (ie: they who sought to lay hold on Jesus), (Mk.11:27)
	12F			left him, and went their way.
15				Then went the Pharisees,

Mt.22	Mk.12	Lk.20	
15B			and took counsel how they might entangle him in his talk.
16	13	20B	And they sent forth (sent out) unto him spies;
16B	13B		certain of the Pharisees (their disciples) and of the Herodians,
		20C	which should feign (ie: to pretend) themselves just men,
	13C	20D	that they might take hold of (to catch him in) his words,
		20E	so that they might deliver him
		20F	unto the power and authority of the governor.
	14	21	And when they were come, they say unto him (they asked him),
16C	14B	21B	saying, Master, we know that thou art true,
		21C	and that thou sayest and teachest rightly;
16E	14C		Neither carest thou for any man (carest for no man),
		21D	Neither acceptest thou the person,
16F	14D		for thou regardest not the person of men,
16D	14E	21E	But teachest the way of God truly (in truth).
17			Tell us therefore, What thinkest thou?
17B	14F	22	Is it lawful for us to give tribute unto Caesar or not;
	15		shall we give, or shall we not give?
	15B		But he (Jesus) knowing their hypocrisy;
18		23	Jesus perceived their wickedness (their craftiness),
18B	15C	23B	and said unto them, Why tempt ye me, ye hypocrites?
19	15D	24	bring/shew me a penny (the tribute money) that I may see.
19B	16		And they brought to him a penny.
20	16B	24B	And he saith unto them, Whose image and superscription hath it?
21	16C	24C	They answered and said unto him, Caesar's.
21B	17	25	And Jesus answering, then saith unto them,
21C	17B	25B	Render therefore unto Caesar the things which be Caesar's,
21D	17C	25C	and unto God the things that/which be God's.
22			And when they had heard these words,
		26	and they could not take hold of his words before the people:
22B	17D	26B	And they marvelled at him (at his answer),
22C		26C	and held their peace; and left him, and went their way.
23			The same day:
23B	18	27	Then came unto him certain of the Sadducees,
23C	18B	27B	which say there is no (deny there is any) resurrection;
23D	18C	27C	And they asked him, saying,
24		28	Master, Moses said/wrote unto us,
24B	19	28B	If a man die, and leave behind a wife having no children,
24C	19B	28C	that his brother should take (marry) his wife,
24D	19C	28D	and raise up seed unto his brother.
25	20	29	Now there were therefore (with us) 7 brethren;
25B	20B	29B	And the 1st. took/married a wife,
25C	20C	29C	and he deceased/died without (having no) issue (ie: seed),
25D			left his wife to his brother:
26	21	30	And the 2nd. took her to wife,
26B	21B	30B	and neither left he any seed (he died childless):
26C	21C	31	And the 3rd. likewise took her, and in like manner the 7 also:
	22	31B	And the 7 had her, and they left no seed (no children), and died.
27	22B	32	And last of all the woman died also.
28	23	33	Therefore in the resurrection, when they shall rise,
28B	23B	33B	whose wife shall she be of them? for all the 7 had her to wife.
29	24	34	And Jesus answering said unto them,
29B	24B		Do ye not therefore err? Ye do err,
29C	24C		because ye know not the scriptures, neither the power of God.
		34B	The children of this world marry, and are given in marriage:
		35	But they which shall be accounted worthy
		35B	to obtain that world, and the resurrection from the dead;
30	25		For in the resurrection when they rise from the dead,
30B	25B	35C	they neither marry, nor are given in marriage:

Mt.22	Mk.12	Lk.20	Jn.12

```
                    36              Neither can they die any more: for
 30C       25C      36B                they are as (equal unto) the angels of God which are in heaven;
                    36C                And are the children of God,
                    36D                   being the children of the resurrection.
 31        26                       And as touching the resurrection of the dead, that they rise:
                    37              Now that the dead are raised, even Moses [was] shewed at the bush;
                    37B                When he calleth the Lord
                    37C                the God of Abraham, and the God of Isaac, and the God of Jacob.
 31B       26B                      Have ye not read
 31C       26C                          that which was spoken unto you by God:  In the book of Moses,
 32        26D                          How in the bush God spake unto him (unto you), saying, I am
 32B       26E                          the God of Abraham, and the God of Isaac, and the God of Jacob?
 32C       27       38              For God is not the/a God of the dead, but the God of the living;
 29B+      27B      38B                     ye therefore do greatly err, for all live unto him.
 33                                 And when the
 33B                                    multitude heard this, they were astonished at his doctrine.

 34                                 But when the Pharisees had heard that he
 34B                                    had put the Sadducees to silence, they were gathered together.
 35        28                       And one of them, a lawyer (one of the scribes) came;
           28B                      And having heard them reasoning together,
           28C                          and perceiving that he had answered them well,
 35B       28D                          asked him, tempting him, and saying, Master, which is
 36        28E                          the great commandment in the law, the first commandment of all?
 37        29                       And Jesus said unto (answered) him,
           29B                      The 1st. of all commandments is,
           29C                          Hear, O Israel; The LORD our God is one LORD:
 37B       30                           And thou shalt love the LORD thy God
 37C       30B                              with all thy heart, and with all thy soul,
 37D       30C                              and with all thy mind, and with all thy strength:
 38        30D                      This is the first and great commandment.
 39        31                       And the 2nd. is like unto it, namely this,
 39B       31B                          Thou shalt love thy neighbour as thyself.
           31C                      There is none other commandment greater than these.
 40                                 On these 2 commandments hang all the law and the prophets.

                    39              Then certain of the scribes
                    39B                 answering said, Master, thou hast well said.
           32                       And the scribe said unto him,                           (Mk.12:28A)
           32B                          Well, Master, thou hast said the truth:
           32C                          for there is one God; and there is none other but he:
           33                           And to love him with all the heart,
           33B                          and with all the understanding, and with all the soul, and
           33C                          with all the strength, and to love his neighbour as himself,
           33D                          is more than all whole burnt offerings and sacrifices.(Hos.6:6)
           34                       And when Jesus saw that he answered discreetly, he said
           34B                          unto him, Thou art not far from the kingdom of God.
           34C      40              And after that no man durst ask him any question.

 41                                 While the Pharisees were gathered together:
 41B                                Jesus asked them,
 42                                     saying, What think ye of Christ? whose son is he?
 42B                                They say unto him, The son of David.
 43        35       41              And Jesus answered and said unto them,                  (Mt.22:42A)
           35B                          while he taught in the temple,
           35C      41B                 How say they (the scribes) that Christ is the son of David?
 43B       36                       For how then doth David himself,
 43C       36B                          by the Holy Ghost (in spirit call him Lord), saying,
                    42                  (And David himself saith in the book of Psalms,)
 44        36C      42B                 The LORD said unto my Lord, Sit thou at my right hand,
```

Mt.22	Mk.12	Lk.20	Jn.12	
44B	36D	43		till I make thine enemies thy footstool. (Ps.110:1)
45	37	44		If David therefore calleth him Lord, and whence is he his son?
46				And no man was able to answer him a word, neither
46B				durst any man from that day forth, ask him any more questions.
	37B			And the common people heard him gladly.

Mt.23				
1	38	45		Then, spake (said) Jesus, unto them in his doctrine,
		45B		in the audience of all the people he said unto his disciples,
1B				(to the multitude and to his disciples).
2	38B	46		Saying, Beware of the scribes,
	38C	46B		who desire/love to walk in long robes (clothing):
2B				The scribes and the Pharisees sit in Moses' seat:
3	Beware of			All therefore whatsoever they bid you observe - observe and do;
3B	the scribes!			but do not ye after their works: for they say, and do not.
4	The scribes			For they bind heavy burdens (Mt.21:30)
4B	and			and grievous to be borne (ie: to undergo/to live up to),
4C	the Pharisees			and lay them on men's shoulders; but they themselves will not
4D	sit in			move them with one of their fingers. (Lk.11:46)
5	Moses' seat.			But all their works they do for to be seen of men:
5B				They make broad their phylacteries
				(ie: via extravagant and literal visible methods, see Ex.13:9.)
5C				and enlarge the borders of their garments.
6	39B	46E		And love the uppermost (chief) rooms at feasts,
6B	39A	46D		and the chief (highest) seats in the synagogues;
7	38D	46C		And love salutations (greetings) in the marketplaces,
7B				and to be called of men, Rabbi, Rabbi.
8				But be not ye called Rabbi:
8B				for one is your Master, even Christ; and all ye are brethren.
9				And call no man your Father upon earth:
9B				for one is your Father, which is in heaven.
10				Neither be ye called Masters:
10B				for one is your Master, even Christ.
11				But he that is greatest among you shall be your servant.
12	Woe!			And ehosoever shall exalt himself shall be abased;
12B	unto			and he that shall humble himself shall be exalted.
13	you scribes			But woe unto you, scribes and Pharisees, hypocrites!
13B	and Pharisees,			For ye shut up the kingdom of heaven against men:
13C	hypocrites.			For ye neither go in yourselves,
13D				neither suffer ye them (that are entering) to go in.
14				Woe unto you, scribes and Pharisees, hypocrites!
14B	40	47		For ye devour widows' houses,
14C	40B	47B		And for a pretence (for a shew) make long peayer(s):
14D	40C	47C		therefore ye shall receive the greater damnation.
15				Woe unto you, scribes and Pharisees, hypocrites!
15B				For ye compass sea and land to make one proselyte,
15C				and when he is made, (Mt.16:12/Mk.8:15/Lk.21:1)
15D				ye make him twofold more the child of hell than yourselves.
16				Woe unto you, ye blind guides, which say:
16B				Whosoever shall swear by the temple, it is nothing; but whosoever
16C				shall swear by the gold of the temple, he is a debtor!
17				Ye fools and blind: for whether is greater,
17B				the gold, or the temple that sanctifieth the gold?
18				And, Whosoever shall swear by the altar, it is nothing; but
18B				whosoever sweareth by the gift that is upon it, he is guilty.
19				Ye fools and blind: for whether is greater,
19B				the gift, or the altar that sanctifieth the gift?
20				Therefore,
20B				Whoso shall swear by the altar,

Mt.23 Mk.12 Lk.20 Jn.12

20C			swaereth by it, and by all things thereon.
21			And whoso shall swear by the temple,
21B			swearest by it, and by him that dwelleth therein.
22			And he that shall swear by heaven, sweareth
22B			by the throne of God, and by him that sitteth thereon.
23			Woe unto you, scribes and Pharisees, hypocrites!
23B			For ye pay tithe of mint and anise and cummin, and have omitted
23C			the weightier matters of the law, judgment, mercy, and faith:
23D			these ought ye to have done, and not leave the other undone.
24			Ye blind guides, which strain at a gnat, and swallow a camel.
25			Woe unto you, scribes and Pharisees, hypocrites!
25B			For ye make clean the outside of the cup and of the platter,
25C			but within they are full of extortion and excess. (Lk.11:38)
26			Thou blind Pharisee,
26B			cleanse first that which is within the cup and platter.
26C			that the outside of them may be clean also.
27			Woe unto you, scribes and Pharisees, hypocrites!
27B			For ye are like unto whited sepulchres,
27C			which indeed appear beautiful outward, but
27D			are within full of dead men's bones, and of all uncleanness.
28			Even so ye also outwardly appear righteous unto men,
28B			but within ye are full of hypocrisy and iniquity.
29			Woe unto you, scribes and Pharisees, hypocrites!
29B			Because ye build the tombs of the prophets,
29C			and garnish (ie: decorate) the sepulchres of the righteous,
30			And say, If we had been in the days of our fathers, we would not
30B			have been partakers with them in the blood of the prophets.
31			Wherefore ye be witnesses unto yourselves,
31B			that ye are the children of them which killed the prophets.
32			Ye then also fulfil the measure of your fathers:
33			Ye serpents, ye generation of vipers, how can
33B			ye escape the damnation of hell (ie: the judgment of Gehenna)?
34			Wherefore, behold,
34B			I send unto you prophets, and wise men, and scribes:
34C			And some of them ye shall kill and crucify;
34D			And some of them shall ye scourge in your synagogues,
34E			and persecute them from city to city:
35			That upon you may come (Gen.4:8,10)(2 Chron.24:20,21)
35B			all the righteous blood shed upon the earth, from the blood of
35C			righteous Abel unto the blood of Zacharias (son of Barachias),
35D			whom ye slew between the temple and the altar. (Lk.11:50,51)
36			Verily I say unto you,
36B			All these things shall come upon this generation.
37			O Jerusalem, Jerusalem, thou that killest the prophets, and
37B			stonest them which are sent unto thee, how often would I have
37C			gathered thy children together, even as a hen gathereth her
37D			chichens under her wings, and ye would not! (Jn.12:46,47)
38			Behold, your house is left unto you desolate. (Gal.4:27)
39			For I say unto you,
39B			Ye shall not see me henceforth, till ye shall say,
39C			Blessed is he that cometh in the name of the Lord.
		Lk.21	
	41		And Jesus sat over against the treasury,
	41B		and beheld how the people cast money into the treasury:
		1	And he looked up,
		1B	and saw the rich men casting their gifts into the treasury,
	41C		and many that were rich cast in much.

```
Mt.23  Mk.12  Lk.21  Jn.12
       42     2              And there came (and he saw also) a certain poor widow,
       42B    2B                 and casting in thither (she threw in) 2 mites (= 1 farthing).
       43                    And he called unto him his disciples,
       43B    3                 and saith unto them, Of a truth (Verily) I say unto you,
       43C    3B                that this poor widow hath cast in more than all they
       43D                      which have cast into the treasury:
       44     4                 For all these have cast in of their abundance
              4B                   unto the offerings of God.
       44B    4C                But she of her penury (she of her want)
       44C    4D                   has cast in all the/her living that she had.        (Lk.15:12)

Mt.24  Mk.13
1      1                     And Jesus went out, and departed from the temple:
1B                           And his disciples
1C                              came to him for to shew him the buildings of the temple.
       5                     And as some spake of the temple,
       5B                       how it was adorned with goodly stones and gifts.
       1B                    One of his disciples saith unto him,
       1C                       Master, see what manner of stones and what buildings!
2      2      5              And he (Jesus) answering said unto him/them,
       2B                    Seest thou these great buildings?
2B                              See ye not all these things? verily I say unto you,
              6                 As for these things which ye behold, the days will come,
2C     2C     6B                   in which there shall not be left here one stone upon another,
2D     2D     6C                      that shall not be thrown down.        (Lk.19:44)

3      3                     And as he sat upon the mount of Olives over against the temple,
3B     3B                       the disciples (Peter, James, John and Andrew) came unto him,
3C     3C     7              And they asked him privately, saying,
3D     4      7B                Master, tell us, when shall these things be?
3E     4B     7C                And what shall be the sign
       4C     7D                   -when all these things shall come to pass (be fulfilled)?
3F                                 -of thy coming, and of the end of the world (ie: age)?
4      5      8              And Jesus answering them began to say, Take heed,
4B     5B     8B                that no man (lest any) deceive you: be ye not deceived,
5      6      8C                For many shall come in my name, saying, I am Christ;
5B     6B                       and shall deceive many.
              8D                And the time draweth near: go ye not therefore after them.
6      7      9              And when ye shall hear of wars and commotions (rumours of wars),
6B     7B     9B                see that ye be not troubled/terrified:
6C     7C     9C                For all these things must needs be (must first come to pass);
6D     7D     9D                but the end is not by and by (the end shall not be yet).
              10             Then he (ie: Jesus) said unto them,
7      8      10B            Nation shall rise against nation, and kingdom against kingdom:
7C     8B     11                And there shall be great earthquakes in divers places,
7B     8C     11B  Beginning    And there shall be famines, and troubles, and pestilence,
              11C   of          And fearful sights and great signs shall there be from heaven:
8      8D          sorrows.        All these are the beginnings of sorrows.
       9      12            But before all these things (take heed to yourselves)
              12B               they shall lay hands on you, and persecute you,
              12C               delivering you up to the synagogues, and in prisons:
       9B                       For they shall deliver you up to councils,
       9C                       and in the synagogues ye shall be beaten.
       9D     12D               And ye shall be brought before rulers and kings for my sake;
       9E     13                and it shall turn to you for a testimony - against them.
       10                    And the gospel must first be published among all nations.
9      11                   But then/when they shall lead you,
9B     11B                     and deliver you up to be afflicted, and to kill you; take no
       11C    14B              thought beforehand what ye shall speak/answer:        (Lk.12:11,12)
```

Mt.24	Mk.13	Lk.21	Jn.12	
		11D	14A	Settle it therefore in your hearts not to premeditate;
		15		for I will give you a mouth and wisdom, (Mt.10:16-20)
		15B		which your adversaries shall not be able to gainsay nor resist:
	11E			But whatsoever shall be given you in that hour, that speak ye;
	11F			for it is not ye that speak, but the Holy Ghost.
		16		And ye shall be betrayed
		16B		both by parents, and brethren, and kinfolks, and friends;
	12			Now the brother shall betray the brother to death, (Mt.10:21-23)
	12B			and the father the son; and the children shall rise up
	12C			against their parents, and shall cause them to be put to death.
		16C		And some of you shall they cause to be put to death.
9C	13	17		And ye shall be hated of all nations for my name's sake:
		18		But there shall not an hair of your head perish.
		19		In your patience possess ye your souls.
10				And then shall many be offended,
10B				and shall betray one another, and shall hate one another.
11				And many false prophets shall rise, and shall deceive many.
12				And because iniquity (ie: the transgression of the law)
12B				shall abound, the love of many shall wax cold. (1 Jn.3:4)
13	13B			But he that shall endure unto the end, the same shall be saved.
14				And this gospel of the kingdom shall be preached
14B				in all the world for a witness unto the nations;
14C				And then shall the end come.
15	14			But when ye therefore shall see the abomination of desolation,
15B	14B			spoken of by Daniel the prophet, (Dan.9:27)(2 Thes.2:4)
15C	14C			standing (where it ought not) in the holy place.
		20		And when ye shall see Jerusalem compassed with armies, then know
		20B		that the desolation thereof is nigh. (Mt.24:15-19,29-31)
15D	14D			Whoso/him that readeth, let him understand. (Lk.19:43,44)
16	14E	21		Then let them which be in Judaea flee to/into the mountains;
		21B		and let them which be in the midst of it depart out;
		21C		And let not them that are in the countries enter thereinto.
17	15			And let him that is on the housetop not go down into the house,
17B	15B			neither enter therein, to take any thing out of the/his house:
18	16			And let him that is in the field
18B	16B			not turn back again for to take up his garment (his clothes).
		22		For these be the days of vengeance
		22B		that all things which are written may be fulfilled.
19	17	23		But woe unto them that are with child,
19B	17B	23B		and to them that give suck, in those days!
		23C		For there shall be great distress in the land,
		23D		and wrath upon this people. (Rom.5:9/Col.3:6/Rev.7:3)
20	18			And pray ye that your flight be not in the winter
20B				neither on the sabbath day (ie: in the sabbath):
21	19			For in those days shall be affliction (great tribulation),
21B		The		such as was not from the beginning of the world (ie: kosmos):
	19B	days		such as was not from the beginning of creation which God created
21C	19C	of the		unto this time, neither shall be/no, nor ever shall be.
22	20	Great		And except that the Lord
22B	20B	Tribulation		had shortened those days, there should no flesh be saved.
22C	20C	be		But for the elect's sake, whom he hath chosen, (Eph.1:4)
22D	20D	shortened.		those days shall be (he hath) shortened. (Rev.7:9)
23	21			Then if any man shall say unto you, (1 Jn.4:1/Ge.16:42/Re.2:2,10)
23B	21B			Lo, here is Christ, or lo, he is there; believe him/it not
24	22			For there shall arise false Christs, and false prophets,
24B	22B			and shall shew great signs and wonders, insomuch that, if it
24C	22C			were possible, they shall deceive/seduce even the very elect.

| Mt.24 | Mk.13 | Lk.21 | Jn.12 |

```
25       23                      But take heed: Behold, I have foretold you all things.
                 24              And they shall fall by the edge of the sword,
                 24B                 and shall be led away captive into all nations:
                 24C                     And Jerusalem shall be trodden down of the Gentiles, (Lk.21:20)
                 24D                         until the times of the Gentiles be fulfilled.
26                               Wherefore if they shall say unto you,
26B                                  Behold, he is in the desert; go not forth:
26C                                  Behold, he is in the secret chambers; believe it not.
27                               For as the lightning cometh out of the east, and shineth even
27B                                  unto the west; so shall also the coming of the Son of man be.
28                               For wheresoever the carcase is
28B                                  there will the eagles be gathered together.    (Lk.17:37)
29B      24                      But in those days,                                  (1 Thess.5:3-6)
29A      24B                     Immediately (ie: anon/shortly/forthwith) after the tribulation,
                 25              There shall be signs in the sun, and in the moon, and in the stars:
29C      24C                     The sun shall be darkened, and the moon shall
29D      25                          not give her light, and the stars of heaven shall fall.
                 25B             And upon the earth distress of nations,
                 25C                 with perplexity; the sea and the waves roaring;
                 26                  Men's hearts failing them for fear, and looking after
                 26B                     those things which are coming on the earth:
29E      25B     26C             For/And the powers of/in the heavens shall be shaken:
30                               And then shall appear the sign of the Son of man in heaven:
30B                                  And then shall all the tribes of the earth mourn,
30C      26      27                  And then shall they see the Son of man coming in the
30D      26B     27B                     clouds of heaven (in a cloud) with power and great glory.
31       27                      And then shall he send his angels with a great sound of a trumpet,
31B      27B                         and they shall gather together the/his elect from the 4 winds,
         27C                             from the uttermost part of the earth
         27D                                 to the uttermost part of heaven:
31C                                  from one end of heaven to the other.
                 28              And when these things begin to come to pass, then look up,
                 28B                 and lift up your heads; for your redemption draweth nigh.
                 29              And he (ie: Jesus) spoke to them a parable:
32       28                      Now learn the parable of the fig tree:
                 29B                 Behold the fig tree, and all the trees;
32B      28B                         When the branch is yet tender, and putteth forth leaves;
                 30                  When they now shoot forth, ye see and know of your own selves,
32C      28C     30B                     ye know that the summer is near (is now nigh at hand).
33       29      31              So ye likewise (in like manner)
33B      29B     31B                 when ye shall see all these things come to pass,
                 31C                     know ye that the kingdom of God is nigh at hand:
33C      29C                             know that it is near/nigh, even at the doors.
34       30      32              Verily I say unto you, that this generation
34B      30B     32B                 shall not pass away, till all these things be done/fulfilled.
35       31      33                  Heaven and earth shall pass away,
35B      31B     33B                     but my words shall not pass away.

36       32                      But of that day and that hour knoweth no man,
36B      32B                         not the angel which are in (of) heaven,
36C      32C                         not the Son, but (ie: if not) the/my Father only.
37                               But as the days of Noe were,
37B                                  so shall also the coming of the Son of man be.
38                               For as in the days that were before the flood,
38B                                  they were eating and drinking, marrying and giving in marriage,
38C                                      until the day - that Noe entered into the ark,       (Gen.7:17)
39       They were destroyed.    And knew not until the flood came, and took them all away;
39B                                      so shall also the coming of the Son of man be.(Gen.6:13)
```

122 | Assembly by John Douma

Mt.24	Mk.13	Lk.21	Jn.12		
40				Then shall	(Mt:26-28/Lk.17:34-37)
40B				2 be in the field; the one shall be taken, and the other left.	
41				2 grinding at the mill;	
41B				the one shall be taken, and the other left.	(Lk.17:37)
	33	34		Take ye heed:	
		34B		to yourselves, lest at any time your hearts be overcharged	
		34C		with surfeiting, and drunkenness, and the cares of this life,	
		34D		and that day come upon you unawares.	(Rev.3:3)
		35		For as a snare shall it come on all them	
		35B		that dwell on the face of the whole earth.	
	33B			Watch and pray: for ye know not when the time is.	(Mk.13:32)
	34			Like unto a man taking a far journey,	
	34B			who left his house, and gave authority to his servants,	
	34C			and to every man his work, and commanded the porter to watch.	
42	35	36		Watch ye therefore:	
	35B			For ye know not when the master of the house cometh, at even,	
	35C			or at midnight, or at the cock-crowing, or in the morning:	
	36			Lest coming suddenly he find you sleeping.	
	37			And what I say unto you I say unto all, Watch!	
42B				for ye know not what hour your Lord doth come.	
43				But know this, that if the goodman of the house had known	
43B				in what watch the thief would come, he would have watched,	
43C				and would not have suffered his house to be broken up.	
44				Therefore be ye also ready:	
44B				for in such an hour as ye think not the Son of man cometh.	
		36B		And pray always, that ye may be accounted worthy	
		36C		to escape all these things that shall come to pass,	
		36D		and to stand before the Son of man.	(Ps.1:5)
		37		And in the day time he was teaching in the temple;	(Lk.19:47,48)
		37B		and at night he went out,	
		37C		and abode in the mount that is called the mount of Olives.	
		38		And all the people came	
		38B		early in the morning to him in the temple, for to hear him.	
45		A wise servant.		Who then is a faithful and wise servant, whom his lord hath made	
45B				ruler over his household, to give them meat in due season?	
46				Blessed is that servant,	
46B				whom his lord when he cometh shall find so doing.	
47				Verily I say unto you,	
47B				That he shall make him ruler over all his goods.	
48		An evil servant.		But, if that evil servant shall say in his heart,	(2 Pe.3:4)
49				My lord delayeth his coming; and shall begin to smite	
49B				his fellowservants, and to eat, and drink with the drunken;	
50				The lord of that servant	
50B				shall come in a day when he looketh not for him,	(Rev.3:3)
51				and in an hour that he is not aware of, and shall cut	
51B				him asunder, and appoint him his portion with the hypocrites:	
51C				There shall be weeping and gnashing of teeth.	
Mt.25					
1				Then shall the kingdom of heaven be likened unto 10 virgins,	
1B				which took their lamps, and went forth to meet the bridegroom.	
2				And 5 of them were wise, and 5 were foolish.	
3		Foolish		They that were foolish took their lamps, and took no oil with them:	
4		and Wise		But the wise took oil in their vessels with their lamps.	
5		virgins.		While the bridegroom tarried, they all slumbered and slept.	
6				And at midnight there was a cry made,	
6B				Behold, the Bridegroom Cometh; go ye out to meet him.	

Mt.25 Mk.13 Lk.21 Jn.12

7		And all those virgins arose, and trimmed their lamps.
8		And the foolish said unto the wise,
8B		Give us of your oil; for our lamps are gone out.
9		But the wise answered, saying,
9B		Not so; lest there be not enough for us and you:
9C		but go ye rather to them that sell, and buy for yourselves.
10		And while they went to buy, the bridegroom came;
10B		and they that were ready went in with him to the marriage:
10C		And the door was shut. (Gen.7:16)
11		Afterward came also
11B		the other virgins, saying, Lord, Lord, open to us.
12		But he answered
12B		and said, Verily, I say unto you, I know you not. (Rev.3:3)
13		Watch therefore, for ye know neither
13B		the day nor the hour wherein the Son of man cometh.
14		For ----------------- as a man travelling into a far country,
14B	To every man	who called his own servants, and delivered unto them his goods.
15	according to	And unto one he gave 5 talents, to another 2, and to another 1;
15B	his ability.	to every man according to his several ability:
15C		And straightway took his journey.
16		Then he that received the 5 talents
16B		went and traded with the same, and made them other 5 talents.
17		And likewise he that had received 2, he also gained other 2.
18		But he that had received 1,
18B		went and digged in the earth, and hid his lord's money.
19		After a long time
19B		the lord of those servants cometh, and reckoneth with them.
20		And so he that had received 5 talents came, and brought other
20B		5 talents: saying, Lord, thou deliveredst unto me 5 talents:
20C		behold, I have gained beside them 5 talents more.
21		His lord said unto him, Well done, good and faithful servant:
21B		Thou hast been faithful over a few things, I will make thee
21C		ruler over many things: enter thou into the joy of thy lord.
22		He that had received 2 talents also came,
22B		and said, Lord, thou deliveredst unto me 2 talents:
22C		behold, I have gained 2 other talents beside them.
23		His lord said unto him, Well done, good and faithful servant:
23B		Thou hast been faithful over a few things, I will make thee
23C		ruler over many things: enter thou into the joy of thy lord.
24		Then he which had received the 1 talent came, and said, Lord,
24B		I knew thee - that thou art an hard man, reaping where
24C		thou hast not sown, and gathering where thou hast not strawed:
25		And I was afraid, and went and hid thy talent in the earth:
25B		lo, there thou hast that is thine. (Lk.19:20,21)
26		His lord answered and said unto him, (Lk.19:22-27)
26B		Thou wicked and slothful (ie: grievous) servant,
26C		thou knewest that I reap where I sowed not,
26D		and gather where I have not strawed (ie: have not scattered):
27		Thou oughtest therefore to have put my money to the exchangers,
27B		and then at my coming
27C		I should have received mine own with usury.
28		Take therefore the talent from him, (Lk.19:26)(Mt.13:12)
29		and give it unto him which hath 10 talents. For unto every one
29B		that hath shall be given, and he shall have abundance: but from
29C		him that hath not shall be taken away even that which he hath.
30		And cast ye the unprofitable servant into outer darkness:
30B		there shall be weeping and gnashing of teeth. (Lk.13:28)

Mt.25	Mk.13	Lk.21	Jn.12		
31				But when the Son of man shall come in his glory,	(Mt.25:19)
31B				and all the holy angels with him,	
31C				then shall he sit upon the throne of his glory:	
32				And before him shall be gathered all nations:	
32B				And he shall separate them one from another,	
32C				as a shepherd divideth his sheep from the goats:	
33				And he shall	
33B				set the sheep on his right hand, but the goats on the left.	
34				Then shall the King say unto them on his right hand,	
34B				Come, ye blessed of my Father, inherit the kingdom	
34C				prepaired for you from the foundation of the world:	
35				For I was an hungred, and ye gave me to eat:	
35B				I was thirsty, and ye gave me drink:	
35C				I was a stranger, and ye took me in:	
36				Naked, and ye clothed me:	(Gen.3:21)
36B				I was sick, and ye visited me:	
36C				I was in prison, and ye came unto me.	
37				Then shall the righteous answer him, saying, Lord, when saw we	
37B				thee an hungred, and fed thee? or thirsty, and gave thee drink?	
38				When saw we thee a stranger, and took thee in?	
38B				Or naked, and clothed thee?	
39				Or when saw we thee sick, or in prison, and came unto thee?	
40				And the King shall answer and say unto them, Verily I say	
40B				unto you, inasmuch as ye have done it unto	
40C				one of the least of these my brethren, ye have done it unto me.	
41				Then shall he say also unto them on his left hand,	
41B				Depart from me, ye cursed,	
41C				into everlasting fire, prepaired for the devil and his angels:	
42				For I was an hungred, and ye gave me not to eat:	
42B				I was thirsty, and ye gave me no drink:	
43				I was a stranger, and ye took me not in:	
43B				Naked, and ye clothed me not:	
43C				Sick, and in prison, and ye visited me not.	
44				Then shall they also answer him, saying, Lord, when saw we	
44B				thee an hungred, or a'thirst, or a stranger, or naked, or sick,	
44C				or in prison, and did not minister unto thee?	
45				Then shall he answer them, saying,	
45B				Verily I say unto you, inasmuch as ye	
45C				did it not to one of the least of these, ye did it not to me.	
46				And these shall go away into everlasting punishment:	
46B				But the righteous into life eternal.	

Mt.26	Mk.14	Lk.22		
1			And it came to pass, when Jesus had finished all these sayings:	
		1	The feast of unleavened bread (called the Passover) drew nigh.	
	1		After 2 days was the passover and of unleavened bread:	
	1B	2	And the chief priests and scribes sought how	
	1C	2B	they might take him by craft, and put him to death (kill him);	
		2C	for they feared the people.	
1B			He (ie: Jesus) said unto his disciples,	
2			Ye know that after 2 days is the passover,	
2B			and the Son of man is betrayed to be crucified.	
3			Then assembled together the	
3B			chief priests, and the scribes, and the elders of the people,	
3C			unto the palace of the high priest, who was called Caiaphas,	
4			and consulted that	
4B			they might take Jesus by subtilty, and kill him.	
5	2		But they said, Not on the feast,	
5B	2B		lest there be an uproar of (among) the people.	

Mt.26	Mk.14	Lk.22	Jn.12	
6	3			Now when Jesus was in Bethany, in the house of Simon the leper,
7D	3B			As he sat at meat (ie: reclined/at the table),
7A	3C			and there came unto him a woman having an alabaster box
7B	3D			of ointment of spikenard, very precious;
7C	3E			And she brake the box, and poured it on his head. (Jn.12:3)
8				But when when his disciples saw it,
8B	4			they (there were some, that) had indignation within themselves,
8C	4B			and said, Why (to what purpose) was this waste of ointment made?
9	5			For this ointment might have been sold for much,
9B	5B			for more than 300 pence, and given to the poor.
	5C			And they murmured against her.
10	6			When Jesus understood it, he said unto them, Let her alone;
10B	6B			Why trouble ye her (the woman)?
10C	6C			for she hath wrought a good work upon me.
11	7			For ye have the poor always with you,
	7B			and whensoever ye will ye may do them good:
11B	7C			but me ye have not always.
	8			She hath done what she could;
12				for in that she hath poured this ointment on my body,
12B				she did it for my burial;
	8B			She is come aforehand to anoint my body to the burying.
13	9			Verily I say unto you, Wheresoever this gospel
13B	9B			shall be preached in/throughout the whole world,
13C	9C			shall also this, that she (this woman) hath done
13D	9D			be told (shall be spoken of) for a memorial of her.
		3		Then entered Satan into
14	10	3B		Judas named Iscariot (being one of the 12)
14B	10B	4		and he went his way unto the chief priests; and communed with
		4B		the chief priests and captains (ie: magistrates), (Acts 16:22)
	10C	4C		how he might betray him unto them:
	11	5		And when they heart it, they were glad,
	11B	5B		and covenanted/promised to give him money.
15				And he (ie: Judas) said unto them,
15B				What will ye give me, and I will deliver him unto you?
15C				And they covenanted with him for 30 pieces of silver.
		6		And he promised, and sought oppertunity to (Lk.22:2)
		6B		betray him unto them - in the absence of the multitude.
16				And from that time he sought oppertunity to betray him;
	11C			And he sought how he might conveniently betray him.
17	12	7		And then came the day (the first day) of unleavened bread,
	12B	7B		when must be killed (they killed) the passover:

> Note: Just a thought!
> On which evening did Jesus and the 12 celebrate the Passover?
> Did the crucifixion take place on Nisan 14, the Passover Day?

Mt.26	Mk.14	Lk.22	Jn.12	
17B	12C			The disciples (his disciples) came unto Jesus, saying unto him,
17C	12D			Where wilt thou that we go
17D	12E			and prepare for thee that thou mayest eat the passover?
	13	8		And he sendeth forth 2 of his disciples (Peter and John),
		8B		saying, Go and prepare us the passover, that we may eat.
		9		And they said unto him, Where wilt thou that we prepare?
18	13B	10		And he said unto them, Go ye into the city;
		10B		And, behold, when ye are entered into the city,
	13C	10C		there shall meet you a man bearing a pitcher of water;
	13D	10D		follow him into the house where he entereth in.
	14			And wheresoever he shall go in,
18B	14B	11		ye shall say unto such a man (the good man of the house).

Mt.26	Mk.14	Lk.22	Jn.12	
18C	14C	11B		The Master saith unto thee, My time is at hand;
18D				I will keep the passover at thy house with my disciples:
	14D	11C		Where is the guestchamber,
	14E	11D		where I shall eat the passover with my disciples?
	15	12		And he shall shew you a large upper room
	15B	12B		furnished and prepared: there make ready for us.
19	16	13		And his disciples did (went forth) as Jesus had appointed them;
	16B	13B		and came into the city, and found as he had said unto them:
19B	16C	13C		And they made ready the passover.

Mt.26	Mk.14	Lk.22	Jn.13	
Now before			1	Now before the feast of the passover,
the feast	14		1B	And when Jesus knew that his hour was come
of the Passover,			1C	that he should depart out of this world - unto the Father,
when			1D	Having loved his own
the even			1E	(which were in the world), he loved them unto the end.
20				Now when the even was come:
	17			In the evening he cometh with the 12, and
20B		14B		He sat down, and the 12 apostles with him.
		15		And he (ie: Jesus) said unto them, With desire I have
		15B		desired to eat this passover with you before I suffer:
		16		For I say unto you, I will not any more
		16B		eat thereof, until it be fulfilled in the kingdom of God.
		17		And he took the cup, and gave thanks,
		17B		and said, Take this, and divide it among yourselves:
		18		For I say unto you, I will not drink
		18B		of the fruit of the vine, until the kingdom of God shall come.
21	18			And as they sat and did eat,
21B	18B			Jesus said, Verily I say unto you,
21C	18C			that one of you which eateth with me shall betray me.
22	19			And they were (began to be) exceeding sorrowful,
	19B			and to say unto him (one by one), Is it I? and another Is it I?
22B				Every one of them began to say, Is it I?
23	20			And he (ie: Jesus) answered and said unto them,
23B	20B			It is one of the 12, he that dippeth
23C	20C			his hand with me in the dish, the same shall betray me.
24	21			The Son of man indeed goeth, as it is written of him:
24B	21B			but woe unto that man by whom the Son of man is betrayed!
24C	21C			It were (had been) good
24D	21D			for that man if he had never been born.
25				Then Judas
25B				(which betrayed him), answered and said, Master, is it I?
25C				He (ie: Jesus) said unto him, Thou hast said.
26	22			And as they did eat (as they were eating),
26B	22B	19		Jesus took bread, and gave thanks, and blessed it,
26C	22C	19B		and brake it, and gave unto them (his disciples),
26D	22D	19C		and said (saying), Take eat; this is my body
		19D		which is given for you: this do in remembrance of me.
		20		Likewise also the cup after supper:
27	23			And he took the cup, and gave thanks;
27B	23B			And when he had given thanks, he gave to them,
		20B		saying, This cup is the new testament (ie: the new covenant)
		20C		in my blood, which is shed for you:
27C	23C			Drink ye all of it: And they all drank of it.
	24			And he said unto them,
28	24B	My blood is		This is my blood of the new testament, which is shed
28B	24C	shed for many.		for many for the remission (ie: forgiveness) of sins.
29	25			But, verily I say unto you,

Mt.26	Mk.14	Lk.22	Jn.13	
29B	25B			I will not drink henceforth (will drink no more)
29C	25C			of the fruit of the vine, until that day when I drink it new
29D	25D			with you in my Father's kingdom (the kingdom of God).
		21		But, behold, the hand of him
		21B		that betrayeth me is with me on the table. (Jn.13:21-30)
		22		And truly the Son of man goest, as it was determined:
		22B		but woe unto that man by whom he is betrayed! (Lk.22:4)
		23		And they began to enquire among themselves,
		23B		which of them it was that should do this thing.
			2	And supper being ended,
			2B	The devil having now put
			2C	into the heart of Judas Iscariot (Simon's son) to betray him;
			3	Jesus knowing that the Father had given all things into his hands,
			3B	and that he was come from God, and goeth to God; (Jn.16:28)
			4	He riseth from supper, and laid aside his garments;
			4B	and took a towel, and girded himself.
			5	After that - he poureth water into a bason,
			5B	and began to wash the disciples' feet, and to wipe them
			5C	with the towel wherewith he was girded.
			6	Then cometh he to Simon Peter;
			6B	And Peter saith unto him, Lord, dost thou wash my feet?
			7	Jesus answered and said unto him,
			7B	What I do thou knowest not now; but thou shalt know hereafter.
			8	Peter saith unto him, Thou shalt never wash my feet.
			8B	Jesus answered him, If I wash thee not, thou hast no part with me.
			9	Simon Peter saith unto him,
			9B	Lord, not my feet only, but also my hands and my head.
			10	Jesus saith to him,
			10B	He that is washed needeth not - save to wash his feet,
			10C	but is clean every whit: And ye are clean, but not all.
			11	For he knew who should betray him;
			11B	therefore said he, Ye are not all clean (ie: pure).
			12	So after he had washed their feet and had taken his garments,
			12B	and was set down again, he said unto them,
			12C	Know ye what I have done to you? (Lk.22:26,27)
			13	Ye call me Master and Lord: and ye say well; for so I am.
			14	If I then (your Lord and Master) have washed your feet;
			14B	ye also ought to wash one another's feet. (Jn.13:34)
			15	For I have given you an example (ie: ensample/pattern),
			15B	that ye should do as I have done to you.
			16	Verily, verily, I say unto you,
			16B	The servant is not greater than his lord; (Jn.14:28)
			16C	Neither he that is sent greater than he that sent him.
			17	If ye know these things, happy are ye if ye do them. (Mt.23:12)
			18	I speak not of you all: I know whom I have chosen:
			18B	But that the Scripture may be fulfilled, He that
			18C	eateth bread with me hath lifted up his heel against me.
			19	Now I tell you before it come,
			19B	that, when it is come to pass, ye may believe that I am he.
			20	Verily, verily, I say unto you,
			20B	He that receiveth whomsoever I sent - receiveth me;
			20C	and he that receiveth me - receiveth Him that sent me.
			21	When Jesus had thus said, he was troubled in spirit,
			21B	and testified, and said, Verily, verily,
			21C	I say unto you, that one of you shall betray me.
			22	Then the disciples
			22B	looked one on another, doubting of whom he spake.

Mt.26	Mk.14	Lk.22	Jn.13	
			23	Now there was leaning on Jesus' bosom
			23B	one of his disciples, whom Jesus loved.
			24	Simon Peter therefore beckoned to him
			24B	that he should ask who it should be of whom he spake.
			25	He then leaning on Jesus' breast saith unto him, Lord, who is it?
			26	Jesus answered,
			26B	He it is, to whom I shall give sop, when I have dipped it.
			26C	And when he had dipped the sop (ie: morsel), (Ruth 2:14)
			26D	he gave it to Judas Iscariot, the son of Simon.
			27	And after sop - Satan entered into him.
			27B	Then said Jesus unto him, That thou doest, do quickly.
			28	Now no man at the table knew for what intent he spake this
			29	unto him. For some of them thought, because Judas had the bag,
			29B	that Jesus had said unto him, Buy those things that we have
			29C	need of against the feast;
			29D	or, that he should give something to the poor.
Judas went out,			30	He (ie: Judas) then having received the sop went out immediately:
and it was night.			30B	And it was night.
			31	Therefore, when he was gone out, Jesus said,
			31B	Now is the Son of man glorified, and God is glorified in him.
			32	If God be glorified in him, God shall also glorify him
			32B	in himself, and shall straightway glorify him.
			33	Little children, yet a little while I am with you.
			33B	Ye shall seek me: And as I said unto the Jews,
			33C	Whither I go, ye cannot come; so now I say to you.
			34	A new commandment I give unto you, That ye love one another;
			34B	as I have loved you, that ye also love one another. (2 Jn.5)
			35	By this shall all men know that (Jn.4:1-3,7,13)
			35B	ye are my disciples, if ye have love one to another.
		24		And there was also strife among them,
		24B		which of them should be accounted the greatest.
		25		And he (ie: Jesus) said unto them,
		25B		The kings of the Gentiles exercise lordship over them; and
		25C		they that exercise authority upon them are called benefactors.
		26		But ye shall not be so:
		26B		but he that is greatest among you, let him be as the younger;
		26C		and he that is chief, as he that doth serve.
		27		For whether is greater, he that sitteth at meat, (Lk.17:7-10)
		27B		or he that serveth? is it not he that sitteth at meat?
		27C		But I am among you as he that serveth. (Jn.13:13-17)
		28		Ye are they which have continued with me in my temptations.
		29		And I appoint unto you a kingdom, as my Father hath appointed
		30		unto me; that ye may eat and drink at my table in my kingdom,
		30B		and sit on thrones judging the 12 tribes of Israel.
30	26			And when they had sung an hymn,
30B	26B			they went out into the mount of Olives.
31	27			And then saith Jesus unto them,
31B	27B			All ye shall be offended because of me this night:
31C	27C			for it is written, I will smite the shepherd:
31D	27D			and the sheep of the flock shall be scattered abroad.
32	28	Peter		But after I am risen, I will go before you into Galilee.
33	29	believed		But Peter answered and said unto him,
33B	29B	in		Though all shall be offended because of thee,
33C	29C	himself!		yet not I, I will never be offended.
		36		Simon Peter said unto him, Lord, whither goest thou?
		36B		Jesus answered him, Whither I go, thou

Mt.26	Mk.14	Lk.22	Jn.13	
			36C	canst not follow me now; but thou shalt follow me afterwards.
		31		And the Lord said, Simon, Simon - behold, Satan hath desired
		31B		to have you, that he may sift you as wheat:
		32		But I prayed for thee, that thy faith fail not:
		32B		and when thou art converted, strengthen thy brethren.
		33	37	And he (ie: Peter) said unto him, Lord,
			37B	Why cannot I follow thee now?
		33B		I am ready to go with thee, both into prison, and to death;
			37C	I will lay down my life for thy sake.
34	30	34	38	And Jesus answered and said unto him,
			38B	Wilt thou lay down thy life for my sake?
34B	30B	34B	38C	Verily, verily, I say unto thee (I tell thee Peter),
34C	30C	34C		that this day (in this night),
34D		34D	38D	the cock shall not crow this day, till/before, that
34E			38E	thou hast denied me 3x:
	30D			before the cock crow 2x,
	30E	34E		thou shalt 3x deny that thou knowest me.
35	31			But he (Peter) speaking more vehemently, said unto him,
35B	31B	You can		Though/If I should die with thee,
35C	31C	count		yet will I not deny thee in any wise.
35D	31D	on us!		Likewise also said they all (all the disciples).
		35		And he (ie: Jesus) said unto them, When I sent you
		35B		without purse, and scrip, and shoes, lacked ye any thing?
		35C		And they said, Nothing.
		36		Then said he unto them, But now, he that
		36B		hath a purse, let him take it, and likewise his scrip: And,
		36C		he that hath no sword, let him sell his garment, and buy one.
		37		For I say unto you, that this that is written must yet be
		37B		accomplished in me, And he was reckoned among the transgressors:
		37C		For the things concerning me have an end. (Mk.15:28/Is.53:12)
		38		And they said, Lord, behold, here are 2 swords.
		38B		And he said unto them, It is enough.
			Jn.14	
			1	Let not your hearts be troubled:
			1B	Ye believe in God, believe also in me.
			2	In my Father's house are many mansions: If it were not so,
I will			2B	I would have told you. I go to prepare a place for you.
come again.			3	And if I go and prepare a place for you, I will come again, and
			3B	receive you unto myself; that where I am, there ye may be also.
			4	And whither I go ye know, and the way ye know. (Jn.14:6;16:28)
			5	Thomas saith unto him, Lord,
			5B	we know not whither thou goest; and how can we know the way?
			6	Jesus saith unto him, I am the Way, the Truth, and the Life:
			6B	no man cometh unto the Father, but by me.
			7	If ye had known me, ye should have known my Father also:
			7B	and from henceforth ye know him, and have seen him.
			8	Philip saith unto him,
			8B	Lord, shew us the Father, and it sufficeth us.
The words			9	Jesus saith unto him, Have I been so long time with you, and yet
that I speak,			9B	hast thou not known me, Philip? He that hath seen me has seen
I speak			9C	the Father; and how sayest thou then, Shew us the Father?
not of			10	Believest thou not that I am in the Father, and the Father in me?
myself.			10B	The Words that I speak unto you I speak not of myself;
			10C	but the Father that dwelleth in me, he doeth the works.
			11	Believe me that I am in the Father, and the Father in me?
			11B	or else believe me for the very works' sake. (Jn.5:36)
			12	Verily, verily, I say unto you,

Mt.26 Mk.14 Lk.22 Jn.14

12B	He that believeth on me, the works that I do shall he do also;
12C	and greater works than these shall he do; (Acts 4:4,7,10)
12D	because I go unto my Father.
13	And whatsoever ye shall ask in my name,
13B	that will I do, that the Father may be glorified in the Son.
14	If ye shall ask any thing in my name, I will do it. (1 Jn.5:14)
15	If ye love me, keep my commandments. (Mt.28:19,20/Rev.22:18,19)
16	And I will pray the Father, and he shall give
16B	you another Comforter, that he may abide with you for ever;
17	Even the Spirit of Truth; whom the world cannot receive,
17B	because it seeth him not, neither knoweth him: (1 Cor.2:14)
17C	But ye know him; for he dwelleth with you, and shall be in you.
18	I will not leave you comfortless: I will come to you.
19	Yet a little while, and the world seeth me no more;
19B	but ye see me: because I live, ye shall live also.
20	At that day ye shall know (ie: understand/perceive/be aware of)
20B	that I am in my Father, and ye in me, and I in you. (Jn.17:21)
21	He that hath my commandments, (Mt.7:21/Mt.24:42/Rev.3:3/Is.55:6)
21B	and keepeth them, he it is that loveth me:
21C	And he that loveth me shall be loved of my Father,
21D	and I will love him, and will manifest myself to him.
22	Judas (not Iscariot) saith unto him, Lord, how is it that
22B	thou wilt manifest thyself unto us, and not unto the world?
23	Jesus answered and said unto him,
23B	If a man love me, he will keep my words (ie: sayings): (Mt.7:24)
23C	and my Father will love him,
23D	and we will come unto him, and make our abode with him.
24	He that loveth me not keepeth not my sayings: (Mt.7:26)
24B	And the word which ye hear
24C	is not mine, but the Father's which sent me. (Jn.7:16)
25	These things have I spoken unto you, being yet present with you.
26	But the Comforter (which is the Holy Ghost), (Acts 2:1-4)
26B	whom the Father will send in my name,
26C	He shall teach you all things, and bring all things
26D	to your remembrance, whatsoever I have said unto you.
27	Peace I leave with you, my peace I give unto you:
27B	not as the world giveth, give I unto you.
27C	Let not your hearts be troubled, neither let it be afraid.
28	Ye have heard
28B	how I said unto you, I go away, and come again unto you.
28C	If ye loved me, ye would rejoice, because I said,
28D	I go unto the Father: for my Father is greater than I.
29	And now I have told you before it come to pass,
29B	that, when it is come to pass, ye might believe.
30	Hereafter I will not talk much with you; for the prince
30B	of this world (ie: kosmos) cometh, and hath nothing in me.
31	But that the world (ie: kosmos) may know that I love the Father;
31B	and as the Father gave me commandment, even so I do.
31C	Arise, let us go.

Jn.15

1	I am the true vine, and my Father is the husbandman.
2	Every branch in me that beareth not fruit he taketh away:
2B	And every branch that beareth fruit,
2C	he purgeth it, that it may bring forth more fruit.
3	Now ye are clean through the word which I have spoken unto you.
4	Abide in me, and I in you. As the branch
4B	cannot bear fruit of itself, except it abide in the vine;

Mt.26 Mk.14 Lk.22 Jn.15

4C	no more can ye, except ye abide in me.
5	I am the vine, ye are the branches:
5B	He that abideth in me, and I in him, the same
5C	bringeth forth much fruit: For without me ye can do nothing.
6	If a man abide not in me,
6B	he is cast forth as a branch, and is withered; and the men
6C	gather them, and cast them into the fire, and they are burned.
7	If ye abide in me, and my words abide in you,
7B	ye shall ask what ye will, and it shall be done unto you.
8	Herein is my Father glorified,
8B	that ye bear much fruit; so shall ye be my disciples.
9	As the Father
9B	hath loved me, so have I loved you: continue ye in my love.
10	If ye keep my commandments, ye shall abide in my love; even as
10B	I have kept my Father's commandments, and abide in his love.
11	These things have I spoken unto you, that
11B	my joy might remain in you, and that your joy might be full.
12	This is my commandment,
12B	That ye love one another, as I have loved you.
13	Greater love hath no man than this,
13B	that a man lay down his life for his friends.
14	Ye are my friends, if ye do whatsoever I command you. (Jn.14:10)
15	Henceforth I call you not servants;
15B	for the servant knoweth not what his lord doeth:
15C	But I have called you friends; for all things
15D	that I have heard of my Father I have made known unto you.
16	Ye have not chosen me, but I have chosen you,
16B	and ordained you, that ye should go
16C	and bring forth fruit, and that your fruit should remain:
16D	that whatsoever ye
16E	shall ask of the Father in my name, he may give it you.
17	These things I command you, that ye love one another.
18	If the world hate you, (Jn.7:7)(1 Jn.3:13)
18B	ye know that it hated me before it hated you.
19	If ye were of the world, the world would love his own:
19B	But because ye are not of the world, but I have chosen
19C	you out of the world, therefore the world hateth you.
20	Remember the word that I said unto you,
20B	The servant is not greater than his lord. (Jn.13:16/Jn.16:2,33)
20C	If they have persecuted me, they will also persecute you;
20D	If they have kept my saying, they will keep your's also.
21	But all these things will they do unto you
21B	for my name's sake, because they know not him that sent me.
22	If I had not come and spoken unto them, they had not had sin:
22B	but now they have no cloke for their sin. (Jn.9:41)
23	He that hateth me, hateth my Father also. (Jn.5:23)
24	If I had not done among them
24B	the works which none other did, they had not had sin:
24C	but now have they both seen and hated both me and my Father.
25	But this cometh to pass, that the word might be fulfilled
25B	that is written in their law, They hated me without a cause.
26	But when the Comforter is come, whom I will send unto you
26B	from the Father, even the Spirit of Truth,
26C	which proceedeth from the Father, he shall testify of me:
27	And ye also shall bear witness,
27B	because ye have been with me from the beginning.
Jn.16	

Mt.26 Mk.14 Lk.22 Jn.16

	1	These things
	1B	have I spoken unto you, that ye should not be offended.
	2	They shall put you out of the synagogues:
	2B	yea, the time cometh, that whosoever killeth you
	2C	will think that he doeth God service.
	3	And these things will they do unto you,
	3B	because they have not known the Father, nor me.
	4	But these things have I told you, that when
	4B	the time shall come, ye may remember that I told you of them.
	4C	And these things I said not
	4D	unto you at the beginning, because I was with you.
	5	But now I go my way to Him that sent me; (Jn.16:10,16,28)
	5B	and none of you asketh me, Whither goest thou?
	6	But because I have said these things unto you,
	6B	sorrow hath filled your heart.
	7	Nevertheless I tell you the truth;
	7B	It is expedient for you that I go away:
	7C	for if I go not away, the Comforter will not come unto you;
	7D	but if I depart, I will send him unto you. (Jn.14:26)
	8	And when he is come, he will reprove (ie: convict/convince)
	8B	the world of sin, and of righteousness, and of judgment:
	9	Of Sin,
	9B	because they believe not on me;
	10	Of Righteousness,
	10B	because I go to my Father, and ye see me no more;
	11	Of Judgment,
	11B	because the prince of this world is judged. (Jn.12:31)
	12	I have yet
	12B	many things to say unto you, but ye cannot bear them now.
	13	Howbeit when he, the Spirit of Truth, is come, he will
	13B	guide you into all truth: for he shall not speak of himself;
	13C	but whatsoever he shall hear, that shall he speak: (Jn.14:24)
	13D	And he will shew you things to come.
	14	He shall glorify me:
	14B	for he shall receive of mine, and shall shew it unto you.
	15	All things that the Father hath are mine: therefore said I,
	15B	that he shall take of mine, and shall shew it unto you.
A little while	16	A little while, and ye shall not see me:
and ye shall	16B	and again, a little while, and ye shall see me,
not see me,	16C	because I go to the Father.
	17	Then said some of his disciples among themselves, What is this
	17B	that he saith unto us, A little while, and ye shall not see me:
	17C	and again, a little while, and ye shall see me:
	17C	and, because I go to the Father?
	18	They said therefore, What is this that he saith,
	18B	A little while? We cannot tell what he saith.
And again a	19	Now Jesus knew - that they were desirous to ask him,
little while	19B	And said unto them, Do ye enquire among yourselves
and ye	19C	of that I said, A little while, and ye shall not see me:
shall see me.	19D	and again, a little while, and ye shall see me?
	20	Verily, verily, I say unto you,
	20B	That ye shall weep and lament, but the world shall rejoice: and
	20C	ye shall be sorrowful, but your sorrow shall be turned into joy.
	21	A woman when she is in travail hath sorrow,
	21B	hath sorrow, because her hour is come:
	21C	But as soon as she is delivered of the child, she remembereth
	21D	no more the anguish, for joy that a man is born into the world.
	22	And ye now therefore have sorrow:

The Gospels of Matthew, Mark, Luke, and John: Merged into One Historic Calendar of Events | 133

Mt.26	Mk.14	Lk.22	Jn.16	
I will			22B	but I will see you again, and your heart shall rejoice,
see you again.			22C	and your joy no man taketh from you.
			23	And in that day ye shall ask me nothing.
And in that day -			23B	Verily, verily, I say unto you, Whatsoever ye (Jn.15:7)
			23C	shall ask the Father in my name, he will give it you.
			24	Hitherto have ye asked nothing in my name:
			24B	Ask, and ye shall receive, that your joy may be full.
			25	These things have I spoken unto you in proverbs: but the time
			25B	cometh, when I shall no more speak unto you in proverbs,
			25C	but I shall shew you plainly of the Father.
			26	In that day ye shall ask in my name:
			26B	and I say not unto you, that I will - pray the Father for you:
			27	For the Father himself loveth you, because ye
			27B	have loved me, and have believed that I came from God.
			28	I came forth from the Father, and am come into the world:
			28B	again, I leave the world, and go to the Father.
			29	His disciples said unto him,
			29B	Lo, now speakest thou plainly, and speakest no proverb.
			30	Now are we sure that thou knowest all things,
			30B	and needest not that any man should ask thee:
			30C	By this we believe that thou camest forth from God.
			31	Jesus answered them, Do ye now believe? Behold,
			32	the hour cometh, yea, is now come, that ye shall be scattered,
			32B	every man to his own, and shall leave me alone:
			32C	And yet I am not alone, because the Father is with me.
			33	These things
			33B	I have spoken unto you, that in me ye might have peace.
			33C	In the world ye shall have tribulation:
			33D	But be of good cheer; I have overcome the world.
			Jn.17	
			1	These words spake Jesus, and lifted up his eyes to heaven,
			1B	And said, Father, the hour is come;
			1C	glorify thy Son, that thy Son also may glorify thee:
			2	As thou hast given him power over all flesh, that he should give
			2B	eternal life to as many as thou hast given him.
			3	And this is life eternal, that they might know
			3B	thee the only true God, and Jesus Christ, whom thou hast sent.
			4	I have glorified thee on the earth:
			4B	I have finished the work which thou gavest me to do. (Jn.4:34)
			5	And now, O Father, glorify thou me with thine own self with
			5B	the glory which I had with thee before the world was.
			6	I have manifested thy name
			6B	unto the men which thou gavest me out of the world: thine they
			6C	were, and thou gavest them me; and they have kept thy word.
			7	Now they have known
			7B	that all things whatsoever thou hast given me are of thee.
			8	For I have given unto them the words which thou gavest me;
			8B	And they have received them,
			8C	And have known surely that I came out from thee,
			8D	And they have believed that thou didst send me. (Jn.16:27)
			9	I pray for them: I pray not for the world,
			9B	but for them which thou hast given me; for they are thine.
			10	And all mine are thine, and thine are mine;
			10B	and I am glorified in them.
			11	And now I am no more in the world,
			11B	but these are in the world, and I come to thee.
			11C	Holy Father, keep through thine own name
			11D	those whom thou hast given me, that they may be one, as we are.

Mt.26	Mk.14	Lk.22	Jn.17	
			12	While I was with them in the world, I kept them in thy name:
			12B	those that thou gavest me I have kept,
			12C	and none of them is lost, but the son of perdition;
			12D	that the scripture might be fulfilled.
			13	And now come I to thee;
			13B	and these things I speak in the world,
			13C	that they might have my joy fulfilled in themselves.
			14	I have given them thy word;
			14B	and the world hath hated them, because
			14C	they are not of the world, even as I am not of the world.
			15	I pray not that thou shouldest take them out of the world,
			15B	but that thou shouldest keep them from the evil.
			16	They are not of the world, even as I am not of the world.
			17	Sanctify them through thy truth: Thy word is truth.
			18	As thou hast sent me into the world,
			18B	even so have I also sent them into the world.
			19	And for their sakes I sanctify myself,
			19B	that they also might be sanctified through the truth.
			20	Neither pray I for these alone, but for them also
			20B	which shall believe on me - through their word;
			21	That they all may be one; as thou, Father,
			21B	art in me, and I in thee, that they also may be one in us:
			21C	That the world may believe that thou hast sent me.
			22	And the glory which thou gavest me, I have given them;
			22B	that they may be one, even as we are one:
			23	I in them, and thou in me,
			23B	that they may be made perfect in one,
			23C	And that the world may know that thou hast sent me,
			23D	and hast loved them, as thou hast loved me.
			24	Father, I will that they also,
			24B	whom thou hast given me, be with me where I am;
			24C	that they may behold my glory, which thou hast given me:
			24D	for thou lovedst me before the foundation of the world.
			25	O Righteous Father, the world hath not known thee: but I have
			25B	known thee, and these have known that thou hast sent me.
			26	And I have declared unto them thy name, and I will declare it:
			26B	that the love wherewith
			26C	thou hast loved me may be in them, and I in them.

Mt.26	Mk.14	Lk.22	Jn.18	
		39	1	When Jesus had spoken these words, he went, as he was wont,
		39B		to the mount of Olives; and his disciples also followed him:
			1B	He went forth (with his disciples) over the brook Cedron,
36	32		1C	and they (Jesus with them) came to a place (where was a garden)
36B	32B			which was called/named Gethsemane,
			1D	into the which he entered, and his disciples.
		40		And when he (ie: Jesus) was at the place,
		40B		he said unto them, Pray that ye enter not into temptation.
36C	32C			And he saith unto his disciples,
36D	32D			Sit ye here, while I shall go and pray yonder.
37	33			And he taketh (took) with him
37B	33B			Peter, and the 2 sons of Zebedee (James and John),
37C	33C			and began to be sore amazed (sorrowful), and to be very heavy:
38	34			And saith he unto them,
38B	34B			My soul is exceeding sorrowful, even unto death;
38C	34C			Tarry ye here, and watch (ie: be vigilant) with me. (1 Pe.5:8)
39	35			And he went foreward, a little farther,
		41		(and he was withdrawn from them about a stone's cast);

Mt.26	Mk.14	Lk.22	Jn.18	
39B	35B	41B		And he kneeled down, he fell (on his face) on the ground, and
	35C			prayed, that, if it were possible the hour might pass from him.
	36			And he said, Abba, Father,
	36B			all things are possible unto thee, take away this cup from me:
39C		42		Prayed, saying, O my Father,
39D				all things are possible with thee (if it be possible),
39E		42B		if thou be willing remove/let this cup (pass) from me:
39F	36C	42C		Nevertheless not what/as I will (not my will),
39G	36D	42D		but what/as thou wilt (but thine, be done).
		43		And there appeared
		43B		an angel unto him from heaven, strengthening him.
		44		And being in an agony he prayed more earnestly:
		44B		And his sweat was
		44C		as it were great drops of blood falling down to the ground.
40	37	45		And when he rose up from prayer, and was come unto his disciples,
40B	37B	45B		and he findeth them asleep/sleeping (sleeping from sorrow).
40C	37C			And saith unto Peter, (Mt.26:37)
	37D			Simon, sleepest thou? couldest not thou watch one hour?
40D				What (ie: So), could ye not watch with me one hour?
		46		And said unto them,
		46B		Why sleep ye? rise and pray, lest ye enter into temptation.
41	38			Watch ye and pray,
41B	38B			Lest ye enter (that ye enter not) into temptation: The spirit
41C	38C			indeed (truly) is willing (ready), but the flesh is weak.
42	39			And again (the 2nd. time) he went away, and prayed,
	39B			and spake the same words,
42B				saying, O my Father, if this cup may not
42C				pass away from me, except I drink it, thy will be done.
43	40			And when he came/returned, he found them asleep again.
43B	40B			for their eyes were heavy,
	40C			neither wist (ie: knew) they what to answer him.
44				And he left them, and went away again,
44B				and prayed the 3rd. time, saying the same words.
			2	Now Judas (which betrayed him) also knew the place: (Mk.14:10,11)
			2B	for Jesus oft-times resorted thither with his disciples.
			3	Judas then, having received a band
			3B	of men and officers from the chief priests and Pharisees,
			3C	cometh thither with lanterns and torches and weapons.
45	41			And then cometh he (the 3rd. time) to his disciples,
45B	41B			And saith unto them, Sleep on now, and take rest:
45C	41C			It is enough; behold, the hour is at hand (the hour is come),
45D	41D			and the Son of man is betrayed into the hands of sinners.
46	42			Rise up, let us be going;
46B	42B			Lo/Behold, he is at hand that betrayeth (doth betray) me.
47	43	47		And immediately, while he yet spake, behold a multitude,
47B	43B	47B		Lo, he that was called Judas (1 of the 12) came,
47C	43C			and with him a great multitude with swords and staves,
47D	43D			from the chief priests and scribes and the elders.
			4	Jesus therefore, knowing all things that should come upon him,
			4B	went forth, and said unto them (ie: the band), Whom seek ye?
			5	They answered him, Jesus of Nazareth.
			5B	Jesus saith unto them, I am he.
			5C	(And Judas also, which betrayed him, stood with them.)
			6	As soon then as he had said unto them, I am he,
			6B	they went backward, and fell to the ground.
			7	Then asked he them again, Whom seek ye?
			7B	And they said, Jesus of Nazareth.

Mt.26	Mk.14	Lk.22	Jn.18	
			8	Jesus answered, I have told you that I am he:
			8B	if therefore ye seek me, let these go their way:
			9	That the saying might be fulfilled, which he spake,
			9B	Of them which thou gavest me have I lost none.
48	44			Now he that betrayed him had given them a token (a sign),
48B	44B			saying, Whosoever I shall kiss, that same is he:
48C	44C			take him (hold him fast), and lead him away safely.
		47C		Judas went before them, and drew near unto Jesus to kiss him.
49	45			And forthwith as soon as he (ie: Judas) was come,
49B	45B			he goeth straightway to him: and he came to Jesus
49C	45C			and saith, Master, Master (Hail Master), and kissed him.
		48		But Jesus said unto him, Judas,
		48B		betrayest thou the Son of man with a kiss?
50				And Jesus said unto him, Friend, wherefore art thou come?
50B	46			Then came they, and laid their hands on Jesus, and took him.
		49		When they (ie: the disciples) which were about him
		49B		saw what would follow,
		49C		they said unto him, Lord, shall we smite with the sword?
51	47	50		And behold, one of them that stood by (which were with Jesus),
			10	Then Simon Peter having a sword,
51B	47B		10B	stretched out his hand, and drew his sword,
51C	47C	50B	10C	and smote (struck) a/the servant
51D	47D	50C	10D	of the high priest, and smote (cut) off his right ear.
			10E	The servant's name was Malchus.
		51		And Jesus answered and said, Suffer ye thus far
		51B		And he (ie Jesus) touched his ear, and healed him.
52			11	Then said Jesus unto him (Peter),
52B			11B	Put up again thy sword into his place (into the sheath):
52C				for all they that take the sword shall perish with the sword.
			11C	The cup which my Father hath given me, shall I not drink it?
53				Thinkest thou that I cannot now pray to my Father,
53B				and he shall presently (ie: immediately)
53C				give me more than 12 legions of angels?
54				But how then shall
54B				the scriptures be fulfilled, that thus it must be?
55				In that same hour:
55B	48	52		Then Jesus answered and said unto them,
55C				-to the multitudes,
		52B		-to the chief priests, and captains of the temple,
		52C		and the elders which were come unto him,
55D	48B	52D		Are ye come out as against a thief,
55E	48C	52E		with swords and with staves for to take me?
55F	49	53		When I was/sat daily with you in the temple teaching,
		53B		ye stretched forth no hands against me,
55G	49B			and ye laid no hold on me (ye took me not):
		53C		But this is your hour, and the power of darkness.
56				But all this was done, that
56B	49C			the scriptures of the prophets might/must be fulfilled.
56C	50			Then they all (all the disiples) forsook him, and fled.
			12	Then the band and the
			12B	captain and officers of the Jews took Jesus, and bound him.
	51			And there followed him - a certain young man,
	51B			having a linen cloth cast about his naked body;
	51C			And the young men laid hold on him:
	52			and he left the linen cloth, and fled from them naked.
57	53	54		And they that had laid hold on Jesus (then took and led him away);
			13	And they led him away to Annas first,

The Gospels of Matthew, Mark, Luke, and John: Merged into One Historic Calendar of Events

Mt.26	Mk.14	Lk.22	Jn.18	
			13B	(for he was father in law to Caiaphas,
			13C	which was the high priest that same year.)
			24	And Annas sent him bound
57B	53B		24B	to Caiaphas (the high priest),
57C				where the scribes and the elders were assembled.
		54B		They brought him into the high priest's house;
	53C			and with him (ie: Caiaphas) were assembled
	53D			all the chief priests, and the elders, and the scribes:
		14		Now Caiaphas was he, which gave counsel to the Jews, (Jn.11:49-52)
		14B		that it was expedient that one man should die for the people.
58	54	54C	15	And Simon Peter followed Jesus afar off;
			15B	And so did another disciple, and
			15C	that disciple was known unto the high priest,
			15D	and went in with Jesus into the palace of the high priest.
			16	But Peter stood at the door without (ie: outside).
			16B	Then went out that other disciple (known unto the high priest),
			16C	and spake unto her that kept the door, and brought in Peter;
58B	54B			even into the palace (ie: court/hall) of the high priest.
		55		And when they had kindled a fire in the midst of the hall,
		55B		and were set down together:
	54D	55C		Peter sat down among them, and warmed himself at the fire,
58C	54C			he sat with the servants, to see the end.
59	55			Now the chief priests, and elders, and all the council
59B	55B			sought for false witness against Jesus,
60	55C			to put him to death; and found none:
60B	56			Yea, though many bear false witness against him,
60C	56B			but their witness agreed not together, yet found they none.
60D	57			At the last there came/arose 2 false witnesses against him,
61	58			and said, we heard him say (this fellow said),
61B				I am able to destroy the temple of God, and to build it in 3 days.
	58B			I will destroy this temple that is made with hands,
	58C			and within 3 days I will build another made without hands.
	59			And even so their witness (ie: testimony) agreed not together.
62	60			And the high priest arose (stood up) in the midst,
62B	60B			And asked Jesus (said unto him) saying,
62C	60C			Answerest thou nothing? What do they witness against thee?
63	61			But Jesus held his peace (and answered nothing). (Is.53:7)
63B	61B			And again the high priest answered (asked him), and said unto him,
63C				I adjure thee by the living God, that thou tell us
63D	61C			whether thou be (art thou) the Christ,
63E	61D			the Son of God (the Son of the Blessed).
64	62			And Jesus saith unto him, I am (thou hast said):
64B				Never-the-less I say unto you,
64C	62B			And/Hereafter ye shall see the Son of man sitting on the right
64D	62C			hand of power, and coming in the clouds of heaven.
65	63			Then the high priest rent his clothes, saying,
65B				He hath spoken blasphemy;
65C	63B			what further need have we of witnesses?
65D	64			Behold, now ye have heard the blasphemy! What think ye?
66				And they answered and said, He is guilty of death,
	64B			(they all condemned him to be guilty of death):
67	65			And/Then some began to spit on him (they did spit in his face),
67B	65B			and to cover his face, and buffeted (fist-punched) him;
67C	65D			and others **smote** (the servants did strike) him with the
68	65E,C			palm of their hands; and to say (said) unto him, Prophesy
68B				unto us, thou Christ, Who is it that smote thee?

Mt.26	Mk.14	Lk.22	Jn.18	
69	66			Now/And as Peter sat without (was beneath) in the palace,
69B	66B			There cometh (came) unto him a damsel,
	66C	56		a certain maid (one of the maids of the high priest),
	67			And when she saw Peter warming himself,
	67B	56B		and she beheld (looked upon) him, as he sat by the fire,
		56C		and earnestly looked upon him;
69C	67C	56D	17	And then saith - the damsel that kept the door unto Peter,
			17B	-Art not thou also one of this man's disciples?
69D	67D			-And thou also wast with Jesus of Galilee (of Nazareth);
		56E		-This man was also with him!
70	68	57	17D	But/And he denied him before them all (he saith) saying,
		57B	17E	Woman, I am not, I know him not;
70B	68B			I know not, neither understand I what thou sayest.
71	68C			And when he went (was gone) out into the porch,
	68D			And the cock crew.
			18	And the servants and officers stood there,
			18B	who had made a fire of coals, for it was cold);
			18C	And they warmed themselves,
			18D	and Peter stood with them, and warmed himself.
			19	The high priest then asked Jesus
			19B	of his disciples, and of his doctrine.
			20	Jesus answered him, I spake openly to the world;
			20B	I ever (ie: always) taught in the synagogue, and in the temple,
			20C	whither the Jews always resort;
			20D	and in secret have I said nothing.
			21	Why askest thou me?
			21B	Ask them which heard me, what I said unto them:
			21C	behold, they know what I said.
			22	And when he had thus spoken, one of the officers which stood by
			22B	struck Jesus with the palm of his hand,
			22C	saying, Answerest thou the high priest so?
			23	Jesus answered him,
			23B	If I have spoken evil, bear witness of the evil;
			23C	but if well, why smitest thou me?
			25	And Simon Peter stood and warmed himself. (Jn.18:18)
	69			And the maid saw him again, (Jn.18:17)
	69B			and began to say to them that stood by, This is one of them.
		58		And after a little while:
71B		58B		Another saw him, and said,
		58C		-Thou art also of them.
71C				-unto them that were there,
71D				This fellow was also with Jesus of Nazareth.
			25B	They said therefore (ie: in response to what they were told)
			25C	unto him, Art not thou also one of his disciples?
72	70		25D	And he denied it again - with an oath,
72B		58D	25E	and Peter said, Man, I am not, I do not know the man.
73	70B	59		And a little (a while) after, about the space of one hour after:
73B	70C			Came unto him they that stood by, and said again to Peter,
73C	70D			Surely thou also art one of them,
73D				-for thy speach bewrayeth thee,
	70E			-for thou art a Galilaean, and thy speech agreeth.
		59B		Another:
			26	One of the servants of the high priest,
			26B	(being kinsman to whose ear Peter cut off), saith;
		59C		Affirmed, saying, Of a truth,

The Gospels of Matthew, Mark, Luke, and John: Merged into One Historic Calendar of Events

Mt.26	Mk.14	Lk.22	Jn.18	
			26C	-Did I not see thee in the garden with him?
		59D		-This fellow also was with him, for he is a Galilaean.
			27	Peter then denied again,
		60		and Peter said, Man, I know not what thou sayest.
74	71			Then, began he to curse and swear, saying,
74B	71B			I know not this man of whom ye speak.
74C	72	60B	27B	And immediately (while he yet spake) the cock crew,
	72B			The 2nd. time.
		61		And the Lord turned, and looked upon Peter.
75	72C	61B		And Peter remembered (called to mind) the Word of the Lord;
75B	72D	61C		how that/which he (Jesus) said unto him,
75C	72E	61D		Before the cock crow 2x, thou shalt deny me 3x.
75D	72F	62		And, when Peter thought thereon, he went out, and wept bitterly.
		63		And the men that held Jesus mocked him, and smote him; (Mt.26:68)
		64		And when they had blindfolded him, they struck him on the face,
		64B		and asked him, saying, Prophesy, who is it that smote thee?
		65		And many other things blasphemously spake they against him.

Mt.27	Mk.15			
1	1			And straightway when the morning was come:
1B	1B	66C		All the chief priests held a consultatation (ie: council/counsel)
1C	1C	66B		with the elders of the people,
	1D	66D		and the the scribes, and the whole council (they came together),
1D				and took counsel against Jesus to put him to death:
		66A,E		And as soon as it was day - they, led him into their council,
		67		saying, Art thou the Christ? tell us.
		67B		And he said unto them, If I tell you, ye will not believe;
		68		and if I also ask you, ye will not answer me, nor let me go.
		69		Hereafter, shall the Son of man
		69B		sit on the right hand of the power of God? (Mt.26:64)
		70		Then said they all, Art thou then the Son of God?
		70B		And he (ie: Jesus) said unto them, Ye say that I am.
		71		And they said, What need we any further witness (ie: testimony)?
		71B		for we ourselves have heard of his own mouth.
	1E			And they bound Jesus.

		Lk.23		
2				And when they had bound him,
2B	1F	1		the whole multitude of them arose, and carried (led) him away:
			28	Then led they Jesus from Caiaphas, ---(on their way)--- to Pilate.
3				Then Judas, which had betrayed him,
3B				when he saw that he was condemned, repented himself,
3C				and brought again the 30 pieces of silver
3D				to the chief priests and elders, saying,
4				I have sinned, in that I have betrayed the innocent blood.
4B				And they said, What is that to us? see thou to that.
5				And he (ie: Judas) cast down the pieces of silver in the temple,
5B				and departed, and went and hanged himself. (Acts 15-20)
6				And the chief priests took the silver pieces,
6B				and said, It is not lawful for to put them into the treasury,
6C				because it is the price of blood.
7				And they took counsel,
7B				and bought with them the potter's field, to bury strangers in.
8				Wherefore that field
8B				was called, The field of blood, unto this day.
9				Then was fulfilled - that, which was spoken by Jeremy the prophet,
9B				saying, And they took the 30 pieces of silver, the price of him
9C				that was valued, whom they of the children of Israel did value;

Mt.27	Mk.15	Lk.23	Jn.18	
10				And gave them for the potter's field, as the Lord appointed me.
2C	1G	1B		And delivered him (ie: Jesus) unto Pontius Pilate the governor:
			28B	Unto the hall of judgment (and it was early).
			28C	And they themselves went not into the hall of judgment, lest
			28D	they should be defiled; but that they might eat the passover.
			29	Pilate then went out unto them,
			29B	and said, What accusation bring ye against this man?
			30	They answered and said unto him,
			30B	If he were not a malefactor (ie: an evil-doer),
			30C	we would not have delivered him up unto thee.
		2		And they began to accuse him, saying,
		2B		We found this fellow perverting the nation,
		2C		And forbidding to give tribute to Caesar, (Mt.22:21)
		2D		saying that he himself is Christ a King.
			31	Then said Pilate unto them,
			31B	Take ye him, and judge him according to your law.
			31C	The Jews therefore said unto him,
			31D	It is not lawful for us to put any man to death:
			32	That the saying of Jesus might be fulfilled, which he spake,
			32B	signifying what death he should die.
			33	Then Pilate
			33B	entered into the judgment hall again, and called Jesus.
11				And Jesus stood before the governor:
11B	2	3	33C	And Pilate (the governor) said unto (asked) him,
11C	2B	3B	33D	saying, Art thou the king of the Jews?
11D	2C	3C	34	And he (Jesus) answered him, and said,
11E	2D	3D		Thou sayest;
			34B	Sayest, thou this of thyself, or did others tell it thee of me?
			35	Pilate answered, Am I a Jew?
			35B	Thine own nation and the chief priests
			35C	have delivered thee unto me: what hast thou done?
			36	Jesus answered, My kingdom is not of this world:
			36B	If my kingdom were of this world, then would my servants fight,
			36C	that I should not be delivered to the Jews:
			36D	But now is my kingdom not from hence (ie: from here).
			37	Pilate therefore said unto him, Art thou a king then?
			37B	Jesus answered, Thou sayest that I am a king.
			37C	To this end was I born, and for this cause came I
			37D	into the world, that I should bear witness unto the Truth.
			37E	Every one that is of the truth heareth my voice.
			38	Pilate saith unto him, What is truth?
			38B	And when he had said this, he went out again unto the Jews,
		4	38C	Then Pilate saith unto them (to the chief priests and the people),
		4B	38D	I find in him (this man) no fault.
12	3			And when the chief priests and elders accused him of many things;
12B	3B			But he (ie: Jesus) answered nothing.
13	4			Then Pilot said unto him (asked him again), saying,
	4B			Answerest thou nothing?
13B	4C			Behold, hearest thou not
13C	4D			how many things they witness against thee?
14	5			But Jesus answered nothing (not a word);
14B	5B			so/insomuch that Pilate (the governor) marvelled greatly.
15	6			Now at that feast
15B	6B			he (the governor) was wont (ie: the custom) to release unto
15C	6C			them (the people) one prisoner,
15D	6D			whom they would (whomsoever they desired).

Mt.27	Mk.15	Lk.23	Jn.18	
16				And they had then,
16B	7			there was the (a notable) prisoner, called/named Barabbas,
	7B			which lay bound with other fellow-insurrectionists, who had
	7C			committed murder in the insurrection (ie: riot/disturbance).
	8			And the multitude crying aloud began to
	8B			desire to do as he had ever (ie: always) done unto them.
17				Therefore when they were gathered together,
17B	9			Pilate said unto them (answered them), saying,
			39	But ye have a custom,
			39B	that I should release unto you one at/in the passover:
17C				Whom will ye that I release unto you?
17D				Barabbas, or Jesus which is called Christ?
	9B		39C	Will ye then, that I release unto you the King of the Jews?
18	10			For he knew that the chief priests, had delivered him for envy.
			40	Then cried they all again, saying, Not this man, but Barabbas.
			40B	Now Barabbas was a robber/murderer. (Acts.3:14)
19				When he (ie: Pilate) was set down on the judgment seat,
19B				His wife sent unto him, saying,
19C				Have thou nothing to do with that just man: for I have
19D				suffered many things this day in a dream - because of him.
20	11			But the chief priests and elders moved/persuaded
20B	11B			the people (multitude), that they should ask - that he
20C	11C			should rather release Barabbas unto them, and destroy Jesus.
21				The governor answered and said unto them,
21B				Whether of the twain will ye that I release unto you?
21C				They said, Barabbas.
22				Pilate saith unto them,
22B				What shall I do then with Jesus, which is called Christ?
22C				They all say unto him, Let him be crucified.
23				And the governor said, Why, what evil has he done?
23B				But they cried out the more, saying, Let him be crucified.
		5		And they were the more fierce,
		5B		saying, He stirreth up the people, teaching throughout
		5C		all Jewry, beginning from Galilee to this place.
		6		When Pilate heard, from Galilee,
		6B		he asked whether the man were a Galilaean.
		7		And as soon as he (ie: Pilate) knew that he (ie: Jesus) belonged
		7B		unto Herod's jurisdiction, he sent him
		7C		to Herod, who himself also was at Jerusalem at that time.
		8		And when Herod saw Jesus, he was exceeding glad:
		8B		for long he had been desirous to see him,
		8C		because he had heard many things of him;
		8D		and he hoped to have seen some miracle done by him.
		9		Then he questioned with him in many words;
		9B		but he answered him nothing.
		10		And the chief priests and scribes,
		11		stood and vehemently accused him. And Herod with his men
		11B		of war set him at nought, and mocked and arrayed him in
		11C		a gorgeous (ie: a goodly) robe, and sent him again to Pilate.
		12		And the same day Pilate and Herod were made friends together:
		12B		for before they were at enmity between themselves.
			Jn.19	
			1	Then Pilate therefore took Jesus, and scourged him.
			2	And the soldiers platted a crown of thorns,
			2B	and put it on his head, and they put on him a purple robe,
			3	And said, Hail, King of the Jews!

Mt.27	Mk.15	Lk.23	Jn.19	
			3B	and they smote him with their hands.
		13		And Pilate, when he had called
		13B		together the chief priests, and the rulers, and the people:
			4	Pilate therefore went forth again, and saith unto them,
			4B	Behold, I bring him forth unto you,
			4C	that ye may know that I find no fault in him.
			5	Then came Jesus forth,
			5B	wearing the crown of thorns, and the purple robe.
			5C	And Pilate saith unto them, Behold the man!
			6	When therefore, the chief priests, and the officers saw him,
			6B	they cried out, saying, Crucify him, crucify him!
	12			And Pilate answered and said again unto them, What will ye then
	12B			that I shall do unto him, whom ye call the King of the Jews?
	13			And they cried out again, Crucify him.
	14			Then Pilate said unto them, Why, what evil has he done?
	14B			And they cried out the more exceedingly, Crucify him.
		14		Said (Pilate) unto them,
		14B		Ye have brought this man unto me, as one that perverteth
		14C		the people: And, behold, I having examined him before you,
		14D		have found no fault in this man
		14E		touching those things where-of ye accuse him:
		15		No, nor yet Herod: for I sent you to him;
		15B		and lo - nothing worthy of death is done unto him.
		16		I will therefore chastise him, and release him.
		17		(For of necessity he must release one unto them at the feast.)
		18		And they cried out all at once,
		18B		saying, Away with this man, and release unto us Barabbas:
		19		(Who for a certain sedition
		19B		made in the city, and for murder, was cast into prison.)
		20		Pilate therefore, willing to release Jesus, spake again to them.
		21		But they cried, saying, Crucify him, crucify him.
		22		And he (ie: Pilate) said unto them the 3rd. time,
		22B		Why, what evil hath he done? (Mt.27:23/Mk.15:14/Lk.23:22)
		22C		I have found no cause of death in him:
		22D		I will therefore chastise him, and let him go.
		23		And they were instant with loud voices,
		23B		requiring - that he might be crucified.
		23C		And the voices of them, and the chief priests prevailed.
			6C	Pilate saith unto them,
			6D	Take ye him, and crucify him: for I find no fault in him.
			7	The Jews answered him, We have a law, and by our law
			7B	he ought to die, because he made himself the Son of God.
			8	When Pilate therefore heard that saying, he was the more afraid;
			9	And went again into the judgment hall,
			9B	and saith unto Jesus, Whence art thou?
			9C	But Jesus gave him no answer.
			10	Then saith Pilate unto him,
			10B	Speakest thou not unto me? Knowest thou not that
			10C	I have power to crucify thee, and have power to release thee?
			11	Jesus answered, Thou couldest have no power against me,
			11B	except it were given thee from above:
			11C	therefore he that delivered me unto thee hath the greater sin.
			12	And from thenceforth Pilate sought to release him:
			12B	But the Jews cried out, saying,
			12C	If thou let this man go, thou art not Caesar's friend:
			12D	whosoever maketh himself a king speaketh against Caesar.

Mt.27   Mk.15   Lk.23   Jn.19

			13	When Pilate therefore heard that saying,
			13B	he brought Jesus forth: and sat down in the judgment seat,
			13C	In a place that is called, Pavement, but in Hebrew, Gabbatha.
			14	And it was the preparation of the passover (about the 6th. hour):
			14B	And he saith unto the Jews, Behold your King!
			15	But they cried out, Away with him, away with him, crucify him.
			15B	Pilate saith unto them, Shall I crucify your King?
			15C	The chief priests answered, We have no king but Caesar.
24				When Pilate saw that
24B				he could prevail nothing, but that rather a tumult was made,
24C				He took water, and washed his hands before the multitude, saying,
24D				I am innocent of the blood of this just person: see ye to it.
25				Then answered all the people,
25B				and said, His blood be on us, and on our children.
		15		And so Pilate, willing to content the people;
			24	And Pilate gave sentence, that it should be as they required:
26	15B	25A,C		Then released he unto them (him, whom they had desired) Barabbas,
		25B		who for sedition and murder was cast into prison.
26B	15D	25D,F		And he (ie: Pilate), to their will (when he had scourged Jesus),
26C	15C,E	25E	16	he delivered him therefore unto them, to be crucified.
27	16		16B	Then they (the soldiers of the governor) took Jesus,
27B	16B		16C	and led him away into the common hall (called Praetorium).
27C	16C			And they call together (gathered) unto him - the whole band.
28				And they stripped him,
28B	17			and they put on (clothed) him in purple (with a scarlet robe),
29	17B			and when they had platted a crown of thorns, and
29B	17C			they put it upon/about his head, and a reed in his right hand:
29C	18			And they bowed the knee before him, and began to
29D	18B			salute (and mocked) him, saying, Hail, King of the Jews!
30	19			And they did spit upon him, and took the reed and smote him
30B	19B			on the head, and bowing their knees worshipped him.
31	20			And when (after that) they had mocked him,
31B	20B			they took the robe (the purple) off from him, and put his own
31C	20C			raiment/clothing on him, and led him out/away to crucify him.
32		26		And as they led him away (as they came out),
			17	and he (ie: Jesus) bearing his cross went forth:
32B	21	26B		And they found (they laid hold upon)
	21D	26D		one who passed by coming out of the country,
32C	21C	26C		A man of Cyrene (a Cyrenian), Simon by name
	21E			(the father of Alexander)
32D	21B,F			and him they compelled to bear the cross:
		26E		And on him they laid the cross,
		26F		that he might bear it after Jesus.
		27		And there followed him a great company of people,
		27B		and of women, which also bewailed and lamented him.
		28		But Jesus turning unto them said,
		28B		Daughters of Jerusalem, weep not for me,
		28C		but weep for yourselves, and for your children.
When they	29			For, behold, the days are coming,
(in the	29B			in which they shall say, Blessed are the barren, and
green)	29C			the wombs that never bare, and the paps which never gave suck.
say to the	30			Then shall they begin to say to the mountains,
mountains,	30B			Fall on us; and to the hills, Cover us.
Fall on us!	31			For if they do these things in a green tree,
	31B			what shall be done in the dry? (Rev.6:16)
	32			And there were
	32B			also 2 other, male-factors, led with him to be put to death.

144 | Assembly by John Douma

Mt.27	Mk.15	Lk.23	Jn.19	
		33		And when they were come to the place, which is called Calvary:
33	22			And they bring him (and when they were come)
33B	22B		17B,D	unto (into) a/the place (which in Hebrew, is) called Golgotha,
33C	22C		17C	which/that is to say (being interpreted), The place of a skull:
34	23			They gave him vinegar (wine) to drink mingled with gall (myrrh).
34B	23B			And when he had tasted there-of,
34C	23C			he would not drink (but, he received it not).
		33B	18	There/Where they crucified him,
38	27	33C	18B	And they crucified with him the 2 other malefactors (thieves),
38B	27B	33D	18C	one on the right hand, and the other on the left,
			18D	and Jesus in the midst.
	28			And the scripture was fulfilled, (Is.53:12)
	28B			which saith, And he was numbered with the transgressors.
35	25			And it was the 3rd. hour, and they crucified him.
			19	And Pilate wrote a title, and put it on the cross.
37	26	38		And over him (his head), the superscription of his accusation:
			19B	And the writing was,
37B	26B	38C	19C	This is Jesus of Nazareth the King of the Jews.
			20	This title then read many of the Jews,
			20B	for the place where Jesus was crucified was nigh to the city:
		38B	20C	And it was written in letters of Greek, Latin, and Hebrew.
			21	Then said the chief priests of the Jews to Pilate,
			21B	Write not, The King of the Jews;
			21C	but that he said, I am King of the Jews.
			22	Pilate answered, What I have written I have written.
	24		23	And, the soldiers, when (ie: after) they had crucified Jesus,
			23B	Took his garments, and made 4 parts,
			23C	to ever soldier a part; and also his coat:
			23D	Now the coat was without seam, woven from the top throughout:
			24	They said therefore among themselves,
			24B	Let us not rend it, but cast lots for it, whose it shall be:
35B	24B			They parted his garments, casting lots upon them,
	24C			what every man should take.
35C			24C	That the scripture might be fulfilled,
35D			24D	which was spoken by the prophet,
35E			24E	which saith, They parted my garment/raiment among them,
35F			24F	and upon/for my vesture they did cast lots. (Ps.22:18)
			24G	These things therefore the soldiers did.
36				And sitting down they watched (ie: to keep) him there. (Mt.27:24)
			25	Now there stood by the cross of Jesus,
			25B	-his mother,
			25C	-and his mother's sister the wife of Cleophas,
			25D	-and Mary Magdalene.
			26	When Jesus therefore saw his mother,
			26B	and the disciple standing by, whom he loved,
			26C	He saith unto his mother, Woman, behold thy son!
			27	Then saith he to the disciple, Behold thy mother!
			27B	And from that hour that disciple took her unto his own home.
		34		And said Jesus,
		34B		Father, forgive them; for they know not what they do.
35B+	24B+	34C		And they parted his raiment, and cast lots.
		35		And the people stood beholding.
39	29			And they that passed by
39B	29B			railed on him (reviled him), wagging their heads, and saying,
40	29C			Ah, thou that destroyest the temple, and buildest it in 3 days,

Mt.27	Mk.15	Lk.23	Jn.19	
40B	30			Save thyself, if thou be the Son of God,
40C	30B			and come down from the cross.
41	31			Likewise also the chief priests mocking
41B	31B			said among themselves with the scribes and elders,
42	31C			He saved others; himself he cannot save.
42B	32			Let Christ the King of Israel (if he be the King of Israel),
42C	32B			let him descend (let him now come down) from the cross,
42D	32C			And we will believe him (that we may see and believe).
43				He trusted in God;
43B				Let Him deliver him now, If He will have him:
43C				for he said, I am the Son of God.
44	32D			And they (the thieves), which were crucified with him,
44B	32E			also reviled him (cast the same in his teeth).
		35B		And the rulers also
		35C		with them derided him, saying, He saved others;
		35D		Let him save himself, if he be Christ, the chosen of God.
		36		And the soldiers also mocked him,
		36B		coming to him, and offering him vinegar,
		37		and saying, If thou be the King of the Jews, save thyself.
		38A+		And a superscription also was written over him in letters
		38B+		of Greek, and Latin, and Hebrew, This is the King of the Jews.
		39		And one of the malefactors which were hanged railed on him,
		39B		saying, If thou be Christ, save thyself and us.
		40		But the other answering rebuked him, saying, Dost not
		40B		thou fear God, seeing thou art in the same condemnation?
		41		And we indeed justly; for we receive the due reward
		41B		of our deeds: but this man hath done nothing amiss.
		42		And he said unto Jesus,
		42B		Lord, remember me when thou comest into thy kingdom.
		43		And Jesus said unto him, Verily,
		43B		I say unto thee, To-day shalt thou be with me in paradise.
45	33	44		Now from about the 6th. hour (when the 6th. hour was come),
45B	33B	44B		and there was darkness over over the whole land (all the earth)
45C	33C	44C		until (unto) the 9th. hour.
46	34			And at about the 9th. hour Jesus cried with a loud voice,
46B	34B			saying, Eli, Eli (Eloi, Eloi), lama sabach-tha'ni?
46C	34C			which is (that is to say) being interpreted,
46D	34D			My God, My God, why hast thou forsaken me?
47	35			And some of them that stood by (that stood there),
47B	35B			when they heard, said, Behold, he (this man) calleth for Elias.
			28	After this, Jesus knowing that all things were now accomplished,
			28B	that the scripture might be fulfilled, saith, I thirst.
			29	Now there was set a vessel full of vinegar:
48	36		29B	And they (one of them) straightway
48B	36B		29C	ran, and took a spunge, and filled it full of vinegar,
48C	36C		29D	and put it upon hyssop (and put it on a reed),
48D	36D		29E	and put it to his mouth, and gave him to drink.
49	36E			The rest said, Let alone (let be), let us see
49B	36F			whether Elias will come to save him (to take him down).
			30	When Jesus therefore had received the vinegar,
			30B	he said, It is finished:
		45		And the sun was darkened,
		45B		And the veil of the temple was rent in the midst.
50	37	46		And when Jesus had cried again with a loud voice
		46B		he said, Father, into thy hands I commend my spirit:
		46C	30C	And, having said thus, he bowed his head,

```
Mt.27   Mk.15   Lk.23   Jn.19
```

50B	37B	46D	30D	and yielded up (gave up) the ghost.
51	38			And, behold, the veil of the temple
51B	38B			was rent (ie: to rend) in twain from the top to the bottom:
51C				And the earth did quake, and the rocks rent;
52				And the graves were opened;
52B				and many bodies of the saints which slept arose,
53				And came out of the graves, after his resurrection, (Rev.22:19)
53B				and went into the Holy City, and appeared unto many.
54	39	47		Now when the centurion (which stood over against him),
	39B			saw that he so cried out, and gave up the ghost:
		47B		Seeing what was done, he glorified God,
		47C		-saying, Certainly this was a righteous man;
	39C			-he said, Truly this man was the Son of God.
54B				And they that were with him (with the centurion), watching Jesus
54C				saw the earthquake, and those things that were done,
54D				They feared greatly,
54E				saying, Truly this man was the Son of God.
			31	The Jews therefore, because it was the preparation,
			31B	that the bodies should not remain upon the cross
			31C	on the sabbath (Jn.18:28/Mk.15:42/Jn.19:14/De.16:6/Num.9:5)
			31D	(For the sabbath day was an high day),
			31E	Besought Pilate that their legs might be broken,
			31F	and that they might be taken away.
			32	Then came the soldiers, and brake the legs of the first,
			32B	and of the other - which was crucified with him.
			33	But when they came to Jesus,
			33B	and saw that he was dead already, they brake not his legs:
			34	But one of the soliers with a spear pierced his side,
			34B	and forthwith came there out blood and water.
			35	And he that saw it bare record (ie: witness),
			35B	and his record (ie: witness/testimony) is true:
			35C	And he knoweth that he saith true (ie: he speaketh truth),
			35D	that ye might believe.
			36	For these things were done, that the scripture (Ps.34:20)
			36B	should be fulfilled, A bone of him shall not be broken.
			37	And again another scripture saith,
			37B	They shall look on him whom they pierced. (Zech.12:10)
		48		And all the people that came together to that sight,
		48B		beholding the things which were done,
		48C		smote their breasts, and returned. (Mt.27:25)
55	40	49		And all his acquaintance, and also the women (many women)
55B	40B	49C		were there beholding (looking on) these things afar off.
56	40C			Among which/whom was Mary Magdalene, and
56B	40D	Little James		Mary the mother of James the less, and of Joses, and Salome,
56C				And the mother of Zebedee's children:
	41			Who also, when he was in Galilee, followed him,
55		49B		that/which followed him (Jesus) from Galilee
55D	41B			and ministering unto (ie: to serve) him.
	41C			And many other women which came up with him unto Jerusalem.
57	42		38	And after this, when the evening was come,
	42B			because it was the preparation (ie: the day before the sabbath);
57B,D	43	50	38B	And behold there came a man named Joseph,
57C	43B	51C	38C	a rich man of Arimathaea (a city of the Jews),
57E			38D	who himself being a disciple of Jesus;
	43C	50B		An honourable counsellor; and he was a good man, and a just,

Mt.27	Mk.15	Lk.23	Jn.19	
	43D	51D		which/who also himself waited for the kingdom of God:
58		51A		And he, this man
		51B		(who had not consented to the counsel and deed of them),
		52	38E	but secretly (for fear of the Jews), he came,
58B	43E	52B		and went in boldly (ie: durst = to dare to) unto Pilate,
58C	43F	52C	38F	and besought (begged/craved) Pilate, that
58D	43G	52D	38G	he might take away the body of Jesus.
	44			And Pilate marvelled if he were already dead:
	44B			And calling unto him the centurion (ie: the captain of 100),
	44C			he asked him whether he had been any while dead.
	45			And when he knew it of the centurion,
	45B			he gave (ie: granted) the body to Joseph:
			38H	and Pilate gave him leave (ie: to give permission):
58E				Then Pilate commanded the body to be delivered (ie: be given).
	46			And he (ie: Joseph) bought fine linen:
	46B	53		And he took (ie: having taken) it/him down:
			38I	He (ie: Joseph) came therefore, and took the body of Jesus.
59				And when Joseph had taken the body;
			39	And there came also Nicodemus,
			39B	(which at first came to Jesus by night), (Jn.3:1,2/Jn.7:50)
			39C	and brought a mixture of myrrh and aloes, about an 100 pound.
59B			40	Then took he/they the body of Jesus,
59C	46C	53B	40B	and wrapped/wound it in the clean linen clothes with the spices,
			40C	as the manner of the Jews is to bury.
			41	Now in the place where he was crucified there was a garden; and
			41B	in the garden a new sepulchre:
60	46D	53C		And laid it in his (ie: Joseph's) own new tomb,
60B	46E	53D		a sepulchre which he had hewn out in the stone/rock:
		53E	41C	wherein never man before was laid.
		42		There laid they Jesus therefore
		42B		because of the Jews' preparation day;
		42C		for the sepulchre was nigh at hand.
60C	46F			And he rolled a great stone
60D	46G			unto the door of the sepulchre, and departed.
		54		And that day was the preparation, and the sabbath drew on.

> Note: It was the day of preparation, and the sabbath drew on. What sort of sabbath was this? There is agreement, that Jesus was crucified on the 14th. day of Nisan. Friday or Wednesday? First we will explore/examine the Friday theary, followed by the Wednesday (mid-week) theary.

Mt.27	Mk.15	Lk.23	Jn.19	
		55		And the women also,
		55B		which came with him from Galilee, followed after:
61	47			And there was Mary Magdalene, and the other Mary (mother of Joses),
61B				sitting over-against (ie: before/in front of) the sepulchre,
	47B	55C		and (they) beheld the sepulchre, where/how his body was laid;
		56		and they returned,
		56B		and prepared spices and ointments.
		56C		And rested the sabbath day (ie: the Saterday sabbath)
		56D		according to the commandment.
62				Now the next day (that followed the day of the preparation),
62B	Saterday sabbath.			The chief priests and Pharisees came together unto Pilate,
63				saying, Sir, we remember that this deceiver
63B				said (while he was yet alive), After 3 days I will rise again.
64				Command therefore
64B				that the sepulchre be made sure until the 3rd. day,
64C				lest his disciples come by night, and steal him away,
64D				and say unto the people, He is risen from the dead:
64E				So the last error shall be worse than the first.

```
Mt.27   Mk.15   Lk.23   Jn.19
65                              Pilate saith unto them,
65B                                 Ye have a watch: go your way, make it as sure as you can.
66                              So they went, and
66B                                 made the sepulchre sure, sealing the stone, and setting a watch.
Mt.28   Mk.16
1       Saterday sabbath.       In the end of the sabbath,
1B                                  as it began to dawn toward the fist day of the week:
```

> Note; This should have been translated,
> In the end of the sabbath(s),
>   as it began to dawn toward the first of the sabbath(s).

```
        1       Saterday        And when the sabbath was past:
1C      1B      Sunday          Came Mary Magdalene,
1D      1C                          and the other Mary (the mother of James, and Salome),
1E                                  to see the sepulchre.
        1D                      They had bought sweet spices,
        1E                          that they might come and anoint him.
```

O——— The Wednesday (mid-week) Crucifixion theory ———————————————————O

```
Mt.27   Mk.15   Lk.23
                55              And the women also,
                55B                 which came with him from Galilee, followed after:
61      47                      And there was Mary Magdalene, and the other Mary (mother of Joses),
61B                                 sitting over-against (ie: before/in front of) the sepulchre,
        47B     55C                 and (they) beheld the sepulchre, where/how his body was laid;
                56                  and they returned.
62                              The next day (that followed the day of the preparation),
62B     Thursday sabbath        The chief priests and Pharisees came together unto Pilate,
63                                  saying, Sir, we remember that this deceiver
63B                                 said (while he was yet alive), After 3 days I will rise again.
64                              Command therefore
64B                                 that the sepulchre be made sure until the 3rd. day,
64C                                 lest his disciples come by night, and steal him away,
64D                                 and say unto the people, He is risen from the dead:
64E                                 So the last error shall be worse than the first.
65                              Pilate saith unto them,
65B                                 Ye have a watch: go your way, make it as sure as you can.
66                              So they went, and
66B                                 made the sepulchre sure, sealing the stone, and setting a watch.
Mt.28   Mk.16
        1       Thursday        And when the sabbath was passed:
        1B,C    Friday          Mary Magdalene, and Mary (mother of James, and Salome),
        1D                          they *** bought sweet spices,
                56B                 and prepared spices and ointments
        1E                              that they might come and anoint him.
                56C             And rested the sabbath day (ie: the Saterday sabbath)
                56D                 according to the commandment.
1                               And in the end of the sabbath,
1B                                  as it began to dawn toward the first day of the week:
```

> Note: This should have been translated,
> In the end of the sabbath(s),
>   as it began to dawn toward the first of the sabbath(s).

```
1C,D,E          Sunday          Came Mary Magdalene, and the other Mary to see the sepulchre.
```
O——O

```
        Lk.24   Jn.20
```

The Gospels of Matthew, Mark, Luke, and John: Merged into One Historic Calendar of Events

Mt.28	Mk.16	Lk.24	Jn.20	
2				And, behold, there was a great earthquake: (Mt.27:51B-53)
2B				for the angel of the Lord descended from heaven, and
2C				came and rolled back the stone from the door, and sat upon it.
3				His countenance was like lightning, and his raiment white as snow:
4				And for fear of him
4B				the keepers did shake, and became as dead men. (they ran?)
	2			And very early in the morning
	2B			the first day if the week (ie: the first of sabbaths),
	2C			they came unto the sepulchre at the rising of the sun.
	3			And they said among themselves,
	3B			Who shall roll away the stone from the door of the sepulchre?
	4			And when they looked, they saw
	4B			that the stone was rolled away: for it was very great.
	5			And entering into the sepulchre,
	5B			they saw a young man sitting on the right side,
	5C			clothed in a long white garment: And they were affrighted.
5	6			And he (the young man/an angel) answered and saith unto the women,
5B	6B			Be not affrighted (fear ye not):
5C	6C			For I know that, Ye seek Jesus of Nazareth, which was crucified:
6	6D			He is not here: for he is risen - as he said:
6B	6E			Behold, come see the place
6C	6F			where they laid him (where the Lord lay).
7	7			But go your way (and go quickly), and
7B	7B			tell his disciples and Peter, that he is risen from the dead;
7C	7C			And behold, he goeth before you into Galilee; there shall ye
7D	7D			see him, as he said unto you: Lo, I have told you.
	8			And they went out quickly, and fled from the sepulchre:
	8B			for they trembled and were amazed (ie: astonished/in a trance)
	8C			neither said they any thing to any man; for they were afraid.
		1	1	Now upon the first day of the week (ie: the first of sabbaths),
		1B	1C	very early in the morning (early, when it was yet dark);
		1C	1B	Cometh/Came they (ie: the women) + Mary Magdalene unto
		1D	1D	the sepulchre, bringing the spices which they had prepared:
		1E		And certain others with them.
		2	1E	And they found (she seeth)
		2B	1F	the stone rolled away (taken away) from the sepulchre.
		3		And they entered in, and found not the body of the Lord Jesus.
			2	Then she (ie: Mary Magdalene) runneth, and cometh
			2B	to Simon Peter, and to the other disciple, whom Jesus loved,
			2C	and saith unto them, They have taken away the Lord out of
			2D	the sepulchre, and "we" know not where they have laid him.
		4		And it came to pass, as they (ie: the women at the tomb)
		4B		were much perplexed thereabout,
		4C		behold, 2 men stood by them in shining garments:
		5		And as they were afraid, and bowed down their faces to the earth;
		5B		They said unto them, Why seek ye the living among the dead?
		6		He is not here, but is risen:
		6B		Remember how he spake unto you when he was yet in Galilee,
		7		saying, The Son of man must be delivered into the hands
		7B		of sinful men, and be crucified, and the 3rd. day rise again.
		8,9		And they remembered his words, and returned from the sepulchre,
8				They departed quickly from the sepulchre with
8B				fear and great joy; and did run to bring his disciples word,
		9B		and told all these things unto the 11, and to all the rest.
		Mean-while	3	Peter therefore (ie: having heard Mary) went forth, (Jn.20:2)
			3B	and that other disciple, and came to the sepulchre.
			4	So they ran both together: And the other disciple

Assembly by John Douma

	Mt.28	Mk.16	Lk.24	Jn.20	
				4B	did outrun Peter, and came first to the sepulchre.
				5	And he stooping down, and looking in,
				5B	saw the linen clothes lying; yet went he not in.
				6	Then cometh Simon Peter following him,
				6B	and went into the sepulchre, and seeth the linen clothes lie,
				7	And the napkin, that was about his head, not lying with
				7B	the linen clothes, but wrapped together in a place by itself.
				8	Then went in also that other disciple, which came first
				8B	to the sepulchre, and he saw and believed. (Jn.20:2)
				9	For as yet they knew not the scripture,
				9B	that he must rise from the dead. (Lk.18:33,34)
				10	Then the disciples went away again unto their own home.
				11	But Mary stood without at the sepulchre weeping: and
				11B	as she wept, she stooped down, and looked into the sepulchre.
				12	And seeth 2 angels in white sitting, one at the head, (Lk.24:4)
				12B	and the other at the feet, where the body of Jesus had lain.
				13	And they say unto her, Woman, why weepest thou?
				13B	She said unto them, Because they have taken away my Lord,
				13C	and I know not where they have laid him.
				14	And when she had thus said, she turned herself back,
				14B	and saw Jesus standing, and knew not that it was Jesus.
				15	Jesus saith unto her, Woman, why weepest thou? Whom seekest thou?
				15B	She, supposing him to be the gardener,
				15C	saith unto him, Sir, if thou have borne him hence,
				15D	tell me where thou hast laid him, and I will take him away.
She heard clearly				16	Jesus saith unto her, Mary. (Eccl.3:4)
				16B	She turned herself,
				16C	and saith unto him, Rabboni; which is to say, Master.
			9		Now when Jesus was risen
			9B		early the first day of the week (ie: first of the sabbaths),
			9C		he appeared first to Mary Magdalene, (Jn.20:11-16)
			9D		out of whom he had cast 7 devils. (Lk.8:2)
				17	Jesus saith unto her (ie: Mary Magdalene),
				17B	Touch me not; for I am not yet ascended to my Father:
				17C	But go to my brethren, and say unto them, I ascend
				17D	unto my Father, and your Father; and to my God, and your God.
			10		And she (ie: Mary Magdalene) went --------------
	9				And as they (ie: the women) went to tell his disciples, (Lk.24:9)
	9B				Behold, Jesus met them, saying, All hail (ie: rejoice/be glad).
	9C				And they came and held him by the feet, and worshipped him.
	10				Then said Jesus unto them, Be not afraid:
	10B				Go tell my brethren that they go into Galilee,
	10C				and there shall they see me. (Mt.28:16,17)

> Note: Mt.28:9A and Mt.28:11A, and compare them with Lk.24:23.
> As they went to tell his disciples (they met Jesus),
>   and (:11) as they were going, some of the watch ---------.
> Perhaps, these verses should read, as follows:
> After they went to tell his disciples (they met Jesus),
>   and, as they were going (again), some of the watch ------.
> For, in Lk.24:23 there is no hint of them having met Jesus.

	Mt.28				
	11				Now when they (ie: the women) were going,
	11B				Behold, some of the watch came into the city, and
	11C				shewed unto the chief priests all the things that were done.
	12				And when they were assembled with the elders,
	12B				and had taken counsel, they gave large money unto the soldiers,

The Gospels of Matthew, Mark, Luke, and John: Merged into One Historic Calendar of Events

Mt.28 Mk.16 Lk.24 Jn.20

13				Saying, Say ye, His disciples
13B				came by night, and stole him away while we slept.
14				And if this come to the governor's ears,
14B				we will persuade him, and secure you.
15	Hush Money!			So they took the money, and did as they were taught:
15B				And this saying
15C				is commonly reported among the Jews until this day.
		18		Mary Magdalene came,
	10B			and told them that had been with him, as they mourned and wept;
		18B		And told the disciples that she had seen the Lord,
		18C		and that he had spoken these things unto her.
	11			And they, when they had heard that he was alive,
	11B			and had been seen of her, believed her not.
		10		It was Mary Magdalene, and Joanna, and Mary (mother of James),
		10B		and other women that were with them,
		10C		which told these things unto the apostles.
		11		And their words
		11B		seemed to them as idle tales, and they believed them not.
		12		Then arose Peter, and ran unto the sepulchre; and stooping down,
		12B		he beheld the linen clothes laid by themselves, and
		12C		departed, wondering in himself at that which was come to pass.
	12			After that he appeared in another form unto 2 of them:
		13		That same day, behold 2 of them,
	12B			as they walked, and went into the country,
		13B		to the village called Emmaus;
		13C		which was from Jerusalem about threescore (3x20=60) furlongs.
		14		And they talked together of all these things which had happened.
		15		And it came to pass, that, while they communed and reasoned,
		15B		Jesus himself drew near, and went with them.
		16		But their eyes were holden - that they should not know him.
		17		And he (ie: Jesus) said unto them,
		17B		What manner of communications are these
		17C		that ye have one to another, as ye walk and are sad?
		18		And the one of them (whose name was Cleophas), answering said
		18B		unto him, Art thou only (ie: alone) a stranger in Jerusalem?
		18C		and know not the things that came to pass in it, in these days?
		19		And he said unto them, What things?
		19B		And they said unto him, The things concerning Jesus of Nazareth,
		19C		which was a prophet
		19D		mighty in deed and word before God and all the people:
		20		And how the chief priests and our rulers delivered him
		20B		to be condemned to death, and have crucified him.
		21		But we trusted that it had been he which
		21B		should have redeemed Israel: (Jn.1:41:Jn.20:30,31/Jn.4:25,26)
		21C		And beside all this, to day is the 3rd. day
		21D		since these things were done.
		22		Yea, and certain women (also of our company), (Lk.24:9)
		22B		made us astonished, which were early at the sepulchre;
		23		and when they found not his body, they came saying, that they
		23B		had also seen a vision of angels, which said that he was alive.
		24		And certain of them which were with us went to the sepulchre, and
		24B		found it even so as the women had said: but him they saw not.
		25		Then he (ie: Jesus) said unto them, O fools (ie: unwise/foolish),
		25B		and slow of heart to believe all that the prophets have spoken:
		26		Ought not Christ to have suffered these things,
		26B		and to enter into his glory?

Mt.28	Mk.16	Lk.24	Jn.20	
		27		And beginning at Moses and all the prohets, he expounded
		27B		unto them in all the scriptures the things concerning himself.
		28		And they drew nigh unto the village, whither they went: (Lk.24:13)
		28B		and he made as though he would have gone further.
		29		But they constrained him, saying, Abide with us:
		29B		for it is toward evening, and the day is far spent.
		29C		And he went in to tarry with them.
		30		And it came to pass, as he sat at meat with them,
		30B		he took bread, and blessed it, and brake it, and gave to them.
		31		And their eyes were opened, and they knew him;
		31B		and he vanished out of their sight.
		32		And they said one to another,
		32B		Did not our heart burn within us, while he talked with us
		32C		by the way, and while he opened to us the scriptures?
		33		And they rose up the same hour, and returned to Jerusalem, and
		33B		found the 11 gathered together, and them that were with them.
	13			And they went and told it unto the residue,
		34		Saying, The Lord is risen indeed, and hath appeared to Simon.
		35		And they told what things were done in the way,
		35B		and how he was known of them in the breaking of bread:
	13B			Neither believed they them. (Lk.24:11)
			19	Then the same day at evening,
			19B	being the first day of the week (ie: first of the sabbaths),
			19C	When the doors were shut
			19D	where the disciples were assembled for fear of the Jews,
		36	24+	And as they thus spake (note: Thomas ------ was not with them),
		36B	19E	Came Jesus himself and stood in the midst of them,
		36C	19F	and saith unto them, Peace be unto you.
		37		But they were terrified and affrighted,
		37B		and supposed that they had seen a spirit.
		38		And he said unto them,
		38B		Why are ye troubled? and why do thoughts arise in your hearts?
		39		Behold (ie: see) my hands and my feet, that it is I myself:
		39B		Handle (ie: touch) me, and see;
		39C		for a spirit hath not flesh and bones, as ye see me have.
		40		And when he had thus spoken, he shewed them his hands and feet.
		41		And while they yet believed not for joy, and wondered,
		41B		he said unto them, Have ye here any meat?
		42		And they gave him a piece of a broiled fish, and of an honeycomb.
		43		And he took it, and did eat before them. (Gen.18:8)
			20	And when he had so (ie: that/this) said,
			20B	he shewed unto them his hands and his side.
			20C	Then were the disciples glad, when they saw the Lord.
			21	Then said Jesus to them again, Peace be unto you:
			21B	as my Father hath sent me, even so send I you.
Receive ye			22	And when he had said this, he breathed on them,
the Holy Ghost.			22B	and saith unto them, Receive ye the Holy Ghost:
			23	Whose soever sins ye remit (ie: forgive/suffer/send away),
			23B	they are (ie: shall have been) remitted unto them; and
			23C	Whose soever sins ye retain (ie: hold/hold fast/keep),
			23D	they are (ie: shall have been) retained.
			24	But Thomas (one of the 12), called Didymus,
			24B	was not with them when Jesus came.
			25	The other disciples therefore
			25B	said unto him, We have seen the Lord.
			25C	But he said unto them, Except I

Mt.28 Mk.16 Lk.24 Jn.20

		25D	shall see in his hands the print of the nails,
		25E	and put my finger into the print of the nails,
		25F	and thrust my hands into his side, I will not believe.
	14	26	And (afterward) after 8 days
		26B	again his disciples were within, and Thomas with them:
	14B		(he appeared unto the 11 as they sat at meat):
		26C	Then came Jesus, the doors being shut,
		26D	and stood in the midst, and said, Peace be unto you.
		27	Then saith he to Thomas,
		27B	Reach hither thy finger, and behold my hands; and
		27C	Reach hither thy hand, and thrust it into my side:
My Lord		27D	and be not faithless, but believing.
and my God!		28	And Thomas answered and said unto him, My Lord and my God.
		29	Jesus saith unto him, Thomas,
		29B	because thou hast seen me, thou hast believed:
		29C	Blessed are they that have not seen, and yet have believed.
	14C		And he upbraided (ie: reviled) them (Mt.11:20/Mt.27:44/James 1:5)
	14D		with their unbelief and hardness of heart, because
	14E		they believed not them which had seen him after he was risen.

44		And he (ie: Jesus) said unto them,
44B		These are the words which I spake unto you, (Lk.18:31-34)
44C		while I was yet with you, that all things must be fulfilled,
44D		which concerning me were written
44E		in the law of Moses, and in the prophets, and in the psalms,
45		Then opened he their understanding,
45B		that they might understand the scriptures, (Lk.24:27)
46		And he said unto them,
46B		Thus it is written, and thus it behoved (ie: must needs/ought)
46C		Christ to suffer, and to rise from the dead the 3rd. day:
47		And that repentance and remission of sins should be preached
47B		in his name among all nations, beginning at Jerusalem.
48		And ye are witnesses (ie: martyr/witness) of these things.

30	And many other signs truly did Jesus in the
30B	presence of his disciples, which are not written in this book:
31	But these are written,
31B	that ye might believe that Jesus is the Christ, the Son of God;
31C	and that believing ye might have life through his name.

Jn.21

	1	After these things
	1B	Jesus shewed himself again to the disciples
	1C	at the sea of Tiberias; and in this wise shewed he himself.
	2	There were together Simon Peter,
	2B	and Thomas called Didymus, and Nathanael of Cana in Galilee,
	2C	and the 2 sons of Zebedee, and 2 other of his disciples.
I go afishing.	3	Simon Peter saith unto them, I go afishing.
	3B	They say unto him, We also go with thee.
	3C	They went forth, and entered
	3D	into a ship immediately; and that night they caught nothing.
	4	But when the morning was now come, Jesus stood on the shore:
	4B	but the disciples knew not that it was Jesus. (Mk.16:12)
	5	Then Jesus saith unto them, Children, have ye any meat?
	5B	They answered him, No.
	6	And he said unto them,
	6B	Cast the net on the right side of the ship, and ye shall find.
	6C	They cast therefore, and
	6D	now they were not able to draw it for the multitude of fishes.

Mt.28 Mk.16 Lk.24 Jn.21

	7	Therefore that disciple
	7B	whom Jesus loved saith unto Peter, It is the Lord.
	7C	Now when Simon Peter heard that it was the Lord,
	7D	he girt his fisher's coat unto him (for he was naked),
	7E	and did cast himself into the sea.
	8	And the other disciples came in a little ship;
	8B	(for they were not far from land, but as it were 200 cubits):
	8C	dragging the net with fishes.
	9	As soon then as they were come to land, they
	9B	saw a fire of coals there, and fish laid thereon, and bread.
	10	Jesus saith unto them, Bring of the fish which ye have now caught.
	11	Simon Peter went up,
	11B	and drew the net to land full of great fishes, 100+50+3=153:
	11C	and for all there were so many, yet was not the net broken.
	12	Jesus saith unto them, Come and dine.
This is now	12B	And none of the disciples durst ask him, Who art thou?
the 3rd. time	12C	knowing that it was the Lord. (Jn.20:16/Lk.24:35)
that Jesus	13	Jesus then cometh,
shewed	13B	and taketh bread, and giveth them, and fish likewise.
himself to	14	This is now the 3rd. time that Jesus shewed himself
his disciples.	14B	to his disciples, after that he was risen from the dead.
	15	So when they had dined,
	15B	Jesus saith to Simon Peter,
	15C	Simon, son of Jonas, lovest thou me more than these?
	15D	He saith unto him,
	15E	Ye, Lord; thou knowest that I love thee.
Feed my lambs.	15F	He saith unto him, Feed my lambs.
	16	He saith to him again the 2nd. time,
	16B	Simon, son of Jonas, lovest thou me?
	16C	He saith unto Him,
	16D	Yea, Lord; thou knowest that I love thee.
Feed my sheep.	16E	He saith unto him, Feed my sheep.
	17	He saith unto him the 3rd. time,
	17B	Simon, son of Jonas, lovest thou me?
	17C	Peter was grieved
	17D	because he said unto him the 3rd. time, Lovest thou me?
	17E	And he said unto him, Lord,
	17F	thou knowest all things; thou knowest that I love thee.
Feed my sheep.	17G	Jesus saith unto him, Feed my sheep.
	18	Verily, verily, I say unto thee, When thou wast young
	18B	thou girdedst thyself, and walkedst whither thou wouldest:
	18C	But when thou shalt be old, thou shalt stretch forth thy hands,
	18D	and another shall gird thee,
	18E	and carry thee whither thou wouldest not.
	19	This spake he, signifying by what death he should glorify God.
	19B	And when he had spoken this, he saith unto him, Follow me.
	20	Then Peter, turning about,
	20B	seeth following, the disciple whom Jesus loved;
	20C	(which also leaned on his breast at supper
	20D	and said, Lord, which is he that betrayeth thee?).
	21	Peter seeing him
	21B	saith to Jesus, Lord, and what shall this man do?
	22	Jesus saith unto him,
	22B	If I will that he tarry till I come,
	22C	what is that to thee? follow thou me.
	23	Then went this saying abroad
	23B	among the brethren, that this disciple should not die:

Mt.28 Mk.16 Lk.24 Jn.21

			23C	Yet Jesus said not unto him, He shall not die; but, If
			23D	I will that he tarry till I come, what is that to thee?
			24	This is the disciple which testifieth of these things, and
			24B	wrote these things: and we know that his testimony is true.
			25	And there are also many other things which Jesus did,
			25B	the which, if they should be written every one,
			25C	I suppose that even the world itself
			25D	could not contain the books that should be written.
			25E	Amen.

16	Then the 11 disciples went away into Galilee,
16B	into a mountain where Jesus had appointed them.
17	And when they saw him, they worshipped him: but some doubted.
18	And Jesus came and spake unto them,
18B	saying, All power is given unto me in heaven and in earth.
19	Go ye therefore, and Teach all nations, baptizing them
19B	in the name of the Father, and the Son, and of the Holy Ghost:
20	Teaching them
20B	to observe all things whatsoever I have commanded you:
20C	And, lo, I am with you alway, even unto the end of the world.
20D	Amen.

	15	And he said unto them, Go ye into all the world,	
	15B	and preach the gospel to every creature.	
	16	He that believeth and is baptized shall be saved;	(Lk.15:7,16)
	16B	but he that believeth not shall be damned.	
	17	And these signs shall follow them that believe;	
	17B	In my name shall they cast out devils;	
	17C	They shall speak with new tongues;	
	18	They shall take up serpents;	
	18B	And if they drink any deadly thing, it shall not hurt them;	
	18C	They shall lay hands on the sick, and they shall recover.	

		49	And, behold, I send the promise of my Father upon you:	
		49B	but tarry ye in the city of Jerusalem,	(Acts 1:4-8)
		49C	until ye be endued with power from on high.	(Acts 2)
	19		So then after the Lord had spoken unto them:	
		50	And he led them out as far as to Bethany,	
		50B	and he lifted up his hands, and blessed them.	
		51	And it came to pass, while he blessed them,	
	19B	51B	He was parted from them,	(Acts 1:9)
	19C	51C	and received (carried) up into heaven;	
	19D		and sat on the right hand of God.	
		52	And they worshipped him,	
		52B	and returned to Jerusalem with great joy:	
		53	And were continually in the temple,	
		53B	praising and blessing God.	
		53C	Amen.	

	20			And they went forth, and preached every where, (Mk.16:15)
	20B			the Lord working with them, (Mt.28:20)
	20C			and confirming the word with signs following.
20D+	20D	53C+	25E+	Amen.

Table of Topics

Page	Topic
159	From Creation.
160	End Time Ideas.
161	How many years = a Generation?
162	The Road Map to the Holy Scriptures.
163	A Change of Priesthood. The Early Church.
164	Where is Truth?
165	A Better/New Covenant.
166	Jesus was Crucified on Nisan 14, the Passover Day.
167	Passover.
168	A Time Bump.
169	What is happening?
170	The Bible Calendar.
171	Creation, BC.11,013.
172	In the beginning (BC.11,013).
173	Immediate & Potential Knowledge.
174	The Signs of the Times.
175	Stories & Events of Parabolic Significance.
176	Sitting On The Fence.
177	A New Era of Sabbath(s). 1 of 3
178	2 of 3
179	3 of 3
180	Signs (the signs of the times).
181	Changing the Times and the Laws?
182	A Ray of Hope for the hopeless.
183	Is there any thing new under the sun?
184	Hearken to the sound of the trumpet.
185	Believe not every spirit.
186	Revelation.
187	The Little Horn.
188	A Woman sitting upon a Beast.
189	Mystery Babylon.
190	How the Times have Changed.

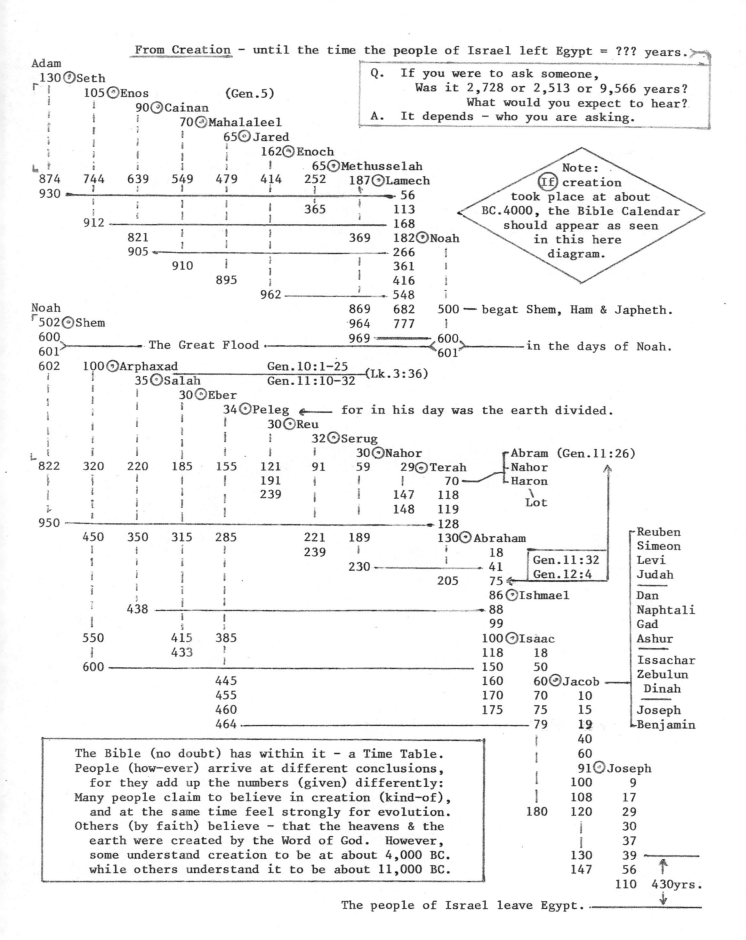

The Gospels of Matthew, Mark, Luke, and John: Merged into One Historic Calendar of Events

End Time Ideas or End Time Prophecies

> End Time Ideas = the result of serious Bible study (compare Scripture with Scripture).
> End Time Prophesies = knowledge obtained via supernatural means (voices, dreams, etc.)

When we read (prayer-fully study) the Bible, and compare Scripture with Scripture,
  having the desire within - to understand more fully, the information presented to us:
Some occurrences are extensively detailed, and we reason within, to what purpose it may so be.
There are many numbers in the Bible (numbers are words), and these too have a purpose/meaning.
There is reference to time:
  The various time spans (including the ages of particular individuals),
    and in relation one to another - they exhibit the evidence of a Bible Calendar.

Many people have devoted much of their time searching and researching the Holy Scripture,
  and have assembled/constructed their Bible Calendars dating back to creation.
However, there is a problem: the date of creation (on the various calendars) are not identical.
  There can only be one creation date.

> It was (for many years) understood/presumed, that the 2nd. coming of Jesus Christ, should
> come to pass 6000 years after creation. For if one day represents 1000 years (2 Pe.3:8),
> then (perhaps) the 6 days of creation could represent 6000 years.
> Lately, there is reason to believe, that the 6000y. theory - will not hold water.

James Usher: according to his calculation creation took place in BC.4004.
  He taught (as do the Jehovah Witnesses in their literature)
    that the children of Israel (ie: the children of Jacob) were in Egypt for 215y. (Ex.12:40)

William Miller: (of the Adventist Church),
  anticipated the 2nd. coming of Jesus to take place betwixt March of 1843 and March of 1844.

The Great White Brotherhood: (a Ukraine based Religion),
  had expectations for November 14 of 1993.

Harold Camping: (a Radio Evangelist, in the USA.),
  expected the 2nd. coming could occur in 1994. And he wrote a book, "1994?"
  and 17y. later he was confident that the Rapture and the End of this world would be in 2011.
  His unique method of calculation (having creation at BC.11013) differs from all others.

The Jehovah Witnesses (although not so named until 1931) were convinced - that,
  (1) The rapture (according to A.H. Macmillan) would occur on September 30, in 1914.
  (2) A resurrection of faithful men of old (Abraham, David, Daniel etc.) in the year 1925.
  (3) What they meant to say, the Millinium (ie: a 1000y. Reign) will begin in 1975.
    (they, at this time, have creation at BC.4026.) (BC.4026+6000y.=AD.1975)
  At this point in time (they appear to have run out of options/time, and) they conclude,
    that, there is ample evidence, that the end (the beginning of the 1000y. Reign) is near:
    And overwhelming it is - as any reasonable person should be aware of.

For all who be convinced, that the Day of the Lord cometh 6000y. after creation: After they
  locate the year of creation (and via calculation) add 6000y. to know the Day of the Lord.
There is one little problem: Every time the 2nd. coming of Jesus is postphoned,
  there is made of necessity a change also of the date of creation.
Now, there has to be a limit some where (like going out on a limb) as to how far one can
    safely continue: It depends upon the information in the Bible, and what it will allow.
Some people now believe that time-wise we already have entered the night time of the 7th. day.
  (Note: when a new day begins at sundown, the night time comes before the day time.)

Exploring, and learning from the Holy Scriptures:
Comparing spiritual with spiritual. (1 Cor.2:13)
When another Bible student (using only the Bible)
  has discovered certain interesting information;
  do not shrug it off, or say, I do not buy it,
  or say, A loving God could not do such a thing.
Take the time needed to properly examine the
  information that is presented, and peradventure you may gain some valuable knowledge from it.

> ──── Believe not every spirit ────
> Try the spirits, if out of God they be.
> There will be false teachers among you.
> Some add, and others take away - making
> changes to the Holy Scriptures, and
> having convincing reasons for so doing.

How many years = a Generation?

The people of Israel (Gen.15:13-16/Ex.12:40,41)
were in a land - that was not theirs, for 430 years (were afflicted for 400 years).
Many people are of the understanding that the people of Israel were in Egypt 430 years.
Others claim - that the Israelites were in Canaan 215 years + 215 years in Egypt.
No doubt, <u>before</u> Jacob entered into Egypt: Abraham, Isaac and Jacob dwelt in Canaan
for a period of 215 years - as sojourners in a land that was as yet not theirs.

We do know - that they came out in the 4th. generation. So how long is a generation?

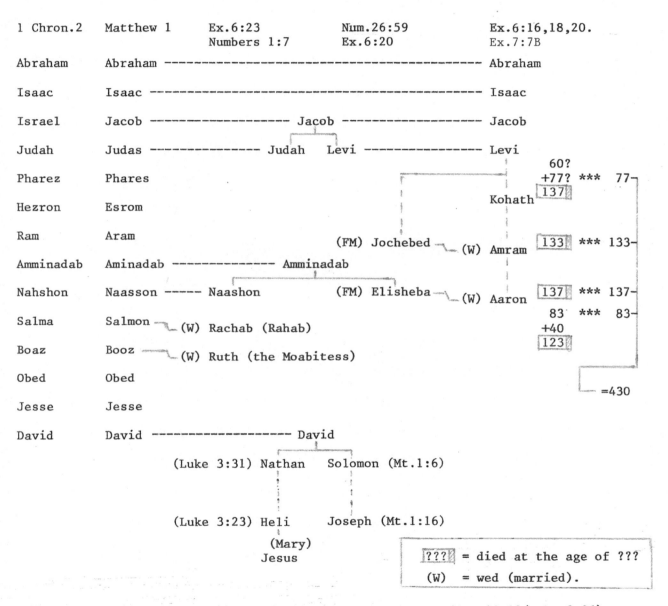

Sometime - A son of, may actually be a ------------. (Gen.11:12/Luke 3:36)
Sometime - A brother, may actually be an ----------. (2 Chr.36:10/2 Kings 24:17)
  Could Kohath peradventure (perhaps) have been the grandfather of Jochebed?

The Bible (the Word of God) was <u>not</u> written conspicuously (ie: easy to understand).

Jesus also spoke in parables - difficult to comprehend (ie: to grasp the meaning of),
  for a specific purpose. (Mt.13:34/Lk.8:10/Rom.10:17/Heb.11:6)

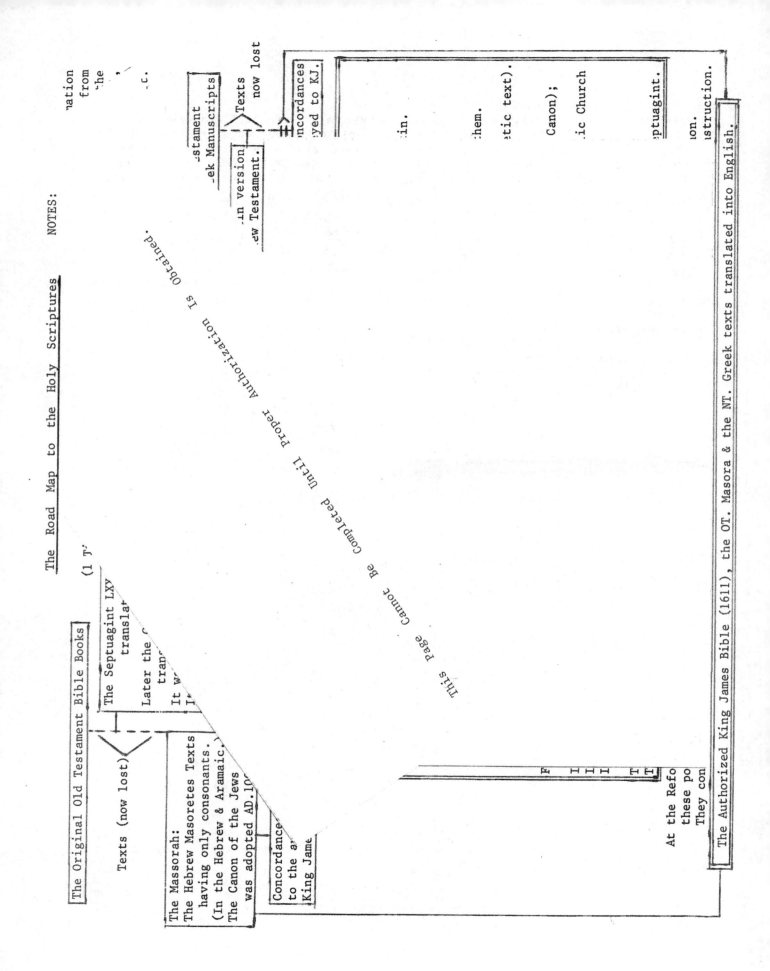

A Change of Priesthood: Jesus Christ being come an High Priest (the reformation).

A change also of the Law: A new era of Sabbath(s):   Salvation had come unto the Gentiles.
The OT. Synagogue era ended, and the NT. Church era began (the vineyard let out to others);
Will the new management be obedient (remain faithful) to the Lord of the vineyard?
                                               (Mt.21:41/Acts 10:15,28,45/Lk.3:16/He.9:10,11)

The Early Church:

   There were 7 churches in Asia: (Bishops & Deacons)   (Phil.1:1)(1 Tim.3:1-13/James 5:14)
     God took note of their activity/performance: A response in writing.   (Rev.1,2,3)
   The Book = The Bible: composed/written over a period of nearly 1500 years, now complete.

> Over time, the pilgrimage of the apostles (ie: the elders who had witnessed the Christ)
>   their lives (their office of bishoprick) had come to an end.
> A new generation, had to face the responsibility and the problems of those days.
> Some of the things that the apostles had said (every thing that God had intended for us
>   to know) was written in The Book (ie: the Bible). And the younger generation also
>   would have recalled many quotations made by the apostles - that were not recorded.
> Keep in mind, that every time a story is repeated from one individual to another,
>   it becomes less credible, and can be applied incorrectly to a particular situation.
> Rightly so: We are warned, not to add or to remove from This Book (ie: the Word of God).

           When changes happen in the world around - every one is touched by these things.
(became)   How will the churches respond/react when worldly customs/ideas come knocking?
           Will they obey the Law of God, or turn to idolatry (as did the nation of Israel).
                                                                   (1 Pe.5:1/Rev.22:18,19)

The Holy Catholic and Apostolic Church: (The Roman Catholic Church)
   The laws/rules were gradually up-dated (adjusted) to meet the circumstances of the times.
   They established a hierarchy (a government) for to oversee, to direct and shepherd their
     members into one Catholic Church. They contend (assert) to have a continuous line of
     pontiffs, starting with Peter, who they believe to have been the very first pope.
   They pray to the Saints - to have them intercede for them on their behalf.
   In addition to their Bible, they also believe in (continue to follow) their traditions:
     And they value tradition to be equal to (or superior to) the Bible itself.
   Now (today) having members in parliament - it gives them a strong voice in politics,
     and thereby giving themselves (their church) special rights and privileges.
                                                 (2 Thes.2:15/Jn.1:42/Mt.16:18/Mk.7:6-8/Eph.2:8,9)

The Great Schism: (AD.1378-1417)
   It all began - when pope Gregory XI had died, and the cardinals elected the next pope.
     But, there was a change of minds, and a different bishop was elected to be the pope.
   Both of these popes had their supporters/followers; and thus, there were 2 popes:
     And for a number of years, these 2 popes had their follow-up popes (2 lines of popes).
   Both sides agreed, that something should be done to correct this unwarranted situation.
     And a council was called, and they developed a theary: that the popes are subject
       to general councils (a new law applied retroactively) annulling previous results.
   So, they declared both lines of popes to be invalid, and they elected a valid pope:
                                     And ------ the Great Schism came to an end.

Another Schism: (East and West)
   The Orthodox Eastern Church, agreed and accepted as ecumenical - the first 7 councils,
     but they rejected the jurisdiction of the bishop of Rome (ie: the pope);
     this was the principle cause for the Orthodox to divide from the Roman Catholics.
   Nevertheless, some of the Orthodox returned, and acknowledged
     the jurisdiction of the pope: And they were called the Eastern Catholics.

More Discontent: (and the possibility/potential for additional division.)
   Some individuals within the Roman Catholic Church were troubled by certain doctrines
     (having to do with acquiring salvation) as they were taught in the Catholic Churches.
     And they protested (creating a bit of a stir) for to bring attention to their cause,
       so that - the necessary changes be made to correct those doctrines in question.
   The Roman Catholic Church having before experienced schisms, decided to take the drastic
     measures required to cut out and end the rebellion/disobedience once and for all:
       The Catholic Church hierarchy did persuade the government to grant them their request;
         and some individuals were apprehended, and burned at the stake.
   Amidst the threat of death, the protest (Protestant) movement continued to grow/expand.
   Later, the Protestants (disagreed among themselves) divided into many different churches.

Where is Truth? (worthy and false prophets)

Every word in the Bible (in the original languages) came from the mouth of God. (Jer.30:2)
God was the author of the Bible: The Bible (in the original languages) was without errors.

When translators (even the most qualified) translate into other languages, they do make errors.
When a new translation is made from the last translation, continuing in a chain-like formation,
 the possibility of error multiplies with each new translation.

A number of Bibles were translated from copies, copied from the original languages (these are
 recommended). One of them is the well known, authorized King James version of the Bible.
Other Bibles, that were translated from translations (these are less trustworthy):
These inferior translations - include many of the modern (up-to-date) Bible translations,
 claiming to be better, because they were translated from older manuscripts.
Some Bibles were translated from copies, copied from the original languages,
 but the translators (having preconceived ideas) decided to omit certain Bible passages.
Many declare the Bible to be the Word of God, but disagree as to what the contents should be.
The Bible translators all have their compelling reasons - why their translation is thé best.

Preachers also have their reasons, as to why their churches are more worthy than other churches.
Stand back and listen to what the preachers say, as they attempt to outdo one another, saying,
 -This network is Saints Sponsored: be sure to sent your support to this ministry. (Mal.3:10)
 -This is the Last Day prophet of God: Submit to God by listening to/obeying me. (Mt.10:41)
Some preachers add/delete, believing that they have the gift to locate and retrieve the Words
 of God - which they believe to be scattered throughout ancient texts, including the Bible.
So where is Truth? Every preacher would have you believe that they are in possession of it.
Many declare the Bible to be the Word of God, but disagree as to what the contents should be.

Before the Bible was completed, God came to certain individuals (prophets) via voices, dreams,
 and visions: But there had to be some way (some method) for the people to distinguish and
 recognize - for to discern the worthy prophets from those who were false prophets.
When some-one claimed to have received a message from God; and he would make his prediction:
If the prediction occurred as predicted, that would be the test to verify him as a worthy
 prophet - provided he did not encouraged the people to follow after other gods. (De.13:1-3)
At Penticost, the apostles (filled with the Holy Ghost) were heard speaking in other languages.
Diversity of gifts, but the selfsame Spirit ------ dividing to every man severally as He will:
 A body has many members, so also is Christ. (1 Cor.12:1-14/Acts 10:34/Gal.3:28,29)
 For by one Spirit we are all Baptized into one body - all made to drink into one Spirit.

After the Bible was completed: (the last/finale chapter was penned about AD.95 to AD.100)
 Every man (hearing the Words of the prophecy of This Book) who shall add unto these things,
  God shall add unto him the plagues that are written in This Book. (Rev.22:18,19)
 And if any man shall take away from the Words of The Book of this prophecy, God shall take
  away his part out of The Book of Life, and out of the Holy City, and from the things which
  are written in This Book. (1 Cor.14:34/Jn.15:10/Rom.13:1-3/Acts 5:29/Gen.1:1/Eph.3:9)

The signs of the modern day false prophets/gospels are not obvious, and difficult to detect.
They could be those that you least expect, and among them that are generally highly regarded.
Here are a few of the false gospel titbits that are taught and fed to the public: When they,
 -Take Bible passages out of context and question/discredit the validity of this Holy Book.
 -Skilfully manipulate the meaning, to make it agree with their man made traditions.
 -Teach, that there are some things that you can do to either trigger or activate salvation.
  A man-made salvation plan (in one way or another) is commonly taught in todays churches.

The authorized King James Bible, was translated from copies copied of the original texts;
 making it a reliable translation in English (there are similar versions in other languages).
A serious Bible student can begin by obtaining an authorized King James Bible; and as reference
 books, A young's Analytical Concordance, and a Strong's Exhaustive Concordance.
Beware of teachers who are pushing inferior Bibles, and Bible Commentaries! (Jer.50:6)
When a Bible and Commentaries are being used - they should be in separate volumes;
 for when students use a Bible Commentary, they tend to be confused, and the statements that
 they thought were from the Bible, were actually the ideas of the author of the commentary.

A Better/New Covenant (different from all others)

Some things are difficult (even impossible) to understand - dependant upon God giving wisdom.

Only the saved (written in the Lamb's book of life) shall inherit the holy city. (Rev.21:27)
He had chosen us (ie: His elect) in him before the foundation of the world. (2 Tim.1:9/Eph.1:4)

2 Books
- (1) The Book(s) of Life (from a creation stand point) contain the names of every-one:
  Over time - many names are blotted out of it. (Rev.3:5/Rev.22:19/Rev.20:15)
- (2) The Book of Life, of the Lamb slain from the foundation of the world: (Rev.13:8)
  Having only the names of the elect - all the Father giveth to Jesus. (Jn.6:37)

Therefore, (in the day of judgment) the names listed in both books will be the same.

How could any-one be saved during the Old Testament era, when the vail was blinding them?
Were many saved during the NT. era, when Christ had removed the vail? (2 Cor.3:14,16/He.10:20)

During the Old Testament era, there were moral and ceremonial laws, that Israel had to perform.
In the NT. the ceremonial laws of the Old Covenant had been fulfilled in Christ (the Messiah).
  and new ceremonial laws (commonly called sacraments) were established;
  and the Christians were commanded to observe them,
    during the NT. church era, under the supervision of the hierarchy of the churches.

During the NT. church era: (1 Jn.4:1/Mt.24:4,5)
When there was disagreement - pertinent to the hermeneutic (interpretation) to the Scriptures,
  the theologians (the wise men) had their work cut out for them: It could result in division.
  Now that the vail has been removed, can there be division? Is Christ divided? (1 Cor.1:12,13)
Today, there are many churches, but their teachings are surprisingly similar!
? Our church has the whole truth - and other churches are found wanting.   (1 Jn.4:6)
? To become saved, one must needs be baptized in water, for baptism now saves us. (1 Pe.3:21)
? Jesus is knocking - you too can be saved, provided you get up and open the door. (Rev.3:20)
? This church is made up of true believers, but the saved in other churches are scarce.
? Nothing is hid from us - for God reveals His mysteries to us in dreams.   (Mt.13:11/Amos 3:7)
? We also have female preachers, for God is not a respecter of persons.   (Gal.3:28/James 2:9)
? God loves everyone - if you reach out to Him, you too shall abtain salvation.   (Jn.3:16)
? The things you can do and know with certainty that you have a place at the banquet in heaven.

In the OT. era, they tried their best to keep the commandments - for fear of being cut off.
In the NT. era, they tried to live a respectable life - for fear of going to hell. (Gen.17:14)
  What did they have in common? They were not particularly focused on pleasing God: (Rom.9:32)
  And saying, If there be <u>no</u> continuous hell, then you might as well do whatsoever pleases you.

The Better/New Covenant (the blood of the Everlasting Covenant).   (Jer.31:31-34/He.13:20,21)
Before the foundation of the world, God chose (elected) everyone whom He intended to save,
  and He gave them to His Son, Jesus Christ (by whom He created all things). (Eph.3:9B/He.1:2)
All the elect, at some point in time (during their pilgrimage on planet earth), shall come into
  the hearing of the Word, and (at the appointed time) God will rescue/save them: As they are
  rescued from the kingdom of Satan, and enter into the kingdom of God - they are indwelled by
  the Holy Spirit (His Spirit beareth witness with our spirit).   (Rom.8:8-16/Rom.9:15/Jn.4:24)
Our works (of faith/belief) that we attribute to ourselves, cannot be counted as a contribution
  to us becoming saved, for we are saved by grace - (a gift). (1 Thess.1:3/Eph.2:4-8/Is.26:12)
When we are saved, His Spirit dwells in us, and He gives us a new heart and spirit; and we will
  have an earnest desire to be submissive to the Will of God, and to do that which is pleasing
  to Him, for He works in us both to will & to do to His good pleasure. (Ez.36:25,26/Phil.2:13)
For some-one to attain salvation - does not depend on the recipient having the ability to re-
  spond, for God is able to save an infant as well as an adult. (Ez.11:19/Rom.9:15/Jn.6:44,37)

Individuals (sometimes families) were saved: Before and after the flood, and during
  the OT. Synagogue era, and again during the NT. Church era, and particularly in the time
  of Great Tribulation (ie: that period of time just prior to the 2nd. coming of Jesus Christ),
  when a great multitude shall be saved.   (Mt.24:21,29,30/Rev.7:9,14)

Watch and Pray (for mercy).   (Rev.3:3/Lk.18:13)
Work out your salvation with fear and trembling.   (Phil.2:12B)

Jesus was Crucified on Nisan 14, the Passover Day

The Feast of Unleavened Bread (which is called the Passover) drew nigh. (Lk.22:1/Ezek.45:21)

D.12) After 2 days (ie: the 14th.) is the passover (and of unleavened bread),
      and the Son of man is betrayed to be crucified. (Mt.22:2/Mk.14:1)
A woman - anointed Jesus on his head (his body) for burial. (Mt.26:6-13/Mk.14:3-9)
That time Judas Iscariot (1 of the 12) went unto the chief priests. (Mt.26:14-16/Lk.22:3-6)

D.13) Then came the first day of unleavened bread (when the passover must be killed)**; and
      arrangement was made to prepare the passover. (Mt.26:17-19/Mk.14:12-16/Lk.22:7-13)
E | Now, when even was come he sat down with the 12; (Mt.26:20/Mk.14:18/Lk.22:14)
V | and (in the evening) they sat, and did eat***. (Mt.26:21-29/Mk.14:18-25/Lk.22:15-38)
E | Now before the Feast of the Passover (ie: the 7 days from D.15 through D.21) ---. (Jn.13:1)
N | Jesus --- washes the feet of his disciples (a for you to do, example). (Jn.13:3-20)
And Judas Iscariot - went out, to betray Jesus: And it was night. (Jn.13:2,21-30)
And when they had sung an hymn, they went into the Mount of Olives; (Mk.14:32/Jn.18:1)
    and they went over the brook Cedron, and into the place named Gethsemane.

D.14) Passover day and unleavened bread (when the passover must be killed). (Ex.12:6-10)
Then came Judas and a band, and officers from the chief priests & Pharisees. And they took
    Jesus to Annas, who sent him to Caiaphas (the high priest); and (Jn.18:3,13,24/Mt.26:57)
      the interrogation and Peter's denials. (Mt.26:58-75/Mk.14:54-72/Lk.22:54-65/Jn.18:14-27)
When the morning was come, the chief priests held counsel with the elders, and the scribes;
    and as soon as it was day, they led him ------. (Gen.1:5A)(Mt.27:1/Mk.15:1A/Lk.22:66-71)
They bound Jesus, and led him from Caiaphas - to the hall of judgment (it was early):
They themselves (however) went not into the judgment hall,
    lest they should be defiled; but that they might eat the passover. (Jn.18:28B/De.16:6)
And Pilate (the governor) went out unto them, --. (Mt.27:2/Mk.15:1B/Lk.23:1/Jn.18:28,29)
Now, they had a custom, that Pilate release unto them one - at the passover. (Jn.18:39,40)
When Pilate heard, Of Galilee, he asked whether the man were a Galilaean.
    And as soon as he knew, that he belonged unto Herod's jurisdiction,
      he sent him to Herod, who himself also was at Jerusalem at that time. (Lk.23:6,7)
    And Herod ---- arrayed him in a gorgeous robe, and sent him again to Pilate. (Lk.23:11)
    The same day Pilate and Herod were made friends: before they were at enmity. (Lk.23:12)
Pilate said to them, I (having examined him) find no fault - nor yet Herod. (Lk.23:14,15)
They cried out all at once, saying, Away with him and release unto us Barabbas. (Lk.23:18)
    Note: 3x Pilate had said to them, that he found no cause of death in him. (Lk.23:22)
It was the preparation of the passover, and about the 6th. hour ------------. (Jn.19:14)
When Pilate saw that he could prevail nothing, he took water and washed his hands before
    the multitude, saying, I am innocent of the blood of this just person: see ye to it.
Then answered all the people, and said, His blood be on us and on our children.
Then released he Barabbas unto them, and he delivered Jesus to be crucified. (Mt.27:24-26)
Jesus (bearing his cross) was led away - to Golgatha (nigh to the city); and (Jn.19:17-20)
    they crucified him, and parted his garments, casting lots. (Mt.27:35/Lev.23:5/Num.9:3)
From about the 6th. until the 9th. hour there was darkness over all the land: (Lk.23:44-46)
Jesus said, Father into Thy hands I commend my spirit, and he gave up the ghost. (Mt.27:50)

E | When Even was come (it was the preparation, ie: the day before the sabbath), (Mk.15:42,43)
V | Joseph (a disciple of Jesus) lay the body in a new sepulchre. (Mk.15:46/Jn.19:38,41)
E | And that day was the preparation, and the sabbath drew on. The women also -------- beheld
N | the sepulchre, and how/where his body was laid. (Mt.27:61/Mk.15:47/Lk.23:54-56)

D.15 — On the sabbath (a high day) they rested (Lk.23:56/Jn.19:31). (The 7 days Ex.13:7)
      The 1st. day of the feast of unleavened bread (ie: the passover feast). (Ezek.45:21)
D.16 —— The 2nd. day
D.17 —— The 3rd. day
D.18 —— The 4th. day
D.19 —— The 5th. day
D.20 —— The 6th. day
D.21 —— The 7th. day, the first and the last day be holy convocations. (Ex.12:16/Lev.23:6-8)
Evening (Ex.12:18)

> Note: Changes are made when the circumstances require that it so be.
> For Jesus and his disciples, the first day of unleavened bread, when
> the passover be killed**, came a day early, on the 13th. of Nisan.
> This, the Last Passover was followed with the First Lord's Supper***

166 | Assembly by John Douma

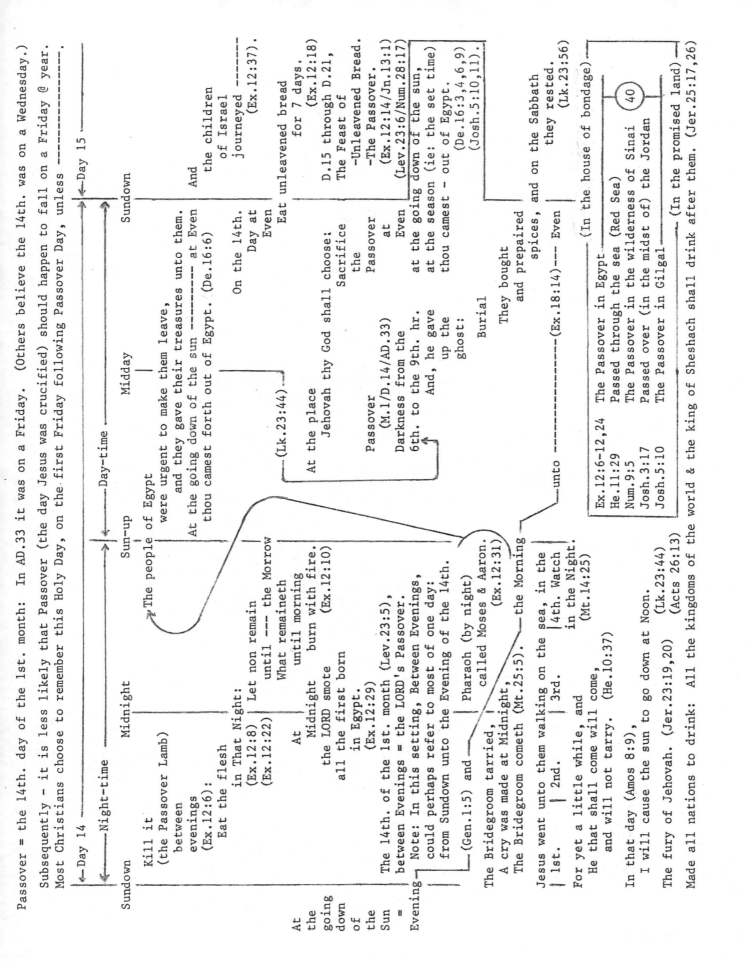

The Gospels of Matthew, Mark, Luke, and John: Merged into One Historic Calendar of Events

A Time Bump (in the midst of Eternity)

Eternity Past

In the beginning
    was the Word, and the Word was with God, and the Word was God. (Jn.1:1)
 Jesus Christ = the only begotten (ie: born) Son of God: In the bosom of the Father. (Jn.1:18)
 God created the heavens and the earth (all things were created by Jesus Christ): (Eph.3:9)
  By the Word of Jehovah were the heavens made; (2 Pe.3:5)
    and all the host of them by the Breath of His mouth. (Ps.33:6)
Before the foundation of the world, God chose all those He intended to save later. (Eph.1:4)
God made man in His own image. Every thing that God had made was very good; (Gen.1:26,27,31)
And God placed the man in a garden - that He had made: Man had the ability to make choices.

Adam ——┬—— God made Adam & Eve in His own image. (Gen.1:27)
     Man (under the influence of Satan) sinned wilfully. (Rom.5:19/Rom.6:23/He.10:26)
   └— Death reigned from Adam to Moses, (Rom.5:14)
    even over them that had not sinned after the similitude of Adam's transgression.
    Sin is not imputed where there is no law. (Rom.5:13)
    As many as have sinned without law shall also perish without law, ————. (Rom.2:12A)

Moses ——┬—— Adopted into the Egyptian culture.
    └— About 450 years until Samuel (the prophet). (Acts 13:17-20)
    The Law of God, given at Mount Sinai. (Ex.19 through Ex.24)(Deut.5:2,3)
    As many as have sinned in the law shall be judged by the law. (Rom.2:12B)
    God works in mysterious ways. (see Rom.5:14-21)(1 Cor.2:7/Eph.1:9/Is.55:9)

Samuel ——┬—— Ministered unto Jehovah before Eli (the priest). (Josh.18:1/1 Sam.1:24/1 Sam.2:11)
    ⎧Yea, all the prophets from Samuel and those that follow after ——————. (Acts 3:24)
    ⎩All the prophets and the law propesied until John. (Mt.11:13)

John ——┬—— The Baptist: The voice of one crying in the wilderness,
    Prepair ye the way of Jehovah, make His paths straight, (Mt.3:3)
     make straight (in the desert) a highway for our God. (Is.40:3)
Jesus Christ, the Messias: His name be Jesus, he shall save His people from their sins.(Mt.1:21)
    Behold, the Lamb of God, which taketh away the sin of the world. (Jn.1:29,36)
    A priest (high priest) forever after the order of Melchizedek (He.5:6)
    The Word of the Oath, which was since the law. (He.7:21,28/Acts 2:29-31/Ps.16:10)
    Change of Priesthood (reformation), changes in the laws. (He.7:12/He.9:10)
Penticost —— A Comforter (the Holy Ghost/the Spirit of Truth), (Jn.16:7/Jn.14:16,26/Jn.15:26)
  whom I will send (proceedeth from the Father) unto you - shall testify of me.

```
┌─────────────────────────────────────────────┬─────────────────────────────────────────────┐
│ On Mount Sinai: (the Law of God)            │ Bethlehem of Judaea (the Lamb of God)       │
│   The presentation of the Old Covenant      │   The revelation of the New Covenant        │
│   The former Ceremonies (sacrifices)        │   The latter Ceremonies (called sacraments) │
│   The OT. Tabernacle/Synagogue era          │   The NT. Church era                        │
│   Circumcision (an act of obedience)        │   Water Baptism (an act of obedience)       │
│   Pass-over + passover feast.               │   The Lord's Supper (in remembrance)        │
└─────────────────────────────────────────────┴─────────────────────────────────────────────┘
```

Adjustments are made from one era to the next: (He.7:12/Nu.3:12,41/2 Thes.2:7,4/Mal.3:6/He.13:8)
 But the Master Plan changes not: Jesus Christ = the same yesterday, and to-day, and for ever.

For, since (during the church era) there was joy in heaven over one sinner coming to repentance;
 but now there is silence in heaven for an 1/2 hour - indicating no-one is becoming saved.
It is the end of the NT. church era, and the beginning of that time of Great Tribulation:
 A period of time (described as a 1/2 hour) when no-one is given salvation: (Rev.8:1/Lk.15:7)
 That time is shortened, and a great crowd is saved from Gr. Tribulation. (Mk.13:20/Rev.7:9-14)
Since the churches (the temple of God) have become an abomination - as is evident in this day:
Now God's Word is proclaimed to all nations (to an exploded population) via alternitive means.
 Signs in the Sun, the Moon, and the Stars: (Amos 5:18-20)(Mt.24:29-31/Lk.21:25-27/Rev.10:7)
The Son of man, coming at the 7th. trump - and the believers are caught up (ie: the rapture).
Judgment: The day of judgment & perdition (damnation/destruction) of the ungodly. (Rom.9:22)
 The heavens pass away (the elements melt), the earth (the works therein burn up). (2 Pe.3:10)
A New Heaven and a New Earth. (Is.65:17/Rev.21:1-4)(Rev.22:10)

Eternity Future

<u>What is happening</u> in the world & in the chuches? (Who is pulling the strings?)

The following information - may be somewhat controversial to some people:
   As you (and your friends) read these pages - read them a section at a time,
     and as you debate, ask yourselves, Do I agree or disagree. And for what reason?
The OT. church (the synagogue) era did come to an end:
   The veil in the temple was torn from the top to the bottom.   (Mt.27:51/Ex.26:33)
   Just because it came to an end, does not mean that there are no synagogues at this time.
And so also shall end - the local congregations, as we have known them through the years.
   Theologians - disagree, if this should occur before or after the Great Tribulation.

The Era of the Synagogue of the Old Testament
- Jehovah ----- chose the nation of Israel, as the husbandmen of His Vineyard. (Lk.20:9-16)
- He (in a spiritual way) was married to Israel. (Jer.3:14/Is.50:1/Mal.2:16)
- <u>Keep all my commandments always</u>, that it be well ------ for ever! (De.5:29)
- (It looked as though they had it made, what could possibly go wrong?)
- But, Israel was unfaithful (committed adultery) they worshipped other gods.
- John the Baptist (he was the Elias which was to come). (Mt.17:12,13)
- The Word was made flesh (God was manifest in the flesh). (1 Tim.3:16/Jn.1:14)
- John baptized with water unto repentance. (Baptized means to be washed.)
- Jesus made the payment for sin - for all the sins of many people.
- The husbandmen --- caught and cast him out of the vineyard, and slew him.
- The Lord of the vineyard - will let it forth to other husbandmen.
- Note: At this time, the Vineyard was not destroyed. (Mt.21:41/Lk.20:16)

The end ----- of the era of the synagogues.

Tarry ye in the city of Jerusalem, until ye be endued with Power from on high. (Lk.24:49B)

Penticost --- The beginning of the NT. church era (of which Christ was the foundation).
   The duty and responsibility for the Vineyard - were given/committed to them.
   They were commanded: Go ye therefore, and <u>teach all nations</u>,
     baptizing them in the name of the Father, of the Son & of the Holy Ghost:
     Teaching them to <u>observe all things whatsoever I have commanded you</u>:
     and, lo, I am with you alway - unto the end of the world. (Mt.28:19,20)
   (It looked as though they had it made, what could possibly go wrong?)

The Era of the Churches of the New Testament

The Bible was completed AD.95 - AD.100 (Rev.22:18,19/Ps.138:2B)

Worldly ideas entered into the assemblies (churches)
- Divorce
- Lottery
- Sunday entertainment
- They cut out parts of the Bible
- They teach a man-made salvation plan (instill a false hope)
- The Command of the Lord is not considered to be the priority.

(Admonishing the Congregations Rev.2:5,16,17.)

They have cast away the Law of the LORD of host. (Is.5:24)
At harvest time: It brought forth wild (poison/stinking) grapes:
   The Vineyard (of His Wellbeloved), He will lay it waste. (Is.5:1-6)

Changes ---------------------- The man of sin (Satan) takes His seat in the Temple of God.
(2 Thess.2:4/Mt.24:15/Mk.13:14/Lk.21:20)

There is silence (no joy) in heaven (Rev.8:1/Lk.15:7)

The days of the Great Tribulation (Mt.24:21-28).

Judgment - at the house of God. (1 Pe.4:17)
First, the tares are bound in fagots:
The wheat - into His barn. (Mt.13:30)

Those days are shortened ------ (Mt.24:22/Mk.13:20)
A great crowd is being saved (Rev.7:9-14)

Come out of her my people. (Rev.18:4)

The Last Trump ------------------------- (1 Cor.15:52/Amos 3:7/Mt.24:37,38/Lk.17:26-29)
   Jesus returns (+ the rapture) immediately after the Great Tribulation. (Mt.24:29-31)
   The judgment and perdition of ungodly men. (2 Pe.3:7/Mt.12:36/He.9:27/Ps.1:5)

The Bible Calendar (how many years are there in one generation?)

In the beginning God created:
All things were made by Him (the Word), and without Him was not any thing made -----.
God - created all things by Jesus Christ: (Eph.3:9 the Authorized King James translation)
    God saw every thing that He had made, and, behold, it was very good.

Adam & Eve were disobedient - they chose to do the one thing that they were told not to do.
    Cain murdered his brother Abel.   Seth was born.   Mankind (in time) multiplied.
And the earth was corrupt before God (filled with violence):
    But Noah found grace (ie: favour) in the eyes of the LORD (ie: Jehovah).
    Noah was a just (ie: righteous) man - perfect in his generation (Noah walked with God).
God said unto Noah, The end of all flesh is come before me -- I will destroy them --------.
And God commanded Noah to build an ark (ie: a very large boat), 300x50x30 cubits,
    for the days of man would be 120 years.   (Gen.6:3,14,15,16)
Noah had 120 years in which to build the ark - approximately 450x75x45 feet in size.
    When Noah began the construction of the ark, he would have been 600-120=480 years old.
Noah was 500 years old: and Noah begat Shem, Ham, and Japheth.   (Gen.5:32;7:11;11:10)
The Great Flood (total deluge): Noah was 600 years old, and Shem was 98 years of age.
Thus - God saved Noah & his family, and of all beasts & fowls & all that creepeth upon earth.
    Noah builded an altar unto the LORD & offered burnt offering of the clean beasts & fowls.
God blessed Noah & his sons: God made a covenant (the bow in the clouds - as a token).
The Tower of Babel - different languages (the LORD scattered them abroad upon all the earth).
    The earth was divided - in the days of Peleg.   (Gen.10:25)

Jehovah commanded Abraham,
    Get thee out of thy country & from thy kindred (from thy father's house),   (Gen.12:1,5)
        unto a land that I will show thee: And Abraham departed, -------------- to Canaan.

    Abraham
        └ Isaac
            └ Jacob (Israel)
                └ the children of Israel

Jacob (130) and his family went from Canaan to Egypt: Joseph (39) was already there.

The children of Israel dwelt in Egypt:
    But in the 4th. generation they shall come hither again: (Gen.15:16/Ex.12:40,41)
    And at the end of 430 years --- the host of the LORD went out from the land of Egypt.

The question is, How many years are there in one generation? Do the math.
    Jacob (Israel)   (when Jacob was 130y. Levi may have been 60y. (or there about).
    └ Levi [137] ----------------- 137-60= 77
            Kohath [133] ------------------ 133
    (Ex.6:16-20) Amram [137] ---------------- 137
    (Ex.7:7) Aaron [123] ----- 123-40= 83

> Ever wonder, as to why the Bible gives such detailed information in some incidents, including the ages of some individuals and not of others?

When we make the necessary calculations - we conclude, that
    Levi could have been 60 years or there about, at the time when Israel came into Egypt;
    And we also know that Aaron was 83 years, when the Israelites departed out of Egypt.

If Levi was 60 when he came into Egypt & he died at 137; he lived in Egypt for 77 years.
    77+133+137+83=430   which is precisely the # of years that the Israelites were in Egypt.

The generations - that Genesis 15:16 refers to
    are the total number of years of the life of a particular individual that is in view.

Mr. Harold Camping, California, USA. has made an earnest study for the Bible Calendar,
    (knowing that a generation could be the complete lifetime of an individual),
    he has concluded that the year of creation was BC. 11013, and the flood in BC. 4990.

Creation: God SPOKE and CREATED - the heavens & the earth / man. (BC. 11013).
6023   Created man in His own image - male/female. (Gen.1:27/Eph.3:9).
                Every thing that He had made ----------- very good. (Gen.1:31).
        The Great Flood (total deluge). Noah (600) & Shem (98) - (BC. 4990)
            Landslides / Animals became trapped & buried (fossils preserved).
2823   Nimrod (the Tower of Babel) - Languages (Ge.10:10 & Ge.11:7-9).
            ⊙Peleg (born to Eber) - (Gen.10:25) --------------- (BC. 3153). **7000**
                The earth was divided (ie: the Continents took shape).
                Peleg (39) the beginning of the Maya Calendar - Aug.11? (BC. 3114).
        75 ⊙Abram » Abraham (Terah age 130) Gen.11:27 --- (BC. 2167)
            Abraham (75) God's Covenant: Go & he went - to Canaan (BC. 2092).
290 **30** ⊙Ishmael (Abraham age 86) Gen.16:16 ----------- (BC. 2081). **4160**
            Circumcision: Abraham (99) & Ishmael (13) -- Gen.17:24,25.
    215 ⊙Isaac - Abraham (100) & Sarah (90) - Gen.17:17;21:4,5. - (BC. 2067).
            Abraham (105)? when Isaac (5)? was weaned / Ishmael mocking.
                NOTE: Weaning could occur, as early as 3 years of age.
        55 Sarah 127? Gen.23:1 (1 Pe.3:6/Titus 2:5/Is.51:1,2,7) (BC. 2030).
            ⊙Jacob » Israel & Esau (Isaac age 60) Gen.25:25,26. -- (BC. 2007).
        130   Abraham 175? BC.1992. Ishmael 137? BC.1944. Isaac 180? BC.1887.
            Jacob (130) & his family - enter into Egypt --- (BC. 1877)
                Jacob 147? --- (BC. 1860). Joseph 110? --- (BC. 1806).
        430 The seed of Abraham entreat-evil for 400y. (Acts 7:6,7). **1290**
            ⊙Moses (Num.26:59) born to Amram & Jochebed - Levites (BC. 1527).
13000   Moses (40) visits his brethren --- he fled. (Acts 7:23)(BC. 1487).
                The burning bush: Message from Jehovah (God Almighty)(BC. 1447).
            The Israelites leave Egypt (end of tribulation) - (BC. 1447)
                Ex.12:37-41 (Gen.15:16). 40 days = 40 years. (Num.14:34). **40**
            Israelites (remnant) invade Canaan. (De.2:7;8:4/Josh.5:6-12)
        480   Joshua - Judges (No King) Samuel (1 Sam.7:15).
                "Give us a King to Judge us" (1 Sam.8:1-7) they demanded!
            King Saul ------ from (BC. 1047) until (BC. 1007).
1440   King David ------ from (BC. 1007) until (BC. 967).
            King Solomon --- from (BC. 971) until (BC. 931). **860**
            The 4th. year of king Solomon's reign (1 Ki.6:1) - (BC. 967).
        36 Death of Solomon (1 Ki.11:42,43/ 2 Chr.9:30,31) - (BC. 931)
                    (the division of the kingdom: Israel 10 & Judah 1).
960   Refer to the Books of Kings and Chronicles. **344**
    322 The destruction of Israel (2 K.17:5,6/ 1 Chr.5:25,26)(BC. 709).
            The death of Josiah (2 Ki.23:30/ 2 Chr.35:23,24) - (BC. 609).
        70 The destruction of Judah (the Temple was burned) - (BC. 587)
                To - serve the king of Babylon 70 years (Jer.25:11/Dan.9:2).
            Darius (the Median) took the kingdom. (Dan.5:28-31) (BC. 539);
                and Cyrus (in his 1st. year) issued a decree. (Ezra 1:1,2).
            Artaxerxes (7th.y) (Ezra 7:1,8,25,9/Dan.9:24) (BC.458)
        ⊙The Messias (the WORD was made flesh) John 1:14 ---- (BC. 7).
                he was circumcised & named Jesus (age 8 days) (Lk.2:21). **2580**
            After 40 days to the Temple in Jerusalem (Lk.2:22-40/Lev.12)
            Death of Herod, the king of Judaea. (Mt.2:1,15) --- (BC. 4).
            The beginning of the gospel of Jesus Christ, the Son of God; **490**
                Jesus - about 30 years of age. (Lk.3:23/Mk.1:1/Num.4:3).
            Jesus was baptized (ie: washed) by John. (Mt.3:13-17) (AD. 29).
                The crusifiction & burial. (Mt.27:24-61) ----- (AD. 33)
            He is risen. (Mt.28:6/Mk.16:6). Seen of them 40 days. (Acts 1:3).
            He was taken (received) up into heaven. (Acts 1:9-11/Mt.24:29-42).
            Pentecost: (Acts 2:1-12/Jn.16:7-11/Jn.14:1-3,16,17,27) - (AD. 33).
            AD.1914 (WW1•1914-1918 & WW2•1939-1945). (AD.70 to AD.1948•Mt.24:32).
            AD.1988 ?(1/2 hr. silence: Rev.8:1/Lk.15:7/Mt.24:22)? AD.1994
            AD.2011 (Gen.7:4 Yet 7 days) x (2 Peter 3:8 One day = 1000 years)

The Gospels of Matthew, Mark, Luke, and John: Merged into One Historic Calendar of Events

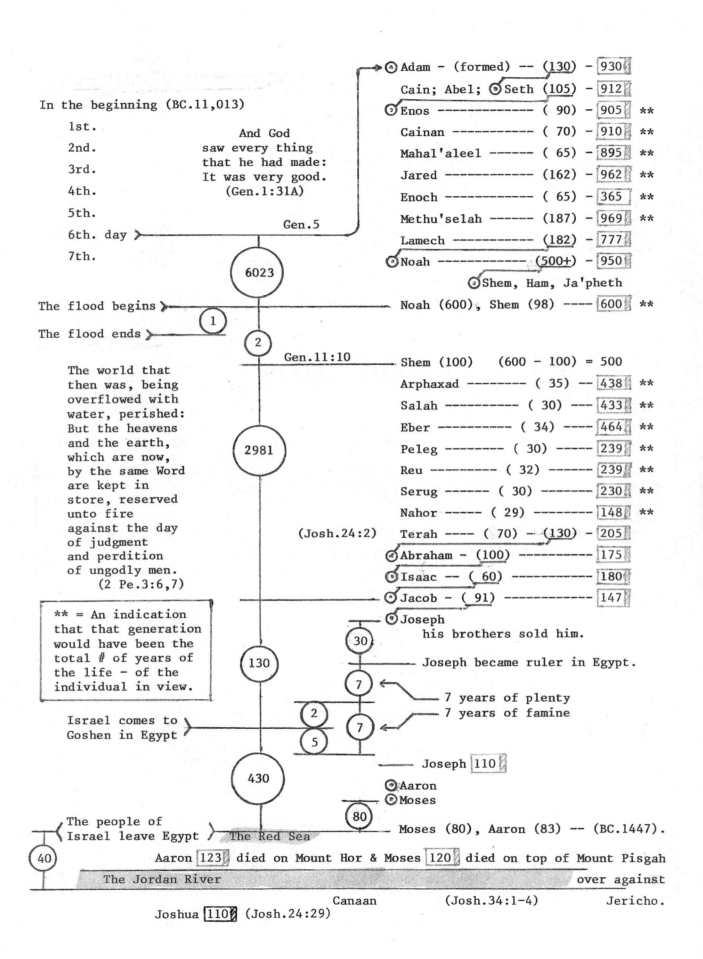

Immediate & Potential Knowledge   (hidden within the Bible)

Eph.3:5 / Amos 3:7 / 2 Thess.2:3,6 / Dan.12:4,10
  Which (ie: the knowledge in the mystery of Christ) in other ages was not made known unto
     the sons of men, as it is now revealed unto His holy apostles & prophets by the Spirit.
  Surely the Lord Jehovah will do nothing,
     but He revealeth His secrets unto His servants the prophets.
  And the man of sin be revealed --------------- that he might be revealed in his time.
  But thou, O Daniel, shut up the words, and seal the book - to the time of the end:
     Many shall run to & fro, and knowledge shall be increased --- the wise shall understand.

Are we today living in that time of the end, when knowledge is increased & the wise understand?

Eccl.8:5,6
  A wise man's heart discerneth both time & judgment,
     because to every purpose (ie: desire/pleasure) there is time & judgment, -------------.

When the King James Bible translators, did translate the O.T. Hebrew, and the N.T. Greek
     into the English language, they made an exceedingly wonderful English translation.
  But - they did make a number of errors, as they made the translation:
    At times another word (of a similar meaning) could have been used;
    At other times - they did not fully understand, and they made a slight alteration.
  For Example:
    Mt.28:1 In the end of the sabbath, as it began to dawn toward the first of the week.
  When properly translated, this verse should read,
     In the end of the sabbaths, as it began to dawn toward the first of the sabbaths.
  Now - It becomes clear, that one era of sabbaths had ended, and a new era of sabbaths began.

  Preachers & teachers - also add to the Scripture, as they attempt to more fully explain.
  For Example, in Mt.24:22/Mk.13:20 Where it speaks concerning the end of days:
     And except those days should be shortened, there should no flesh be saved.
    When they add just the one word "alive", the meaning is incorrectly changed - to,
     And except those days should be shortened, there should no flesh be saved alive.

Today there are many newer translations of the Bible (supposedly improved - so they all claim).
Actually - they copied the errors, and did iron out any area that was not to their taste.
  Just stop & think, of the words "copy rights", and it all begins to make a lot of sense:
  In my opinion, the devil had a hand in some of these soothing translations (2 Cor.11:14,15)

What, if it so came about - as you were diligently searching (examining) the Holy Scripture,
     comparing scripture with scripture - to more fully understand its spiritual message:
  And so doing, you came to (lighted upon) some verses, that required more research;
     and upon additional examination, you realized that you had learned a valuable lesson.
  If the information that you acquired - could also be a valuable lesson to others,
    What are you going to do with that crucial data?
    Would you keep it to yourself (bury it in the sand), or would you share it with others:
  What if the information was critical - would you take the time to warn others?
What is it that a good watchman must do? Run & hide, or blow the trumpet? (Ezek.33:6/Rev.3:3)

Some people teach - that no one can know when the time of the end shall be,
  and that it would be a mistake to be sidetrackt by it - since it is non of our business.
  However, when we read Heb.10:25 we are told - it is possible, to see the day approaching.

There are Bible passages that cannot be fully understood - until a certain era in time:
  These verses (or commandments) are addressed unto His/My people (His beloved),
     who will inhabit the earth during the final days (the days of the great tribulation).

The LORD (ie: Jehovah) is in His holy temple (Hab.2:20):
  This saying was also used to identify the Lord's house in the era of the N.T. churches;
     for to remind the people of the presence of the LORD in the N.T. church (ie: assembly).
  The presence of the Lord - in His holy temple/the temple of God/the holy place.   (Mt.18:20)

The Signs of The Times

2 Peter 3:5-8
   For they (the scoffers) willingly are ignorant of - that by the Word of God
      the heavens were of old, and the earth standing out of the water and in the water:
      Whereby the world that was then was being overflowed with water, perished.
   But, the heavens and the earth which are now, by the same Word are kept in store,
      reserved unto fire against the day of judgment and of the perdition of ungodly men.
   But beloved, be not ignorant of this one thing,
      that one day is with the Lord as a 1000 years, and a 1000 years as one day.

In view are 2 end times (2 different judgments):
   (1) The end of life in the days of Noah (the old world)   (2 Peter 2:5 & 3:5,6)
   (2) The final end (the day of judgment and the perdition of the ungodly)   (2 Peter 3:7)
   (3) One day (with the Lord) is = to a 1000 years, and a 1000 years = to one day.
   It appears as if something is lacking, the # of days to represent the # of 1000y. periods.
   Noah (after building the ark for 120y.) had only 7 more days until the time of the flood.
   If 7 was the hidden # (and no thing had been overlooked in the assembly of this Calendar),
      then (the flood BC.4990 + 7 days of a 1000 years) the end should have been in AD.2011.
We do know with certainty that Jesus shall return: The question remains, when will this be?
And we wonder, and continue to pray for wisdom, and for correction when we make errors.

Matthew 24:15   How can someone see the day approaching?
   When ye therefore shall see the abomination of desolation (spoken of by Daniel the prophet),
      stand in the Holy Place, -----------. (His holy temple/the temple of God/the holy place)

2 Thess.2:3-8   The change (alteration/modification/substitution) within the temple of God.
   For ----- iniquity (ie: sin) --- had already been at work:
   Only He (ie: the Holy Spirit) who now letteth (ie: withholdeth/restricts/limits),
      until He (ie: the Holy Spirit) be taken (ie: be finished/arise) out of the midst:
   Then shall that Wicked (ie: unlawful/lawless) (man of sin/son of perdition) be revealed;
      who opposeth and exalteth himself above all that is called God, or that is worshipped;
      so that he as God sitteth (takes seat/rules) in the Temple of God - as if he were God:
   Whom the Lord shall consume with the spirit of His mouth,
      and shall destroy with the Brightness of His coming, | Note: sentences may be
   Whose coming is after (ie: against) | shortened & rearranged.
         the working of Satan with all power and signs and lying wonders.

So you knew, or so you thought - until the facts were uncovered!   (1 Jn.4:1)

Faith Healers (who believe, that the end justifies the means),
   have their ways of performing their magical tricks, and they call them miracles.

For some time (for days) the Roman Catholics (on short wave)
   set their normal programing aside, to make way for a special advertisement blitz
      to promote, and make others aware of the movie, called, The Passion of the Christ.
   They strongly emphasized (more or less compelled), that everyone
      must needs go and see this all time important, and super terrific film by Mel Gibson.
   A slip of the tongue, uncovered the driving force behind all the hype generated.
   Mel (a fellow Roman Catholic) was expected to dish out (donate) a significant portion
      of the profit to his church.

The United Church (Crossroads) went out of their way to give tribute to Jack Leighten.
   And him they honoured as they recalled the days of his youth, giving praise to someone
      who (later in life) honoured and promoted those of evil/reprobate mentality. (Ro.1:21-32)

Come out of her, my people;   (Rev.18:4/Jer.50:28,29)
   That ye be not partakers of her sins, and that ye receive not of her plagues.
   Now, where would you expect to find those people, referred to as, My people?
      My people (ie: the believers) would be found (as expected) in the churches:
   But now they are commanded (warned), Come out of her.   (Rev.18:2-24/Mt.24:2)
   Remove (ie: flee) out of the midst of Babylon!   (Jer.50:6,8,10/Jer.51:6,7,8,11)

Stories & Events of Parabolical Significance

In the Bible there are stories and actual events, that
   convey an heavenly message, or predict some event that must (in time) come to pass.

An actual event (in Luke 5) took place at the lake of Gennesaret (ie: the sea of Galilee),
     it was also a picture of what would take place <u>during</u> the church era of the NT.
Jesus stood by the lake, and the people pressed upon him to hear the word of God.
   And he saw 2 ships standing by the lake, and the fishermen had gone out - washing nets.
   And he entered into one of the ships, which was Simon's,
      and prayed (ie: asked) him that he would thrust out a little from the land.
   And Jesus sat down, and taught the people out of the ship.
When Jesus had left speaking, he said to Simon,
   Launch out into the deep, and let down your nets for a draught (ie: a catch).
Simon (eventhough they had toiled all night and had taken nothing) did as Jesus had asked.
When they had let down the net - they enclosed a great multitude of fishes: their net brake.
They, then beckoned unto their partners (companions) in the other ship to come and help them.
   And they came - and they filled both ships, so that they began to sink.

Note: The 2 ships loaded with fishes (near sinking), is a picture of the NT. churches:
     The churches - were the external kingdom of God, and it had a multitude of members.

The NT. church era (the Bible teaches) shall come to an end at the appointed time.
2 Thess.2:2,3,7. The Temple of God, <u>before</u> the Day of the Lord Jesus is at hand.
     He letteth (ie: restrains) <u>until</u> <u>he</u> <u>be</u> <u>taken</u> out of the way (ie: the midst).

   There will come an ending
   The Holy Spirit
   The time of the end (taken = finished)

μέσου
Example: Luke 17:11
passed through the midst.
(passing through & <u>out</u>)

Rev.18:4. Come <u>OUT</u> of her my people, lest ----.

John 10:2,3. He that entereth in by the door is the shepherd of the sheep.
(Jn.18:37C)   To him the porter openeth; and the sheep hear his voice:
(Lk.5:11)   And he calleth his own sheep by name, and leadeth them <u>OUT</u>.

An actual event (in John 21) took place at the sea of Tiberias (ie: the sea of Galilee),
     it was also a picture of what would take place <u>after</u> the church era of the NT.
Together were Simon Peter, Thomas, Nathanael, the sons of Zebedee, and 2 other disciples;
   they - entered into a ship immediately, and went fishing: that night they caught nothing.
But when the morning was now come, Jesus stood on the shore (they knew not that it was Jesus).
   Then Jesus saith unto them, Children, have ye any meat? They answered him, No.
   And Jesus said, Cast the net on the right side of the ship, and ye shall find.
They cast therefore: And now they were not able to draw it - for the multitude of fishes.
When Simon was told, It is the Lord; he girt his fisher's coat, and cast himself into the sea.
   The other disciples came in a little ship; (for they were not far from land,
      but as it were 200 cubits), dragging the net with fishes.
As soon as they were come to land - they saw a fire of coals, and fish laid thereon, and bread.
Jesus saith unto them, Bring of the fish which ye have now caught.
Simon went up & drew the net full (153 great fishes) to land: So many, and the net brake not.
Jesus saith unto them, Come dine.
   (Non of the disciples durst ask him, Who art thou? knowing that it was the Lord.)
   Jesus then cometh, and taketh bread, and giveth them, and fish likewise.

Note: An empty net (No harvest - pictures a time when no one is becoming saved).
     A net full (A great harvest - pictures a time when a great crowd is being saved).
     They draged the net full (153 great fishes) as it were 200 cubits towards the land.
     Simon went up, and drew the net to land. No boats (ie: churches) were being used.

──── The Last Trump (the 2nd. coming & the rapture) ────
Judgment:
The 7 vials, In them the wrath of God is filled-up (ie: accomplished/finished).
                           (Rev.15:1/Rev.16:17) It is done.

Sitting On The Fence (staying on the side lines, waiting - until after)

When a Bible student prayerfully searching the Holy Scriptures, exploring the numbers, making
calculations - feeling confident, that the world may end at a particular time (year/day):
And he feels obligated to share his findings with others, so they, can voice their findings.
But the spectators sitting on the fence, are afraid of making errors, and do nothing. And they
remain on the side lines - so they can make their decisions after the fact: And then join
which ever party be on the winning side. In their opinion, one cannot be too careful.
Now, if the idea presented by the Bible student happens to be correct, then those on the fence
are ready/prepaired, to quickly join in, and say, We knew all along that your findings/ideas
were altogether correct: Look at what we have accomplished!
But, if the findings later turned out to be defective (not as expected), then those on the
fence are ready/prepaired, and immediately jump - all over the Bible student,
and say, How could you? You false prophet. Now, look at what you have done!

Are you afraid: Like-minded to those spectators on the fence, idly sitting by, and (Prov.22:13)
having - a wait and see, attitude? Or, are you Watching, and Praying for wisdom and mercy?
And realize, that we being human (on our part) can and do make errors. But as we compare
Scripture with Scripture, and we continue to learn - also from previous errors. (2 Tim.3:16)
But --- seal the book - to the Time Of The End: Many shall run to and fro (ie: Perhaps, many be
looking/searching for purpose/meaning/truth/understanding?), and knowledge shall be increased. -- Many shall be purified, and made white, and tried; but the wicked shall do wickedly:
And none of the wicked shall understand; but the wise shall understand.   (Dan.12:4,10)

The Israelites were Watching/Praying and Waiting (longing) for the Messiah to come and deliver
them: He came unto his own, and his own received him not.   (Jn.1:11-13/Acts 1:6)
The Last Days, began with the coming of Jesus Christ to planet earth, about 2000 years ago.
Jesus completed his mission on earth - he finished the work assigned to him by his Father.

Every one (in the hearing of the Word of God) is commanded to Watch!
In Matthew 24, we can read about, The Day Of The Lord:
And in :36, But of that day and hour knoweth no-one --------- but my Father only.
:42, Watch therefore, for ye know not what hour your Lord doth come.
And, in Revelation 3:3 is written, If therefore thou shalt not Watch,
I will come on thee as a thief, and thou shalt not know what hour I will come upon thee.

It appears as if there is contradiction betwixt these Bible passages: Read them carefully.
One appears to say, there is no way any one could know when the Day of the Lord shall be.
And the other (Rev.3:3) suggests, If - thou shalt Watch,
I will not come on thee as a thief, and thou shalt know what hour I will come upon thee.

Note: The word "hour" could also be translated, time, or season (ie: hour/time/season).
Now examine these passages again, knowing that, hour, could also read, time or season.
Matthew 24:36, But of that day and hour (the precise day and hour) knoweth no-one ------.
:42, Watch therefore, for ye know not what hour (ie: season) your Lord does come.
Revelation 3:3, If therefore thou shalt Watch,
I will not come on thee as a thief,
and thou shalt know (recognize) what hour (ie: season) I will come upon thee.

All are commanded to Watch, regardless as to when they should live during the Last Days, so
that, when the final hour (ie: season) arriveth - they may know/understand, that the Day of
Lord be at hand: And shall see (ie: beware of) The Day approaching. (Mk.13:33-37/He.10:25)

Now learn the parable of the Fig Tree;   (Mt.24:32/Mk.13:28)
when the branch is yet tender, and putteth forth leaves, ye know that summer is nigh:
When ye shall see ALL these things (Mt.24:13-33) know that it (Mt.24:3) is near - at the doors.
When ye -- see the Abomination of Desolation -- stand in the Holy Place, ---- understand/think!
The Holy Place (the Temple of God) can only refer to the Churches (the local assemblies), where
Satan (who has been loosed) now, as the man of sin (appearing as an angel of Light), has
taken His seat - shewing himself that he is God.   (2 Thes.2:2-12) (2 Cor.11:14/Rev.20:3)
Many preachers, teach some truth - but out of context, making the congregation to believe all
is well: Teaching a man-made salvation plan (instill in them a false hope), giveth the
Temple goers (not having the love of the truth) a sense of security, peace and safety.
Today we are in the final season, are you still sitting on the fence - waiting it out?

A New Era of Sabbath(s)

> In the end of the Sabbath(s), as it began to dawn toward the first of the Sabbath(s). (Mt.28:1)

People Puzzle: Trying to understand, how the events unfolded that Sunday morning, when Jesus arose from the grave (in AD.33) early the first of Sabbath(s).

> All indications are, that only a short time period elapsed, as people went to and from the sepulchre (some of them running).

Mary Magdalene and the other Mary (mother of Joses, James and Salome), they (Mk.15:47 & 16:1)
    Saw where and how the body of Jesus was placed in the sepulchre (ie: tomb/grave).
      And they returned, and prepared spices and ointments. (Lk.23:56)
  On the sabbath they rested, according to the commandment. (Lk.23:56/Ex.20:10)

On the first of the Sabbath(s): It was very early (only a glimmer of light).
    They took with them, the sweet spices and ointments - that they had bought/prepared;
      and they made their way to the sepulchre, that they might anoint him. (Mk.16:1)
And, behold, there was a Great Earthquake! (Mt.28:2-4)

One can only imagine their state of mind:
Trying to make sense of all those things, that had happened so quickly.
And possibly a lack of sleep, and in a daze - trying to make sense of it all.

And as they went, they wondered, who shall roll away that (very great) stone? (Mk.16:3,4)
When they arrived at the tomb (to their surprise) they saw that the stone was rolled away.
    And entering into the sepulchre, they saw a young man (an angel). (Mk.16:5/Mt.28:5)
And he (the angel) answered and said to the women, Fear not ye: Ye seek Jesus of Nazareth,
    which was crucified; he is not here/he is risen: Behold the place where the Lord lay.
    But go your way, tell his disciples ------------. (Mt.28:5/Mk.16:6,7)
And they went out quickly, and fled from the sepulchre (for they trembled and were amazed),
    neither said they any thing to any - for they were afraid. (Mk.16:8)
And, they (again) and certain others with them - went to the sepulchre,
    and they brought with them (again) the spices which they had prepared. (Lk.24:1)
  Note: When people are in larger numbers - they tend to be more brave/courageous.
And when they arrived at the sepulchre, they found the entrance (the door-way) open:
    So, they entered in, but they found not the body of the Lord Jesus. (Lk.24:3)
    Mary Magdalene ran to Simon Peter and the other disciple (that Jesus loved), --. (Jn.20:2)
The women (who remained at the tomb) were perplexed;
    and, behold, two men stood by them in shining garments. (Lk.24:4)
    The men reminded them of the words of Jesus, how he spake, ----------------. (Lk.24:5-7)
        And they remembered his words. (Lk.24:8,9/Mt.28:8)
And they (the women at the tomb) returned from there - and went and told the 11, and the rest.
Now (after the women had left), Mary Magdalene came to the tomb with the 2 disciples:
  And when they (the 2 disciples) saw that the tomb was empty,
    they believed (what Mary Magdalene had told them), and they went home. (Jn.20:8,10)
    For as yet they knew not the Scriptures, that he must rise from the dead. (Jn.20:9)
Mary Magdalene remained (still standing) without at the sepulchre weeping:
  She stooped - to look inside the sepulchre, and she saw 2 angels --------.
    And they say unto her, Woman why weepest thou? And she told them why! (Jn.20:13)
  And, she turning herself back: Some-one behind her! Who could it be?
      And he (ie: Jesus) asked her, Woman why weepest thou? Who seekest thou?
    She knew not that he was Jesus,
      (she thought him to be the gardener);
      and she saith, If you have born him
      hence, tell me where thou hast
      laid him: I will take him away!

> Jesus was risen early the first of the Sabbath(s), he appeared first to Mary Magdalene, out of whom he had cast 7 devils. (Mk.16:9)

    Jesus said, Mary. She turned and said, Rabboni (ie: Master)! (Jn.20:14-16)
And after they (the women) told his disciples,
  as they went, behold, Jesus met them, saying, All hail ----------- Be not afraid:
    Go tell my brethren, that they go into Galilee, and there they shall see me. (Mt.28:9)
It was Mary Magdalene, Joanna, and Mary (mother of James), and the other women with them,
  who told these things unto the apostles. (Lk.24:10,11)
  And their words seemed to them as idle tales, and they believed them not.

Page 2 of 3

Matthew (28:1)	Mark (15:47)	Luke (23:55)	John (20:1)
Mary Magdalene & the other Mary	Mary Magdalene & Mary (mother of Joses, James, Salome)	The women from Galilee	Mary Magdalene

> It appears that Mark and Matthew are referring to the same Mary & Mary. Luke is referring to a group of women. John focuses only on Mary Magdalene.

Joseph (of Arimathea) a disciple of Jesus besought Pilate to take the body of Jesus.
Nicodemus brought a mixture of myrrh and aloes. (Lk.23:50-53/Jn.19:38-42)
They wound the body of Jesus in linen clothes with the spices ----- in a sepulchre.

```
                They beheld where  -------  They saw how his
                    he was laid.                body was laid.
                                             They returned and
                                              prepared spices
                                              and ointments.
                                             The sabbath drew on.
```

An High Day (Jn.19:31)   On the sabbath
                                                        they rested.   (Lk.23:56/Ex.20:10)

```
In the end of
    the sabbath(s)
    (ie: Saterdays)
As it began
    to dawn toward
    the first of         When the sabbath
    the sabbath(s)           was past,
    (ie: Sundays).       (they had bought
                             sweet spices)

They came to see  ---  They went
    the sepulchre.         to the sepulchre.
```

> And behold there was a great earth-quake; for
>   The angel of the Lord descended from heaven - rolled back the stone & sat upon it.
> The keepers (ie: watchers) for fear of him did shake, and became as dead. (Mt.28:2-4)

```
                        They (Mary & Mary)
                            came unto the sepulchre:
                        They looked, and saw that
                            the stone was rolled away.
The angel  ----------   A young man
    answered & said,        sitting on the right side
Fear not ye  ----           in a long white garment.
    See where he lay.   He saith, be not afraid,
Go  ---  Tell               behold the place
    his disciples           where they laid him.
    he is risen, and    Go - Tell his disciples and
    goeth before            Peter that he goeth before
    you into Galilee.       you into Galilee; and
                        There shall ye see him.
                        They - fled from the sepulchre,
                            (for they were afraid); and
                        They told no-one
```

Mary Magdalene
  & the other Mary
  (it would appear) must
  have joined the other women,
  and they went to the tomb.

They came unto the
    sepulchre, bringing
    the spices which
    they had prepared.   Mary Magdalene
(And certain others   seeth the stone
    with them). Lk.24:1   taken away
The stone was rolled away - from the sepulchre.
They entered & found
    not the body: ————————→ Mary Magdalene
                                   runneth
And they (the women)
    were

178 | Assembly by John Douma

	much perplexed.	
	And - behold two men stood by them in shining garments:	
	They said unto them, He is not here, but is risen:	and cometh to Simon Peter, and the other disciple (whom Jesus loved) and saith unto them, They have taken away the Lord ---:
They departed quickly ————————————	Remember how he spake ——————. And they remembered. They returned from the sepulchre, to tell the eleven and the rest.	And we know not where they have laid him. Peter - and the other disciple came to (and went into) the sepulchre ————. (Seeing = believing?) Then - went again to their own home.
from the sepulchre with fear and great joy:		Mary stood without at the tomb weeping, stooping looketh in and seeth 2 angels.
And did run to bring his disciples word.		Jesus was behind her. Jesus reveals himself
And as (ie: after) they went to tell his disciples Jesus met them:	Having risen early the first of the week, Jesus appeared first to Mary Magdalene ————————————————— (out of whom he had cast 7 devils). Mk.16:9	to Mary Magdalene.
He saith unto them, All hail --- Be not afraid; Go, tell my brethren that they go into Galilee, and there they shall see me.		
Now, when they were going, Behold, some of the watch came into the city, and shewed unto the chief priests all the things that were done. Being assembled with the elders and having taken counsel, They gave large money unto the soldiers, saying, Say ye that his disciples came by night and stole him while we slept: ————. So they took the money, and did as they were taught.	→ It was Mary Magdalene ———— Joanna, Mary (of James), And other women with them, who told these things unto the apostles. And - they believed them not. Then arose Peter, and ran unto the sepulchre; and stooping down, he beheld the linen clothes laid by themselves: And he departed, wondering in himself ——.	Mary Magdalene came, and told the disciples that she had seen the Lord, And that he had spoken these things unto her.(Jn.20:18)
1 Cor.15:5-8 He was seen of Cephas, then of the twelve, after that above 500, after that of James, then all the apostles, & last of all of me also.	Two of them walking -- into the country. (Jesus appeared in another form.) ——→	Two - went that same day to --- Emmaus. They talked - of all that which had happened. As they communed and reasoned, Jesus drew near. And (later) their eyes were opened, ——————; and he vanished out of their sight.
	And they rose up that same hour, and returned to Jerusalem, and found the eleven ———, and them that were with them, Saying, The Lord is risen indeed, and hath appeared to Simon. And they told what things were done in the way, and how he was known of them in breaking of bread. (Lk.24:33-35) The same day at evening, the first of the Sabbath(s) ———————— As they spake, Jesus himself stood in the midst of them, and saith unto them, Peace be unto you. (Lk.24:36/Jn.20:19)	

S I G N S

The Signs Of The Times.

> A Sign = a Token, or Miracle/Wonder.
> Ensample (example), a Pattern.
> A Wonder, is perhaps best described as a thing of Awe.
> A Covenant (a Promise), is set-up by one or more parties.

A Sign of (1) A covenant (promise), or agreement made in the past, and is of relevance after.
(2) Something to come later:
    (A sound is heard, but the object making the sound is still out of sight.)

A Sign, may be something visible (an object or an action) to impress, or alert/trigger the mind
  to recall a particular matter of vital importance - that must be considered (kept in mind).
  The Thing: may be a ring, or it may be a string, or it could be almost any thing!

Diversity (variation) of Signs:
  A Man — and what happened unto him.   (Jonah 1:17)(Mt.16:4/Mt.12:39,40/Lk.11:29,30)
         — acting the part (resembling), that which must befall later.   (Ez.12:1-7,11,26-28)
  That Time, when a prediction comes to fulfilment.   (Ex.3:12)
  A heap of stones.   (Gen.31:44-49/Josh.4:1-7)
  The Bow (rain-bow) in the clouds.   (Gen.9:11-17)
  The Sabbath (the Saterday Sabbath) was a sign.   (Gen.2:3)(Ex.31:13,17)
  The sign of circumcision.   (Gen.17:9-14/Rom.4:11)
  The Lights in the firmament of the heaven.   (Gen.1:7,14)(Jer.10:2)
  The blood on the Side Posts and on the Lintel (the upper door post/header).   (Ex.12:7,22,13)
  For a sign unto thee upon thy hand, and for a memorial between thine eyes. (Ex.13:9/Mt.23:5)
  The Son of man be a Sign unto this generation.   (Lk.11:30)

In those days, that Jesus resided on earth (in this world),   (Mt.2:1,23/Acts 22:8)(Mt.16:1-4)
  the Pharisees and the Sadducees (it appears) were unable to discern the Signs of those Times.
So what are (if there be any) the Signs of the Times for This Day?   (Lk.12:56/Lk.21:34/Rev.3:3)
According to certain Bible teachers, we have no clue - Jesus shall come as a thief in the night.
Actually, the Bible points out to us - some things are expected from us (we are commanded to
  act) when the 2nd. coming of the Son of man is imminent - at the door.
When ye see "all" these things (in Mt.24:14-33), know that it is near, even At The Door!
  The abomination of desolation - stand in the Holy Place ----, flee! (Mt.24:15,16/Gen.19:17)
  The man of sin/son of perdition (Satan) - as God   (2 Thes.2:3-12)(Mt.13:15/Rev.18:4/Jn.10:3)
    sitteth (takes seat/rules) in the Temple of God, shewing himself that he is God.
  Woe unto them that call evil good, and good evil -------.   (Is.5:20)(Mt.19:17)
  For if we sin wilfully, after that we have received the knowledge of the Truth,
    there remaineth no more sacrifice for sins.   (He.10:26/He.6:4-6)
  False prophets (showing signs and wonders);
    insomuch that, if it were possible, they should deceive the very elect.   (Mt.24:24)

Stand back/observe, look and take note: how the forces of evil are dominant - at this time.
The momentum of evil has infiltrated Governments, Schools, Churches, and other organizations.
In the past the Bible was consulted - when the laws were tabled:
  But as of late, the tables are turned, and now they call evil good, and good evil.
  The Bible has been outlawed, it is (has become) an obstacle (a stumbling block) to society.
The Line dividing Right from Wrong is moving to & fro - like a brush, painting everything grey.
  It is now common practise (lawful) to exterminate the unwanted pre-born human beings.
  Those who waltz/dance to the beat of Sodom are granted a voice (a special status) to exhibit
    their strange affection/behaviour in public - and are given privileged protection by law.

What shall be the Sign of thy coming, and the end of the world? (Mt.24:3B,15,29-31/Mk.13:14-28)
Ask yourself, Immediately after the Great Tribulation - Why does (what could cause) the sun
  to darken, that the moon give no light, and the stars fall from heaven?
Perhaps we can picture it in this manner:
When Jesus is coming (about to appear), the brightness of the Glory of God (just prior to his
  appearance) is much brighter than the radiance of the sun, making the sun black/obsolete;
  And all the tribes of the earth shall mourn.
  And they shall see the Son of man coming in the clouds of heaven with power and great glory.
It is a mystery: We shall not all sleep, but we shall all be changed, in a moment, in the
  twinkling of an eye, at the last trump: for the trumpet shall sound, and the dead shall be
  raised incorruptible, and we shall be changed. (1 Cor.15:51,52/Mt.24:29-30/Ps.1:5/Mt.10:28)
We - look for New Heavens and a New Earth wherein dwelleth Righteousness.   (2 Pe.3:10-13)

Changing the Times and the Laws? (a different Code of Conduct.)

At the preent time (in the beginning of the 21st. century) the traditional values are being
   challenged in trying times, when we are told/expected to smile and be tolerant. (Dan.7:25)
Subtil spirits have conned people to become successful (be a somebody) via ill-conceived means.
Many (politicians, lawyers, judges and others) have signed up - to having their conscience
   seared, and to abandon sound traditional values - based upon the Holy Scriptures. (Mt.4:9)

(1) Abortion (to terminate the Life of a pre-born.)
   The concoction of evil mentality. Their feet are swift to shed blood. (Rom.3:15-18/Is.59:7)
   Surprisingly (having a broad view),
     many who abort their young - later in life use extreme methods to become with young.
     More are the children of the desolate than the children of the married wife. (Is.54:1)
   In accordance with the laws of man, the unwanted pre-born are judged axe worthy. (Ez.16:38)

(2) The Gay Life-style, is pictured to be an honourable alternative to traditional marriage.
   The homosexual/lesbian community proudly wave a banner,
     having the colours of the Bow In The Cloud (an Everlasting Covenant of Almighty God).
   They (by their actions) announce publicly, We Know the truth of the Word of God,
     and His blood be on us and our recruits. (Mt.27:25/Rom.1:21,22,32)

(3) Evolution (having the earmark of religion), is now taught in schools instead of Creation.
   The Religion of Evolution: (what the preachers of this religion are inclined to avoid.)
   In the beginning there was no-thing. But, miraculously (out of no-where) Some-Thing was,
     about the size of a pin-head (or it may only have been the size of a Pin Prick).
   Please bear with me, there is more to come - this was only the beginning! (Ps.2:1/Jer.7:24)
   And in time: Miracle, after miracle, after miracle - until the required building blocks
     were established. Now we are getting somewhere, now there is some-things to build with.
   The action and re-action among these building blocks, making way for more blocks, and one
     thing led to another - things were beginning to take shape. All this took place (not in
     only 6 days, but) over a very, very long time!
   Evolution came about over millions of years, and in time there was man (a more intelligent
     animal). The wisdom/knowledge of man has excelled (evolved) greatly - so that, we now
     can trace our roots back to when it all began: When Some-Thing was. (Rom.1:20/Ps.2:1-4)

In our time, the traditional values from the past are revised - to please the antichrists.
If now, the majority of the people were to voice their discontent; would it make a difference?
   They (the politicians, lawyers and judges) find ways to manipulate the democratic process:
   Some court cases are fixed, and results are pre-determined by the way the jury is selected.

The wrath of God is revealed from heaven against all ungodliness and unrighteousness of men
   who hold the Truth of God in unrighteousness, ----------------. (Rom.1:18/Is.24:5/1 Tim.4:2)
For the invisible things of God (His eternal Power and Divinity), from the creation of the
   world are clearly seen/understood by the things that are made: and they be without excuse.
   Professing themselves to be wise - they became fools,
     and changed the Glory of the uncorruptible God into an image,
     made like corrubtible man, and to birds, and fourfooted beasts, and creeping things:
     Wherefore God also gave them up, to -------------. (See Rom.1:20-24)

> Note: And/So God (Jehovah God), gave them up/over (they gave themselves over)
> Concerning the Israelites at Mount Sinai: (Ps.106:19-21/Ex.32:1-4)(Ex.32:22/Ex.17:4)
>   -unto their own hearts' lusts. (Ps.81:12)
>   -to worship the host of heaven. (Acts 7:41,42)
> Concerning the inhabitants of Sodom, Gomorrha, Admah and Zeboim: (De.29:23)
>   -to uncleaness/vile affections (ie: unnatural same-sex behaviour). (Rom.1:24,26)

The inhabitants of Sodom, Gomorrha, Admah and Zeboim, through the lusts of their own hearts,
   became lesbians/homosexuals; dishonouring their own bodies between themselves, for they
     changed the natural use into that which is against nature. (2 Pe.2:10,12/Rom.1:24-26)
   These giving themselves over to fornication, and going after strange flesh, are set forth
     for an example, suffering the vengeance of eternal fire. (Jude :7)(Lk.3:17/Mk.9:43,45)
   And turning these cities into ashes (condemned them with an overthrow), making them an
     ensample (ie: an example) unto those that "After" should live ungodly. (2 Pe.2:6)
Note: "After" = To-day, when the creature is worshipped/served more than the Creator. (Ro.1:25)
Choose "This Day" whom ye will serve? As for me and my house we will serve Jehovah. (Jos.24:15)

A Ray of Hope (for the hopeless)

The Bible is its own dictionary:
To better understand the meaning of the words, we observe their use else-where in the Bible.
Numbers are words: their significance is determined by the circumstances in which they be used.
The Bible is a treasure-trove of information for people of all ages, to read and to learn from.
A Young's Analytical Concordance, and a Strong's Exhaustive Concordance may be of assistance.

If you are depressed/lonely, instead of popping pep pills, or happy drugs, or create some kind
    of god for your pleasure - read the Bible and listen to what God Almighty has to say to you.
    Use pen & paper (making notes) trying to understand: Keep trying!   (Acts 17:11)(2 Tim.3:16)

> Learning is a process, and we categorize our findings, as
>   (1) Data (the various passages/information gathered together on a particular subject.)
>   (2) Conclusions (the results arrived at following serious Bible study.)
>   (3) Dogma (what we understand/consider to be unquestionable facts.)

As we prayerfully search/study the Holy Scriptures - we arrive/come to certain conclusions:
But, as we continue our studies, comparing Scripture with Scripture (spiritual things with
    spiritual), we soon realize (although we were sure we understood), that, our findings need
    correction - to be in sink with the remainder of the Bible: And we keep trying!   (2 Pe.1:20)
The Bible has within (hidden within) potential information; to be revealed progressively:
Certain Bible passages cannot be properly/fully understood spritualy, until the time should
    come, when the believers (who be living in a particular season) will experience the Bible
    prophecy being fulfilled, and recognize the signs of those times.   (Hab.2:3/Dan.12:4,10)
The Author of the Bible often speaks to the reader/listener in parables (proverbs/allegory).
  For example: (Are you able to detect the spiritual significance of this parabolic speech?)
    Pray without ceasing.   (1 Thes.5:17)
    Except a man be born again, he cannot see the kingdom of God.   (Jn.3:3/1 Pe.1:23/1 Jn.3:9)
    I will make you fishers of men.   (Mt.4:19/Mk.1:17)
    Behold, the Lamb of God.   (Jn.1:29,36/Acts 8:32/1 Pe.1:19)
    And washed us from our sins in his own blood.   (Rev.1:5/1 Cor.6:11/1 Pe.1:18,19)

Many people are dumb-founded
  by the words found in Ex.20:5, and repeated in Ex.34:7/Num.14:18/De.5:9.
I Jehovah thy God am a jealous God,
    Visiting the iniquity of the fathers upon the children unto the 3rd. and the 4th. generation
        of them that hate me, ---------------.
  (Note: Two different limits/boundaries are given, "Unto the 3rd. and the 4th. generation".

> ——— Unto the 4th. generation ———
> The 4th. (for example, the 4 corners of the earth) = to the very ends of/all inclusive.
> All we (conceived and born in sin) are guilty -------.   (Ps.58:3)
> All have sinned. The wages of sin is death. (we deserve to be destroyed.)   (Rom.3:23)
> I am unable to save myself, I am helpless: My situation is hopeless! (Ro.6:23/Ro.7:24)

  And Ex.20:5 continues,
    And, shewing mercy unto thousands of them that love me and keep my commandments.

> ——— Unto the 3rd. generation ———
> The 3rd. (almost, but not to the very end of) = an allowance for mankind to be hopeful.
> That narrow margin betwixt the 3rd. and the 4th. giving a ray of hope for the hopeless.
> To-day is the day, for sinners to cry out and say, Lord save me!   (He.4:7/Mt.14:30)
> A Great Crowd (out of the Great Tribulation) are saved. (Rev.7:9,14/1 Jn.5:14/Rom.9:15)

The Mystery (hid from ages, and from generations, but) now revealed to His saints;
  to whom God would make known (the riches of the Glorious Mystery) to the gentiles:
    which is Christ in you - the Hope of Glory.   (Col.1:26,27)(Acts 10:12-15,28B)
In Christ Jesus ye are all one: Circumcised and uncircumcised, Jew and Greek/Gentile;
    bond and free, Barbarian and Scythian; male and female.   (1 Cor.12:13,14/Gal.3:28/Col.3:11)
If ye love me - keep my commandments!
    Thou shalt love the Lord thy God ---. Thou shalt love thy neighbour ---.   (Mk.12:30,31)
    Let your women keep silence in the churches.   (1 Cor.14:34.35/1 Tim.2:11,12)
    Abstain from meats offered to idols,
        and from blood, and from things strangled, and from fornication.   (Acts 15:29)

Is there any thing new under the sun?

Every one is encouraged to read the Bible - but not every one will understand.   (1 Col.1:9B)
The commandments (pertinent to the era that one lives in) must be obeyed. (1 Jn.2:4/Jn.14:15)
   God is the author of the Bible.
   The Bible is God's law-book for mankind.
   The Bible, in the original writing (now lost) were free of errors.
     Copies, copied from copies of the originals - can be found in museums.

The Bible translators had the difficult task to translate the Bible into other languages.
And at times (due to a lack of understanding) they did not do as well, as they set out to do.
Occasionally we may find a Bible passage and question the word(s) the translators have used.

It so happened, that (while listening on Short Wave Radio) I heard repeatedly (over and over),
   that Satan is a god! some will add, that he is a god with a small "G", (a small "G" god).
The god of this world (2 Cor.4:4) could have been translated, The God of this age.
There is One God, and no other; although, there be those who are called gods.   (1 Cor.8:4-6)
   (1) There are many (whether in heaven or in earth) that are called gods. (Jn.10:34/Ps.82:6)
   (2) Them that are made/created by people (idols), these be so-called gods.   (Ps.96:4,5)

Who is, The God of this age? My initial thought, God Almighty has to be The God of all ages!
Later, it dawned on me, that, O God (ie: the God) of this age - is no other than Jesus Christ:
Our Lord Jesus Christ is The God of this present age (ie: the New Testament era);   (Is.9:6,7)
   And he must reign, until He hath put all enemies under his feet. (1 Cor.15:24-28/He.10:13)
     (Now, when he saith all things - He that did put all things under him is excepted.)
The last enemy that shall be destroyed is death.   (1 Cor.15:26,54/Rev.21:4-8/Rev.20:14,15)
And when he shall have put down all rule, and all authority, and power:
   and when all things be subdued unto him, then shall the Son also himself be subject
     unto Him that put all things under him, that God may be all in all.

Many in the Temple of God (the modern day churches of this day), believe in themselves; and,
   they are not interested/obedient to the whole counsel of God: they have cut-out/eliminated
   the Bible passages, that (according to their way of thinking) are said to be outdated.
And they are confident, that they possess the intelligence needed to make wise decisions, and
   they (of themselves) are capable to discern Evil from Good (Immoral from Moral); (Is.5:20)
   and there is no need for publicans and sinners to change - for God loves every-one.
And because they have not the love of the Truth, God has send them a strong delusion, that
   they should believe a lie. The man of sin takes His seat in the Temple of God! (2 Th.2:10)
Among the churches today, the United church is in the lead travelling the broad way that leads
   to condemnation/judgment, having women and homosectual preachers as their counsellers.
   Other churches also (as did the United church) have found pleasure in unrighteousness.
Q. What would you expect to happen when the blind follow the blind?   (Mt.15:14/Lk.6:39)

There also be them who are on a mission to proof that the Bible need not be taken seriously.
To them (as they see it), the Bible is a collection of ideas (stories and opinions) from
   various authors that were bound into a book. And they question the purpose of the laws,
     for they fail (they are blind), to understand the spiritual significance. (Lev.21:5)
These (having the spirit of the world), in their minds - believe themselves to be intelligent;
   and when they speak, they so do with such confidence, that their followers (even when they
   understand it not, they) pre-sume that they must know what it is they be talking about.

Every one of us have sinned (made errors) knowingly or unknowingly.   (1Jn.1:8,10/Mt.6:6-13)
We must repent, asking, our heavenly Father for mercy.   (Lk.15:18,19/Rom.9:15,16/Rom.11:5-7)

> All Scripture is given by inspiration of God; and is profitable for doctrine,
> for reproof, for correction, for instruction in Righteousness.   (2 Tim.3:16)

From time to time, all we (due to something we said or did) are subject to correction.
The first in need of correction are the teachers - so they can properly educate the students.
Some people, after they have erred (and are corrected), will acknowledge their error and make
   correction, and others quietly make changes - and continue their vocation.
When-ever changes (new teachings) are introduced, these are said to be, "New Life".
Q. Which sinners do you think would be more appreciative?   (Lk.7:40-50)

Hearken to the sound of the trumpet

Every-where, all over this world, changes are happening at an alarming rapid pace.
And (it appears as if), since approximately AD.1988,
   that the rulers on planet earth have injected the inhabitants with a persuasive serum,
   a potion - to lul the people into believing whatsoever it is they instruct them to believe.
Those things which our parents taught us to be good/respectable, are now judged to be immoral;
   and what we understood as evil, the same is now tolerated/encouraged, and even promoted.

> Hear, O Earth! Behold, I will bring evil upon this people - the fruit of their thoughts,
>   because they have not hearkened unto my words, nor my law, but rejected it.   (Jer.6)

There are 2 royal movements, a liberal movement, and a conservative movement;
   and, both these - speak lies at one table: (Dan.11:27)
   This they can do, because they make the laws, also the law that gives them immunity.
And when the laws (rules) are constructed they allow for provisions,
   (including exemptions/escape clauses, and loop holes),
   to determine whom the law shall deter, and to whom it may be beneficial.

The rulers on planet earth are determined to make sweeping changes:
And thus far, they have cut out the Lord's prayer and side-swept the 10 commandments,
   to prepair (make way) for a, New World Order
   (a passage that all the inhabitants of this planet must adhere to - according to the law).
   The very structure of society (the nature of right and wrong) are challenged and changed;
      making it more favourable to the wealthy, and more tolerable to radicals and extremists.

The extremists and radicals are making their voices heard, and they come with their demands:
   Having mastered the process, "How to manipulate the public and achieve your goals";
   They, knowing (the ideal sequence), where and how to begin, and how to proceed,
      for to trick the public to agree to something - that they really do not want.
And next, some polititian (one of their own kind) may display sympathy toward their cause:
And they engage the courts;
   and (even they are astonished to discover, that) they have friends in high places.
And, due to political wranglen, the tables are over-turned, and the laws are held hostage:
And in the process - the radicals (or the extremist) are granted what they had demanded;
   even-though, the public in general, may not be content with what is being forced onto them.
   But what can the public do? when those governing lack common sense and display madness!
First: We were told (led to believe), If the population continued to increase as they have,
   the earth could not produce ample victuals to provide for all the population of this world.
Next: The radicals successfully moved (did succeed) to change the law,
   and abortion was legalized: the pre-born of mankind were declared to be axe worthy.
   (Note: the MAIN reason to legalize abortion had to do with, CONVENIENCE.)
   These (so-called) honourable politicians were brainwashed, by the lies they had been told.

The extremist would have you believe, that the sea level shall rise due to the melting of ice.
   But they fail to inform you, that, when floating ice melts - it will not raise the ocean.
The wealthy extremists (professional liars, scare-mongers) would have you to believe, that
   the poor (those at the bottom of the pyramid) must preserve - to combat climate change:
   How-ever, the wealthy (if they be willing to pay more) can use as much as they desire.
In reality, money is no obstacle to the rich, and the poor have no choice but to cut back.

For the extremists and the radicals to obtain their goals, they either exaggerate and/or lie;
   and the governing authorities fall on their faces - to accommodate and to appease them.
   They have one more obstacle to overcome, ie: to have the Bible officially declared invalid.
Scientists have decided (based on if & probability) that this planet is billions of years old.
Children are forced-fed the religion of evolution, and by so-doing deny the Creator Almighty.
And they (the children) are also taught (it is in-grained in their mindset), that,
   having 2 mommies or 2 daddies are a good alternative - for a healthy family envirenment.
Corruption and deception has infiltrated into government, courts, schools and the churches.
And it appears that governments are possessed by an evil entity, and are catering to Lucifer.
The spiritual realms (we cannot see), but there be a host of wicked ghosts in the air, and by
   their effect on humans - we (in our day) can know that they are busy and active. (Eph.2:2)

Believe not every spirit

The Author of the Bible alerts (commands/warns) us!
Beloved, believe not every spirit, but try the spirits whether they be of God;
   because many false prophets are gone out into the world. (1 Jn.4:1-3)(1 Jn.2:18)(2 John :7)
Nearly 2000y. ago there were many antichrist(s), evidence that they were in the Last Time.
   Every spirit that confesseth that Jesus Christ is come in the flesh is of God. (1 Cor.8:6)
   Every spirit that confesseth not that Jesus Christ is come in the flesh is not of God.

The commandment, To Try (to test) the spirits, is some-what puzzling: (2 Cor.11:13-15)
   How can I (or others) be obedient, when we are unable to fully understand the instructions?
   Therefore, I have prayerfully consulted the Bible, comparing spiritual with spiritual.

> Every one goeth through a learning phase to arrive at the truth. (Acts 20:27)
> At times others may have discovered some things that we may have over-looked.
> To come to a full understanding, one has to consult the whole counsel of God.

In our day: Many profess (make confession) to know God, but in their works they deny Him,
   being abominable, and disobedient, and unto every good work reprobate.   (Titus 1:16)
   And false/deceitful prophets are transformed as ministers of righteousness.   (2 Cor.11:14)

Bible teachers/counsellors (having pre-conceived ideas) select Bible passages - out of
   context from the remainder of the Bible, to which they add their own spin,
   to make it say what they choose to make it say - to compliment their life-style.

Example:
(1) There is neither male or female, for ye are all one in Jesus Christ.
This statement comes directly from the Holy Scriptures; how could any-thing be more correct?
However, when it be taken out of context (isolated) from the remainder of the Bible,
   it makes an environment (a set-up) for a strong delusion, that they should believe a lie.
All we have sinned: (Rom.3:23/Rom.5:12/Rom.14:23)(1 Jn.1:10)(De.24:16)
God is not a respecter of persons in the way He gathereth the elect from all nations; for the
   elect of God are saved by grace, whether they be Jew, Greek, slave, free, male or female.

(2) Judge not that ye be not judged.
This passage can easily be mis-interpreted, and used/exploited for unrelated personal reasons.
All judgments are not equal (not the same), it depends on what sort of judging is in view.
   Every one has to make judgment - to determine right from wrong.   (Lk.7:43)(1 Cor.11:13)
There is a judgment, that we are to refrain from: Judge not,   (Mt.7:1/Rom.3:23/1 Jn.1:8-10)
   for wherein thou judgest another, thou (who doest the same) condemnest thy-self. (Rom.2:1)
   That all may be condemned who believe not (did not commit to) the truth.   (2 Thes.2:12)
The judgment to damn (ie: condemn to hell-fire/Gehenna) is not for sinners to make. (Mt.10:28)
Some people use the expression, Judge not that ye be not judged, to divert attention away from
   existing repetitive sin - giving them a license to continue in their sinful behaviour.
Also, it is not advantageous to repeatedly remind others of past errors of which they
   may have repented - for all of us may have a few skeletons hidden away in our own closet.
And besides, we know not the hearts of others, or their dying confessions.
Therefore judge no-thing before the time, until the Lord come,   (1 Jn.1:8/Rom.3:23)
   who both will bring to light the hidden things of darkness, and will make manifest
   the counsels of the hearts: Then shall every man have praise of God. (1 Cor.4:5/Rom.2:16)

There also be certain catchy expressions in circulation:
   -God loves the sinner, but not the sin.
   -Come as you are, for God loves all.
And when spoken, they (although deceptive in nature), have the ring of genuine and loving
   hospitality - to make believe that all is well, peace and safety: (1 Thes.5:3)(2 Tim.4:3,4)
   And it sounds like music - appealing to the unlearned/broadminded having itching ears.

In this day, Try the spirits (what sort of spirit motivates individuals): Beware! (Mt.7:15)
   What is taught, but particularly take note of what they Do Not Teach!   (Acts 20:27)
   Is tantalizing music incorporated to indulge the audience into a spirit of acceptance?
   Do they teach that salvation can be obtained in ways other than Jesus Christ? (Acts 4:12)
All who profess to know God the Father, and deny that Jesus is the Christ are liars. (1 Jn.2)

Revelation

Many Bible Students have tried (spent a lot of time) to understand the last book of the Bible.
As we struggle to understand Revelation, we have to admit that we see through a glass darkly,
  when prominent/distinguished Bible Students arrive at different conclusions. (1 Cor.13:12)
    Progressive Revelation, only allow us to understand - as the Spirit of God gives wisdom.
The 1000 year time periods (as described in Revelation 20);
  Are these, to be understood literally, as periods of time that consist of 1000 years?
  Or, may these be pictures of (resembling) periods of time - of which the duration may vary?
Also, was Revelation written in cronological sequence? Some say, it is, and others disagree.

As I now understand, the 1000 year terms, are pictures of un-known durations of time.
And, in my opinion, Revelation is probably in cronological sequence, but there is more to it.

> In a particular space of time (at the same time - so to speak);
> Various events may occur at the same time (a span of time), but, in different locations;
>   and different observers (at the same event) have varied accounts from different views:
> To record the various statements of the various accounts from the different viewers;
> One, repeatedly has to go back in time - to the beginning (or, part way back),
>   and make another pass over the same time period (span of time),
>   and add another event or account until the recording is completed.

The time spans may vary in duration, and thus we move to & fro, until we arrive at the End.

Jesus was born in Bethlehem of Judaea, and circumcised on the 8th. day.   (Mt.2:1/Lk.2:21)
  Jesus (later) was baptized by John the Baptist - in the Jordan River.   (Mt.3:5,6,13-17)
  Jesus ministered: preaching the gospel of the kingdom of God.   (Mk.1:14,15/Mt.11:2-6)
  The Son of man (before he had been crucified) had Power to forgive sin.   (Mt.9:6-8)
Jesus died, and arose from the dead: went up into heaven, is seated at the R.H. of God.
      (1 Cor.15:25) for he must reign, till He hath put all enemies under his feet.
      (Lk.1:31-33) Jesus -------, and of his kingdom there shall be No End ------»

Satan is bound   ├─Satan   The 2nd. coming of the Son of man (+ the rapture).
(Rev.20:2,3,7)   is
←──1000 years──→   loosed,   The Last Day: (Jn.11:24/Jn.6:39,40,44,54)(Jn.12:48)
                         The Great   His servants are rewarded. (Rev.2:11)
Christ, became   Tribulation Judgment unto the dead. (Rev.11:18,19)
the 1st.fruits
(1 Cor.15:20)

  The Lamb opening the seven seals.
    The sounds of the 7 trumpets.
        (7 sealed thunders)   The 7 Vials (the last plagues)
                                  of the wrath of God. (Rev.16)
           (2 Pe.2:9)
                                Death/Hell cast in the lake of fire. (Re.20:14)
                                The lake of fire = The 2nd. death.   (Rev.21:8)
  Jesus (in Heaven), seated
    on the Right Hand of the Father......Delivers the Kingdom to God. (1 Cor.15:24)-»

Then be The End, when Christ shall have delivered up the Kingdom to God, even the Father,
   for he must reign, until He hath put all enemies under his feet. (1 Cor.15:24,25/Ps.110:1)
And he (Jesus) shall reign ---- for ever; and of his kingdom (Lk.1:33) there shall be No End-»

What is the 1st. Resurrection? (Rev.20:5B, takes us back to Rev.20:4)
And I saw thrones, and they that sat upon them, judgment was given unto them:
And I saw the souls of them that were beheaded for the witness of Jesus, and the Word of God,
   which had not worshipped the beast, neither his image,
     neither had received his mark upon their foreheads, or in their hands:
   And they lived and reigned with Christ a 1000 years.
Blessed and Holy is he   (Rev.20:6) (Rev.2:11,7/Rev.3:5,21)
   that hath part in the 1st. Resurrection - on such the 2nd. death hath no power:
   And they (ie: the priests of God, and of Christ) shall reign with him a 1000 years.
After The End of time is Eternity - which is time-less.
Some Bible Students have concluded that the 1000y. reign (Rev.20:4E) is an Everlasting reign-»
He hath made us unto our God, kings and priests - and we shall reign on the earth. (Rev.5:10)

The Little Horn

The Bible gives us numerous hints, concerning the final days; and thus we are encouraged
to continue searching the Scriptures - perhaps additional information may be revealed.
The Bible points out to us, that knowledge shall increase and the wise shall understand.

At different intervals (in the past), it was thought that certain political figures were
expected to be the antichrist: but all the possibilities were proven to be incorrect.

Some have suggested the antichrist may be Barack Obama (the President of the United States).
Could Barack Obama be the Little Horn (Dan.8:9), a king of fierce countenance?
What do we know about this man called Barack Obama - if that be his real name?
When a white policeman had a confrontation (dealt with) a man, who happened to be black.
 And the black community cried out to Barack to save the black individual.
And Barack (not knowing the circumstances) rapidly accused the white policeman for unjustly
 creating problems for a peaceful law-abiding black man.
At some point, someone must have corrected Barack - explaining to him the situation:
 Barack suggested that they not go to court, but settle their differences over a beer.
 And Barack Obama was voted to become the President of the United States of America.

Barack chose to have his family attend a racist church, taught by the reverent Wright.
He also has racism characteristics - provided one can meet the level of his blackness.
Since January 20, 2009 Barack has been governing his country some-what as a dictator.
Some may conclude that he is a crafty king of fierce countenance (ie: a powerful prescence).

Yet 3 kings in Persia (Dan.11:2), and a <u>4th.</u>   In the reign of Darius, and Cyrus. (Dan.6:28)

  The Ram (with 2 horns) = Media and Persia   (Dan.8:20)

  The He Goat = Greece (King #1)   (Dan.8:21)   A mighty king. (Dan.11:3,4)

And for it (out of this nation),
 (Dan.8:8,22), shall stand up 4 kingdoms, (four notable ones toward the 4 winds of heaven).

                            Passage   --- The kings of the North,
And out of one of them   of   and of the South.   (Dan.11:5)
 a king of fierce countenance: time.
 (Dan.8:8-12,23-25)   A Little Horn ---------- Yea, he magnified himself
                                                    even to the prince of the host;
                           (2300) days.   against the Prince of princess.
The Vision (Dan.8:14,26)   ---- From the time the Daily be taken away,
 of the Daily   (1290)   (Dan.11:31)   (Dan.12:11,12)
 (Evening and Morning),   until,
 is true (ie: is certain).   (1335)   -- The Abomination
                                                    that maketh desolate be set up.
                                   (45)   Blessed is he that waiteth. (D.12:12)
 (2300 days = 6.3 years?)   *A time of trouble/tribulation?
Then shall the Sanctuary be cleansed. ---------- The End shall be at the appointed time.

When we study the Bible (which was written over a period of about 1500 years), and read
 about future events: and we debate, which events have, or have not been fulfilled as yet.
Jacob (in the land of Canaan) was in great tribulation, as he was unable to escape the dearth.
All who confess Jesus as their Saviour, will have tribulation. (Acts 7:11/Jn.16:33/Mt.24:29)
Just prior to the 2nd. coming of our Lord - be the climax, the Greatest of all Tribulations.
*Reading Daniel 12:1,11,12 it appears (to me) that the time of Great Tribulation be 45 days.
After the Little Horn magnifies himself - there be 2300d. until the Sanctuary be cleansed.
They who believe that all roads lead to the same destination are spiritually blind.
We are to live righteously, looking for that blessed hope, and glorious appearing of the
 great God and our Saviour Jesus Christ. Blessed is he that waiteth/endureth unto the End.
The actions of the wicked (to root-out/silence Christians) shall be cut short/end abruptly.

The Gospels of Matthew, Mark, Luke, and John: Merged into One Historic Calendar of Events

A Woman sitting upon a Beast with 7 Heads and 10 Horns

There were those that had access to the Throne of God, and Satan came among them. (Job 1:6)
   In heaven (before God), Satan accused our brethren, but they over came ----. (Rev.12:7-11)
A Great Red Dragon, with 7 heads & 10 horns; and his tail drew 1/3 part of the stars of heaven
   and cast them down to earth. (Rev.12:3,4)

                                 7 heads = 7 kings: Egypt
                                                               Assyria
The Beast/Satan (Who Was) ---- (R.17:8) ----   Five are fallen   Babylon
                                                                             Med.Per.
Jesus was Victorious,   (Rev.17:10)   Greece
   and the Devil/Satan was bound. (R.20:2) ---- 6 ---- And One Is ---- Rome
   (One of the heads of the Beast was wounded)

   A time span pictured as (a 1000y.) ---------   The New Testament Church era:
                                                       Over time changes were incurred.
            (That Is Not)   (for better or for worse?)
                                                       And they tolerated Evil.

The head wound had healed,
   and Satan (the Beast) was loosed. (R.20:7) ---- 7 -------- And One Is To Come. (Rev.17:10)
      (And Yet Is)   8 | 10 Horns
War: The beast & the false prophet were taken   The 10 horns = 10 kings:
   and cast into the Lake of Fire. (R.19:19,20) ---- These 10 shall receive power as kings
The Beast (Satan) is the eighth. (R.17:8,11) ---- for One hour with the Beast: and,
Another beast, with 2 horns like a lamb: and he   they give their Power and Strength
   causeth all to receive the Mark. (R.13:11-18)   unto the Beast. (Rev.17:12,13)
The 10 horns (10 kings) make war with the Lamb; and the Lamb shall overcome them. (R.17:10-14)
   Babylon is fallen, is fallen. (Rev.14:8)
   The 10 horns shall hate the whore sitting upon the Beast, and shall destroy her. (R.17:16)
   Come out of her my people (be not partakers of her sins), and receive not of her plagues.
   Her sins have reached unto heaven, and God has remembered her iniquities.
   Her plagues shall come in One day, death, and mourning, and famine; and she shall be
      utterly burned with fire: for strong is the Lord God who judgeth her. (Rev.18:4-8)
The Devil that deceived them (The nations in the 4 corners of the earth - who compassed the
   camp of the Saints about.), was cast into the Lake of Fire and brimstone, where the beast
   and the false prophet are, and be tormented day and night for ever and ever. (Rev.20:7-10)
   All those not written in the Book of Life were cast into the Lake of Fire. (Rev.20:15)

Notes:
The Beast with 7 heads and 10 horns, is a metaphorical figure - the representation of Satan.
   -when Satan is bound (the Beast is no-where), the Beast (so to speak) is out of the picture.
   -when Satan is loosed, the Beast re-appears.
The description of various animals (like a Leopard, the feet of a Bear, the mouth of a Lion),
   used to describe this Beast with 7 heads and 10 horns - are the visual representations
   (ie: are pictures) of how Satan disguises/camouflages himself, as he roams about on earth.
And the 8th. (belongs unto the 7), it is the Beast himself (ie: Satan himself). (Rev.17:11)

The beast & the false prophet convinced men (via miracles) to receive the Mark of the Beast;
   and many have made a pact with the devil: all sorts of goodies in exchange for their soul.
But, near the End (at the climax), when men (are not asked, but) are commanded by the law, to
   receive the Mark of the Beast (denounce Jesus Christ), if you hope to buy/sell. (Rev.19:20)
                                                                                 (Rev.13:17)
Who is this Woman (that Great City) which is called Babylon?
As we read, How she began, and What she became - we get a sense of the direction she is going.
   -The Light of the candle was in her = a Shining Light, for every-one to See.
   -The voice of harpers, musicians, pipers, trumpeters = all together making a joyful noise.
   -In her was heard the voice of the Bridegroom and the Bride = as they made their vows.
   -The sound of the millstone = indicating that they had plenty (no shortage) of sustenance.
But, over time (as generations come and go) things will change (not always for the better):
Babylon became an habitation of devils, and in her was found the blood of prophets, and
   of saints, and of all that were slain upon the earth. (Rev.18:2,24)(Rev.17:16-18)
The 10 horns shall hate the whore, and shall make her desolate, and naked, and shall eat her
   flesh, and burn her with fire: For God hath put in their hearts to fulfil his will, and to
   agree, and give their kingdom unto the Beast - until the words of God shall be fulfilled.

Mystery Babylon (Babylon the Great/that Great City)

Many have searched the Scriptures, to try and understand - who this famous woman be!
And, even-though the Bible has painted an extensive description of what she has become;
  And yet we are unable to come to an aggreement, as to what or who this woman represents.
It is as though (as I have heard say), One cannot see the forest because of all the trees.

The phrase, "The Light of the Candle", is rarely found in the Bible. (Jer.25:10/Rev.18:22-24)
It is my understanding (according to the situations it is utilized), that   (Is.1:21,9,26,27)
  it has to do with the Spirit of God making a grand entrance, as in a New Beginning.

  For example:
  (1) The Ark of the Covenant journeyed among/with the children of Israel into Canaan:
      And it was placed in the Temple (a house called by My Name), Jehovah's House.

      Later Nebuchadnezzar invaded Judah, and took Jerusalem, and the Temple was burned.
      We read about all the people of Judah, and all the inhabitants of Jerusalem:
        I will take from them the voice of mirth, and the voice of gladness;
        The voice of the bridegroom, and the voice of the bride;
        The sound of the millstone, and the Light of the Candle.   (Jer.25:2,10)

  (2) Jesus Christ descended from heaven to earth: Jesus was born in Bethlehem.
      Jesus (on earth) finished all his Father assigned to him, and he returned to heaven.
      At Penticost, the Holy Spirit made the grant entrance descending upon the apostles.

      Q. How does the performance of our churches compare with the Early Churches?

Note: Because it is not possible to take away from people - the things that they have not;
       Therefore, we may know that there was a city,   (Is.1:21)
         having been blessed by God, later became Mystery Babylon the Mother of harlots.
And we read concerning that Great City, Mystery Babylon the Great:
  The voice of the harpers, musicians, pipers and trumpeters shall be heard in thee no more.
  No craftsman (of whatsoever craft) shall be found any more in thee.
  The sound of the millstone shall be heard no more at all in thee.
  The Light of the Candle shall shine no more at all in thee.
  The voice of the bridegroom, and of the bride shall be heard no more at all in thee;
    -For thy merchants were the great men of the earth,
    -For by thy sorceries were all nations deceived.
  And in her was found the blood
    of prophets, and of saints, and of all that were slain upon the earth.   (Rev.18:21-24)

> Note: When someone breaks one of the laws, he is guilty of all: he has broken the law.
>   So too perhaps, as one sheds the blood of a saint, he is guilty of all blood shed.

Babylon the Great is fallen, is fallen, and is become the habitation of Devils. (Rev.18:2,4)
Come OUT of her My People! partake not of her sins, that ye receive not of her plagues.
Now, if we knew where My People were, then the identity of Babylon the Great could be solved.

Mystery Babylon the Great, the mother of harlots and abominations of the earth.   (Rev.17:5)
The Great Whore that sitteth upon many peoples, multitudes, nations and tongues: (Re.17:1,15)
  With whom the kings of the earth have committed fornication, and   (Rev.17:2)
  The inhabitants of the earth have been made drunk with the wine of her fornication.

Some say, that USA. could be Mystery Babylon - where, had been the Light of the Candle.
Although the USA. had a beginning based upon Christian principles (ie: the Bible);
  but to say, that the Light of the Candle was in her exclusively, is not possible.
  It is more probable, that the USA. may be the 7th. head of the Beast.   (Rev.17:10,12-14)

The 10 horns (ie: the 10 kings), shall receive power as kings one hour with the Beast.
  These make war with the Lamb: the Lamb (Lord of lords/King of kings) shall overcome them.
  These 10 kings shall hate the whore, and burn her with fire.   (Rev.17:12-14/Rev.18:8)
Also (at the 7th. Vial), she receives the cup of the wine of the wrath of God.   (Rev.16:19)
Note: The Wrath of God is filled up (fulfilled/finished) in the 7 last plagues. (Rev.15:1)

How the Times have Changed.

A One Room Schoolhouse in the country:
Where I attended a public school, grades 5 through 8 (1956-1960).

We walked to school, and played outside during recess (exercise programs were for the birds).
We brought our own lunches (in lunch boxes) to school, which we/our moms had prepared.
In school, we prayed the Lord's Prayer every morning (believing the Bible to be God's Word).
   We sang, God saved the Queen, our National Anthem, Hymns of praise, and folk songs.
One teacher (Mrs. Curtis) taught grades 1 through 8, and there were approximately 35 students.
   At certain intervals a music teacher (Mrs. Sweet) would come and give us music lessons.
   In the classroom: on the stage, at the front - were the teacher's desk, and a piano.
   We also had a portable library (a case with books) which was exchanged every-so-often.
In school we were taught to Read, to Write, and do Arithmetic; and also Right from Wrong.
The school was not the place to play with toys - at home we had our Meccano and Lego sets.

Out in the front yard was a long handle water pump.
   And out, away from one side of the school building was the woodshed.
   Behind the school, and off to the other side were 2 outhouses - used summer and winter.
And, at the back (a short way behind), and toward one side, was an Orange Hall;
   and that is where we (with permission) were allowed to exhibit our Christmas programs.
A wood burning stove, was used to heat the one room red brick school structure.
A large bell in the steeple: The Ding, Dong, alerted us when-ever recess came to an end.
   When entering, select either the girls or the boys cloakroom - to enter the classroom.
A water cooler was positioned upon a table:
   A row of hooks supporting cups, one for each student - identifiable with their names.
   During the cold days of winter, the teacher would make/provide us with a cup of hot soup.
Back then the schools were built to last, and all things were managed very efficiently; and
   when the property taxes were due - only a small segment was identified as school taxes.
All we, poor country folk - trying to make ends meet: And we were content with the simple
   things in life: We had the basics, a tube radio, and a telephone (crank to ring the bell).

There was one event that took place in our school, that caught my attention: Let me explain!
It was just before noon (1959/1960), and we were about to get our lunch boxes to have lunch:
   (That day it was cool enough, so that it was not practical to eat lunch outside.)
The teacher was standing in front facing us, and she was holding in front of her a picture;
   the picture was of adequate size - so all of us could see, as she moved it about.
That picture was not a pretty sight, for it shewed severely undernourished/hungry children,
   whose rib cages were clearly evident; and she wanted the opinion/approval from us students,
   whether she should put the picture up, for us to see - as we were eating our lunches.
At the time I was convinced, that no-one would agree that she put it up for us to look at;
   But the technique she applied, "How to begin, and how to proceed", proved me to be wrong!
First, the teacher asked a young child (in one of the lowest grades);
   who apparently, believed that the teacher expected her to answer, Yes: and she so answered.
Next, the teacher asked someone near unto the first (they may have been friends),
   and that child agreed (with the first), that the picture be displayed during lunch time.
   And this got the ball rolling, and the direction did not change - as she
   continued, gradually moving (through the various grades) into the highest grade:
   All of us were very tolerant, as we agreed to some-thing (I am sure) no-one really wanted.

Now, in our day, deceptive methods are used to get the ball rolling - for us to condone evil.
The inhabitants are misled/brainwashed to become tolerant to those things which be contrary.

It has been said, If you neglect your right to vote - you forfeit your right to criticize.
But what should a citizen do, when the only individual having a moral bone in his body,
   also demonstrates a diverse/comical; and the occasional odd behaviour in a drunken stupor.
   And one debates, which is the lesser of the 2 evils - and whom to vote for, if any!
Those who cut parts out of the Bible (the Bible phobics), accuse others of having homo-phobia.
All who thumb their noses at the Bible, and the Author there-of, be in danger of hell-fire.

All we have sinned! Are we repentant?   (Lk.15:21/Lk.18:13)   John Douma
Father, I have sinned against heaven, and before thee, and in thy sight,   Delta,
   And am no more worthy to be called Thy son: -------------------.   Ontario.

CPSIA information can be obtained
at www.ICGtesting.com
Printed in the USA
BVHW01*0954090718
521161BV00015B/628/P